How Second Languages are Learned

An Introduction

A comprehensive introduction to how people learn second languages (L2s), this textbook approaches the topic through five problems the L2 learner has to solve: 'breaking into' the L2; associating forms with meanings; learning sentence structure; learning phrasal and sentential meaning; and learning the use of the L2 in context. These problems are linked throughout to the L2 acquisition of lexis, morphology, syntax, semantics, phonetics/phonology and language-use in a reader-friendly way, using key studies to build a comprehensive picture of how L2s are learned. 'In a nutshell' summaries of chapter sections provide helpful signposts to the developing argument, whilst end-of-chapter activities encourage the reader to reflect on the ideas presented, analyse data and think creatively about the problems encountered. The roles of innate knowledge, input, and the age at which learning starts are also considered. This essential textbook will enable students to think objectively about language, and will be an asset to any introductory course on second language acquisition

ROGER HAWKINS is Emeritus Professor in the Department of Language and Linguistics at the University of Essex. His research into how second languages are learned spans over 30 years. His publications include *Second Language Syntax: A Generative Introduction* (2001), *Approaches to Second Language Acquisition* (1994) and *French Grammar and Usage* (2015) with Richard Towell.

How Second Languages are Learned

An Introduction

Roger Hawkins

University of Essex

CAMBRIDGE
UNIVERSITY PRESS

CAMBRIDGE
UNIVERSITY PRESS

University Printing House, Cambridge CB2 8BS, United Kingdom

One Liberty Plaza, 20th Floor, New York, NY 10006, USA

477 Williamstown Road, Port Melbourne, VIC 3207, Australia

314–321, 3rd Floor, Plot 3, Splendor Forum, Jasola District Centre, New Delhi – 110025, India

79 Anson Road, #06–04/06, Singapore 079906

Cambridge University Press is part of the University of Cambridge.

It furthers the University's mission by disseminating knowledge in the pursuit of education, learning, and research at the highest international levels of excellence.

www.cambridge.org
Information on this title: www.cambridge.org/9781108475037
DOI: 10.1017/9781108565875

First published 2019

Printed in the United Kingdom by TJ International Ltd. Padstow Cornwall

A catalogue record for this publication is available from the British Library.

Library of Congress Cataloging-in-Publication Data
Names: Hawkins, Roger (Roger D.), author.
Title: How second languages are learned : an introduction / Roger Hawkins.
Description: Cambridge, United Kingdom ; New York, NY : Cambridge University Press, 2019. | Includes bibliographical references and index.
Identifiers: LCCN 2018022951 | ISBN 9781108475037
Subjects: LCSH: Second language acquisition.
Classification: LCC P118.2 .H3658 2019 | DDC 418.0071–dc23
LC record available at https://lccn.loc.gov/2018022951

ISBN 978-1-108-47503-7 Hardback
ISBN 978-1-108-46843-5 Paperback

For Lenny, Katherine, Isabelle and Robin
growing up in a multilingual world

CONTENTS

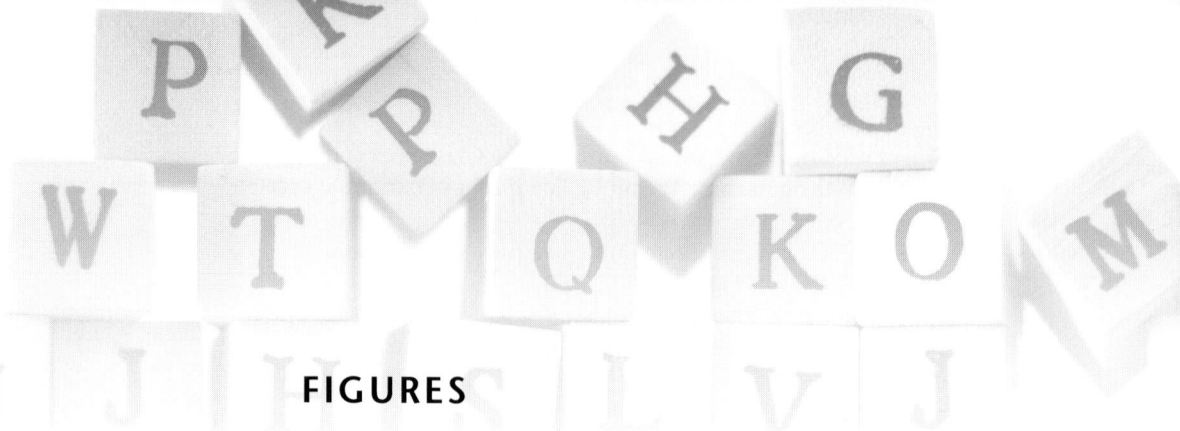

FIGURES

TABLES

PREFACE

Second language (L2) speakers of English can be heard saying things like the following, where the native speaker equivalent is given in the right-hand column:

L2 Speaker	Native Speaker
1. Who want this egg?	Who wants this egg?
2. He bring umbrella with him	He brought an umbrella with him
3. He wake up and shaked the girl	He woke up and shook the girl
4. No very good	It isn't very good
5. Is the café is open?	Is the café open?
6. I sink zis is yours	I think this is yours

Such differences between L2 speaker speech and native speaker speech are not idiosyncratic. Many L2 learners of English go through stages of development where they allow a verb not to agree with a subject (1), omit articles where they are needed (2), do not inflect the verb appropriately for past tense (2 and 3), use *no* where *isn't* is required (4), copy rather than move a verb in questions (5), or use substitutes for some of the more difficult sounds of English (6). Similar systematic divergence from the target language by L2 speakers is found in the learning of other languages. Patterns like these provide clues to the linguistic knowledge that underlies them – the mental grammars of L2 speakers. And patterns of linguistic behaviour that change over time provide clues to how the mental grammars of L2 speakers develop.

This book introduces the reader to a range of examples of the use of language by L2 speakers in a number of different languages and some of the hypotheses that have been made about the mental grammars that give rise to this use. The aim is to build an overall picture of what is currently known about how second languages are learned.

Because readers may be new to this area of enquiry, three strategies have been used in the text to help with the assimilation of and engagement with the facts and ideas. Firstly, 'in a nutshell' summaries of preceding sections appear at frequent intervals. These act as signposts to the main points being made in each section. Secondly, end-of-chapter activities are designed to encourage active reading. These activities also aim to develop the ability to interpret data drawn from the primary literature on second language learning and to foster creative thinking about the significance of those data. Thirdly, the concluding remarks at the end of each chapter give an overview of what the chapter has been about. Additionally, a glossary of key terms and conventions is provided at the end of the book.

There are probably more people today who learn second, third or more languages than at any time in the past. It is hoped that this book will give you an insight into how they do it.

ACKNOWLEDGEMENTS

I am grateful to many people who have enabled me to write this book. Firstly to the researchers, too many to name individually, whose work I report. Without their efforts to document the language of second and third language speakers and to propose and test hypotheses about the knowledge that underlies that language there would be no book. Secondly to my colleagues and former colleagues at the University of Essex (and particularly Martin Atkinson, Bob Borsley, Harald Clahsen, Claudia Felser, Florence Myles, Andrew Radford and Monika Schmid) from whom I have learned a lot about linguistics, language acquisition and second language learning. Thirdly to Malcolm Todd, whose ability to identify inconsistency and incoherence in a text is without parallel. Finally, but not least, to the undergraduate and postgraduate students with whom I have discussed and exchanged ideas over many years. Their feedback has often helped clarify my own thinking about how second languages are learned.

1 Second Language Learning: the Nature of the Task

1.1 Can Anyone Learn a Second (Third, Fourth, …) Language?

Some people are apparently very good at learning languages beyond the one(s) they acquire in infancy. The nineteenth-century British explorer Sir Richard Burton claimed to have spoken more than forty languages and dialects (Farwell, 1963). There are also 'linguistic savants', people who, despite a number of cognitive impairments, have a precocious ability to learn languages. Christopher, a linguistic savant studied by Smith and Tsimpli (1995), has a number of cognitive impairments that make it difficult for him to find his way around or deal with everyday tasks like doing up buttons or shaving. However, 'he can read, write and communicate in any of fifteen to twenty languages' (1995: 1). In contrast to these examples, other people appear to be rather poor at language learning. In 2008, the *Guardian* newspaper reported the attempts of a French teacher at a London school to motivate a Vietnamese boy in his bottom French class, Tommy, for an upcoming French exam. In doing so he was presented with a challenge:

> I told him it wasn't too late. I insisted he could still pass French even at this stage. Tommy scoffed. You learn Vietnamese in three months, he said, and I'll learn French. (*Education Guardian*, Tuesday 26 August 2008, p. 4)

The 52-year-old teacher accepted the challenge, and passed an Institute of Linguists first-level certificate in Vietnamese three months later. Unfortunately, Tommy was not so successful. He failed his French exam with an even lower grade than he was originally predicted to get.

Examples like these sometimes lead to the belief that a special talent is needed to learn languages beyond one's native language. This is not the case. For the majority of people successful second language learning is entirely realistic. Where second, third or further languages need to be acquired for an individual to function normally in society, they mostly can be acquired.

Stenzel (2005) reports the case of the Wanano, a people living along the Vaupés river in South America on the border between Colombia and Brazil. It is the social norm among the Wanano to marry someone outside their language group, because speakers of the same language are regarded as brothers and sisters. As in most societies, to marry a brother or sister would be incest. It is also the norm for the wife to move to the husband's village and to learn the husband's language. The children of such marriages grow up speaking both languages. Because other wives moving to the same village may speak different languages, other languages may also be learned. In addition, there is a local lingua franca, Tukano, used for communicating with other indigenous communities, and Portuguese and Spanish for communicating with speakers from elsewhere in Brazil and Colombia. A language census conducted in 2002 with thirty-eight Wanano males aged between 12 and 65 shows that individuals speak on average six languages (Stenzel 2005: 20–1).

This is not an isolated example. Similar multilingualism can be found in other parts of the world. Erard (2012: 199) reports the following description of family language use by a woman living in southern India:

> We speak Hindi a lot … All of us speak Telegu, but when more of us are together, we speak Tamil. Then, when we get even more together, we speak Kannada.

It appears, then, that many people can achieve good levels of communicative ability in a second language (henceforth referred to as L2) given the motivation to do so, the opportunity to interact with samples of the target language, and sufficient time for such encounters to turn into acquired mental linguistic knowledge, as the Wanano people, those living in southern India and Tommy's teacher show. The willingness to interact with samples of the target language, and to do so over long periods of time, appear to be key factors. It is interesting to note that Tommy, a Vietnamese speaker, had already been highly successful in acquiring English, where presumably motivation was high and access to samples of English easy for him. Indeed, his success in using English could well have been one cause of his lack of success in French. As his teacher observes, 'it did not help that he preferred to spend the [French] lesson chatting', presumably in English.

Furthermore, Farwell's description of how Burton set about learning a new language suggests high levels of motivation and engagement with the language over a sustained period of time:

> First he bought a simple grammar and vocabulary and underlined the words and rules he felt should be remembered. Putting these books in his pocket, he studied them at every spare moment during the day, never working more than 15 minutes at a time. By this method he was able to learn 300 words a week. When he acquired a basic vocabulary, he chose a simple story book and read it, marking with a pencil any new words he wanted to remember and going over these at least once a day. Then he went on to a more difficult book, at the same time learning the finer points of the grammar … When native teachers were available, he claimed that he always learned the 'swear words' first and laughingly said that after that the rest of the language was easy. (Farwell, 1963: 30)

Modern examples of 'hyperpolyglots' (obsessive acquirers of L2s) appear to confirm that time spent in the company of the L2 is a major factor in its acquisition. Erard (2012: 117) describes one such hyperpolyglot, Alexander Arguelles, who spends around ten hours a day working to maintain the languages he speaks, devoting most time to revising the languages he knows best (English, Arabic, French, German, Latin, Chinese, Spanish, Russian and Korean) but also devoting some time to forty other languages.

This book assumes that, for many people, acquiring L2s is a natural extension of human linguistic ability. Given the right opportunities and sufficient time, good levels of communicative ability in an L2 can be achieved. It aims to show how people do this. You will discover that there are remarkable similarities in the way people who speak different first languages and are acquiring different L2s go about the task, although there are also clear influences from their first language. The accumulation over the past fifty to sixty years of observations from carefully-designed empirical studies has led to the proposal of various hypotheses and theories about L2 learning. Several of these will be outlined and evaluated against the available evidence. Since many people learn L2s in a classroom setting, the relationship between the samples of language they encounter (the 'input') and what they learn will also be discussed, as will the often-asked question: 'What is the best age to learn an L2?' Two further topics that will be addressed are how speakers of L2s use their knowledge in real time, and the role that context plays in L2 learning.

The aim in this chapter is to outline the task facing the L2 learner. This will be presented as a number of 'problems' that the learner has to solve. The discussion starts with how learners 'break into' the L2 in the first place; that is, how they identify its words and assign them the right meanings. A second problem is distinguishing appropriate from inappropriate combinations of words in phrases, clauses and sentences. When words combine to form phrases, those phrases sometimes have meanings that go beyond those of the individual words. Identifying such cases constitutes a third problem. A fourth problem is identifying the way that sentences link to each other in verbal exchanges and written texts. Finally, an L2 learner needs to work out the variety of language to use in specific situations.

1.2 Cracking the Code: the Segmentation Problem

At birth, children with normal hearing ability are confronted with continuous strings of sounds produced by the people around them. To acquire the language(s) that those people are speaking the child has first to identify recurring portions of the sound continuum that are potentially meaningful. S/he then has to associate those chunks of sound with actual meanings. Further, the child has to discover how those sound-meaning chunks – the words of the language – can be combined and recombined to create the multiplicity of new messages s/he will want to understand or will want to communicate to others every day. This is a formidable challenge.

To illustrate, imagine you are an infant living in a community that speaks West Greenlandic (Fortescue, 1984). You will hear people uttering strings of sounds like the following:

1. qimmipinnittuquppai

Even if you can work out from the non-linguistic cues available in the context that it means 'The dog killed the people', you do not know which section of the string might correspond to 'dog', which to 'people' and which to 'kill'. Given that in some languages the verb ('kill') can come at the beginning of a sentence (like Welsh), perhaps some portion of *qimmipin* … means 'kill'? On the other hand, in languages like Japanese and Turkish the verb comes at the end of a sentence, so perhaps some portion of … *tuquppai* means 'kill'. And which bits of sound refer to 'dog' and which bits to 'people'?

Exactly the same 'segmentation problem' faces the L2 learner. Classroom L2 learners are usually helped by having their attention consciously drawn to sound–meaning correspondences and the order in which constituents occur (often with written support). But even if you know consciously that *qimmip* is 'dog', *innit* is 'people' and *tuquppai* is 'kill', such explicit knowledge is difficult to access when trying to 'catch' what native speakers are saying, or produce utterances yourself (as anyone who has learned an L2 on the basis of a 'read-then-listen/speak' method will know). What you need is an ability to automatically segment the fast stream of speech you hear into its meaningful components.

It appears that humans have such an unconscious analytical capacity that is available to infants and older L2 learners alike. This capacity is the ability to analyse rapidly a continuous stream of speech into its component sounds, like the [q], [i], [m] and so on from example (1), and to retain a memory of the frequency with which they co-occur. The unconscious tallying of the frequency with which individual sounds occur together is important because sounds co-occur more frequently within words than between words. To illustrate, the probability of hearing the sequence [kæt] 'cat' as a recurring string in sequences like *thecatlikesmilk* is greater than the probability of hearing other sequences of adjacent sounds that cross word boundaries: [ðək] 'thec', [ætl] 'atl' or [tlai] 'tli'. If language learners retain a memory for such co-occurrence frequencies, it provides them with an important cue to the identification of words from a continuous sequence of sounds: an important step in solving the segmentation problem.

Research has demonstrated that adults not only retain a memory of the frequency of co-occurrence of sounds from novel strings, but also do so very rapidly. Saffran et al., (1996b) invented a language that consisted of six 3-syllable 'words' like *bidaku, padoti, tupiro* and *golabu*. These words were combined and repeated to form a continuous string as in (2) that was recorded in a female voice.

2. bidakupadotigolabupadotibidakugolabupadoti …

English-speaking participants in their study (undergraduate student volunteers) were told that the language contained 'words', but were not told what they were.

After 21 minutes of listening to the speech stream, participants were presented with a word decision task. They heard pairs of syllable strings where one was a 'word' from the continuous stream they had been listening to (like *bidaku*), and the other either a 'non-word' made up from syllables that never followed each other in the listening phase (like *dadopi*) or a 'part-word' created from two syllables of a 'word' plus a random syllable (such as *bidado*). Participants were asked to decide which of the two strings 'sounded more like a word from the language' (Saffran et al., 1996b: 613) by pressing a key on a computer keyboard. The results show that participants were significantly above chance in identifying both 'words' and 'part words', although they were less certain about the latter (unsurprisingly, since they only partially resembled 'words' in the language they had been listening to).

Saffran et al. interpret these results as showing that adult language learners are sensitive to the probability with which one syllable will follow another in the speech stream. In the stream of sounds they heard, only *da* could follow *bi*, and only *ku* could follow *da* (because *da* is the central syllable in *bidaku*). By contrast, *bi* could be preceded by any of *ti, ro, bu*, and *ku* could be followed by any of *pa, tu, go*. The adult participants unconsciously computed the 'contingencies' between these syllables very rapidly to identify recurring, stable sound sequences in the input they encountered.

In a similar study with 8-month-old infants using the duration of fixation of the infants' gaze on a blinking light to determine whether they were distinguishing words from non-words (Saffran et al., 1996a) the same results were found.[1] So, at a level of perception below conscious awareness, adult L2 learners have the same capacity as infants to compute and retain a memory for recurrent chunks of sound in the stream of speech they are exposed to. The ability to identify such chunks that are potentially meaning-bearing forms in a target second language is an important step in solving the 'segmentation problem'.

Section 1.2 in a Nutshell
Adults have an unconscious mental capacity for computing the frequency with which sounds co-occur in the speech stream that contributes to their identification of word-like sequences. They share this capacity with infants. The ability to identify word-like sequences that are potentially associated with stable meanings is an important step in acquiring a new language.

---

[1] In the blinking-light procedure an infant sits on a parent/carer's lap and looks at a blinking light on a facing wall while listening to a continuous sequence of invented words, as in (2). At the end of two minutes the light is switched off and another starts blinking on a side wall. This new light is accompanied either by one of the invented words the infant has just been listening to, or a non-word. The average time the infant spends looking at this second blinking light while hearing words is compared with the time spent looking while hearing non-words. Saffran et al. found that the infants studied spent significantly longer looking when they heard non-words than when they heard 'words', suggesting that they were distinguishing the two.

1.3 Matching Form and Meaning: the Categorisation Problem

In real languages, recurrent strings of sounds (or sequences of written symbols) can be associated with three types of meaning, and working out which of these form–meaning relations is appropriate is a second problem to solve.

Some strings are associated with meanings that uniquely identify people, things, ideas, actions, states, locations and qualities in the world (real or imagined). For example: *student, book, freedom, walk, know, in, smooth*, etc., are all recurrent strings in English with uniquely identifiable meanings. Other strings (including those that consist of just one sound segment) have meanings that modify strings with uniquely identifiable meanings. This is the case, for example, with the English articles *the* and *a*, whose function is to indicate whether the uniquely identifiable meanings of nouns (like *student, book*) are to be understood as definite or indefinite: *I saw the student* (a definite description of a particular person – I expect you, the reader, to know who I am talking about); *I saw a student* (an indefinite reference to a person who is a member of the class 'student').

Forms that have a meaning-modifying function need not be words in their own right (although *the* and *a* are). They can attach to strings with uniquely identifiable meanings as affixes. For example, in the strings *students, books, freedoms*, the final *-s* is an affix that turns the reference of *student, book* and *freedom* from singular to plural.

Yet other strings of sound mark a dependency between forms. For example, the *-s* affix of the English string *sings* marks a dependency between *sing* and the constituent that typically precedes it (the **subject** of *sing*). This constituent must be third **person** (i.e. not *I* or *you*) and singular (i.e. not *they*): *He sings* and *She sings* are fine, but **I sings* and **They sings* are not fine in standard varieties of English. (Note that this *-s* has the same form as the meaning-modifying plural *-s*, as in *songs*, but the two have different functions.) Dependency-marking strings are often affixes.

The L2 learner must associate recurrent strings of sounds/written symbols that have been identified with one of the categories of meaning: uniquely identifiable, meaning-modifying or dependency-marking. That is, they have to solve a 'categorization problem'.

Where samples of the L2 that are encountered are written, it appears that L2 learners initially deal with the categorisation problem primarily by retaining a memory for form–meaning correspondences where uniquely identifiable meanings are involved. DeKeyser (1995) has shown that in the initial stages of learning a new language, the extent to which adults can identify meaning-modifying and dependency-marking forms simply from exposure to samples of the target language is quite limited.

Like Saffran et al. (1996a, 1996b) DeKeyser used the 'invented language' technique, but unlike the language used by them, his language, called Implexan, had properties that were more like those found in real languages. There were ninety-eight words with uniquely identifiable meanings, for example the nouns *melaks* 'apple', *perakt* 'book', and the verbs *wulas* 'peel', *wost* 'read'. In addition, there was a meaning-modifying affix that could attach to nouns and that changed their reference from singular to plural (like English *-s*): *melakson* 'apples', *perakton* 'books'. There were also dependency-marking affixes, one that necessarily attached to verbs when the subject of the verb was female:

3   a.   Mari wostin.   'Mary is reading'
    b.   Rober wost.   'Robert is reading'

Another attached to nouns when they followed the verb (i.e. when they were the verb's direct object):

4   a.   Mari wostin peraktus.   'Mary is reading a book'
    b.   Rober wost peraktus.   'Robert is reading a book'[2]

DeKeyser exposed a group of thirteen adults to this language over twenty training sessions of 25 minutes each. In each session participants saw the same 124 photographs depicting simple actions paired with a written sentence of Implexan (for example, a photo of a woman reading a book paired with the sentence *Mari wostin peraktus*), although the order in which the photographs were presented varied in each session. (Note that this is a written 'language', unlike the spoken 'language' in the Saffran et al. studies. Further, the segmentation problem is greatly reduced because the words of the language are already identified by spaces between letter strings). To stimulate the active processing of meaning in Implexan, participants were presented at regular intervals with additional pictures, some of which were accompanied by sentences whose nouns or verbs did not match the picture. Participants were asked to indicate whether the sentence matched the photo, yes or no. (The affixes were always appropriate during the training phase).

At the end of the training period, participants were asked to produce sentences in Implexan themselves to describe photos. Eight of these could be described using sentences that had been encountered during the training phase, but thirty-six were new photos requiring new combinations of nouns, verbs and affixes. Results showed that participants were very good at using previously encountered sentences to describe previously encountered photos (89.5% accurate). They were also very good at using previously encountered [noun + affix] and [verb + affix] strings to describe new photos (87.3% accuracy). But when they had to use new [noun + affix] or [verb + affix] combinations to describe new photos, their accuracy dropped to 33.3%. DeKeyser observes that 'a score of 33.3% is about what one would expect by chance' (1995: 393). They either failed to add affixes to nouns and verbs where they were required, or overused an affix where it was not required. In the latter case, all the errors involved the overuse of the plural affix *-on* in contexts where the referent of the noun was singular. This is strongly suggestive of a failure by the participants to identify the function of *-on* as a plural marker.

---

[2] This description of Implexan is simplified, as is the description of DeKeyser's experiment. For full details see DeKeyser (1995).

These results suggest that while the participants had retained a memory for recurrent strings of co-occurring letters (rather than sounds as in the Saffran et al. study) with uniquely identifiable associated meanings, they had not identified the meaning-modifying and dependency-marking affixes within those letter strings. DeKeyser concludes that the participants' unconscious knowledge of the rules underlying the distribution of the affixal forms 'was ... virtually non-existent' (1995: 393).

1.4 Identifying Possible and Impossible Word Combinations: the Syntax Problem

Another important feature of 'real' languages that an L2 learner has to acquire is the range of ways in which meaning-bearing strings of sounds (or letters) can be combined, and the kinds of combinations that are not possible. In simple **declarative** (statement) sentences in English, verbs appear after their subjects and before their objects: *Today Mary*[subject] *plays hockey*[object]. In West Greenlandic the verb appears at the end of the sentence: *Today Mary hockey plays*. In German, the verb marked for tense and agreement with the subject appears in second position in main clauses (*Today plays Mary hockey*), but at the end of a clause that is subordinate to the main clause (e.g. *Molly said that today Mary hockey plays*). If the subordinate clause comes first in the sentence, its verb appears at the end of that clause, and the tensed/agreeing verb in the main clause immediately follows (because it is in second position after the initial subordinate clause): *Whenever Mary hockey plays, wears she a mouth guard*. The rules that determine the appropriate combinations of words in a language (and exclude inappropriate combinations) are known as its **syntax**.

Rebuschat (2008) (reported in Williams 2009: 331) used a quasi-invented language to examine how quickly adult learners might identify possible and impossible word combinations in a target language. His quasi-invented language consisted of English word-forms with German word order. He presented his English-speaking adult participants (with no previous knowledge of German) with 120 sentences, where the three word orders described above were distributed equally. Their 'training' in the language involved making judgements of the plausibility of the meaning of each sentence (i.e. there was no explicit reference to word order in participants' encounters with the language). After they had made judgements on the 120 sentences, they were given a 'surprise' test in judging whether the word order in a new set of sentences was **grammatical** or ungrammatical (in the invented language they had just encountered). Results show that participants were above chance in accepting patterns of word order combination found in the training sentences, even though the vocabulary was different, but responded randomly to word orders that were ungrammatical. Williams concludes that 'there was rapid incidental learning of abstract word order patterns, but ... no learning of the actual verb placement rules' (2009: 331). In other words, L2 learners in the initial stages can compute and remember linear orders of words in the samples of language they encounter, but their failure to use that information to identify possible and impossible word order patterns suggests that it may be more difficult for them to solve the 'syntax problem' at this very early stage of exposure, the problem of determining the syntactic rules that give rise to particular word orders and not others.

Sections 1.3 and 1.4 in a Nutshell
When L2 learners have identified recurrent strings of sounds (or letters) in the stream of speech (or in connected text), they need to establish what kinds of meaning they have. Those meanings fall into one of three categories: (i) uniquely identifiable; (ii) meaning-modifying; (iii) dependency-marking. In the second and third cases, the forms involved are often affixal. The establishment of form–meaning associations was referred to as the 'categorisation problem'. A study by DeKeyser (1995) of the initial learning of an artificial language (with the characteristics of a 'natural' language) suggests that learners have considerably more difficulty categorising strings that have a meaning-modifying or dependency-marking function (and are also affixes) than categorising strings that have a uniquely identifiable meaning. Results from a study by Rebuschat (2008) suggest that when L2 learners initially encounter novel syntax in an L2 they can apply it to new vocabulary, but they do not immediately infer impossible from possible word orders.

1.5 Working Out the Meaning of Word Combinations: the Semantics Problem

When the syntactic rules of a language combine words into phrases, composite meanings are created. Unremarkably, combining the English words *a, red* and *ball* into *a red ball* creates a phrase that refers to an object that is both a ball and red. Sometimes, however, the meaning of phrases goes beyond the meanings of the individual words of which it is composed. *A heavy smoker* could indeed be a person who is both a smoker and heavy, but more usually it has the meaning 'someone who smokes heavily'. The ambiguity arises not just from the meanings of the words themselves, but from their meanings in conjunction with the structure of the phrase into which they have been combined. Speakers of English know that *heavy* can be understood as modifying the meaning of *smoker* in two ways. The first is additive: it adds the meaning 'heavy' to an entity in the world described as a 'smoker', in the same way that *red* adds the meaning 'red' to an entity in the world described as a 'ball'. The second is qualitative: *heavy* qualifies the activity engaged in by the entity referred to; that is, 'smoking'. The entity is someone who 'smokes heavily'.

Determining the meanings of word combinations created by the syntactic rules of a language is the job of **semantics**. One of the tasks facing the L2 learner is identifying how composite meanings are derived from the individual meanings of words that have been combined into phrases and sentences. As in the case of the 'categorisation problem', solving the 'semantics problem' may take some time. An illustration of the development of such knowledge is provided in a study by Anderson (2008) of the identification of the additive and qualitative meanings of adjective–noun combinations in French by L2 learners whose L1 is English.

Unlike English, the majority of adjectives in French follow the noun they qualify, for example *un ballon rouge* (literally 'a ball red'), *un voyage fatigant* (lit. 'a journey tiring'). A handful of adjectives typically precede the noun, for example *un vieux château* ('an old castle'), *un bon professeur* ('a good teacher'). There is, however, a set of adjectives that can both precede and follow a noun, but change their meaning with their position. Some examples are given in (5) (from Anderson 2008: 13). In these cases the meaning is qualitative when the adjective precedes and additive when the adjective follows.

5 a. un **cher** bijou 'a cherished jewel'   un bijou **cher** 'an expensive jewel'
   b. un **ancien** roi 'a former king'   un roi **ancien** 'an ancient king'
   c. un **pauvre** village 'a pitiful village' un village **pauvre** 'a poor village'
   d. une **grande** gymnaste 'a great   une gymnaste **grande** 'a tall
       gymnast'   gymnast'

Anderson investigated whether English learners of French at different proficiency levels were sensitive to the difference in meanings associated with the different position of eight adjectives in phrases like these. He elicited their intuitions by asking them first to read stories that favoured either the qualitative interpretation or the additive interpretation, and then to rate sentences containing adjective + noun or noun + adjective as 'fine' or 'odd'. For example, one of the stories was about an old lady distributing some of her possessions to her relatives before she dies, but who keeps an imitation diamond that cost little but is of great sentimental value to her. This favours the qualitative 'cherished jewel' interpretation of the word order *cher bijou*. If participants have understood the relationship between the order of adjective and noun and meaning, they should find a sentence containing the phrase *son cher bijou* 'her cherished jewel' fine and a sentence containing the phrase *son bijou cher* 'her expensive jewel' odd. Participants were mainly classroom learners of French in their second, third and fourth year of study at an American university, or university graduates (the advanced group). There was also a **control group** of French native speakers. The results are presented in table 1.1.

The important information to look at in these results is not the absolute ratings of the test items as 'fine' (i.e. whether participants rate the expected cases as 100%

TABLE 1.1 Ratings (%) of Adj + N and N + Adj word orders as 'fine' in contexts favouring qualitative or additive meanings (based on Anderson, 2008: 16, Table 4 and Appendix B).

	Qualitative Meaning		Additive Meaning	
	Adj + N %	N + Adj %	Adj + N %	N + Adj %
2nd year (n = 29)	55	56	64	60
3rd year (n = 24)	57	51	64	56
4th year (n = 20)	59	39	52	70
Advanced (n = 20)	82	12	36	76
Native speakers (n = 27)	79	3	51	64

n = number of participants

TABLE 1.2 Difference in ratings of 'fine' to Adj + N and N + Adj word orders in contexts where a qualitative meaning or an additive meaning is favoured

	Qualitative Meaning	Additive Meaning
	Difference	Difference
2nd year (n = 29)	−1	−4
3rd year (n = 24)	6	−8
4th year (n = 20)	20	18
Advanced (n = 20)	70	40
Native speakers (n = 27)	76	13

'fine') but rather the relative ratings of the phrases that are expected to be 'fine' compared with those that are expected to be 'odd'. If participants have acquired the knowledge that some adjectives in French can precede and follow nouns and have different meanings when they do so, they should be making a clear distinction between these cases. It would be unrealistic to expect to find absolute judgements of 'fine' and 'odd' in a task where participants are asked to rate sentences that are all grammatical in the context of stories that only favour one or other meaning, but cannot categorically rule out the alternative meaning. There is plenty of room for participants to create their own, unexpected interpretation of the context.

The relative ratings can be considered by subtracting the percentage ratings of 'fine' for the unexpected orders from the percentage ratings of 'fine' for the expected orders in table 1.1. The percentage point differences are presented in table 1.2.

The sizes of the differences show that the native speakers of French, who provide a baseline or control measure against which the L2 speakers can be compared, make a very strong distinction when the meaning is qualitative. Adjective + noun order is greatly preferred with this meaning (a 76-point difference). They make much less of a distinction between the two word orders when the meaning is additive (a 13-point difference), with a slight preference for noun + adjective order.

Only the advanced L2 speakers really show the same pattern of response (and in fact associate noun + adjective order more strongly with an additive meaning), although the fourth-year learners are beginning to make a connection between the order of adjectives and nouns and the qualitative/additive meaning distinction. The early second- and third-year learners appear not yet to have identified the connection between word order in the French noun phrase and meaning. In this case, solving the 'semantics problem' does not appear to happen until learners are of quite advanced proficiency.

Section 1.5 in a Nutshell

The 'semantics problem' facing L2 learners is to identify how, in the target language, the meaning of individual words interacts with the structure of phrases to produce composite meanings. A study of the acquisition by L2 learners of the meanings of some French adjectives when they precede and follow nouns (Anderson, 2008) suggests that solving the 'semantics problem' may require considerable exposure to the language.

1.6 Identifying the Relevance of Extra-Sentential Information – the Context Problem

This section considers two ways in which the use of language is affected by factors beyond the immediate sentence. A further task facing the L2 learner is identifying these extra-sentential context effects.

1.6.1 The Discourse Problem

Knowledge about properties internal to sentences is not the only kind of knowledge that an L2 learner needs to have to become communicatively competent in the target language. Linguistic dependencies that hold across sentences in conversations, monologues, and other extended uses of language commonly referred to as 'discourse' also need to be identified. For example, languages have different ways of indicating, in a current sentence, information that is recoverable from preceding discourse and information that is not and is new. In English, new information often comes at the end of the current sentence, and already known information at the beginning. For example, in the following scenario the second possible response to the question just doesn't sound right because *my cousin* is the new information but it appears in a position normally occupied by already-known information:

6. Speaker A: Whom did the news surprise?

    Speaker B: (a) The news surprised my cousin.

                (b) #My cousin was surprised by the news.

(# means that the sentence is infelicitous in this context. It is a perfectly acceptable sentence in other contexts: *What surprised your cousin? My cousin was surprised by the news.*)

Another device in English for signalling information that is new in the discourse is known as 'left dislocation', as in the following examples from Geluykens (1992: 10):

7 a. **Your friend John**, I saw **him** last night.

   b. **That play, it** was terrible!

Here, a phrase has been moved to the front of the sentence, and a pronoun inserted in the position in which it is interpreted (*your friend John* is interpreted as the object of the verb *see; that play* is interpreted as the subject of the description *was terrible*). Geluykens shows that in the majority of cases in English such fronted phrases 'represent information which is highly irrecoverable' (1992: 53), in other words effectively 'new' information.

Donaldson (2011: 406) has argued that left dislocation in French, which has a similar structure to English (as shown in the examples of (8)), and is considerably more frequent than in English (at least in spoken French), serves a different function. It signals information that is not new, but is already known from discourse.

8 a. **Ton**   **ami**   **Jean**,   je   **l'**   ai   vu   hier   soir.
      Your   friend   Jean,   I   him   have   seen   yesterday   evening

   b. **Cette**   **pièce**,   **c'**   était   affreux!
      That   play,   it   was   terrible

In a study of eight-and-a half hours of free conversation between near-native speakers of French (whose L1 is English) and native speakers, Donaldson found that of 408 left dislocation constructions produced by the near-native speakers, 77% of them referred to information encountered in previous discourse. This proportion was identical to the proportion of references to previous discourse information in the 421 left dislocations produced by the native speakers. The challenge facing English learners of French in this case is not just to acquire the form that left dislocation takes in French, but also to identify the different function it serves, compared with English, in signalling discourse information. To do this, learners have to keep track of what information has gone before and then choose appropriate sentence structures for expressing the current message. It appears that very advanced proficiency speakers of L2s can do this (although keeping track of discourse information probably exceeds the computational resources of less proficient learners; for further discussion of this, see chapter 8).

1.6.2 The Sociolinguistic Variation Problem

A fundamental characteristic of language appears to be that different forms should not have the same meaning. In instances where two forms look as if they have the same meaning, it is usually the case that they are used in different contexts. For example, Crystal (1995: 164) observes that although *rancid* and *rotten* both qualify nouns referring to foodstuffs and both mean 'has badly deteriorated/ become inedible', they differ in the nouns with which they can co-occur: *rancid* is used with *butter* and *bacon, rotten* with *apples* and *tomatoes.* Here the context that determines the distribution of *rancid* and *rotten* is linguistic. But the choice of forms that appear to have very similar meanings can also be determined by non-linguistic factors that can be grouped under the general heading of 'social context of language use'. It is highly unlikely that the Secretary General of the United Nations would greet a delegate with 'Hey dude, what's up?' This is inappropriate in a professional context, although it may be appropriate in the context of a young skateboarder greeting a friend. In a professional context one is more likely to say 'Hello, how are things going?' Both expressions have the same intended meaning, but their use is conditioned by the social context in which a speaker finds her-/himself.

Identifying the features of social context that might be relevant to deciding which forms to use is a further challenge for the L2 learner. It will be referred to here as the 'sociolinguistic variation problem'. As in the case of the 'discourse problem', long exposure to the target language may be necessary to determine the relevance of the context in which target language forms are used.

A study by Rehner, Mougeon and Nadasdi (2003) of the use of the two pronouns *nous* and *on* with the same meaning 'we' by L2 learners of Canadian French shows an apparently persistent failure by them to identify the distribution of these forms in the spoken language. Participants were forty-one English-speaking classroom learners enrolled in a French immersion programme in the anglophone province of Ontario. In French immersion programmes, students are taught 'content' subjects through the medium of French for a proportion of the school day. In Ontario, the students in question experienced French immersion in 50 per cent of their classes in grades 5 to 8 (when they were aged ten to thirteen) and 20 per cent in the following grades. Rehner et al. studied learners who were in grades 9 (aged around fourteen) and 12 (aged around seventeen). They counted the proportions of use of *nous* and *on* in samples of the speech of the Canadian French-speaking teachers, who were the primary source of spoken language input for the learners, the distribution of *nous* and *on* in the textbooks that the learners were using, and the distribution of *nous* and *on* in the learners' own speech when they had an interview with a native speaker of French who asked 'nonchallenging, noninvasive questions about the students' daily activities' (2003: 135). The results are presented in table 1.3.

TABLE 1.3 Use of *nous* and *on* with the meaning 'we' by teachers, in textbooks and by L2 learners (based on Rehner et al., 2003: 146, Table 11).

	Teachers	Textbooks	Learners
Nous	80/478 (17%)	81/147 (55%)	642/1452 (44%)
On	398/478 (83%)	66/147 (45%)	810/1452 (56%)

It can be seen from table 1.3 that the teachers predominantly use *on* in speech, which according to Rehner et al. reflects the general trend in the speech of Canadian French speakers. By contrast, the learners use *nous* and *on* in their speech in roughly equal proportions. This is not dissimilar to the proportions of use of these forms in the written language they are exposed to via the textbooks. It suggests that the learners have so far failed to identify the difference in the frequency with which *nous* and *on* are used in the spoken language versus the written language.

Section 1.6 in a Nutshell

To become communicatively competent in an L2, you need knowledge not only of the internal properties of sentences (word meanings, grammatical versus ungrammatical word combinations, the composite meanings that arise from word combinations) but also how discourse and the context of language use affect the choice of linguistic forms. A study by Donaldson (2011) shows that speakers of English who are near-native speakers of French have identified the 'known from discourse information' function of French left dislocation. However, knowledge of the effect of extra-sentential properties may require long exposure to the target language. A study of the knowledge of the different uses of French *nous* and *on* (with the meaning 'we') in spoken and written French by highly proficient English speakers in French classroom immersion programmes found that they had not yet identified the difference in the use of these forms in the written and spoken language.

1.7 A Note on L2 versus L3, L4 ... Learning

While the task facing the learner of a third language (L3), fourth language (L4) ... is the same as that facing the L2 learner (solving the segmentation problem, the categorisation problem, the syntax problem etc.), it has become clear in recent years that there are differences in the way L3, L4 ... learners respond to that task. For example, in L2 learning a question arises about whether the first language influences the way that the learner approaches the segmentation, categorisation, syntax etc. problems. But in L3 learning the question is whether the L1, L2 or both are influential, and whether the learning of an L3 might have a reverse influence by changing already-acquired knowledge of the L2. The focus in this book is primarily on L2 learning. However, at some points studies of L3 learning will be briefly considered, and it should be noted that there is growing interest among researchers in how learners acquire third languages (Cabrelli Amaro et al., 2012).

1.8 Is Learning an L2 Good for You?

Michael Gove, the British Secretary of State for Education in 2011, expressed the view that 'there is a slam-dunk case for extending foreign language teaching to children aged five' (*The Guardian*, Friday 30 September 2011). He went even further, saying 'it is literally the case that learning languages makes you smarter. The neural networks in the brain strengthen as a result of language learning.' Was he right? Does learning an L2 make you smarter?

There are obvious ways in which speaking a second, third or more languages brings personal benefits. One is the satisfaction of being able to say something, however little, in the local language of a country one is visiting. Another is that speaking more than one language widens career options because many organisations and businesses need people who can communicate on the ground with their international partners, clients or customers in their own language. A third is that learning another language is typically accompanied by an increase in our understanding of the community that uses that language, contributing to our knowledge of how societies work.

Two less obvious potential benefits of speaking two or more languages, that more directly relate to whether speaking an L2 makes us smarter, have been extensively investigated in recent years. These are the impact of bilingualism on **executive control** and **cognitive reserve**. Valian (2015: 5) defines executive control as the mental processes that 'manage, integrate, regulate, coordinate or supervise other cognitive processes, such as attention and visual perception'. Cognitive reserve refers to the ability of the brain to compensate for damage to its neural structure, particularly from diseases that cause dementia. In both cases it has been claimed that bilingualism has a positive impact.

Executive control has been measured by a variety of tests that are assumed to reflect its workings. These include the 'Simon test', the 'Stroop test', and a 'colour–shape test'.

In the Simon test a participant is presented with coloured rectangles on a computer screen, and is required to press a key when a rectangle of a particular colour appears. For example, pressing a key with the left hand when a green rectangle appears and pressing a key with the right hand when a red rectangle appears. The rectangles appear randomly on the left or the right of the computer screen, and it has been found that in general people are faster at pressing a key with the left hand when the green rectangle appears on the left of the screen than when it appears on the right, and faster at pressing a key with the right hand when the red rectangle appears on the right of the computer screen than when it appears on the left.

In the Stroop test participants are presented with colour words like *red, blue, green* etc., either in a font colour that matches the word (e.g. the word *red* in a red font) or in a different font colour (e.g. the word *red* in a blue font). They are asked to name the font colour each time a word is presented. It has been generally found that people are faster at naming a colour when it matches the word than when it does not.

In the colour–shape test participants are shown shapes (like rectangles, squares, triangles, and so on) in different colours. Initially they are asked to name either the colour or the shape, but at certain intervals they are asked to switch, naming the shape if they have been naming the colours, or naming the colours if they have been naming the shapes. It has been found that participants generally take longer to name either colour or shape just after they have been asked to switch.

Each of these tasks requires a participant to juggle two pieces of perceptual information, selecting only one for the task at hand, thereby involving executive control. In the Simon test participants juggle with colour (red versus green) and location on the screen (left versus right), ignoring screen location to produce the correct answer. In the Stroop test participants juggle linguistic information (the name of a colour) and visual information (actual colour), and have to ignore misleading linguistic information to produce the correct answer. In the colour–shape test participants need to switch from one kind of perceptual information (colour) to another (shape) to produce the right answer. Ignoring some perceptual information to focus attention on just the percept that is relevant, or switching attention from one type of perceptual information to another, are assumed to be exactly the kinds of functions performed by executive control.

A number of studies have found an increased performance by bilingual speakers on these tests compared with monolinguals. In the Simon test it has been found that bilinguals are faster than monolinguals in pressing the key both when the hand and location on the screen are congruent (e.g. left hand/left of screen location) and when they are incongruent (e.g. left hand/right of screen location) (Bialystok, Craik, Klein and Viswanathan, 2004). In the Stroop test bilinguals have been shown to be faster than monolinguals in naming the font colour of colour words when the two do not match (i.e. when the word *red* is presented in a blue font) (Bialystok, Craik and Luk, 2008). Children asked to sort cards showing coloured shapes by colour and then re-sort them by shape are typically not able to do so until the age of four or five. Before that age they continue sorting by colour after being asked to switch. Bialystok (1999) has found that bilingual children acquire the ability to switch earlier than monolingual children. She argues that this 'ability to switch criteria [from colour to shape, or shape to colour] for the sorting decision and attend to the new feature while the irrelevant feature remains salient is an aspect of executive control' (2009: 5). The implication is that being bilingual promotes the development of executive control in young children.

It is more difficult to measure what facilitates cognitive reserve since the processes that give rise to it are not well understood (Valian, 2015: 8). Research has focused on outcomes: comparing people with neural damage and the mitigating effects of being a bilingual speaker. Bialystok, Craik and Freedman (2007), for example, found that dementia manifests itself in bilinguals on average four years later than in monolinguals, suggesting that regularly speaking two or more languages throughout life in some way bypasses the potential effects of physical decline in the brain.

However, caution is needed in interpreting studies that seem to suggest clear benefits of speaking a second language on executive control and cognitive reserve – making us smarter, in Michael Gove's words. Firstly, nearly all the work reported above has been conducted with bilinguals – people who are communicatively proficient in two or more languages and typically use them on a regular basis throughout life. It is not clear whether learning an L2 to a low level of proficiency, using it irregularly, or learning an L2 in later life will produce the same benefits, although there are studies that show that learning an L2 in adulthood leads to changes in neural networks (Li et al., 2014), as Gove speculated.

Secondly, Valian (2015) has conducted an extensive review of the work on executive control and cognitive function and alongside studies that show clear benefits of bilingualism, like those described above, there are many that find no differences between monolinguals and bilinguals. For example, Gathercole and her colleagues (2014) conducted a study in Wales with bilingual Welsh–English speakers and monolingual English speakers across the lifespan (children, teenagers, younger and older adults) using the Simon test and a card sorting test, and found no differences in performance between the bilinguals and the monolinguals.

In the case of cognitive reserve, Valian (2015: 13) distinguishes two types of study. The first is retrospective, where bilingual individuals who already have cognitive impairment are compared with monolinguals with cognitive impairment. The second is prospective, where a large sample of older bilinguals and monolinguals who are not cognitively impaired are followed over a number of years, typically four to ten. During this period some participants will develop dementia and the differences between the bilinguals and monolinguals can be compared. Valian's review of these studies finds that while the retrospective studies 'find a protective effect of bilingualism' (2015: 13), the prospective studies do not.

Valian also notes that bilingualism is not the only factor that may promote executive control processes and cognitive reserve. There are also positive correlations with musical training, experience playing video games, aerobic exercise, number of leisure and social activities engaged in, and other non-linguistic factors. The interpretation she gives of why some studies fail to find an effect for bilingualism on tests of executive control or outcomes for cognitive reserve is that the benefits of these other factors in monolinguals are equal to the benefits that may be conferred by speaking two or more languages. Speaking two languages brings cognitive benefits, but it is just one of a number of mentally challenging experiences that bring benefit. She concludes that 'consistent cognitive challenge, in any form, generally yields better performance on tests of executive function and generally yields more successful (i.e. less demented) aging' (2015: 4). So to slightly modify Michael Gove's speculation, learning languages is one of a number of mental activities that might make you smarter by improving/maintaining your executive control processes and adding to your ability to compensate for dementia in later life.

Section 1.8 in a Nutshell

'Executive control' is the set of mental processes that manage and coordinate cognitive processes like attention and visual perception. 'Cognitive reserve' is the ability of cognitive processes to compensate for physical damage to the brain, particularly from diseases that cause dementia. Tasks measuring executive control typically require the juggling of two pieces of perceptual information, suppressing one of them in favour of the other, for example suppressing the linguistic information provided by the word *red* to name a different font colour in which it is printed, e.g. 'blue'. A number of studies have found that bilingual speakers have enhanced performance on these tasks compared with monolinguals. However, if there are such benefits they seem to be for those who use two languages on a regular basis throughout life. It is not clear whether learning an L2 to a low level of proficiency or learning an L2 later in life has the same effect. And there are other studies that find no such differences between bilinguals and monolinguals (e.g. Gathercole et al., 2014). There are similarly mixed results in the case of cognitive reserve. Retrospective studies, looking at the age of onset of dementia in monolinguals and bilinguals, have found that it is on average four years later in bilinguals. Prospective studies, where monolinguals and bilinguals are studied longitudinally from a point before they show signs of dementia, find no difference between the two groups. Other kinds of cognitively challenging experience may also enhance executive control and compensate for dementia (Valian, 2015).

1.9 Concluding Remarks

Although some individuals may be exceptionally good at learning second languages (and some rather poor), for the majority of people it is perfectly possible to successfully acquire languages beyond their mother tongue(s), and to do so throughout life. Willingness to interact with samples of the target language over long periods of time appears to be a key factor. In engaging with the target language there are five key problems that an L2 learner has to solve:

- the segmentation problem – how to break into the continuous speech stream to identify recurrent meaningful components
- the categorisation problem – identifying which recurrent strings of sound have uniquely identifiable meanings, like *student, walk, in, smooth*, which have a meaning-modifying function, like **tense** or **number**, and which mark dependencies, like agreement between a third person singular subject and a verb in the present tense in English
- the syntax problem – working out which combinations of words are grammatical and which are ungrammatical in the target language
- the semantics problem – identifying the meanings of phrases that go beyond the meanings of the individual words of which they are composed
- the context problem – working out how grammatical properties interact with information previously supplied by discourse, and with different social and stylistic contexts.

Subsequent chapters introduce the reader to a selection of empirical findings that shed light on how L2 learners deal with these problems.

ACTIVITIES

1. TEST YOURSELF

(i) Which of the following meaning-modifying and dependency-marking properties did DeKeyser (1995) include in his invented language Implexan?

- *Meaning-modifying:* past tense, plural, possessive, definite
- *Dependency-marking:* subject–object agreement, verb–object agreement, adjective–noun agreement, subject–verb agreement

(ii) What underlies the ambiguity of the phrase *a heavy smoker*?
(iii) When is the symbol # used?
(iv) What do you understand by the terms 'executive control' and 'cognitive reserve'?

2. SEGMENTING STRINGS OF LETTERS

Will Saffran et al.'s experiment (section 1.2) also work if the input is a continuous string of letters, rather than sounds? The string of letters below is made up of a number of words. Read the string carefully from beginning to end. When you have read the complete string, you will be asked to decide what the words are.

Pronounce the vowels as follows:

u – *oo* as in *soon*	i – *ee* as in *see*
e – as in *egg*	a – *ah* as in *car*
o – *oh* as in *so*	

and give every syllable the same amount of stress, e.g. lú-mé-fú-só-kí-rí … and so on.

> **lu-me-fu-so-ki-ri-te-bo-da-lu-me-fu-so-ki-da-lu-me-ri-te-bo-fu-so-ki-fu-so-ki-ri-te-bo-da-lu-me-ri-te-bo-da-lu-me-fu-so-ki-da-lu-me-ri-te-bo-fu-so-ki-fu-so-ki-ri-te-bo-da-lu**

Choose the item in the following pairs, (a) or (b), that sounds more like a word from the language (Don't look back at the long string. Make a decision on the basis of whether the string feels like a word):

(i)	(a) ridafu	(b) ritebo
(ii)	(a) dalume	(b) teluso
(iii)	(a) kiluri	(b) fusoki

The answer is given at the end of the activities.

3. WHAT IS ACQUIRED FROM EXPOSURE TO SAMPLES OF LANGUAGE?

DeKeyser (section 1.3) found that, at the end of their exposure to Implexan, his participants were accurate in using previously-encountered [noun + affix] and [verb + affix] strings to describe photos, but only performed at chance level in using new [noun + affix] or [verb + affix] combinations. Similarly, Rebuschat (section 1.4) found that his participants, after 120 exposures to English-with-German-word-order, were above chance in deciding that word orders they had encountered were grammatical, but performed randomly in rejecting ungrammatical word orders.

What explanation would you give for this?

4. SEMANTICALLY AMBIGUOUS SENTENCES

Explain how the meaning of the following sentences goes beyond the meaning of the individual words of which they are composed:

 (i) Everyone in the room speaks two languages.
 (ii) He's a French teacher.
 (iii) I almost read a book last night.
 (iv) She's a light sleeper.

5. DATA ANALYSIS

Below are two transcripts of the English speech of a native speaker of Italian, 'Andrea', who was working in London as a waiter (Klein and Perdue, 1992: 91 and 101). The first sample was collected after he had been in London for six months, the second sample twenty months later. Andrea was acquiring English primarily on the basis of interaction with other speakers of English.

Assuming that what Andrea says is a direct reflection of the range of his knowledge of English, describe the development that takes place between the first and second data collection points in relation to his knowledge of pronouns (forms like *I, he, she, they* ...), verbs and definite/indefinite articles (*the/a*).

Transcript (a) (6 months after arrival). Andrea is describing a scene involving a man and two women cooking when a fire breaks out (... = pauses):

> every people happy in the cooking ... tea ... biscuit ... one man ... I dunno ... for the window ... the man thinks for ... no possible from the door. This man one idea from the window but when this man is in the cooking the door is open from the very quickly fire brigade

Transcript (b) (26 months after arrival). Andrea is describing a scene from the Charlie Chaplin film *Modern Times*.

> well after ten days they meet again and she tell him that she find, found one house for their, for them, and they go together to see this house. This house is a very old house all in wood in one field near one lake and they stay in this house, well they stay there.

Hint: There is only one pronoun *I* in the first transcript, and this may even be part of a rote-learned **formula** *Idunno*. Andrea's knowledge of pronouns is more differentiated in the second transcript. The task is to describe how they are differentiated, and therefore what he might have acquired between the first data collection point and the second. Discuss the development of his knowledge of verbs and articles in the same way.

Answer to activity 2: the words are *ritebo, dalume, fusoki.*

FURTHER READING

For more on obsessive language learners ('hyperpolyglots') see:

> Erard, M. 2012. *Babel no more: the search for the world's most extraordinary language learners.* New York: Free Press.

A useful and quick introduction to first and second language acquisition can be found in:

> Lightbown, P. M. and Spada, N. 2013. *How languages are learned.* Fourth Edition. Oxford: Oxford University Press.

For a detailed introduction to first language acquisition see:

> Guasti, M. T. 2016. *Language acquisition: the growth of grammar.* Second Edition. Cambridge, MA: MIT Press.

For a recent introduction to syntax see:

> Koeneman, O. and Zeijlstra, H. 2017. *Introducing syntax.* Cambridge: Cambridge University Press.

For an introduction to semantics see:

Hurford, J. R., Heasley, B. and Smith, M. B. 2007. *Semantics: a coursebook*. Second Edition. Cambridge: Cambridge University Press.

For a recent collection of papers on L3 learning see the following, although the studies reported in this collection assume familiarity with current research into L2 learning and are probably best read when you are familiar with the contents of the current book:

Cabrelli Amaro, J., Flynn, S. and Rothman, J. (eds) 2012. *Third language acquisition in adulthood*. Amsterdam: John Benjamins.

For more on bilingualism and its possible effects on other cognitive capacities see:

Bialystok, E., Craik, F. I. M. and Luk, G. 2012. Bilingualism: consequences for mind and brain. *Trends in Cognitive Sciences*, 16, 240–50.

And for the specific effects of bilingualism on aging see:

Bialystok, E. and Sullivan, M. D. (eds) 2017. *Growing old with two languages: effects of bilingualism on cognitive aging*. Amsterdam: John Benjamins

2 How Words and their Parts are Learned

In chapter 1 it was suggested that one of the challenges facing L2 learners is to determine which of three kinds of meaning are associated with recurrent strings of sounds/written symbols that have been segmented from the target language: uniquely identifiable, meaning-modifying or dependency-marking. This was described as a categorisation problem. In this chapter evidence is examined that bears on how L2 learners deal with the categorisation problem.

2.1 Associating L2 Forms with Uniquely Identifiable Meanings

One view of human cognition is that there is a part of the mind where 'concepts' are stored independently from linguistic forms. This view is consistent with findings from studies of people who have suffered linguistic impairment as the result of brain damage through illness or injury. Hart et al. (1985), for example, report a study of a 34-year-old man (MD) who had suffered a stroke with surprisingly specific effects on his mental capacities. They discovered that when MD was presented with pictures of fruit, vegetables and other objects, he had difficulty naming the fruit and vegetables, but not the other objects. When MD was asked to sort seventy-five randomised pictures into piles on the basis of the categories 'fruit', 'vegetable', 'animal', 'vehicle', 'food product', he made errors in the 'fruit' and 'vegetable' categories, but not the others. However, when MD was presented with pairs of pictures which included fruit and vegetables, and simultaneously heard a word corresponding to one of the pictures, he made no errors in selecting the appropriate picture. These findings suggest that the association between the concepts that MD has for fruit and vegetables and the linguistic names that he has for them has been impaired by his stroke. When he sees a fruit or vegetable he cannot always find the right name for it. However, the association in the other direction is unimpaired. If he hears words like *apple, pear, potato, bean* he can appropriately call up the concept with which the word is linked.

Concepts are mental representations of entities that have been perceived or imagined. In the context of language acquisition, when learners identify the meaning of a recurrent string of sounds/written symbols, they are making an

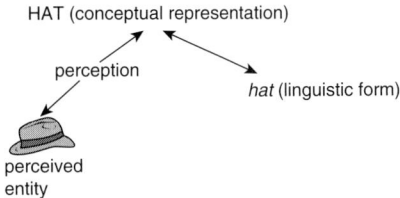

Figure 2.1 The relationship between linguistic forms and what they refer to

association between that string and a conceptual representation, not directly between the string and the entity it refers to (real or imagined). This view of the association between forms and uniquely identifiable meanings is illustrated in figure 2.1. Through encounters with a given entity that has a particular form and function, for example an object that protects or adorns the head (a 'hat'), a person establishes a memory for that object: a conceptual representation. A capitalised HAT stands for the conceptual representation in figure 2.1. This conceptual representation is associated with a linguistic form (a sequence of sounds or letters) represented by an italicised *hat*. The associations between HAT and the perceived entity and between HAT and the linguistic form *hat* work in both directions. Seeing a hat will activate the concept HAT, and this concept will only be associated with objects that can function to protect or adorn heads, not with objects that can hold liquids (jugs) or carry goods (bags), for example. Conversely, hearing (or reading) the form *hat* will activate the concept HAT; and the activation of HAT will call up the linguistic form *hat*. In the stroke victim MD it appears that while hearing or seeing forms like *apple, potato* activated the corresponding concepts, activation of the concepts did not automatically activate the link to the linguistic forms.

People who are proficient speakers of an L2 will know many thousands of such associations. How do they acquire this knowledge? There are a number of conceivable possibilities. Potter et al. (1984) considered two of them. In the first, L2 *forms* are mapped directly to equivalent *forms* in the L1, as illustrated in figure 2.2(a), where Mandarin Chinese is the L1 and English the L2 (the Mandarin equivalent of English *hat* is *maozi*). In the second, L2 *forms* are associated directly with the conceptual representation for HAT, as illustrated in figure 2.2(b).

Potter et al. tested these two possibilities with native speakers of Chinese who were highly proficient in English. They measured the time it took them to name objects in pictures using English (their L2) compared with the time it took them to translate words from Chinese (their L1) into English, for example to translate *maozi* as *hat*. They reasoned that if the scenario depicted in figure 2(a) is correct, speakers should be faster in translating words from the L1 to the L2 than in naming objects in pictures in the L2. This is because more mental processing steps are involved in naming. In naming, an informant first has to associate the picture with the conceptual representation, then access the L1 form, and finally access the L2 form connected to it. However, in translating from *maozi* to *hat*,

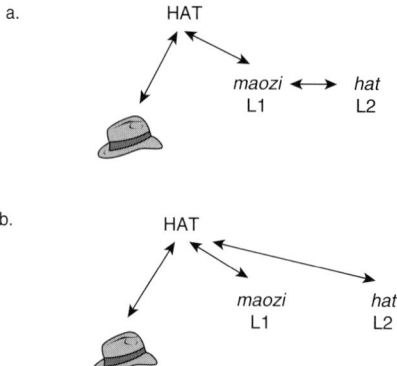

Figure 2.2 Two Ways in Which L2 Forms Might Be Learned

once the written symbol for *maozi* has been recognised, the only step required is the activation of the link with the L2 English form. If the scenario illustrated in figure 2(b) is correct, no difference in response times is expected between naming and translation because the number of processing steps an informant has to go through is about the same. In naming, the object in the picture is associated with the conceptual representation and then directly with the L2 form. In translating, the L1 form is associated with the conceptual representation, which in turn is associated with the L2 form.

Potter et al. found that participants' response times were the same in naming the objects depicted in pictures and in translating L1 words into the L2, consistent with the second scenario. This might suggest that when L2 learners initially associate recurrent strings of sounds/written symbols with uniquely identifiable meanings, they make direct links between L2 forms and conceptual representations.

However, Kroll and Curley (1988) replicated Potter et al.'s experiment both with L2 learners who were relatively experienced in the L2 (had been learning for more than two years) and with novice learners (with less than two years' experience). They found that while the participants with more than two years' exposure to the L2 performed in the same way as Potter et al.'s participants, taking about the same amount of time to name objects in pictures and translate L1 words into the L2, the participants with less than two years of exposure were faster in translation than in picture naming. This is consistent with the scenario depicted in figure 2.2(a) and led to the conclusion reported by Kroll and Stewart (1994: 151) that 'there is a developmental shift in second language learning from reliance on word-to-word connections to reliance on concepts'.

In other words, the initial phase in the learning of the uniquely identifiable meanings of L2 forms involves a direct linking between an L2 form and an L1 form, with the meaning of the L2 form being the conceptual representation that the L1 form is associated with. However, with time and repeated encounters with the L2 form in contexts that give clues to its meaning, the form becomes directly associated with its own conceptual representation, which may be the same conceptual representation with which the L1 form is associated.

2.2 Persistence of the Connections between L2 Forms and L1 Words

Kroll and Stewart (1994) provide evidence that although the organisation of L2 words in the mental lexicon changes from one initially based on connections between L2 and L1 forms to one where L2 forms are directly connected to their own conceptual representations, nevertheless L2 form-to-L1 form connections remain, although weaker. The evidence for this comes from a meaning-based interference effect when speakers translate words from the L1 to the L2, but not when they translate from the L2 to the L1.

The interference effect appears in native speakers when they are asked to name objects in sets of pictures. They are generally slower to do so when those objects are conceptually related than when they are random. For example, they are slower in naming a set of pictures depicting the objects 'mitten', 'hat', 'jacket', 'shirt', all items of clothing, than in naming a set of pictures depicting the unrelated objects 'hat', 'carrot', 'toe', 'cello'. It is known that words with similar conceptual representations are stored close together in memory (see section 2.3 below for discussion). And it is also known that when a word is accessed from memory it tends to activate other words with which it is stored. Kroll and Stewart argue that because conceptually-related words activate each other they are competitors in the naming task. A speaker has to suppress related, but inappropriate, words for a given object in order to produce the appropriate one, and this takes time. When a speaker has to name a random set of objects, there are no connections between the words that describe them, there are no words that need to be suppressed and naming is faster. Thus there is a meaning-based interference effect in naming a list of related objects.

Exploiting this interference effect, twenty-four L1 speakers of Dutch with high proficiency in L2 English were asked to translate lists of English words into Dutch and Dutch words into English. Some of the lists were conceptually related (clothing, vegetables, parts of the body) while others were random. Results showed that participants were slower at translating lists of words from Dutch to English when they were conceptually related than when they were random, but participants were equally fast in translating from English to Dutch, regardless of the type of list. Kroll and Stewart interpret these findings to mean that when translating a word in L1 Dutch to L2 English the connection between the Dutch word and its conceptual representation is first activated and the concept activates the connection to the English word. But in translating a word in L2 English to L1 Dutch, the level of conceptual representation is by-passed; the connection between the English form and a Dutch equivalent word that was established in early acquisition is used.

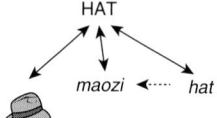

Figure 2.3 A revised model of the way L2 forms are stored in memory in proficient L2 speakers (Mandarin Chinese is the L1 and English the L2) (adapted from Kroll and Stewart, 1994: 158, Figure 3)

This suggests that although connections between conceptual representations and L2 forms increase in strength with proficiency, nevertheless L2 form-to-L1 form connections persist.

Figure 2.3 illustrates the relationship between L2 forms, L1 forms and conceptual representations in later L2 acquisition. The thick arrows represent stronger connections than the dotted arrow.

Sections 2.1 and 2.2 in a Nutshell
Experimental studies that have looked at the time it takes L2 speakers to respond in naming objects in the L2 and in translating L1 words into the L2 and L2 words into the L1 suggest that early-stage learners associate L2 forms directly with equivalent L1 forms. As they become more proficient, L2 forms are associated directly with their own conceptual representations (uniquely identifiable meanings), but the connections between L2 and L1 forms persist, although they are weaker.

2.3 The Organisation of L2 Form–Meaning Pairs in a 'Mental Lexicon'

Words are pairings of linguistic forms with conceptual representations. Being able to comprehend and produce sentences in an L2 requires knowing thousands of words. This stock of remembered words is often referred to as a **mental lexicon**. Acquiring an L2 mental lexicon is a major challenge. This section looks first at how the mental lexicon is organised in native speakers, and then considers whether L2 learners store words in the same way.

2.3.1 Organisation of Words in the L1 Mental Lexicon

How do native speakers of a language store words? In principle, there are a number of possibilities. For example, they could be stored as a random list: *sock, leaf, happy, fish* etc. Alternatively, they could be stored in alphabetical order: *[f]ish, [h]appy, [l]eaf, [s]ock* etc. Listing by alphabetical order is the method used by most dictionaries. Yet again, words could be stored in the order in which they were acquired. And there are other conceivable possibilities.

As it turns out, words in native speakers' mental lexicons are typically grouped together by the grammatical category they belong to (noun, verb, adjective etc.), by similarity of meaning (their conceptual representations) and to a lesser extent by the similarity of their forms. The groupings are usually thought of as a set of connections between words, so that when one word is accessed, words with which it has connections are also 'activated' (i.e. retrieved from memory at the same time). Similarity of meaning can take a number of forms: words with the same meanings (**synonyms**) are connected, e.g. *sofa–couch, help–aid, quick–fast*; words with opposite meanings (**antonyms**) are connected, e.g. *new–old, tall–short, black–white*; words whose meanings describe entities of the same type are connected, e.g. *salmon–trout–cod–herring–haddock*. These are all types of *fish*, and are known as **hyponyms** of the superordinate noun *fish*. Meaning connections between words can also be less well defined, largely being determined by a speaker's knowledge of the contexts in which a word is used. For example, *leaf* might activate other nouns whose meaning makes one think of 'leaves': *tree, plant, caterpillar, book* ('leaves of paper') and so on.

Where words are members of the same grammatical category, they are generally in complementary distribution in sentences, as illustrated in (1):

1. The child looked at the $\begin{bmatrix} \text{sofa} \\ \text{cat} \\ \text{leaf} \\ \text{tree} \end{bmatrix}$ in the picture

Sofa, cat etc. are all nouns and form a paradigm. Where words in a paradigm share meaning connections, these are described as paradigmatic connections. Other connections between words in the lexicon can be determined by the frequency with which they appear together sequentially in sentences. In these cases, connected words typically belong to different grammatical categories. If you hear the phrases *tall ship, black coffee, green energy* often enough, this may lead to connections being established between the words involved, so that hearing *tall* will not only activate *short* but also *ship*, and so on. Because these connections are the result of the frequent co-occurrence of words in syntactic structures, they are often referred to as syntagmatic connections, and the phrases themselves as collocations.

Connections may also be established between the *forms* of words, regardless of their meaning. Words that have the same number of syllables, have main stress on the same syllable and have segmental sounds in common may activate each other. For example, a form like **si***lence* (with stress on the first syllable) might be connected to forms like **sci***ence*, **sy***phon*; con**nec***tion* (with stress on the second syllable) to forms like col**lec***tion*, cor**rec***tion*, and so on.

How is it known that native speakers group words in the mental lexicon in this way? One source of evidence comes from **Word Association Tests** (WATs). In a WAT, an informant hears a list of prompt words and is asked to respond quickly after each word with the first word that comes to mind. Here is an example:

2. | **Prompt** | **Possible informant response** |
|---|---|
| new | old |
| fish | cod |
| break | glass |
| potato | onion |
| brother | sister |
| attach | tie |

The assumption underlying WATs is that the responses that informants produce reflect the connections they have with the prompts in memory. If words are remembered randomly, responses will be random. If they are remembered in the alphabetical order of the forms that realise them, a prompt like *potato* might elicit the response *potent* rather than *onion*. If words are stored by grammatical category or by frequency of co-occurrence in speech, prompts will elicit responses that are paradigmatically or syntagmatically connected. Indeed, the responses obtained in such tests tend to be of the latter kind. For example, in a WAT conducted with 1,000 native speakers of English by Jenkins (1970) over half of the informants responded to prompts like *hammer* (noun), *high* (adjective), *white* (adjective), *king* (noun) with the words *nail* (noun), *low* (adjective), *black* (adjective), *queen* (noun), all responses that are in the same syntactic category and semantically related to the prompts.

Section 2.3.1 in a Nutshell
The words (pairings of linguistic forms with conceptual representations) in a native speaker's mental lexicon may be connected to other words of the same grammatical category that have related meanings (paradigmatic connections), to words with which they collocate frequently (syntagmatic connections) and to words that are similar in form. When one word in a network of connections is accessed, the others are also activated (retrieved from the mental lexicon at the same time).

2.3.2 Organisation of Words in the L2 Mental Lexicon

Do L2 speakers store words in the same way as native speakers? Evidence from WATs suggests that, when words are well known, they do. When words are less well known, those words are stored differently.

Wolter (2001) conducted an English WAT with thirteen L1 speakers of Japanese of at least high intermediate proficiency in English, and nine native speakers.

There were forty-five prompts with equal numbers of nouns, adjectives and verbs. Responses were classified into four categories: paradigmatic (*sofa–couch*, *leaf–tree*, ...), syntagmatic (*soft–pillow*, *green–energy*, ...), responses based on 'similarity of sound or that were unclassifiable', and no response. The overall proportions of responses in each of these categories are presented in table 2.1.

Both groups show similar proportions of syntagmatic responses to the prompts, but the native speakers are more likely to produce meaning-based paradigmatic responses, and the L2 speakers more likely to produce responses based on similarity of sound with the prompt or no classifiable connection. It looks, then, as if L2 speakers remember L2 words more on the basis of the frequency of co-occurrence of words in sentences and the similarity of their sound structure than on the basis of membership of the same grammatical category and similarity of meaning.

However, following the WAT, Wolter asked participants to rate the prompts in terms of how familiar they were, and re-calculated the proportions of responses only for prompts that were very familiar to participants. He also gave the native speaker group a second WAT where the prompts were relatively infrequent words of English. The proportions of responses by both groups to familiar prompts, and the responses of the native English group to infrequent prompts are given in table 2.2.

The responses of the L2 participants to prompts they are familiar with look more like those of native speakers, with higher proportions of responses with

TABLE 2.1 Proportions of responses (%) by type in a WAT (based on Wolter, 2001: 56, Figure 4)

	No. of Responses	Paradigmatic (%)	Syntagmatic (%)	Similar Sound/ Other (%)	No Response (%)
Japanese (n = 13)	579	19.7	37.7	35.1	7.6
English (n = 9)	402	51.7	41.0	7.2	0

TABLE 2.2 Proportions of responses (%) by type of the L2 group to 'familiar' prompts, and of the English participants to 'infrequent' prompts (based on Wolter, 2001: 57–60, Figures 5 and 10)

	No. of Responses	Paradigm. (%)	Syntagm. (%)	Similar Sound/ Other (%)	No Response (%)
Japanese (familiar prompts)	268	35.4	54.1	10.4	0
English (familiar prompts)	284	48.9	39.8	11.3	0
English (infrequent prompts)	404	38.1	32.4	27.2	2.2

meaning-based paradigmatic connections to the prompts and fewer similar sounding or unclassifiable responses. Furthermore, the native speaker responses to the infrequent prompts look more like those of the L2 speakers to the test overall, where around half of the prompts were to varying degrees unfamiliar to them.

These results suggest that when words are less well known, both by L2 speakers and native speakers, connections by frequency of co-occurrence and similarity of form increase and connections by grammatical category and similarity of meaning decrease.

Integrating these findings with those of the studies by Kroll and Curley (1988) and Kroll and Stewart (1994), the picture that emerges of the L2 lexicon can be represented as in figure 2.4 (where for illustrative purposes English is the L1 and French the L2). Initially, French forms are connected to perceived English equivalent words. There is no direct connection between French forms and conceptual representations. However, learners do make connections between forms in the L2 that sound the same (like *chapeau* 'hat' and *crapaud* 'toad' in figure 2.4). In later acquisition, when L2 learners have become more familiar with L2 forms, they are associated directly with conceptual representations (as in the L1 mental lexicon). Paradigmatic connections with words in the same semantic field are established (like *chapeau* 'hat', *gant* 'glove' and *écharpe* 'scarf' in figure 2.4), as are syntagmatic connections with frequently encountered collocates (such as *chapeau melon* 'bowler hat' and *chapeau de paille* 'straw hat' in figure 2.4). However, the connection between L2 form and L1 word remains, although it is weaker.

a. *Storage of Recently Acquired L2 Forms*

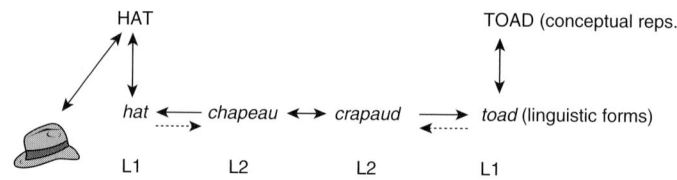

b. *Storage of 'Familiar' L2 Forms*

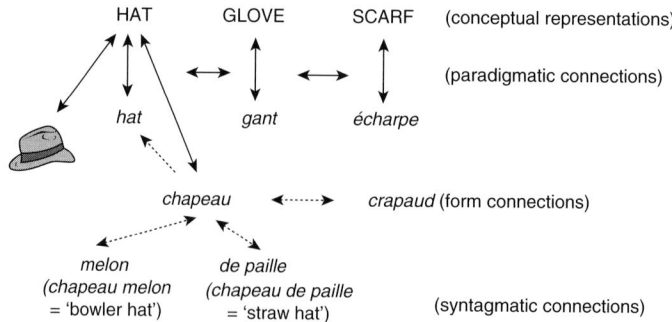

Figure 2.4 A revised model of the acquisition of L2 words with uniquely identifiable meanings

2.4 Associating L2 Forms with Meaning-Modifying Functions

The learners of Implexan in DeKeyser's (1995) study (see section 1.3) had apparently not had enough exposure to the language to enable them to categorise the meaning-modifying and dependency-marking function of forms like *-on* (plural marker) and *-in* (subject–verb dependency marker). This section considers how L2 learners come to associate forms with meaning-modifying functions when they have had sufficient exposure.

An interesting example is provided in a study by Wode (1981: 250–63) of the developing use of English by his four German-speaking children during a period the family spent in the United States. One of the properties he looked at was how the children developed knowledge of the meaning-modifying plural affix *-s*. The function of *-s* is to change the reference of count nouns from individual entities to sets of entities, for example *apple–apples, egg–eggs, book–books*. He found that two of his children initially used just one form of the word *egg* to express both singular and plural. But they differed in whether the form ended in *-s* or not. His son Heiko used the word *egg* to refer both to 'one egg' and 'more than one egg':

3 a. Heiko: How many egg you have?
               I want two egg.

Another son, Lars, used *eggs* for both meanings:

   b. Lars: Who want this eggs?
              You give me one eggs

At this stage in their development, although Heiko and Lars have associated the form *egg(s)* with a uniquely identifiable meaning, they have not yet worked out the function that *-s* has in English.

A bit later on, when the children had had more exposure to English, they each acquired the other form, so both were now saying *egg* and *eggs*. At this stage Heiko used *eggs* exclusively to mean 'more than one egg' (e.g. 'I want two eggs'). But he did not always use it, so *egg* continued to mean 'one egg or more than one egg'. He was optionally saying 'I want two egg/I want two eggs'.

For Lars, who initially used the single form *eggs* to mean both 'eggs' or 'just one egg', a rather surprising change occurred when he learned the form *egg*. He no longer used *eggs* to mean 'one egg'. Instead, it now only meant 'more than one egg'. But he used the newly learned word *egg* to mean both 'one egg' and 'more than one egg'. So at this second stage of development, Lars's performance had become just like that of Heiko. The development of the two boys' use of the singular and plural forms *egg/eggs* is represented diagrammatically in (4).

4. Heiko   Lars

   egg [singular/plural]   *eggs* [singular/plural]

        ↓   ↓

   egg [singular/plural]   *egg* [singular/plural]

   eggs [plural]   *eggs* [plural]

This example turns out to be quite representative of what happens when L2 learners begin to acquire the meaning-modifying or dependency-marking functions of forms. Once a form-function correspondence has been identified (as in the case of plural *-s*), when a learner uses the form it will have the identified function. But the form is not always used in the contexts where native speakers obligatorily require it. It alternates with some other form of the word. In the case of Heiko and Lars, the affix-less form *egg* alternates with *eggs* in plural contexts, but only *egg* is used in singular contexts. This kind of optionality, where two forms of the same word can be used in contexts where just one is required in the target language, is a pervasive characteristic of L2 learner performance, as will become clear as the chapter proceeds.

Section 2.4 in a Nutshell
When forms are associated with a meaning-modifying function, they may at first be under-generalised, alternating with another form of the same word in contexts where the meaning-modifying form is obligatory in the target language. The other form is used optionally in more than one context.

2.5 Associating L2 Forms with Dependency-Marking Functions

The way that L2 learners come to associate L2 forms with dependency-marking functions can be illustrated from another study of artificial language learning conducted by Williams (2005). The findings suggest that learners may have unconscious linguistic predispositions that drive their analysis. In the study, forty-one native and non-native speakers of English were exposed to a language that was English but with four novel determiners ('determiners' are forms that appear in the same position in sentences as the words *the, a, this, my*): *gi, ro, ul, ne*. Participants were told that 'in this language, each time an object is mentioned, it is necessary to specify how far away it is from the subject of the sentence, whether it is "near" or "far"' (2005: 282). *Gi* and *ro* always appeared with near objects, *ul* and *ne* with far objects, as illustrated in the following examples:

5   a. When I was out for a walk, I petted gi dog and it bit me.
   b. The researchers studied ul bees from a safe distance.

In other words, participants were given explicit information about the meaning-modifying function of *gi, ro, ul, ne*.

In the exposure phase of the experiment, participants were asked to listen to 144 sentences containing the novel determiners, and for each determiner to press a button indicating whether it meant 'near' or 'far'. This ensured that they were actively engaged in processing the meaning of each of the new determiners during their exposure to this 'language'. Unknown to them, however, in addition to their meaning-modifying function, the four determiners also encoded a dependency: *gi* and *ul* only co-occurred with animate nouns like *dog, bee, lion*, while *ro* and *ne* only co-occurred with inanimate nouns like *sofa, television, table*. That is, the novel determiners also served to mark a dependency between the determiner and the noun based on animacy (just as the *-s* in *She sings* marks a dependency between the verb and its subject based on person and number).

Following exposure, participants were shown sentence fragments like *The lady spent many hours sewing …* with two possible completions: *gi cushions* or *ro cushions*. They had to choose the appropriate completion for the sentence. Here *gi* and *ro* are both appropriate in terms of 'nearness', but *ro* is the form that is used with inanimates, not *gi*. The results show above-chance selection of the animacy-appropriate determiner, suggesting that participants had unconsciously tallied the frequencies with which *gi* and *ul* co-occurred with animate nouns, and *ro* and *ne* with inanimate nouns.

What is particularly interesting in this study is that participants needed to know firstly that a determiner-like form can express a dependency between it and a property of a following noun, and secondly that 'animacy' is a potentially relevant **feature** in dependency-marking. If learners are linguistic 'blank slates' when they start learning, there is no reason to expect them to identify a dependency-marking function of the four determiners in addition to the meaning-modifying function.

Furthermore, there is a potentially large number of properties that could be the target of that dependency, and not just animacy: *gi* and *ul* could co-occur with words of one syllable (*dog, bee*) and *ro/ne* with words of more than one syllable (*sofa, cushion*); *gi* and *ne* could co-occur with nouns if they are in the first five words in a sentence (*I was amazed when gi bird ate from my hand; I looked up at ne clock*), *ul* and *ro* are used elsewhere (*I was distressed by the smell of ul pig*, etc.); *gi* and *ul* could co-occur with nouns describing creatures that can fly (*gi birds, ul bees*), while *ne/ro* co-occur with other nouns (*ne clocks, ro boxes*); among others. A learner would have to compute all of these possibilities and determine that 'animacy' was a greater-than-chance possibility on the basis of 144 exposures to the language. This seems fairly implausible and might suggest that language learners already know in some sense that when there are alternative forms apparently serving the same meaning-modifying function this may be because they also have a dependency-marking function, and that 'animacy' is a feature that could be relevant to the categorisation of forms. They bring this knowledge to the task of learning a new language.

Section 2.5 in a Nutshell

L2 learners know in advance of exposure to a new language that it may use forms to mark dependencies between constituents in sentences. Where they find more than one form apparently serving the same meaning-modifying function, they may hypothesise that a dependency-marking function is also involved. Additionally, learners know that the animacy or inanimacy of the entities referred to by nouns is more likely to be relevant to dependency marking than other conceivable properties, such as the number of syllables a word is composed of, the linear position it occupies in a sentence, or whether it describes a flying, rather than a non-flying, entity.

2.6 Development of Knowledge of L2 Verb Forms

In many languages, the time reference of the event or state of affairs described by a sentence is reflected in the form that the verb takes. Such reference can be to a defined period of time, such as prior to the moment of speaking (or writing), simultaneous with the moment of speaking, or some time in the future. Verb forms that refer to a defined period of time are known as **finite** forms. Alternatively, a form of the verb can indicate that an event or state of affairs has no defined time reference; such forms are **non-finite**. In (6a–b), different finite forms of the English verb *write* signal defined time reference: past in the case of

(6a), non-past in the case of (6b).[1] In (6c), the form *to* marks the verb as non-finite and signals that the time reference is not specified. These changes in the form of the verb have a meaning-modifying function, determining whether the event/state of affairs described has a defined time reference or not.

6 a. She *wrote*[finite, past] novels.

  b. She *writes*[finite, non-past] novels

  c. She likes *to*[non-finite] *write* novels.

A study by Prévost and White (2000) examined the use of finite and non-finite verb forms in the L2 French of two L1 speakers of Arabic (Zahra and Abdelmalek) over a three-year period of naturalistic acquisition in France. In French, non-finite verb forms involve an affix, just like finite verb forms (and unlike English where the non-finite marker is the independent form *to*), as illustrated in (7):

Finite		**Non-finite**	
7 a. (Elle) parl-e	'(She) speaks'	parl-er	'to speak'
b. (Nous) vend-ons	'(We) sell'	vend-re	'to sell'
c. (Vous) part-ez	'(You) leave'	part-ir	'to leave'

While both speakers knew finite and non-finite forms of French verbs, they did not use them in the same way as native speakers. Two illustrative examples are given in (8) from a transcript of a fragment of speech from Zahra, who is describing a film clip (from the Charlie Chaplin film *Modern Times* – Klein and Perdue 1992: 244–5):

8 a. après   i   *parler*   Charlie   li   fille

     after   he   **to-speak (non-finite)**   Charlie   the   girl

     'Then Charlie speaks to the girl'

     (Native French: 'Après/Puis Charlie *parle* à la fille')

  b. après   Charlie   i   *monte*   …   la   maison

     after   Charlie   he   **goes (finite)** into …   the   house

     'Then Charlie goes into the house'

     (Native French: 'Après Charlie *entre* dans la maison')

Prévost and White discovered that the different use being made of finite and non-finite forms by Zahra and Abdelmalek was not random. Whereas non-finite forms were used in around a quarter of finite positions in sentences, finite forms were rarely overused in non-finite positions. (Typical non-finite positions include following a finite verb (*Il veut partir* 'He wants *to leave*') and following a preposition (*pour vendre la maison* 'in order *to sell* the house'). This pattern was common to both speakers, as table 2.3 shows.

---

[1] You might think that 'non-past' should really be 'present' or 'future', since many reference grammars use the past–present–future distinction. However, some verbs with the affix -*s* can refer to the future as well as to the present: *She leaves tomorrow, The course starts next week*. For this reason the assumption made here is that finite time reference in English divides into 'past' and 'non-past'.

TABLE 2.3 Use of finite and non-finite verb forms by two L2 speakers (based on Prévost and White, 2000: 119, Table 7)

	Non-Finite V in Finite Contexts	Finite V in Non-Finite Contexts
Zahra	224/755 (23%)	2/156 (1%)
Abdelmalek	243/767 (24%)	17/278 (6%)

The findings suggest that the two speakers are aware of the distinction between finite and non-finite *positions* in sentences, and of the finite function of some verb *forms*. However, they are not aware that verbs ending in *-er, -re, -ir* are restricted to non-finite positions. The state of their knowledge can be summarised as in (9).

9. **Position**

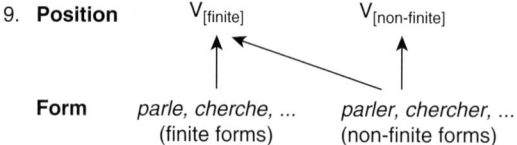

Form	*parle, cherche, ...*	*parler, chercher, ...*
	(finite forms)	(non-finite forms)

If they were not aware of the finite/non-finite distinction, an equal distribution of overused non-finite forms in finite positions and finite forms in non-finite positions would have been expected.

This pattern of use is not something for which Zahra and Abdelmalek will have evidence from the speech and writing they are exposed to. Native speakers of French typically do not use non-finite verb forms in finite positions in sentences. At the same time, this kind of optionality in the use of forms is similar to that observed in the marking of plurality in English by Heiko and Lars (section 2.4). When finite forms are used, they are typically used in appropriate finite contexts. But those forms are not always used in contexts where native speakers require them. They alternate with non-finite forms.

A pattern of overuse of some verb forms but not others, similar to that found in L2 French by Prévost and White, occurs in the acquisition of English as an L2. Consider the transcript in (10) of a story told by an L1 speaker of Japanese. This is a story she has just listened to, read by a native speaker of English. She was asked to retell the story as accurately as she could.

10. Mr Jones always read the weather forecast in the morning newspaper. When it forecast raining he bring umbrella with him. When it forecast sunshine he doesn't wear coat. Unfortunately, sometimes weather forecast is not correct. When he arrive at work he ... his clothes are wet because he didn't bring umbrella, but sometimes he feels shivering because he doesn't wear coat.

Where native speakers of English would attach the affix *-s* to verbs with uniquely identifiable meanings (*read-s, forecast-s, bring-s, arrive-s*) this speaker does not do so (except in the case of the verb *feels*), using an affix-less form of the verb instead.

At the same time, she does use an appropriate form of the verb *do* in *he doesn't wear (a) coat*, and appropriate forms of the verb *be* in *(the) weather forecast is not correct* and *his clothes are wet.* In this context, *do* and *be* are 'support' verbs, used to signal both meaning-modifying, non-past time reference and dependency-marking agreement with the subject of the sentence: third person singular (*does, is*) and plural (*are*). *Does* in this use is known as an auxiliary verb (it accompanies a verb with a uniquely identifiable meaning when it is negated: *doesn't wear*). *Is/ are* are forms of what is called the **copula** verb *be.* The copula provides a link between the subject of a sentence and an adjective, prepositional phrase or noun phrase complement, e.g. *She is wealthy* (adjective), *She is at the office* (prepositional phrase), *She is an accountant* (noun phrase).

A contrast in the use of appropriate forms of the copula and auxiliary verbs in finite contexts and overuse of affix-less verbs with uniquely identifiable meanings in finite contexts is a pervasive characteristic of the early English of L2 speakers from a variety of L1 backgrounds. For some L2 learners this pattern of usage may persist, even when they are highly proficient in other areas of English grammar (see section 2.7 for discussion).

Table 2.4 compares the findings from three studies of the use of English verb forms by L2 speakers from different L1 backgrounds, of different ages, learning English in different contexts. Haznedar (2001) reports a case study of a Turkish-speaking child learner of English, Erdem, who was four years old when he was first exposed to English at a nursery school in the UK. Erdem learned English through immersion (interaction with native speakers) first at the nursery school then at an infant school over the next eighteen months. Haznedar recorded his speech production in play or conversation roughly three times per month over this period, and counted his use of verb forms. The data in table 2.4 are from her sample 33, which was recorded about one year after Erdem's first exposure.

The data from Ionin and Wexler (2002) are counted from the recordings of conversations with twenty L1 Russian speakers, children who were first exposed to English in the US at ages ranging from 3 years 9 months to 13 years 10 months. Again acquisition was through immersion in the language at school.

TABLE 2.4 Rates of omission of copula and auxiliary *be* forms, and use of affix-less forms of verbs with uniquely identifiable meanings in obligatory contexts

Study	N	Omissions		Affix-less Verb Forms		
		Cop *be*	Aux *be*	Irreg past	Reg past	3p -*s*
L1 Turkish (Haznedar, 2001)	1	3/132 (2%)	10/84 (12%)	19/34 (56%)	11/12 (92%)	66/87 (76%)
L1 Russian (Ionin and Wexler, 2002)	20	69/431 (16%)	158/479 (33%)	193/460 (42%)	101/174 (58%)	250/321 (78%)
L1 Basque/Span CLIL learners*	27	1/113 (1%)	2/106 (2%)	—	21/44 (48%)	190/267 (71%)
L1 Basque/Span Non-CLIL*	23	1/107 (1%)	11/102 (11%)	—	2/9 (22%)	110/153 (72%)

*García Mayo and Villarreal Olaizola (2011); CLIL = Content and Language Integrated Learning

The last two rows in the table present data reported in a study by García Mayo and Villarreal Olaizola (2011) of Basque–Spanish bilingual speakers learning English in a classroom context in northern Spain. The data reported are from participants who had been learning English in the classroom since the age of eight, and were collected when they were aged fourteen to fifteen. The 'CLIL' group had been following a 'Content and Language Integrated Learning' programme for a year, in addition to normal classroom English lessons. The CLIL programme involves the study of standard school curriculum subjects (e.g. geography, technology or religion) through the medium of English. The data come from recordings of participants retelling a picture story in English.

The results in the columns present the proportions of non-native-like use of verb forms in **obligatory contexts**. That is, contexts where, if a native speaker had said the same thing, a particular verb form would normally be required. For example, the grammar of (standard) English forces a native speaker who wants to convey the message 'there is a spider in the bath' to use the verb form *is*; this form cannot be omitted, and no other form will do: *There a spider in the bath;* *There am a spider in the bath*. The cases reported are non-target omissions of forms of copula *be* and auxiliary *be* (auxiliary *be* accompanies a verb with an *-ing* affix that describes an event in progress: *The student is reading*), and non-target use of affix-less verbs where the intended reference is past tense (subdivided into verbs that take the regular **inflection** *-ed* (*walked, phoned, cooked*) and those that have irregular forms (*went, bought, drove*)), or where the intended reference is non-past and the subject is third person singular.

It can be seen that there is a common pattern of use of verb forms across these learners from different backgrounds, of different ages and learning in different contexts. The appropriate forms of copula and auxiliary *be* are used in many of the contexts where they are required, and in all the studies are used in a considerably more target-like way than verbs with uniquely identifiable meanings that require affixes. These L2 learners use a high proportion of affix-less verb forms in such contexts.

Two striking features of these observations are the following. Firstly, the pattern of use of verb forms is unrelated to the use of forms in the learners' L1s. In all of the L1s represented, verbs with uniquely identifiable meanings have affixal forms, but not all of them have equivalents of copula and auxiliary *be*. Ionin and Wexler (2002: 108) observe that 'Russian lacks an overt *be* copula in the present tense and has no *be* auxiliary in any tense except for the compound future tense. However, Russian does have affixal inflection in all tenses. Thus the … paradigm that the L2 learners are acquiring first is precisely the one that is not fully available in their native language.'

The second striking feature is that when meaning-modifying/dependency-marking affixes are used by L2 speakers, they are typically used in appropriate contexts. Ionin and Wexler (2002: 107) also counted the number of overuses of *-ed* and *-s* by their participants and found no overuse of *-ed*, and four non-target-like uses of *-s*, out of eighty uses (5%). When L2 learners are using inflected forms productively, they appear to know what they mean, even though they fail to use them in all the contexts where they should.

This is similar to the finding that, although Heiko and Lars were using both forms *egg* and *eggs*, they knew that the *-s* inflection meant plural. Optionality for them involved the use of the bare N *egg* to mean both singular and plural, not the optional use of *-s*. Similarly, Zahra and Abdelmalek knew that finite forms of verbs are largely restricted to finite positions. Optionality for them involved using non-finite forms of verbs in both non-finite and finite positions.

Might this commonality in development be the result of L2 learners having unconscious linguistic predispositions that determine to some extent how they go about categorising forms? The possibility that L2 learners already know some of the properties of language before acquisition begins, leading them to entertain some hypotheses but not others, was raised in section 2.5 in connection with the treatment of the invented determiners *gi, ro, ul, ne* by learners studied by Williams (2005). It will be considered in more detail in chapter 3, in relation to the development of verb forms, where some potential explanations for the early use of verb-related forms are considered.

Section 2.6 in a Nutshell
When L2 learners identify the meaning-modifying or dependency-marking function of affixal forms in early stages of learning the target language, they typically use them appropriately, but not in all the contexts where they are required (obligatory contexts). Another form of the same word lacking the affix can also appear in these contexts. This optionality in the use of forms was observed in the case of two L2 learners of French (with L1 Arabic) and the use of past and non-past affixal forms in English by L2 learners from a variety of backgrounds. This behaviour is similar to that of Heiko and Lars acquiring meaning-modifying plural *-s* in English, described in section 2.4. At the same time, little optionality was seen in the early use of appropriate forms of 'support' verbs like copula and auxiliary *be*.

2.7 Persistent Non-Target Use of English Verb Forms and the Role of the L1

In discussing how L2 learners acquire target L2 forms with uniquely identifiable meanings (sections 2.1–2.3) it was implicit that the first language of the learner played an important role. Initially, L2 *forms* are associated with ('connected to') L1 form–meaning pairings. Subsequently, L2 forms become associated with their own abstract conceptual representations. In the acquisition of meaning-modifying and dependency-marking forms (sections 2.4–2.6) a combination of unconscious knowledge about linguistic properties that might be relevant (like 'finiteness', 'animacy') and input from the target language appeared to be involved. However, there is evidence that a learner's L1 may also play a role in the acquisition of meaning-modifying and dependency-marking forms, perhaps inhibiting the development of target-like use, leading to persistent optionality.

A well-known example in the L2 research literature is that of a native speaker of Chinese known as Patty, studied by Lardiere (2007). Lardiere recorded samples of Patty's free speech after ten years of immersion in English in the US, and on two further occasions after eighteen and a half years of immersion, and counted her use, in obligatory contexts for use, of finite non-past forms of *be*, irregular and regular past tense forms of lexical verbs (i.e. verbs with uniquely identifiable meanings), and her use of third person singular present tense *-s*. The frequency with which these forms are supplied across all three recordings is presented in table 2.5.

As found in other studies, when Patty uses inflected forms, they are typically used correctly. Hence optionality in her performance is asymmetrical. Bare lexical verbs can appear in finite contexts as well as non-finite contexts, but inflected forms only appear in finite contexts. Her use of forms of *be* is nearly target-like.

By contrast, other L2 speakers appear able to achieve a level of proficiency where inflected verb forms are used in a close-to-target way. A study by White of a Turkish speaker known as SD (White 2003b: 134), after eleven and a half years of immersion in English in Canada, shows that she was producing past tense forms in 81 per cent (318/392) of obligatory contexts and third person singular present tense *-s* in 79 per cent (215/271) of obligatory contexts.

There are good grounds for claiming that the persistent optionality shown in the production of inflected verb forms by speakers like Patty, in contrast to speakers like SD, is the result of L1 influence. Chinese verbs inflect neither for tense nor for subject–verb agreement. By contrast, Turkish verbs have forms that express both tense and subject–verb agreement. The presence of inflected verb forms in the L1 appears to facilitate the use of such forms in an L2. The absence of such forms in the L1 appears to inhibit their use in the L2, whatever the precise cause of this inhibition. Some possible explanations are considered in chapter 3 and in section 7.3.2.

TABLE 2.5 Use of verb forms in obligatory contexts by Patty (based on Lardiere, 2007: Tables 3.5–3.6, 4.11a–4.11b)

Non-Past *be*	Irregular Past Tense	Regular Past Tense	3p *-s*
166/185 (90%)	135/293 (46%)	8/138 (6%)	3/68 (4%)

2.8 Concluding Remarks

In this chapter we have seen that to meet the challenge of acquiring L2 forms with uniquely identifiable meanings (forms in English like *hat, new, break, under*, and so on) early-stage learners first associate those forms directly with L1 forms and their conceptual representations. This was shown in an experiment by Kroll and Curley (1988) comparing response times in picture naming in the L2 and translation of L1 words into the L2. Early-stage learners were faster in translation than in picture naming. As learners become more proficient, they link L2 forms to independent conceptual representations. However, weak connections between L2 and L1 forms remain. This was shown in an experiment by Kroll and Stewart (1994) where advanced proficiency L2 speakers were faster in translating lists of conceptually-related words (belonging to categories like clothing, vegetables, parts of the body) from the L2 to the L1 than from the L1 to the L2.

L2 words are initially stored together in the mental lexicon on the basis of the similarity of their forms. For example, L2 learners of French will store words like *chapeau* 'hat' with similar sounding words like *crapaud* 'toad', *chapelle* 'chapel'. As the learner's proficiency increases, connections between words that co-occur frequently in input (syntagmatic connections) grow, for example in L2 English *soft* might be stored with *fruit, egg* if a learner hears 'soft fruit' and 'soft egg' frequently enough. When proficiency increases further, connections are established between words of similar meaning belonging to the same grammatical category (noun, verb, adjective, preposition) (paradigmatic connections). For the L2 learner of French, *chapeau* 'hat' will be stored with words like *gant* 'glove', *écharpe* 'scarf' and other items of clothing.

The above suggests that the organisation of the L2 mental lexicon is not fixed but fluid, with connections between items changing (strengthening or weakening) as the learner encounters more input. Furthermore, some items will go through the stages of being stored by form, syntagmatically and then paradigmatically, before others. It will depend entirely on how frequently a learner encounters items in input or uses them her-/himself. Wolter's (2001) notion of 'familiarity' is relevant here. Words that are familiar to the learner are more likely to be stored paradigmatically than less familiar words.

When L2 learners begin to associate L2 forms with meaning-modifying or dependency-marking functions they may not use those forms in all the contexts required by the target language. For example, once the child L2 learners of English studied by Wode (1981) had identified English *-s* as a plural marker, they did not use it in all the contexts where nouns had plural reference. They sometimes used the default uninflected form, saying *two eggs* and *two egg*. However, while the bare noun was overgeneralised (that is, used optionally in plural contexts), nouns inflected with the affix *-s* were rarely used in non-plural contexts.

A study by Williams (2005) suggested that L2 learners may be predisposed to expect some forms in a target language to mark dependencies between constituents, such as subject–verb or verb–object agreement. Learners of a semi-artificial language based on English were presented with input containing two forms with apparently the same meaning-modifying function, *gi* and *ro* meaning 'near', *ul* and *ne* meaning 'far'. The learners identified *gi* and *ul* as marking a dependency with animate nouns, and *ro* and *ne* as marking a dependency with inanimate nouns. This suggests not only that L2 learners have a predisposition to expect to encounter forms that have a dependency-marking function in language, but also to expect specific values to be associated with the dependency, like an animate/ inanimate contrast.

The chapter concluded by looking at the L2 development of meaning-modifying and dependency-marking forms associated with verbs. The pattern of optionality in the use of bare verb forms (like *arrive, write*) and accurate but under-use of meaning-modifying/dependency-marking affixal or **suppletive forms** (like *arrived/arrives, wrote/writes*) in early development was found to be pervasive and common to learners from different L1 backgrounds. At the same time, in the L2 acquisition of English, little optionality was seen in the early use of appropriate forms of copula and auxiliary *be*. In later development there appears to be evidence of L1 influence on the use of meaning-modifying/dependency-marking forms. Learners whose L1s lack affixal meaning-modifying/dependency-marking forms appear to persist more with the optional use of bare verb forms and under-use of meaning-modifying/dependency-marking affixes by comparison with learners whose L1s also have such forms.

In chapter 3 a number of possible explanations for these observations will be explored.

ACTIVITIES

1. TEST YOURSELF

(i) How are L2 forms associated with uniquely identifiable meanings stored in the mental lexicon (a) when they are initially identified by the learner; (b) when they have become familiar?

(ii) How did the plural marking of English nouns emerge in the speech of two children studied by Wode (1981)?

(iii) What evidence emerged in a study of initial learning of an artificial language by Williams (2005) that L2 learners might have innate dispositions that they bring to the learning task?

(iv) Is the acquisition of English finite verb forms by L1 speakers of Russian influenced by their L1?

2. REACTION TIMES TO HOMOGRAPHS

Dijkstra et al. (2000) asked speakers of L1 Dutch and L2 English to read a list of randomly organised Dutch and English words on a computer screen. They had to press a button every time they thought the word was an English word. The speed with which the participants responded (their 'reaction times') was measured for each press of the button. Some of the words in the list were unique to English, for example the word *home*. Others had the same form in both Dutch and English (homographs), but had different meanings. For example, English *room* is also a Dutch word, but in Dutch it means 'cream'.

Dijkstra et al. found that the reaction times of the participants in pressing the button were longer for the homographs, like *room*, than for the English words that had no counterpart in Dutch.

Are these findings consistent with or problematic for the proposal in sections 2.2 and 2.3 about how words are stored in the mental lexicon?

3. ANALYSING THE RESULTS OF A WORD ASSOCIATION TEST

Write down the first word you think of to each of the following prompts (taken from Zareva and Wolter 2012: 67):

second	blanket	toxic
hunger	beaten	pillar
sweep	concede	weaken

(i) Assign the prompts and your responses to their grammatical category (e.g. *wet* is an A(djective), *grass* is a N(oun), *sit* is a V(erb)).

(ii) Classify your responses as 'paradigmatic', 'syntagmatic', 'similar in sound' or 'other'.

(iii) What conclusions do you draw about how these words are stored in your mental lexicon for English?

4. EFFECTS OF SEMANTIC CLUSTERING ON WORD LEARNING

Tinkham (1997) investigated whether L2 learners find it easier to acquire new words when they form 'semantic clusters' or when they are in unrelated sets. He created the following four sets of words:

Set 1: Semantically-related co-hyponyms of the same grammatical category, like *apple, pear, nectarine, peach, plum, apricot* (all nouns)

Set 2: Thematically-related words of different grammatical categories like *frog* (N), *pond* (N), *hop* (V), *croak* (V), *green* (A), *slimy* (A)

Set 3: Semantically unrelated words of the same grammatical category like *cigar, wolf, lace, stone, chain, fuel* (all nouns)

Set 4: Semantically unrelated words of different grammatical categories like *hill* (N), *menu* (N), *behave* (V), *serve* (V), *stubborn* (A), *brief* (A)

Each English word in these sets was paired with an invented word, for example *moslee* – 'peach', *iddek* – 'stubborn'. Tinkham trained forty-eight students at a US university to learn the invented words paired with their English meanings. The method used for training was based on guessing the meaning of an invented word, e.g. '*moslee* means ___ ?' or recalling the new word given a definition, e.g. 'The word for "stubborn" is ___ ?' Success in learning was measured by how many trials (encounters with the invented words) a participant needed to successfully recognise that *moslee* means 'peach' or to recall that the word for 'stubborn' is *iddek*.

Tinkham found that participants trained on set 1 took statistically significantly longer to reach the criterion of full success in recognising and recalling the invented words (7.89 mean trials) than those trained on set 2 (4.35 mean trials). And participants trained on set 3 required statistically significantly fewer trials to reach the criterion (4.89 trials) than participants trained on set 4 (5.74 trials).

How do you interpret these findings, given the conclusions drawn from WAT findings about how words are stored in the mental lexicon?

5. THE USE OF THE WORD 'GUYS' BY HEIKO AND LARS (SECTION 2.4)

Both Heiko and Lars initially used the word *guys* to refer to singular and plural. *Come on you guys!* could therefore be a call of encouragement to just one person, as well as to several people.

A little later, both boys started using the word *guyses* to refer to several people: *Come on you guyses! Guyses* was never used to refer to just one person, although *guys* continued to be used with both singular and plural meaning. By the end of the family's stay in the United States, Heiko had established the target English contrast, using *guy* only for singular reference, and *guys* only for plural reference (although Lars had not).

(i) How would you explain the creation of the form *guyses* by these children?

(ii) Describe the development in Heiko's knowledge of the relationship between singular–plural meaning and the forms *guy, guys, guyses* during his stay in the United States.

6. PRODUCTION OF ENGLISH VERB FORMS BY A SPEAKER OF JAPANESE

Below is a transcript of the spoken English of an L1 Japanese speaker with twenty-eight years of immersion in English in the United States. She is describing her experience of a tornado in Tampa, Florida (data from Kumpf, 1984):

> First time Tampa have a tornado come to.
> Was about seven forty-five.
> Bob go to work, n I was inna bathroom
> and ... a ... tornado come shake everything
> Door was flyin open.
> I was scared.
> Hanna was sittin in window ...
> Hanna is a little dog. French poodle. I call Baby.
> Anyway, she never wet bed, she never wet anywhere.
> But she was so scared an cryin,
> run to the bathroom, come to me,
> an she tinkle, tinkle, tinkle all over me. (laugh)
> She was so scared.
> I see somebody throwin a brick onna trailer
> wind was blowin so hard
> ana light ... outside street light was on
> oh I was really scared.
> An den second stop (= 'and then in a second it stopped').
> So I try to open door. I could not open.
> I say, 'Oh my God, what's happen?'
> I look window
> Awning was gone.

(i) Identify all tokens of finite lexical verbs (i.e. those with a uniquely identifiable meaning), copula and auxiliary *be*. Make a reasoned guess about whether the lexical verbs are being used in an intended past or non-past context. Count the number of omissions of copula and auxiliary *be*, and the number of bare lexical verb forms used, in contexts where copula, auxiliary or inflected (i.e. 'non-bare') forms of lexical verbs would be required by native speakers. Create a table of the following form to display your results:

	Omissions		Bare Verb Forms		
	Cop *be*	Aux *be*	Irreg past	Reg past	3p -*s*
L1 Japanese (n = 1)					

(ii) What conclusions do you draw from the findings?

FURTHER READING

For more discussion of the properties of the L2 mental lexicon, see:

Singleton, D. 1999. *Exploring the second language mental lexicon*. Cambridge: Cambridge University Press.

Juffs, A. 2009. Second language acquisition of the lexicon. In W. C. Ritchie and T. K. Bhatia (eds) *The new handbook of second language acquisition*. Bingley: Emerald Group Publishing, pp. 69–88.

Slabakova, R. 2016. *Second language acquisition*. Oxford: Oxford University Press, chapter 9: Acquisition of the mental lexicon.

3 Exploring the L2 Learning of English Verb Forms

One of the challenges facing L2 learners is to acquire the meaning-modifying and dependency-marking forms of the target language. As the observations made towards the end of chapter 2 suggest, L2 learners of English initially use such forms optionally, and this may continue even when a speaker is of otherwise quite high proficiency. The following is a transcript of the English speech of a native speaker of Mandarin Chinese who varies between using meaning-modifying past tense forms (e.g *gave, pushed*) and uninflected verb forms that could have either intended past-tense or intended non-past tense reference. The speaker was a post-graduate student at an English-speaking university with a good level of general proficiency in English. He is describing a segment from the Charlie Chaplin film *Modern Times* in which Charlie, a girl and a policeman are being driven to the police station in an open-backed police van. The alleged crime is the theft of a loaf of bread. The speaker refers to Charlie as 'the gentleman' and consistently uses the pronouns *he/him* to refer to the girl.

> So er the gentleman <u>give, gave</u> his seat to the, to the girl and er <u>ask</u> him, <u>ask</u> him '<u>Do</u> you remember me and er er the bread'? So er the girl <u>imagine</u> er of course the girl's <u>know</u> him. And er and er he <u>cried</u>. The gentleman <u>give</u> her a handkerchief. So maybe they <u>talking</u> about something and er the girl <u>feel</u> angry or such like at this. So he <u>want</u> to escape. So he <u>pushed</u> the police out … so erm they <u>are</u> er they <u>are flied</u> out the car. There <u>are</u> three people fly the car: the gentleman, the girl and the policeman. Er, so erm the gentleman <u>wake up</u> and er and <u>shaked</u> the girl, and <u>told</u> her 'now <u>is</u> your chance to escape'. Er so they <u>run</u>, they <u>ran</u> away, and er when they <u>go, went</u> through the house and they <u>sawed</u> a nice grass. They <u>sit</u>, they <u>sat</u> on there.

While this speaker produces target-like meaning-modifying past tense forms (*gave, cried, pushed, told, ran away, went, sat*) in what are probably intended obligatory contexts for past tense use, and two unexpected forms (*shaked, sawed*), he also uses bare verb forms where an inflected form is required (*ask, imagine, know, give, feel, want, wake up*). There are two examples of the target use of copula *be* (*There are three people, now is your chance*), and one example of a missing auxiliary *be* (*they talking*).

The pattern of use of verb forms by this speaker is partly consistent with the typical pattern that is found across L2 learners of English:

- When verbs with the affixes *-ed/-s* (e.g. *walked, walks*) and irregular verb forms (e.g. *wrote*) are used, they are used accurately. But they are not used in all the contexts required by the target language; bare verb forms (e.g. *walk, write*) are used in contexts where English requires inflected forms;
- Forms of copula and auxiliary *be* are used in a highly target-like way, although forms of auxiliary *be* are typically omitted more often than forms of copula *be*;
- In later L2 development, persistent optionality may result from L1 influence. Where an L1 lacks meaning-modifying/dependency-marking inflections, speakers of that L1 may persistently alternate between bare verb forms and inflected forms in the L2.

A number of accounts have been proposed to explain these observations. Five of these will be considered in this chapter. The aim is to give the reader a sense of how research into L2 development is conducted. To understand these accounts it is first necessary to be a bit more precise about what is meant by the term 'word' and the structure of words.

3.1 The Structure of Words

3.1.1 The Minimal Meaningful Unit is the Morpheme, not the Word

Each of the following is usually called a 'word': *walk, walks, walked, write, writes, wrote, book, books*. It is clear, though, that they are not all of the same type. *Walk, write* and *book* have no internal structure. They cannot be divided into smaller meaningful units: **wa* and **lk*, **wri* and **te*, or **bo* and **ok* do not mean anything. By contrast, *walks, walked, writes, wrote* and *books* do have internal structure: *walks* and *writes* can be divided into *walk + s, write + s* (*-s* a marker of non-past tense and a dependency between the verb and a third person singular subject); *walked* and *wrote* are the surface realisation of *walk, write* and a meaning-modifying 'past tense' component; *books* can be divided into *book + s* (*-s* a meaning-modifying plural marker).

A 'word', then, can consist of one or more meaningful components. The minimal meaningful unit is known as the **morpheme**. *Write* and *book* are morphemes. But so is the affix *-s* attached to *book* that expresses meaning-modifying plural number, and the affix *-s* attached to *walk, write* that expresses meaning-modifying non-past time reference and agreement with a third person singular subject.

But consider *walked* and *wrote*. Each involves a verb and a meaning-modifying past tense morpheme. But while *walked* can be transparently analysed into the two component morphemes *walk* and *-ed*, it is not possible to transparently analyse *wrote* into two bits. And yet the relationship between the verb and the past tense morpheme is the same in both cases. This shows that morphemes need to be distinguished from the forms that realise them; *wrote* is the form that realises a merger of the morpheme that has the meaning 'put marks on a surface to express a linguistic message' and the morpheme that means 'event or state that occurred prior to the moment of speaking'. In other words, *wrote*, just like *walked*, is of the structure illustrated in (1):

1 a. *wrote* ↔ {write} + {tense$_{\text{finite, past}}$}
  b. *walked* ↔ {walk} + {tense$_{\text{finite, past}}$}

From now on the convention of using curly brackets to indicate morphemes will be adopted. (1a) is interpreted as: '*wrote* is the form that realises the merger of the morpheme {write} and the morpheme {tense}, which has the values "finite" and "past"'.

Similarly, *walks, writes* are the forms that realise the merger of {walk}, {write} and the morpheme {tense}. This time {tense} has both the values 'finite' and 'non-past' and values agreeing with the 'person' and 'number' of a subject noun or pronoun morpheme: 'third person' and 'singular'. *Books* is the form that realises the merger of {book} and a {number} morpheme with the value 'plural':

2 a. *walks* ↔ {walk} + {tense$_{\text{finite, non-past, 3 person, singular}}$}
  b. *writes* ↔ {write} + {tense$_{\text{finite, non-past, 3 person, singular}}$}
  c. *books* ↔ {book} + {number$_{\text{plural}}$}

Words may consist of a single morpheme (simple words) or two or more morphemes (complex words). Morphemes that have a uniquely identifiable meaning, like *write, book, happy, tomorrow*, are often called **lexical morphemes** in the linguistic literature. Morphemes that are meaning-modifying or that mark a dependency between other morphemes are called grammatical or functional morphemes.

3.1.2 Reconsidering the Storage of 'Words' in the Mental Lexicon

Recognising that the minimal meaningful unit in word formation is the morpheme, and that morphemes are abstract units realised by forms, requires revising the model of how words are stored in the mental lexicon outlined in chapter 2 (sections 2.1–2.3). There the link between a form and its meaning (a conceptual representation) was direct. Now, however, the relationship between forms and conceptual representations is mediated through morphemes. The difference between the earlier view of lexical storage and this revised view is illustrated in (3) in the case of a form with a uniquely identifiable meaning, *write*. Conceptual representations are represented in capitals, morphemes in curly brackets and forms in italics.

3. *Two views of word storage in the mental lexicon*

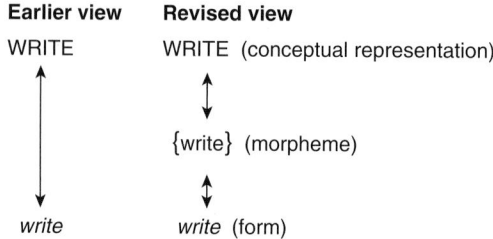

A consequence of the revised view is that there are now two lexicons: a lexicon of morphemes that are connected to conceptual representations, and a lexicon of forms that realise those morphemes. To distinguish the two, the lexicon of morphemes will continue to be referred to as the **Lexicon**, but now with a capital L, while the store of forms will be referred to as the **Vocabulary** (Embick and Noyer, 2007). It is important to keep the technical use of the term Vocabulary distinct from the everyday use of 'vocabulary' to mean a list of words. Whenever Vocabulary is used in this book it will start with a capital letter and it will refer to the store of linguistic forms that realise the morphemes that are stored in the Lexicon.

Meaning-modifying morphemes also mediate between forms and conceptual representations, as illustrated in (4):

4.

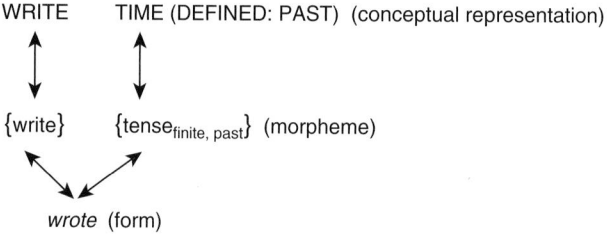

Dependency-marking forms (like the -*s* that marks a dependency between the verb and its subject in English) do not have a conceptual representation of their own. Rather, they 'mirror' values associated with morphemes that are connected to conceptual representations. In the case of dependency-marking -*s*, while its tense value comes directly from a conceptual representation of time, its third person and singular number values mirror those of the subject of the sentence:

5.

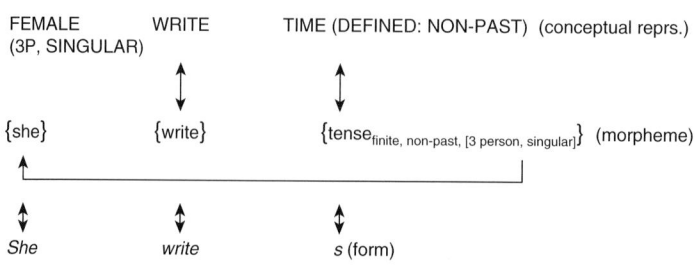

Section 3.1 in a Nutshell

Morphemes are the minimal meaningful units from which sentences are constructed. Simple words consist of one morpheme, complex words of two or more. Morphemes that have uniquely identifiable meanings are lexical morphemes, meaning-modifying and dependency-marking morphemes are functional morphemes. Morphemes need to be distinguished from the forms that realise them. Morphemes are stored in the Lexicon, the forms that realise them are stored in the Vocabulary. Both lexical morphemes and meaning-modifying functional morphemes are associated with conceptual representations. Dependency-marking functional morphemes are not associated with conceptual representations but mirror (in other words, copy) the values of morphemes that are.

3.2 The Non-Target Use of English Verb Forms by L2 Learners: the Problem Restated

With the understanding now of how forms are related to morphemes, how morphemes are associated with conceptual representations, and how morphemes can combine to form complex words, what account can be given for the observations about the use of English verb forms by L2 speakers summarised in the introduction to this chapter? Five possibilities will be considered.

3.2.1 Apparent, but Not Real, Optionality

One possibility to consider first is that the optional use of bare forms of lexical verbs is only apparent. Learners acquire a unique form for a particular meaning. In some cases this happens to look like an inflected form. In others it happens to look like an uninflected form. For example, a learner might acquire the form *writes* and the form *walk*, saying *She writes* and *She walk*, but never saying *She write* and *She walks*. This possibility is implausible, given that it would lead to overuse of *writes* in cases like *I writes*, which Ionin and Wexler (2002) found to be extremely rare (see section 2.6). But it can also be shown that L2 speakers do optionally use inflected and bare forms of the same verb. Table 3.1 presents the use of bare and inflected lexical verb forms used in obligatory past tense contexts by Haznedar's (2007) informant Erdem at sample 33 (i.e. after about one year of exposure to English).

Although Erdem uses some verb forms that are uniquely bare or are uniquely inflected for past tense, there are five verbs where he alternates between a bare form and a past tense form.

TABLE 3.1 Distribution of bare and inflected lexical verb forms in intended past tense contexts (based on Haznedar, 2007: Appendices 1 and 2)

Bare Verb Forms	Inflected Verb Forms		
Unique	Optional		Unique
Close, Crash (2), Jump (2), Show, Look, Fall, Get (3), Give (2), Shoot, Take (2), Watch (2), Draw, Drive, Eat	Buy (2)	Bought	Died, Wrote (3)
	Find	Found	
	Say	Said (8)	
	Make	Made (8)	
	Come	Came (2)	

3.2.2 A 'Miscategorisation of Verb Forms' Account of Optionality

A second possible account of optionality in the early use of verb forms proposes that learners associate inflected forms of lexical verbs with meanings that are not those associated with the same inflected forms by native speakers. This gives the appearance of optionality.

Verbs, or verbs and their complements, universally describe a small number of situations, real or imagined, that can be defined in terms of three binary distinctions (Comrie, 1976). One is whether the situation is dynamic or static. When someone *enters a room* the situation described is dynamic, requiring 'energy' on the part of the subject (Robison, 1995). When someone *lives in a house* the situation described is static. A second distinction is whether the situation described includes a clear endpoint or not. The phrase *run a mile* includes reference to an endpoint. However, if someone *runs every day*, while there certainly will be some physical limit, no endpoint is specified by the verb and its complement. This distinction is referred to in the linguistic literature as telic (from the Greek *telos* 'end') versus atelic ('having no endpoint'). The third distinction is whether the situation described takes place over time or is over in an instant. For example, *writing a book* and *finding a key* are both telic (describing a situation with an endpoint) and dynamic (requiring energy from the subject). But writing a book is likely to take some time while finding a key happens in an instant (as opposed to looking for a key which might take hours). This distinction is referred to as durative versus punctual. These situation-describing features encoded by verbs and their complements are known as **situation aspect** (sometimes also called inherent or lexical aspect).

The **Aspect** Hypothesis (Li and Shirai, 2000) proposes that L2 learners initially categorise the inflected forms of verbs in terms of the situation aspect they express, whatever the real function of those forms in the language. So, for example, Robison (1995) claims that the inflected forms of lexical verbs that mark the past tense in native grammars of English initially mark punctual events in L2 learners' grammars (like *found the key*); the *-s* that signals third person singular non-past tense in native grammars initially marks non-dynamic, atelic, durative situations in L2 grammars (like *lives in a house*); and the *-ing* that signals an event in progress in native grammars marks dynamic, atelic, durative events in L2 grammars (like *is running at the moment*).

Here is an example from Robison (1995: 358) consistent with this claim. This is a transcript of a sample of L2 speech in which the intended time reference is past. Note that the speaker only uses an inflected past tense form in the case of *went to the church*, a description of a punctual event, but not in the case of *talk about religion* or *study in the library*, which are durative activities. ("…" represents a pause.)

6. I … **went to the … church** every … Mondays … (we) … teacher … a group of the students … I **taking [= 'talking'] about religion** … in a group … and … **study in the library**

With longer exposure to the target language, learners should notice that inflected verb forms that they have so far restricted to verbs describing punctual events, and others that they have restricted to durative events, are used with a wider range of verbs by native speakers. This will lead them to re-categorise the inflections, and it will appear as if the inflections are 'spreading' to other verb types: 'an emerging inflection initially marks a given aspectual category and then spreads to adjoining categories' (Robison, 1995: 345).

The core observation of the Aspect Hypothesis, then, is that L2 learners initially use their existing knowledge of types of situation that verbs and their complements can describe to determine the meaning of inflected verb forms. However, it is not the whole story, as the following analysis of the English past tense verb forms used by Erdem (the L1 Turkish-speaking learner of English studied by Haznedar, 2001; 2007) illustrates. Costello and Shirai (2011) counted the number of past tense forms of verbs used by Erdem by type of situation described (dynamic, telic, etc.) over an eighteen-month period. The results are presented in table 3.2, where 'sample' refers to data collection points over the eighteen months.

Initially (samples 8–12) there are very few verbs used, and no past tense inflected forms. When past tense inflected forms emerge, in samples 13–17, they are only used with dynamic, telic, punctual verbs (like *find, break*). But there are also very few other types of verb used by Erdem at this stage in his development. From sample 18 onwards, past tense inflected forms of other verb types are being used, and in fact are used more with verbs describing durative dynamic telic situations (*wrote a book, baked a cake*) than with verbs describing punctual dynamic telic situations.

Strikingly, though, the number of bare verb forms that optionally appear in intended past tense contexts remains quite high across all verb types. The Aspect Hypothesis does not explain this.

TABLE 3.2 Proportions of verbs used with a past tense inflection out of total number of verbs in intended past tense contexts (adapted from Costello and Shirai, 2011: 477, Table 4)

Sample	Dynamic Telic Punctual e.g. *found*	Dynamic Telic Durative e.g. *wrote a book*	Dynamic Atelic Durative e.g. *played*	Non-Dynamic Atelic Durative e.g. *liked*
8–12	0/12	0/1	0/11	0
13–17	8/40 (20%)	0/1	0/12	0
18–31	58/177 (33%)	15/28 (54%)	6/24 (25%)	0/3
32–39	94/260 (36%)	50/54 (93%)	5/35 (14%)	5/13 (39%)
40–45	162/349 (46%)	28/32 (88%)	31/79 (39%)	30/43 (70%)

3.2.3 A 'Limitation in Language Processing Capacity' Account of Optionality

One account that aims to explain persistent optionality appeals to a limitation on L2 speakers' capacity for processing language in real time. It proposes that when L2 speakers are productively using forms that realise functional morphemes, even though they may not use them in all contexts required by the target language, they have acquired the abstract morpheme. Erdem has the morpheme $\{tense_{finite, past}\}$ in his mental Lexicon by sample 33, even though he is not consistently producing past tense forms (see table 3.1 above). A problem arises, however, in his ability to access the appropriate forms to realise $\{find\} + \{tense_{finite, past}\}$, $\{play\} + \{tense_{finite, past}\}$, etc. from the Vocabulary (the mental store of forms). Instead of retrieving *found, played*, he produces *find, play*. Why does he do this?

Entries in the Vocabulary need to be specified for the morphemes with which they are associated. It is important that *write* is associated with $\{write\}$ and not $\{read\}$, and that *wrote* is associated with $\{write\} + \{tense_{finite, past}\}$ and not $\{write\} + \{tense_{non-finite}\}$. *She wrote a novel* cannot have the meaning 'She read a novel', and **She wanted to wrote a novel* is not a grammatical sentence of English.

At the same time, for the sake of efficient language use, the specification of forms for the morphemes they are linked to should not be over-elaborate. Many linguists argue that forms have the minimal specification necessary to ensure they are matched with the appropriate morpheme, and no more. For example, *wrote* and *writes* need to be specified as in (7), where ↔ means 'realises':

7. **Form**   **Specification**
   wrote   ↔ $\{write\} + \{tense_{finite, past}\}$
   writes   ↔ $\{write\} + \{tense_{finite, non-past, 3 person, singular}\}$

However, in all other finite contexts *write* is used: *I write, you write, they write*. It would be redundant to specify *write* for each one of these cases (finite, non-past, 1 person, singular; finite non-past, 2 person, singular; finite non-past, 3 person, plural). It is simpler to specify that *write* is used in any finite context where *wrote* and *writes* are not used. In other words, *write* is an **elsewhere form**, used whenever *wrote* and *writes* are not:

8. **Form**   **Specification**

   wrote   ↔   {write} + {tense $_{finite,\ past}$}

   writes ↔   {write} + {tense $_{finite,\ non\text{-}past,\ 3\ person,\ singular}$}

   write   ↔   {write} + {tense $_{finite}$}

But now, because *write* is unspecified for particular values of {tense $_{finite}$}, it could potentially realise any combination of {write} + {tense $_{finite}$}, including those cases realised by *wrote* and *writes*. It is necessary, therefore, that *wrote* and *writes* are selected before *write* is. There is an ordering, then, in the accessing of forms from the Vocabulary to realise abstract morphemes. More specified forms must be selected before elsewhere forms. In mature native speakers, this ordering usually operates seamlessly. In L2 learners of English, particularly less proficient speakers, it does not. Sometimes during speech production the demands of constructing a message and associating that message with morphemes and forms to produce a fully target-like utterance exceed the speaker's working memory capacity. The result is that speakers access the elsewhere form in contexts where more specified forms are required.

This account, proposed by Haznedar and Schwartz (1997), Prévost and White (2000), is known as the Missing Surface Inflection Hypothesis. More specified forms become 'temporarily irretrievable from the [Vocabulary] … due to processing reasons or communicative pressure' (Prévost and White, 2000: 129).

The Missing Surface Inflection Hypothesis not only offers a potential explanation for the overuse of affix-less verb forms by early L2 learners of English, but also for the overuse of non-finite forms in finite contexts by early L2 learners of French (non-finite forms are elsewhere forms), and Heiko's and Lars's overuse of English bare count nouns in plural contexts (bare count nouns are elsewhere forms).

It is not entirely clear how the Missing Surface Inflection Hypothesis deals with the markedly lower incidence of optionality in the use of forms of copula and auxiliary *be* illustrated in table 2.4. It would appear that *are* and *be* are potential elsewhere forms, if *is* and *am* are as specified in (9):

9. **Form**   **Specification**

   is   ↔   {be} + {tense$_{finite,\ non\text{-}past,\ 3\ person,\ singular}$}

   am   ↔   {be} + {tense$_{finite,\ non\text{-}past,\ 1\ person,\ singular}$}

   are   ↔   {be} + {tense$_{finite}$}

   be   ↔   {be} + {tense}

However, *be* and *are* do not appear to be used in contexts where *is* and *am* are required. Rather, *is* and *am* are omitted.

Furthermore, the influence of the L1 on persistent optionality in later L2 development would require some additional account. The Missing Surface Inflection

Hypothesis assumes that where learners are productively using forms that realise functional morphemes, they have acquired the abstract functional morpheme. The capacity of L2 learners to access the appropriate form should then be the same, regardless of L1 background.

3.2.4 A 'Morphological Deficit' Account of Optionality

An alternative account for optionality assumes the same separation between a Lexicon of abstract morphemes and a Vocabulary of forms. It differs in that it assumes that in early L2 development learners do not have representations for functional morphemes. They initially learn inflected forms of lexical morphemes like *wrote* as an alternative to the form *write* when the intended message refers to an event or state of affairs in the past. Similarly, they learn *writes* as an alternative to *write* when the intended message refers to an event or state of affairs that is not in the past and involves a subject that is third person and singular.

In other words, rather than knowing that English has a functional tense morpheme that determines the selection of certain forms, L2 learners know that the lexical verb morpheme can potentially take a different form depending on the meaning of the message:

10.

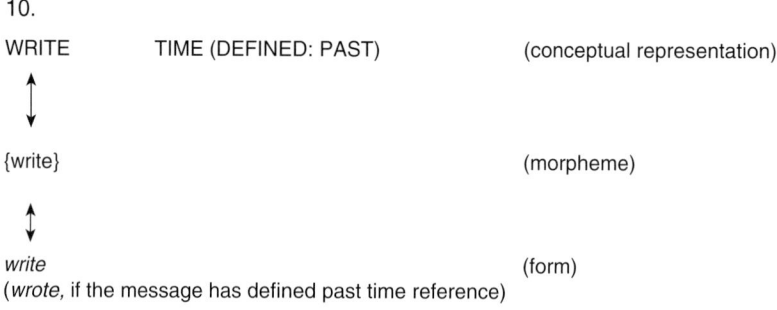

WRITE   TIME (DEFINED: PAST)   (conceptual representation)

{write}   (morpheme)

write   (form)
(*wrote*, if the message has defined past time reference)

Knowledge about inflected forms and their meaning is derived from experience. On this account bare verb forms are **default forms** that L2 learners encounter most frequently in the samples of language they are exposed to and then use in any context. Default forms are different from the elsewhere forms of the Missing Surface Inflection Hypothesis, which are defined morphologically as having under-specified features by comparison with more specified forms. Learners replace the default form by one of the inflected forms to the extent that they can compute the relevant contextual information (whether past or non-past tense reference is intended, what the person and number of the subject are) and match it to the information in the Vocabulary. If the demands of constructing a meaningful message take up all of a learner's processing capacity, the contextual information required to access inflected forms will not be computed, and the default verb form will be selected.

With longer exposure to the target language there will come a point where encounters with and use of the inflected forms trigger the establishment of an independent abstract morpheme. For example, repeated exposure to or use of forms like *played*, *wrote* in past tense contexts will at some point trigger a {tense$_{\text{finite, past}}$} morpheme in the learner's Lexicon.

On the assumptions of this Morphological Deficit Hypothesis (McCarthy, 2008) it is predicted that verbs inflected with -*s* might be produced less often than verbs inflected with -*ed* in obligatory contexts because the appropriate use of -*s* requires the computation of more contextual information (not only the intended time reference of the clause, but also the person and number of the subject) than the appropriate use of -*ed*. And this pattern is found in a number of studies (see table 2.4).

Persistent optionality, on this account, could be linked to the existence of a similar abstract functional morpheme in the L1. Where an L1 has, say, an abstract morpheme for {tense} (as in the case of the Turkish speaker of English described in section 2.7), identification of its values in the L2 might take place more quickly than where a learner's L1 lacks such a morpheme (as in the case of the Chinese speaker of English also described in section 2.7).

The lower incidence of optionality in the use of copula and auxiliary *be* results from *is* being the default form. It is the form most frequently encountered by L2 learners in the samples of language they are exposed to, rather than *be*.

3.2.5 A 'Feature Re-Assembly Over Time' Account of Optionality

The final account of optionality considered in this chapter assumes the same separation between abstract morphemes and forms as the Missing Surface Inflection and Morphological Deficit hypotheses. The Feature Re-Assembly Hypothesis (Lardiere, 2009a, b) assumes that there is a universal set of linguistic features like [past], [non-past], [singular], [plural], [1, 2, 3 person] which language learners, both first and second, know unconsciously to be relevant for constructing morphemes in any of the world's languages. This knowledge is part of the linguistic predispositions that humans have for language learning. However, languages vary in which features they select to encode in morphemes and how selected features are combined. For example, while English has selected the features [past] and [non-past] as values of its finite tense morpheme, it is arguable whether Mandarin Chinese has an abstract tense morpheme at all. In Mandarin, the tense interpretation of a sentence is determined by context, for example through the use of adverbs of time. The same verb form can co-occur with both past and non-past reference, as illustrated in (11):

11. Zuotian ⎤
     Jintian ⎬ wo   gen   mama   yiqi   **qu**   waimian   chi
     Mingtian ⎦

     Yesterday ⎤
     Today   ⎬ I   with   mother   together   **go**   outside   eat
     Tomorrow ⎦

     'Yesterday I **went** out for dinner with mother'
     'Today **I'm going** out for dinner with mother'
     'Tomorrow **I'm going** out for dinner with mother'

By contrast, both Mandarin and English have a productive plural affixal morpheme: *-men* in Mandarin and *-s* in English. But *-men*, unlike *-s*, is optional in plural contexts, is restricted to co-occurring with human nouns that are definite in reference, and cannot be used when the noun is modified by a numeral (Lardiere, 2009a: 197).

The challenge facing the language learner is to identify, from the samples of language encountered, which features from the universal set the target language has selected to construct its morphemes, and how morphemes are mapped to forms. The particular challenge facing the L2 learner is that a selection of features and a mapping to forms has already occurred in the L1. And we have seen that initially L2 learners associate L2 linguistic forms with L1 forms and their morphological and conceptual representations (sections 2.1 and 2.2). Learners therefore have to work out (unconsciously, of course) whether features selected for the L1 are also appropriate for the L2, whether they need to be re-organised, and whether new features have to be selected. In other words they have to re-assemble the abstract level of morphemes that exists in the L1 into a set of morphemes that is appropriate for the L2.

To illustrate, using the verb *xie* 'write', a Mandarin speaker learning English has to go from a representation for the past tense illustrated in (12a) to that illustrated in (12b):

12 a.

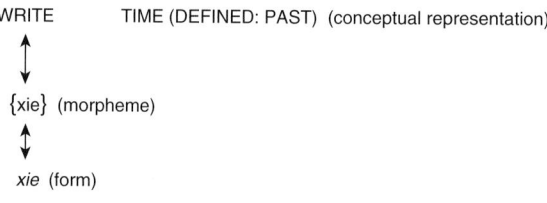

     b.

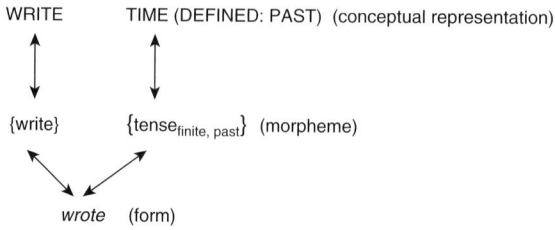

The Mandarin learner not only has to learn that *write* takes the form *wrote* in finite past tense contexts, but also that it must do so obligatorily. This takes time. The Feature Re-Assembly Hypothesis proposes that optionality arises where learners have not definitively fixed the mapping between the features of the abstract morpheme and forms that realise the morpheme.

An example is offered by Choi and Lardiere (2006) for the L2 acquisition of question words in Korean by native speakers of English. In English, the *wh*-forms in questions like *Who came?, What did you buy?* can only be interpreted as question words. The equivalent *wh*-forms in Korean can be interpreted either as question words or as the indefinite expressions 'someone', 'something' in a declarative sentence. Which interpretation is appropriate is determined by two verbal inflections: *-ci* (question) and *-ta* (declarative), as illustrated in (13), in the case of *mues* 'what?; something' (examples from Lardiere 2009a: 186). (Top = Topic, Nom = Nominative Case, Acc = Accusative Case, Decl = Declarative.)

13   a.   John-un   Mary-ka   mues-ul   sassnun   -ci   an   -ta

         John-Top   Mary-Nom   thing-Acc   bought   -Q   know   -Decl

         'John knows what Mary bought'

    b.   John-un   Mary-ka   mues-ul   sass   -ta   -ko   an   -ta

         John-Top   Mary-Nom   thing-Acc   bought   -Decl   -that   know   -Decl

         'John knows that Mary bought something'

It appears that whereas in English the morpheme *what* encodes both the interrogative feature [Q] and the semantic feature [non-human thing], the Korean form *mues* only encodes the semantic feature [non-human thing]. Its interpretation as a question word or an indefinite expression is determined by *-ci*, which has the feature [Q], and *-ta*, which has the feature [Decl]. English speakers learning Korean have to recognise that the [Q] feature that is part of the representation of *wh*-words in English is located in a verbal inflection in Korean.

Choi and Lardiere (2006) investigated how successful English-speaking learners were in doing this. Eighty intermediate-proficiency and twenty-four advanced-proficiency speakers participated. The intermediate-proficiency participants were significantly better at interpreting the interrogative interpretation than the indefinite one, suggesting that they had 'apparently failed to observe the interpretive contingency between the [indefinite expression and *-ta*]' (Lardiere, 2009a: 187). The advanced-proficiency speakers were better at identifying the indefinite interpretation, with four of them performing in a target-like way. This is an example of feature re-assembly posing a challenge for L2 learners that may not be resolved until they are highly proficient in the target language.

Section 3.2 in a Nutshell

Five possible accounts of the optional use of English verb forms by L2 speakers were discussed in this section:

The 'apparent, but not real optionality' account proposes that learners acquire the inflected forms of some verbs and the uninflected forms of others, and this gives the appearance of optionality in their productions. However, empirical evidence suggests that L2 speakers do optionally use different forms of the same verb in the same linguistic context.

The Aspect Hypothesis proposes that L2 learners do not initially use functional morphemes associated with the verb with their target language meaning but use them to reflect the verb's aspectual properties. For example, *-ed* is used with verbs that describe punctual events, *-s* is used with verbs that describe non-dynamic, atelic, durative situations, *-ing* is used with verbs that describe dynamic, atelic, durative events. While this is consistent with observations about the very early stages of L2 development, it does not explain continued optionality in later stages of development.

The Missing Surface Inflection Hypothesis assumes that when L2 learners use forms of functional morphemes productively, if optionally, they have acquired the abstract morphemes with their target language features. Optionality arises when speakers' working memory capacity is overloaded by the demands of communication. Speakers access elsewhere forms rather than the more highly specified forms required by the target language.

The Morphological Deficit Hypothesis proposes that the optional use of verb forms indicates that the underlying abstract morphemes have not yet been established. Different forms of the same verb are stored in the Vocabulary with information about the contexts in which they can appear. This account assumes that when L2 learners' working memory capacity is under pressure from the demands of communication, they access a default form, which is the one encountered most frequently in input. There will come a point where the abstract morpheme will be triggered through repeated encounters with the forms. Persistent optionality in advanced proficiency is linked to the absence of a counterpart morpheme in a learner's L1.

The Feature Re-Assembly Hypothesis assumes that there is a universal set of morphological features, like [past], [non-past], [singular], [plural], [1, 2, 3 person], that are part of human linguistic predispositions. These features guide language learners in establishing morphemes in the target language. The challenge for the L2 learner is to identify those features that the target language uses to construct its morphemes, and re-assemble the features of morphemes that have been transferred from the L1 to match the feature configurations of morphemes in the L2. Optionality arises where the features have not yet been fully (re)-assembled.

3.3 Which of the Five Accounts of L2 Learners' Use of English Verb Forms is Correct?

The hypothesis that L2 speakers do not really use competing verb forms in the same context (e.g. *She find it/She found it* in a past tense context) but have learned unique forms for each verb (e.g. *find* (but not *found*), *bought* (but not *buy*)) was shown to be empirically inadequate (section 3.2.1).

The Aspect Hypothesis is a promising account of the use of verb forms by learners at very early stages of learning an L2 (section 3.2.2). However, it cannot account for the kind of optionality in the use of forms that has been found in later development illustrated in table 2.4 and table 3.2. Three different accounts for this later kind of optionality were described. All three make the same assumption about the organisation of the mental lexicon: forms and the meanings they express are mediated by abstract morphemes.

The Missing Surface Inflection Hypothesis argues that L2 speakers at this stage have the same mental representations for lexical and functional morphemes as native speakers, but they have a problem accessing some of that knowledge (the forms that are stored in the Vocabulary) when demands on their memory capacity are high (section 3.2.3). It does not offer an account of why L2 learners might show more optionality in the use of the English third person singular non-past form -*s* than the forms of the past tense, nor why there might be L1 influence on persistent optionality. Additional assumptions would need to be made in both cases. It is not clear how it explains the much lower rates of optionality in the case of copula and auxiliary *be*.

The Morphological Deficit account proposes that where L2 learners show optionality they have not yet established functional morphemes in the Lexicon, but have stored inflectional forms in their Vocabularies with a specification of the message contexts in which they can appear (e.g. intended past tense reference, intended non-past reference where the subject is a third person singular noun or pronoun) (section 3.2.4). Again the extent to which an L2 speaker can access these forms depends on the demands put on their working memory by the need to compute other information relevant to sentence production. The Morphological Deficit Hypothesis can account for a difference in the rate of optionality in the use of the third person singular non-past -*s* and past tense forms in terms of a computational problem. Selecting a non-past third person singular form involves computing more features of the context than selecting a past tense form, hence more default verb forms appear in such contexts. It may also be able to give an account of L1 influence on persistent optionality. L2 learners whose L1s have counterpart abstract morphemes to the target language establish L2 morphemes more quickly than learners whose L1s lack a counterpart morpheme.

Unlike the Missing Surface Inflection Hypothesis, the Morphological Deficit Hypothesis accounts for the much lower rates of optionality in the use of copula and auxiliary *be* because *is*, rather than *be*, is the default form, the one most frequently encountered in input and therefore the form that is accessed first from learners' Vocabularies.

L1 influence on persistent optionality follows directly from the Feature Re-Assembly Hypothesis (section 3.2.5). Where an L1 and L2 have similar feature configurations for specific morphemes the challenge facing the L2 learner will be less than where the L1 and L2 configurations are very different, or where the L2 has a morpheme for which there is no counterpart in the L1. An L1 speaker of Turkish has fewer steps to go through to establish the appropriate features for the English past tense morpheme than an L1 speaker of Mandarin Chinese.

One of the problems for the Feature Re-Assembly Hypothesis is constraining it so that it is says more than that L2 learners transfer properties of their L1 to the L2 which then need to be changed. A number of proposals have been made for doing this.

Slabakova (2009: 321) and Cho and Slabakova (2014: 166) have proposed that there is a 'cline of difficulty' in feature re-assembly. If a particular property in the L1 is determined contextually, as for example in the case of tense in Mandarin Chinese, a speaker of that language will have more difficulty acquiring a morphological realisation of that property in an L2 than a speaker of a different L1 that also has a morphological realisation (like Turkish). A speaker of an L1 with a morphological realisation of a property acquiring an L2 with a morphological realisation will have more difficulty if the features of that morpheme are configured differently than a speaker of an L1 where the features are configured similarly. For example, this predicts that a speaker of Mandarin Chinese learning Korean will have less difficulty acquiring the verbal-inflection-determined interpretation of the interrogative/indefinite expression *mues* 'what? non-human thing' than English speakers because Mandarin has a similar distribution of features.

A second kind of constraint, alluded to by Lardiere (2009a: 219), is a universal feature hierarchy whereby some features are more accessible than others and tend to appear earlier in acquisition than others. For example, Harley and Ritter (2002) have argued that, in the case of pronouns, **gender** is hierarchically dependent on number. If a language encodes gender in its pronouns it will also encode number. This implicational fact about the world's languages also seems to affect language acquisition: L1 learners of a language that has both number and gender distinctions in its pronoun system acquire the number property before the gender property. From the perspective of the Feature Re-Assembly Hypothesis, the feature hierarchy might also determine that an L2 learner will establish the number feature of pronouns in the L2 before the gender feature.

Finally, constraints on feature re-assembly may appear from empirical studies of L2 learner development where those features that are relatively easy to re-assemble and those that take longer are identified. An example is provided in a study by Mai and Yuan (2016). They investigated the acquisition of a construction in Mandarin Chinese by English speakers that is the equivalent of the English cleft construction *it is/was ... that*, for example *It is tomorrow that she arrives*. This has the function of drawing attention to new information in the sentence (known as 'focus' – see section 8.3 for discussion). The constituent that immediately follows *is/was* is the new information: *I thought you said she was arriving today? No, it's tomorrow that she arrives*. The Mandarin counterpart is *shi ... de* (example from Mai and Yuan, 2016: 248):

14. Mali   shi   zuotian   qu   Meiguo   de
    Mary   be   yesterday go   America de
    'It was yesterday that Mary went to America'

However the use of this construction is more restricted than the English *it is/was ... that*. It is incompatible with verbs or adjectives whose meanings are static, like *know, be angry*, and it has obligatory past tense reference when the focused constituent is an adverb or other phrase optionally added to the verb phrase (known as an 'adjunct'). To explain this difference between Mandarin and English, Mai and Yuan assume that *shi ... de* has the features [past] and [telic]. By contrast, English *it is/was ... that* does not have these features, although [past] and [telic] are of course present elsewhere in English, [past] on the {tense} morpheme and [telic] on lexical morphemes like {find}, {reach}.

Mai and Yuan tested a group of adult learners of Mandarin, with L1 English, who started learning Chinese in early adulthood, and a group of native speakers. The L2 speakers were of low intermediate, high intermediate and advanced proficiency. Several tasks were used to test awareness of the constraints on the use of the *shi ... de* construction. Only the results from an acceptability judgement task are reported here. Participants were asked to rate grammatical and ungrammatical sentences (i.e. use with non-past tense and atelic verbs/adjectives) involving *shi ... de*. The rating scale was from 1 (completely unacceptable) to 4 (completely acceptable). Mean ratings of the unacceptable items are presented in table 3.3. Scores close to 1 indicate awareness of the features [past] and [telic] that constrain the use of *shi ... de*.[1]

The English speakers come to recognise with proficiency that *shi ... de* is not compatible with non-past interpretations. There is a gradual decline in positive ratings from the lower intermediate to advanced level, suggesting that the [past] feature has been assigned to *shi ... de*. However, there is much less recognition of the ungrammaticality of *shi ... de* in atelic contexts, suggesting that the [telic] feature takes longer to establish. As Mai and Yuan observe, although both [past] and [telic] are available in English, they need to be assembled in a novel way, and it appears that the [past] feature is assembled before the [telic] feature. Empirical studies like these provide evidence about which features may be re-assembled early and which features later in L2 development.

---

[1] I thank an anonymous reviewer for advice about the constraints on the *shi ... de* construction in Mandarin. For reasons not germane to the discussion here, the data from more high intermediate and advanced proficiency participants were analysed for the atelic condition than the non-past condition.

TABLE 3.3 Mean rating of *shi* ... *de* in non-past and atelic sentences (based on Mai and Yuan, 2016: 263–4, Tables 3 and 4)

	*Non-Past		*Atelic
Natives (n = 15)	1.10	Natives (n = 15)	1.68
Advanced (n = 14)	1.88	Advanced (n = 17)	2.52
High Interm. (n = 17)	2.06	High Intermed. (n = 21)	2.73
Low Intermed. (n = 10)	2.78	Low Intermed. (n = 10)	2.95

3.4 Concluding Remarks

This chapter has described in detail five accounts of observations about optionality in the use of English verb forms by L2 speakers. The aim was to give a sense of how research into L2 development is conducted. It is based on proposing hypotheses (which are in essence informed guesses) and then testing them against empirical data. Some hypotheses turn out not to give sufficient coverage of the data. This is the case of the 'apparent, but not real, optionality' account, which can be shown to be wrong. Others offer interesting accounts of some aspects of the observations and are therefore worth pursuing. All four of the other accounts considered have their strengths and weaknesses. At the time of writing there is no single account that convincingly trumps the others in terms of coverage and elegance, although the Feature Re-Assembly Hypothesis is being actively investigated by a number of researchers for its potential explanatory power. A sixth account which suggests that optionality in the production of functional morphology may be to some extent the result of pronunciation problems for L2 speakers (the Prosodic Transfer Hypothesis) will be discussed in section 7.3.2. In chapter 4 attention turns to how L2 learners deal with the 'syntax problem': the acquisition of the sentence structure of the target language.

ACTIVITIES

1. TEST YOURSELF

(i) What is the difference between the Lexicon and the Vocabulary, as defined in this chapter?

(ii) What does the Aspect Hypothesis propose? Is it a good explanation of observed optionality in the use of English verb forms by L2 speakers?

(iii) Why is the 'underspecification' of forms in the Vocabulary important for the Missing Surface Inflection Hypothesis?

(iv) How do the Missing Surface Inflection and Feature Re-Assembly Hypotheses differ from the Morphological Deficit Hypothesis?

(v) What kinds of constraints need to be imposed on the Feature Re-Assembly Hypothesis to make it an interesting proposal for explaining optionality in the speech of L2 speakers?

2. IDENTIFYING MORPHEMES

Identify the morphemes in the following sentences, and label them as lexical (L) (with uniquely identifiable meanings) or functional (F) (with meaning-modifying or dependency-marking functions), e.g. *strode* → {stride} (L) + {tense$_{finite, past}$} (F).

 (i) Benny strode into the room, breathing heavily.
 (ii) He had seen the soldiers climbing the hill in the distance.
(iii) She would try to remember the circumstances under which the promise was made.
(iv) How many times were they asked to return their library books?

3. IDENTIFYING VERBAL ASPECT

Classify the situation aspect of each lexical verb or verb phrase in the sentences of activity 2 using the categories dynamic–static, telic–atelic, durative–punctual:

> e.g. *stride:* dynamic, atelic, durative
> breathe
> see the soldiers
> climb the hill
> try
> remember the circumstances
> make a promise
> ask
> return the library books

4. DATA ANALYSIS 1

Below is the text of a story that an L2 speaker of English (whose L1 is Japanese) was asked to listen to and retell.

> **Original Story**
> Once upon a time there was a man from my street who drank too much.
> He would visit a pub I know well after work, and only leave the pub when it closed. When he got home he would knock the coat-stand over, sing songs and frighten the cat. One day he stopped drinking. He joined a gym, ran a mile every day, and started eating fresh fruit. He became so full of energy that when he got home after work he would throw the door open, knocking the coat-stand over, sing songs and frighten the cat.

The informant listened to the story twice, and was shown a set of prompts on a computer screen (*man, pub, home, coat-stand, songs, cat, gym, mile, fresh fruit*). Here is the informant's retelling (… indicates a pause):

The Story Re-told

Once upon a time there's a man who … drink too much. He … goes to the pu, pub every day, every night and he … come back when the pub close. He … when he back home he … always knock the coat-stand and sing a song and play with cat. One day he … stop drinking and he … he … goes to the gym, run a mile and eat fresh fruit every day. He … he's full of energy, so when he … go home after work he throw the door open and knock coat-stand, sing a song and play … with cat.

Analyse this speaker's use of verb forms. Is the pattern of use what you would expect for an L2 learner of English? Give reasons for your answer.

5. DATA ANALYSIS 2

The transcript below is of a conversation in English with an L1 speaker of Korean with more than ten years' residence in an English-speaking environment (Ahn, 2010):

I was collapsed … then ambulance came and I never come back, so that was really all my classmates and, and lecturers are very … um sorry for me, and then but I've been hospital for two years and then I've been home and then hospital you know, all like that, and then for yeah another five years so nearly seven, eight years I've been at home.
… my mother's still ali, alive but she's just a housewife like me yeah … but she look after grandchildren and then she living very life … she helping lots of people. I think I come after my mother for that matter. She always help other people who need her, she never refuse.

Make three lists: (i) of all the verb forms used in finite contexts, together with their subjects; (ii) of all intended singular nouns; (iii) of all intended plural nouns. (Focus on full nouns, like *ambulance*, and ignore pronouns.) What conclusions do you draw from the lists for the different hypotheses discussed in this chapter? Organise your results in the form of a table, as illustrated below:

Subject + finite verb	Singular nouns	Plural nouns
I was	ambulance	Classmates

6. L1 INFLUENCE ON THE USE OF L2 VERB MORPHOLOGY

The data in table (i) are taken from a study by Stauble (1984). They represent the use of English verb forms by four L1 speakers of Japanese (two of lower intermediate proficiency in English and two of advanced proficiency) and four L1 speakers of Spanish (again two of lower intermediate proficiency in English and two of advanced proficiency). The data were collected from two hours of spontaneous speech between the researcher and each participant. The scores represent the percentage of target-like use of copula *be*, auxiliary *be*, irregular past tense (e.g. *ran*), regular past tense (e.g. *walked*) and third person singular present tense -*s* (e.g. *runs*) by these speakers. J are the L1 Japanese participants, S the L1 Spanish participants.

On the basis of the differences in the use of forms by the Japanese and Spanish speakers, can you infer any potential influence of the first language?

Table (i) Target-like use (%) of English verb forms (based on Stauble, 1984: 344–9, Tables 6 and 8)

	Cop *be*	Aux *be*	Irreg past	Reg past	3p -*s*
Lower Intermediate					
J1	23	10	8	0	2
J2	19	0	9	3	0
S1	59	17	4	0	2
S2	88	7	3	0	0
Advanced					
J3	90	58	53	22	19
J4	85	72	71	18	10
S3	94	96	53	4	56
S4	97	94	85	24	56

FURTHER READING

For a concise introduction to the structure of words (**morphology**), see part II of:

Radford, A., Atkinson, M., Britain, D., Clahsen, H. and Spencer, M. 2009. *Linguistics: an introduction*. Second Edition. Cambridge: Cambridge University Press.

For more on 'aspect' see:

Comrie, B. 1976. *Aspect: an introduction to the study of verbal aspect and related problems*. Cambridge: Cambridge University Press.

For more on the separation of abstract morphemes from their forms, and feature underspecification of forms in the Vocabulary see:

Halle, M. and Marantz, A. 1993. Distributed morphology and the pieces of inflection. In K. Hale and S. J. Keyser (eds) *The view from building 20*. Cambridge, MA: MIT Press, pp. 53–109.

Harley, H. and Noyer, R. 1999. Distributed morphology. *Glot International*, 4, 3–9.

For other researchers' perspectives on the topics dealt with in this chapter see:

Slabakova, R. 2016. *Second language acquisition*. Oxford: Oxford University Press, chapter 7: Acquisition of (functional) morphology.

Snape, N. and Kupisch, T. 2017. *Second language acquisition: second language systems*. New York: Macmillan Palgrave, chapter 2: Acquisition of verbal morphosyntax and chapter 3: Acquisition of nominal morphosyntax.

4 How Sentence Structure is Learned

Imagine you are in an art class drawing a picture of a landscape, using crayons. You discover you have lost the blue crayon. You might say, in dismay:

1 I don't have a blue crayon!

As a proficient speaker of English, you would not say:

2 a. *I a crayon blue not have!
   b. *Not I have blue crayon a!

This is because your knowledge of English involves mental rules that tell you that some combinations of morphemes produce acceptable phrases while others do not. These mental rules are the **syntax** of English. Second language learners have to acquire the syntactic rules of the target language – the syntax problem referred to in section 1.4. (For an explanation of what morphemes are, see section 3.1.) This chapter describes some of the things we know about how L2 learners deal with this problem.

4.1 The Form of L2 Speakers' Early Utterances

When L2 learners begin to produce utterances in an L2, those utterances are often different from those of proficient speakers, raising the possibility that L2 speakers have different syntactic rules. To illustrate, consider the following examples of spontaneous speech from a study by Ellis (1988) of two Punjabi-speaking children, aged between ten and thirteen, studied over two school years. They were beginners at the start of the study, classroom learners for whom 'English was not only taught as a subject, but also used as a medium of instruction' (1988: 25). The examples all involve 'sentential **negation**', that is the denial of information conveyed in a statement, e.g. *I have a blue crayon → I don't have a blue crayon*. The intended meanings of the utterances are given in the right-hand column. The first example has the same intended meaning as sentence (1) above:

3. | **Utterance** | **Presumed intended meaning** |
| --- | --- |
| me no blue | 'I don't have a blue crayon' |
| red, no | 'I don't have a red one' |
| no very good | 'It isn't very good' |
| no sir finish | 'I haven't finished, sir' |
| I'm no drawing chu | 'I'm not drawing a "chu"' (not clear what 'chu' means) |

Two striking features of these utterances are: firstly, the use of *no* as a sentential negator, where the target form is *n't/not*. *No* in standard English is the form used to reply to a yes–no question (an 'anaphoric' negator): *Do you have a blue crayon? – No*. Secondly, that the presence of a verb is optional, where in equivalent utterances in the target language it is obligatory.

The use of *no* as a sentential negator is found widely in studies of early L2 learners of English. Ellis (1988: 30) compares the utterances of his Punjabi speakers with those of L1 speakers of German in studies by Wode (1976), of naturalistic learners, and Felix (1981), of classroom learners. These learners produce utterances like:

4 a. no play baseball
  b. lunch is no ready
  c. it's no my comb
  d. Britta no this … no have … this

The optionality of tense-inflected verbs is also a characteristic of early L2 learner utterances, in affirmative declaratives ('statements') as well as negative declaratives. Here are some examples from Erdem, the Turkish child learner of English studied by Haznedar (2001):

5. | Investigator: | Where is your dad now? |
| --- | --- |
| Erdem: | My dad school. |
| Investigator: | Where are we going now? |
| Erdem: | Newcastle going. |

Myles (2005) has studied the early productions of twelve- to thirteen-year-old classroom learners of L2 French in the UK and found that, in a picture description task, 45 per cent of utterances with sentence-like meanings lacked verbs. Where verbs were used, they often appeared to be part of unanalysed chunks ('**formulas**'), that is, a sound sequence that can be analysed into several morphemes in the target language, but which is a single morpheme for the learner. As an example, Haznedar (2001) suggests that *it is a/it's a* may be an unanalysed chunk for Erdem in cases like the following:

6. | Investigator: | What is the cat doing? |
| --- | --- |
| Erdem: | *Itisa* playing. |
| Investigator: | What are these? |
| Erdem: | *Itsa* banana. |
| Erdem: | *Itsa* I don't know |

In an earlier study, Myles and her colleagues (Myles et al., 1999) also found considerable use of unanalysed chunks in the development of questions in L2 French by sixteen adolescent classroom learners over the first two years of exposure (roughly 254 hours). Participants were exposed to (target) question constructions like the following through role play and drilling:

7 a. Quel   âge   as-tu?   'How old are you?'
        What   age   have-you?

   b. Comment   tu   t'   appelles? 'What's your name?'
        How   you   self   call?

   c. Où   habites-tu?   'Where do you live?'
        Where   live-you?

Myles et al. then looked at participants' use of question forms in 'semi-spontaneous' dialogues between pairs of learners at six sampling points over the two years of their exposure to French. The data collected were divided into three types:

• Questions using the forms participants had been drilled in as unanalysed chunks
• Novel question constructions without verbs, e.g.

   Où la piscine?   'Where the swimming pool?'
   Jaune?   'Yellow?' (i.e. Is it yellow?)
   La dame à la stade?   'The lady at the stadium?' (i.e. Is the lady at the stadium?)

• Novel question constructions with verbs (mostly in non-finite forms), e.g.

   Je manger douze   heures? 'Do I eat at 12 noon?'
   I   to-eat 12   hours?

   Tu   et   moi   visiter   le   cinéma? 'Shall you and I go to the cinema?'
   You and me   to-visit the   cinema?

The results are presented in table 4.1. It can be seen that over the two-year period of development, while the number of unanalysed chunks decreases, the proportion

TABLE 4.1 Proportion of French question types used by 16 informants at six sampling points over two years (based on Myles et al., 1999: 69)

Question Type	1	2	3	4	5	6
Chunk	143/186	264/418	47/111	214/483	261/622	40/264
	(77%)	(63%)	(42%)	(44%)	(42%)	(15%)
Novel	41/186	129/418	53/111	235/483	287/622	182/264
Verb-less	(22%)	(31%)	(48%)	(49%)	(46%)	(69%)
With Verb	2/186	25/418	11/111	34/483	74/622	42/264
	(1%)	(6%)	(10%)	(7%)	(12%	(16%)

of question sentences where verbs are present remains fairly low. The big change is in the production of novel question constructions that lack verbs.

Section 4.1 in a Nutshell

The syntax of L2 learners' early utterances can be very different from that of proficient speakers. Utterances may lack tense-inflected verbs and include unanalysed chunks. In early L2 English, *no* is used as a sentential negator by many speakers.

4.2 The Phrase Structure of Early L2 Utterances

What are the syntactic rules that early L2 learners use that lead them to produce utterances like *me no blue*, and what rules must they acquire to produce utterances like *I don't have a blue crayon* and exclude utterances like **I a crayon blue not have*?

The approach that will be followed here in answering these questions assumes that L2 learners unconsciously know how syntactic rules work in general before they start learning the target language. This is because the way that syntactic rules work is universal to human language, and possibly one of the linguistic predispositions that humans bring to the task of language learning (see chapter 5 for discussion of linguistic predispositions). However, knowing how the general rules apply in specific languages is something that has to be learned on the basis of experience.

One of the things L2 learners know already is that the thousands of morphemes they will need to learn to become proficient speakers are associated with a small number of morpheme categories like N(oun), V(erb), A(djective), P(reposition), Adv(erb), D(eterminer) and a few others. It is these morpheme categories that are used by syntactic rules to construct sentences, rather than the individual morphemes themselves.

A second thing they know is that one of the rules of syntax, referred to in recent syntactic theory as Merge, combines morpheme categories into phrases to create the phrase structure of a sentence. By hypothesis, this rule is highly constrained. It never involves more than two constituents, so that the structure of phrases is binary: each phrase consists of only two immediate constituents. One of the constituents is the main constituent or head of the phrase. This is the important word that gives its name to the phrase.

One argument in support of binary Merge is that it captures the ambiguity of phrases like *American football coach*. This can either refer to someone who coaches American football or to a football coach who happens to be American, and who coaches, say, soccer players. In the first case the adjective *American* merges first with *football* to produce the noun phrase [$_{NP}$ *American football*] which then merges with *coach* to produce another noun phrase [$_{NP}$ [$_{NP}$ *American football*] *coach*]. In the second case the noun *football* first merges with the noun *coach* to produce a noun phrase [$_{NP}$ *football coach*] which then merges with the adjective *American* to produce another noun phrase [$_{NP}$ [$_A$ *American*] [$_{NP}$ *football coach*]]. Merger of all three categories simultaneously (ternary Merge) would not distinguish the two possible meanings.[1]

To illustrate, consider how Merge produces the phrase structure of *I don't have a blue crayon*. For the purposes of exposition it is easiest to start building the phrase structure from the end of the sentence, moving towards the beginning: *blue*, an A, and *crayon*, an N, merge to form a Noun Phrase (NP), where N is the head.[2]

8.

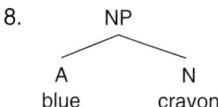

Merge can combine individual morpheme categories with phrases to form larger phrases. For example, a common assumption in recent syntactic theory is that morphemes associated with the D category ({the, a, this, my, some, ...}) head the phrase created when a D merges with an NP (Koeneman and Zeijlstra, 2017: 100–5). This means that the phrase *a blue crayon* has the structure in (9):

9.

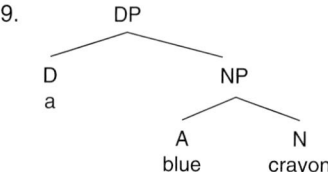

The DP [$_{DP}$ a blue crayon] merges with a V which heads a Verb Phrase (VP):

10.

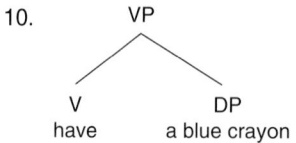

VP merges with a category Neg (with which the form *n't* is associated) to form a Neg Phrase (NegP):

11.

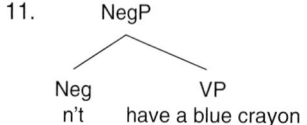

---

[1] For a general introduction to syntactic structure see Koeneman and Zeijlstra (2017) or Radford (2009). The rationale for binary Merge is discussed in Koeneman and Zeijlstra in section 2.3 and in Radford in section 2.2.

[2] It should be noted that the order in which the building of phrase structure is discussed here is unlikely to be how speakers really construct sentences when they are speaking. They are more likely to start from the beginning of the sentence. For a comprehensive overview of what is involved in speaking, see Levelt (1989).

NegP merges with the category Tense (with which the form *do* is associated) to form a Tense Phrase (TP):

12.

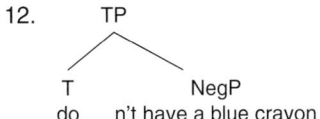

TP merges with a ProN(oun) category, with which morphemes like {I, you, she, he, we, etc.} are associated. This ProN is not, however, normally assumed to be the head of the phrase. T remains the head, and so ProN merges with TP to create an extended TP[3]:

13.

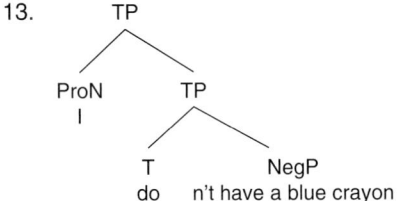

Finally, recent syntactic theory assumes that TP merges with a C(omplementiser) category to form a Complementiser Phrase (CP), whose head is C. Phrases whose head is a C are clauses:

14.

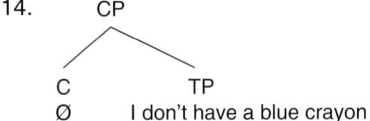

As illustrated in (14) the presence of a CP layer of structure is not audible/visible in main declarative clauses in English because there is no overt form. It can become so, though, in embedded (subordinate) clauses where the form *that* may realise C:

15.

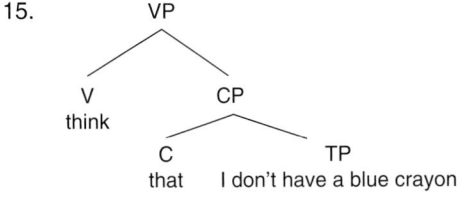

C is also the locus of information about the type of clause that it heads: declarative, interrogative (question), embedded. The complete phrase structure for *I don't have a blue crayon* is:

---

[3] The interested reader will find discussion of the reason why TP remains the head of the phrase in Radford (2009), section 2.3.

16.

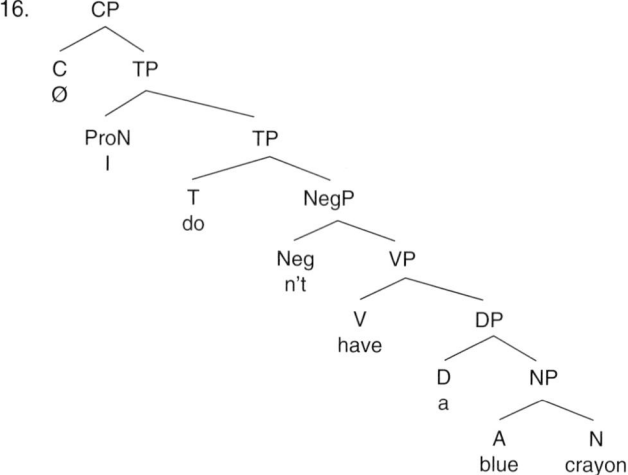

Although knowledge of the morpheme categories and knowledge that one of the syntactic rules is binary Merge may be two of the linguistic predispositions that people have for learning language, what is not given by these predispositions is either the morphemes associated with the morpheme categories ({I, n't, have, a, etc.}) or the ordering of constituents within phrases. Languages differ in both of these cases. While the first person singular subject pronoun in English is *I*, in French it is *je*, in Mandarin Chinese it is *wo*. Word order also has to be learned on the basis of experience. Consider some of the possibilities in the case of the DP:

17 a.

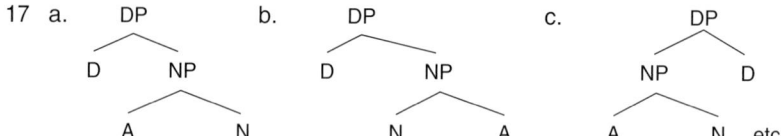

(17a) is the order found in English (*a blue crayon*), (17b) the order found in French for many adjectives (*un crayon bleu* 'a pencil blue'), (17c) the order found in Bulgarian (*siniya pisalka ta* 'blue pen the') where *ta* (the definite article) is a member of the D category (Bulgarian has no indefinite article equivalent to English *a*), and so on.

Given this account of how Merge creates the phrase structure of sentences like *I don't have a blue crayon*, how does it operate in the case of the Punjabi-speaking learner of English who produced *me no blue* with the intended meaning 'I don't have a blue crayon'? What is the phrase structure of this expression, and how did the learner arrive at this structure?

In view of the assumptions about linguistic predispositions made above, having learned the forms *me, no, blue* from exposure to English, the learner will have assigned these to morpheme categories:

18 a. me   ↔   ProN
    b. no   ↔   Neg
    c. blue   ↔   A

She also knows that the phrase structure of *me no blue* results from binary Merge. There are now two possibilities that could be considered for the phrase structure that underlies this utterance:

(i) Her early syntax only involves the merger of categories to which specific, overt morphemes have been assigned:

19.

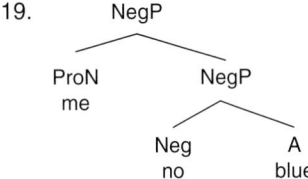

(ii) She has the full syntactic representation for the target English clause that native speakers have, but some of the categories have no morphemes to realise them. The phrase structure that underlies *me no blue* is like that in (20):

20.

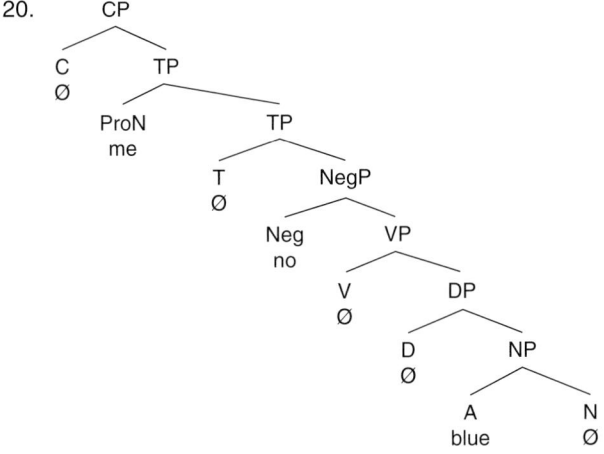

These two possibilities, (19) and (20), correspond to two well-known hypotheses in the second language research literature about how L2 learners in the early stages of acquiring a target language deal with the 'syntax problem'. The hypothesis corresponding to (20) essentially assumes that in addition to knowing about morpheme categories, binary Merge and headedness, learners already know the full phrase structure for clauses up to CP. This is one of the linguistic predispositions they bring to the task of language learning. The learner then only has to identify the morphemes of the target language that are associated with particular morpheme categories and the order of constituents within phrases. Their pre-existing linguistic knowledge instructs them in how to build clauses. This is known as the Full Access Hypothesis (Epstein et al., 1996; White, 2003a, chapter 3). Full Access is access to Universal Grammar, the name given to the linguistic predispositions that humans have. Universal Grammar will be discussed in more detail in chapter 5.

The hypothesis corresponding to (19) does not assume that Universal Grammar specifies the full phrase structure of clauses before learning begins, although it still assumes that learners bring pre-existing knowledge about morpheme categories, binary Merge and headedness to the learning task. On this view, the only morpheme categories that are present in early phrase structure are those for which the learner has overt evidence from the target language. Given that the research described in section 1.3 suggests that learners tend initially to identify form–meaning pairings associated with lexical morphemes before those associated with functional morphemes (meaning-modifying/dependency-marking forms), early productions by L2 learners will consist primarily of the merger of lexical morphemes like N, A, V into larger phrases. Neg here, realised by *no*, is assumed to be a lexical morpheme. Merger with the categories T and C will only come later when morphemes belonging to these categories have been identified. This view of the early phrase structure of L2 learners' productions is known as the Minimal Trees Hypothesis, more recently renamed Organic Grammar (Vainikka and Young-Scholten 2007; 2011). 'Minimal Trees' because initially there are no layers of structure with invisible exponents, 'Organic Grammar' because phrase structure grows organically with time, as a function of learners identifying morphemes associated with a wider range of morpheme categories.

Section 4.2 in a Nutshell

The thousands of morphemes that an L2 learner needs to acquire to become a proficient speaker are assigned to a small set of morpheme categories (N, V, A, P, Adv, D, Neg, Tense, ProN, C). Syntactic rules apply to morpheme categories and not individual morphemes. The syntactic rule Merge combines just two syntactic objects (morpheme categories or phrases) into a phrase headed by one of those objects. In other words it is a binary rule. Knowledge of morpheme categories and knowledge of binary Merge are two of the linguistic predispositions that people have for language learning; individual morphemes and the ordering of constituents within phrases have to be learned from exposure to the target language.

There are two possibilities for the phrase structure of early L2 utterances like *me no blue* ('I don't have a blue crayon'): a Minimal Trees structure where only morpheme categories for which the learner has evidence from exposure to the target language are merged; or a hypothesised full phrase structure for a clause known by the L2 learner from linguistic predispositions where some of the categories have no morpheme to realise them.

4.3 Development of L2 Learners' Knowledge of Sentential Negation

How does an L2 learner develop from producing utterances like *me no blue* to utterances that more clearly resemble *I don't have a blue crayon*? Although there is no evidence available about how the Punjabi-speaking learners studied by Ellis (1988) used sentential negation when they became more proficient in English, there is evidence about how L2 learner knowledge of sentential negation might develop over time from other studies.

The data in table 4.2 are from Stauble (1984), who reports the use of English sentential negation in the spontaneous speech of six L1-Spanish and six L1-Japanese speakers, four of whom were of lower intermediate proficiency, four of intermediate proficiency, and four of advanced proficiency. Although the performance of each participant is sampled at a single moment in time, assuming that performance is representative of learners at those three proficiency levels allows a picture of possible development to be constructed.

The data are presented as proportions (%) of different construction types used in intended sentential negation contexts, and based on at least ten tokens of each type produced by the participants. For example, of S1's intended sentence negations involving the copula, 86 per cent involve the sentential negator *no* and the

TABLE 4.2 Proportions (%) of types of sentential negation used by L2 speakers at different proficiency levels (based on Stauble, 1984: 338–9, Table 5)

	Low Intermediate				Intermediate				Advanced			
	S1	S2	J1	J2	S3	S4	J3	J4	S5	S6	J5	J6
Copula												
no + Ø	86	58	-	78	9	-	-	-	-	-	-	
n't/not + Ø	-	-	-	-	-	18	79	50	-	5	3	25
no + be	14	25	-	-	64	-	-	-	-	-	-	-
n't/not + be	-	-	-	-	-	-	-	-	-	-	3	-
be + no	-	17	-	11	-	9	7	-	-	-	-	-
be + n't/not	-	-	-	11	18	73	14	50	100	95	94	75
Lexical V												
no + V	87	94	64	79	40	14	-	5	-	-	-	-
n't/not + V	-	-	11	-	-	-	10	13	-	-	2	-
unanalysed don't	13	6	24	21	60	81	90	26	15	13	12	7
analysed don't	-	-	-	-	-	-	-	33	24	46	45	56
analysed didn't	-	-	-	-	-	-	-	13	42	35	29	17
analysed doesn't	-	-	-	-	-	-	-	-	17	3	11	16

S = Spanish participants, J = Japanese participants. 'Unanalysed don't' refers to uses like *She don't like tea, He don't come yesterday*, where inflected forms of *do* are required in English: *She doesn't …, He didn't …*

absence of a form of *be* (e.g. *she no clever*) while 14 per cent involve *no* followed by a form of *be* (e.g. *she no is teacher*).[4]

The utterances of the low intermediate proficiency learners are similar to those of the Punjabi-speaking learners (and the German-speaking learners studied by Wode (1976) and Felix (1981)). The majority involve *no* as a sentential negator (*me no blue, no play baseball*). In cases where a form of copula *be* would be required by native speakers of English, it is absent in the speech of the L2 speakers. However, *n't/not* is beginning to be used with forms of *be* by one of the learners (J2), and *don't* is beginning to be used with lexical verbs by all the learners, although it is generalised to third person singular present tense and past tense contexts (*She don't like tea, He don't come yesterday*). This is referred to as 'unanalysed *don't*'.

The emergence of *n't/not* appears to coincide with greater use of forms of *be* and *do* to the left of the sentential negator. This occurs at some point between low intermediate and intermediate proficiency. This might follow from learners either merging a newly-identified T category with NegP (as Minimal Trees would propose) or newly identifying morphemes that realise an already-present T category (as Full Access would propose), as illustrated in the case of *don't* in (21).

21. **Low Intermediate Proficiency**   **Intermediate Proficiency**

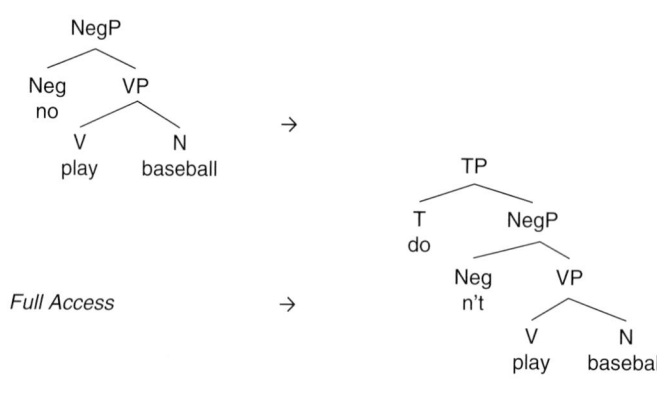

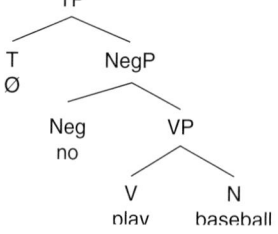

For a while, learners appear optionally to produce utterances like *she no is clever/she isn't clever, I no play baseball/I don't play baseball*, as in the case of S3. But between intermediate and advanced proficiency, utterances that lack a verb and involve *no* as the sentential negator decrease, so that target *isn't/am not/aren't* predominate, and the features of T that are associated with meaning-modifying past and non-past tense, and dependency marking number and person (in subject–verb agreement) are realised by *don't–didn't–doesn't*.

Section 4.3 in a Nutshell

The acquisition of the syntax of English sentential negation by L2 learners appears to be driven both by linguistic predispositions and by learning from experience: knowledge from linguistic predispositions that binary Merge can create phrases from a small set of morpheme categories; and learning individual morphemes that are associated with those morpheme categories from experience with the target language. Initially lexical morphemes are identified, and the form identified as the sentential negator is *no*. Later, morphemes associated with the category T are identified, and *n't/not* replaces *no* as the realisation of the category Neg.

4.4. The L2 Acquisition of Constructions that Involve Movement

4.4.1 Movement of T and V

The rule Merge combines morpheme categories with other morpheme categories or phrases until a clause is formed. Another syntactic rule, **Move**, has the ability to re-arrange the phrases constructed by Merge. In discussing sentential negation in section 4.3, it was proposed that T merges with a NegP to produce sentences like (22):

22. She [$_T$ does [$_{NegP}$ n't have a blue crayon]]

In affirmative ('non-negative') declaratives, *do* disappears and the lexical verb, *have* in this case, is inflected for tense:

23. She has a blue crayon

There are reasons for thinking that the phrase structure underlying (23) is exactly the same as that underlying (22), with T merging with the VP *have a blue crayon*. The only difference is the absence of a NegP:

24.

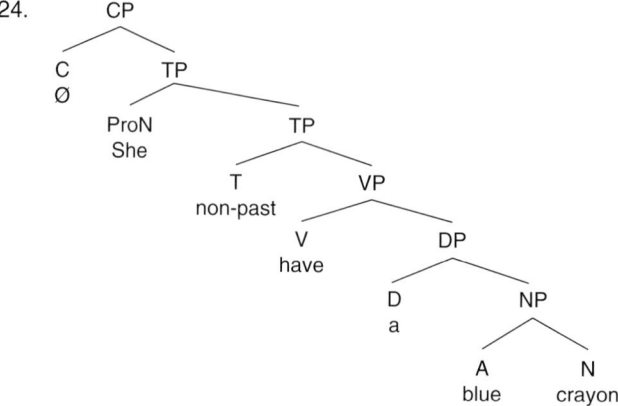

One reason is that it allows a unified account of the phrase structure of finite and non-finite variants of the same clause in English. In non-finite clauses T appears to the left of the verb and is realised by *to*: *She expected [$_T$ to [$_{VP}$ have a blue crayon]].*

But now finite T somehow has to merge at the right edge of V to produce *has*. There are two possibilities. Either Move lowers T to V, or it raises V to T. The position of VP-modifying adverbs, as in *She **usually** has a blue crayon*, suggests that Move lowers T to V, as illustrated in (25) (e for 'empty' indicates the position from which a constituent has moved):

25.

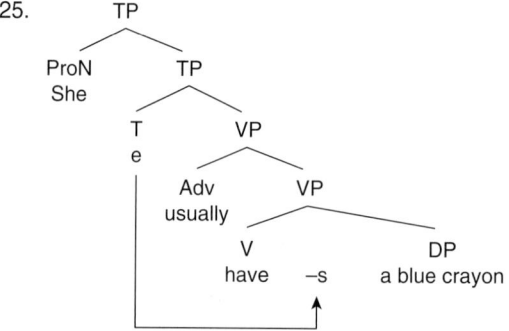

If V were raised to T by Move, the ungrammatical sentence **She has usually a blue crayon* would result. The lowering of T to V produces the grammatical *She usually has a blue crayon*.

While Move lowers T to V in English affirmative declarative clauses involving lexical verbs like *have, prefer, like, use* (*She has/had a blue crayon, She prefers/preferred a blue crayon*), the presence of a sentential negator blocks movement. As we have seen, in such cases *do* is inserted directly into T to carry T's inflection. There is a similar insertion of *do* when T raises to C to form a yes–no question (*Does she have a blue crayon?*):

26.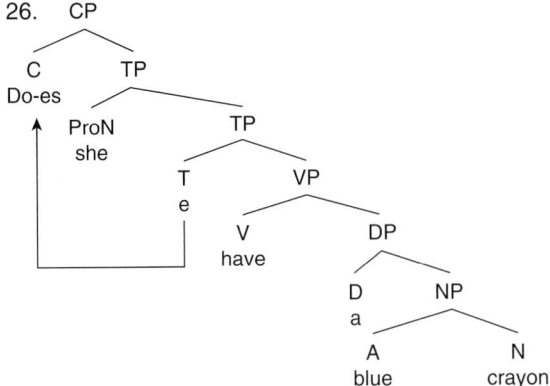

It seems that lexical verbs in English are fixed in their VP and are not affected by the syntactic rule Move. When the T category cannot be lowered to V, either because there is an intervening sentential negator or because T has already moved to C in questions, *do* must play the role of the verb. These observations are captured by the proposal that T is a category that is separate from V, and merges with VP in the formation of clauses.

Non-lexical verbs – copula *be*, the auxiliaries *be* and *have* and modal verbs like *must, can, will* – are different from lexical verbs in terms of their syntactic properties. Modal verbs appear to belong to the category T, rather than V. They do not co-occur with non-finite *to: They were thought *to must leave, He expected her *to can write the letter.* This is in contrast to the copula and auxiliaries: *They were thought to be ready/to be leaving/to have left.* Furthermore, they always come first in a sequence of verbs: *She must have been drawing a picture/*She has must been drawing a picture.* As a consequence of being members of T, modal verbs appear to the left of the sentential negator and move with T to C in questions: *She mustn't have a blue crayon, Can she draw a picture?* The insertion of *do* in these sentences is ungrammatical: *She doesn't must have a blue crayon, *Does she can draw a picture?*

Copula *be* and the auxiliaries *be/have* appear to be members of the category V. When they co-occur with modals they appear in the typical position in which lexical verbs appear: to the right of the sentential negator and VP-modifying adverbs: *She must**n't usually** be late, She ca**n't often** have drawn a picture like that.* However, they differ from lexical verbs in that, when they are finite, Move can raise them from their VPs to T, as illustrated in (27):

27.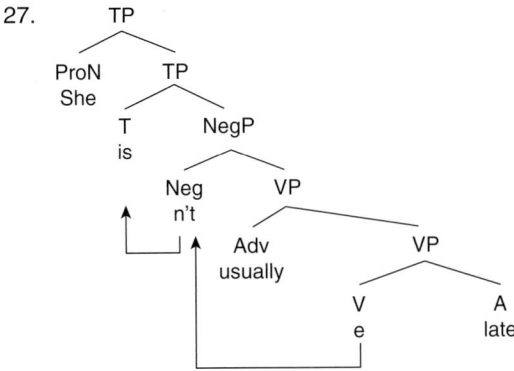

The tree in (27) shows the copula being moved to the Neg head before moving to the T head. This is another of the hypothesised linguistic predispositions that learners have: knowledge that Move can only operate in 'local' steps, moving a category to the next closest category, and from that category to a higher category. (See Radford, 2009, section 1.5 for discussion of 'locality' as a fundamental property of our linguistic knowledge.)

While Move, and the locality constraint on it, are part of a learner's pre-existing knowledge, the categories to which it can apply are language-specific and have to be learned. Although Move cannot raise finite lexical verbs to T in English, finite lexical verbs in French are raised to T. While this is not obvious from simple affirmative declarative clauses like (28a), it becomes clear that lexical verbs are raised when there is a sentential negator (the form *pas* in French) (28b), or a VP-modifying adverb (28c), or in yes–no questions (28d):

28 a. Marie   aime   les   pâtes
       Marie   likes   the   pasta
       'Marie likes pasta'

    b. Marie   aime   pas   les   pâtes
       Marie   likes   not   the   pasta
       'Marie doesn't like pasta'

    c. Marie   mange   souvent   les   pâtes
       Marie   eats   often   the   pasta
       'Marie often eats pasta'

    d. Aime-t-elle   les   pâtes?
       Likes-she   the   pasta?
       'Does she like pasta ?'

Note that the lexical verb appears to the left of the negator *pas*, to the left of the adverb *souvent*, at the very left edge of the sentence in the question.

Given these assumptions, a second language learner does not have to learn that there is a syntactic rule that can move constituents from the position where they are first merged to other positions. This is part of a learner's linguistic predispositions. But the categories that allow movement do need to be learned, because these are language-specific. Acquiring this knowledge may take time, and may be influenced by the categories that allow movement in the L1. Such a case is described in section 4.4.2

Section 4.4.1 in a Nutshell

L2 learners know as part of their linguistic predispositions that there is a syntactic rule Move. However, they have to learn from exposure to the target language to which morpheme categories it can apply. In English it applies to finite Tense (T), which is lowered to the right edge of lexical verbs in affirmative declarative clauses when no other verbs (copula *be*, auxiliary *be* and *have*, modal verbs like *must*) or negation are present. Modal verbs belong to the category T, so when they are present no movement occurs. When modal verbs are not present and the first verb in the VP is copula *be*, or auxiliary *be* or *have*, it moves to T. The presence of negation in English blocks the movement of T to lexical verbs and the support verb *do* is inserted to host the affixal forms that realise T. *Do* is also inserted when T moves to C in questions. Movement is hypothesised to occur in local steps, from head to head. In French, lexical verbs move to T, just like copula and auxiliary verbs. Evidence for this comes from the location of VP-modifying adverbs, the location of negation and the possibility of moving lexical verbs to C in questions.

4.4.2 The L2 Acquisition of T and V Movement in French and English

White (2003a: 130) reports a study of L1 French adolescent learners of L2 English after two years of classroom instruction. She gave them a preference task where they were asked to judge the grammaticality of pairs of English sentences involving sentential negation (*The boys don't like the girls*/*The boys like not the girls*), yes–no questions (*Do you like pepperoni pizza?*/*Like you pepperoni pizza?*) and VP-modifying adverbs (*Linda always takes the metro*/*Linda takes always the metro*). Observe that all the examples that are grammatical in English would be ungrammatical in French, and all the examples that are ungrammatical in English would be grammatical in French. White also compared the performance of the L2 learners with a control group of native English speakers of the same age. The percentages of rejections of the ungrammatical sentences are shown in table 4.3.

The French learners are very successful in recognising the ungrammaticality of the French pattern of verb placement in English with negation and question formation. But they are notably different from the native controls in assuming the grammaticality in English of sentences like *Linda takes always the metro*, consistent

TABLE 4.3 Rejection (%) of the ungrammatical English sentences (based on White, 2003a: 130, Box 4.5)

	Negation	Question	Adverb
L2 learners (n = 72)	85	86	23
Native speakers (n = 29)	98	97	95

with them having transferred verb movement from their L1 into their grammars for English. They have not yet identified the fact that lexical verbs do not move over VP adverbs.

White accounts for these observations by proposing that agreement properties (which up to now we have been assuming are features of T) in fact belong to a separate Agr(eement) category that merges with VP. The AgrP constituent created can merge with Neg or, if Neg is not present, with T. The specific structure that White assumes is illustrated in (29):

29.

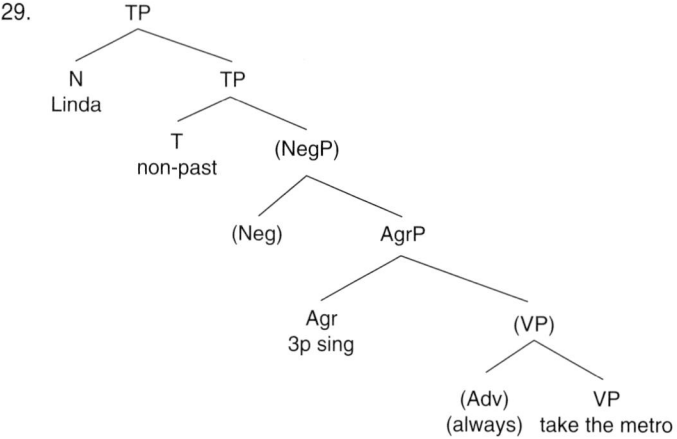

Whereas T and Agr in English are lowered to the lexical V (when Neg is absent), lexical Vs in French are raised to Agr, then to Neg (if present) and finally to T. White argues that the pattern of responses of the French learners of English shown in table 4.3 can be accounted for if learners initially assume that English is like French, rapidly identify the fact that Agr cannot move to T in English, but have not yet identified the fact that the lexical V cannot move to Agr. If lexical Vs can move to Agr, sentences like *Linda takes always the metro* result. But if they cannot then move to T, they will appear to the right of negation, and will not move to C in questions.

By proposing an explicit linguistic description of the kind of knowledge that needs to be acquired in English in relation to negation, adverb placement and question formation, an account can be given of what might at first look like unexpected development in the way that native speakers of French learn the sentence structure of English.

However, White's proposal does not work all that well in explaining how English speakers appear to acquire verb movement in French. A grammaticality judgement task used by Hawkins et al. (1993) with seventy-nine intermediate proficiency learners found that while participants were accurate in locating lexical verbs with negation (*Marie aime pas les pâtes* 'Marie doesn't like pasta'), 40 per cent of them allowed both the French and English location with VP-modifying adverbs (*Marie mange souvent les pâtes*/*Marie souvent mange les pâtes* '*Marie eats often pasta/Marie often eats pasta'). This is a finding replicated by Rogers (2009) in a study of English-speaking learners of French at several proficiency levels, also using a grammaticality judgement task. Her high intermediate proficiency group (who had had six years of classroom input) accepted English-like lexical verb placement with negation in only 8 per cent of cases, but accepted the English-like location of verbs with VP-modifying adverbs in 38 per cent of cases.

If English learners have identified the fact that finite lexical verbs in French move to Agr to Neg to T, to account for the acquisition of verb location with Neg, then verbs should also move to T when VP-modifying adverbs are present. But characteristically, intermediate proficiency learners optionally allow the verb to move or to stay in the VP.

One way of reconciling the observations about French learners of English and English learners of French is to go back to the phrase structure where there is a single T category (rather than the two categories T and Agr), as illustrated in (30).

30.

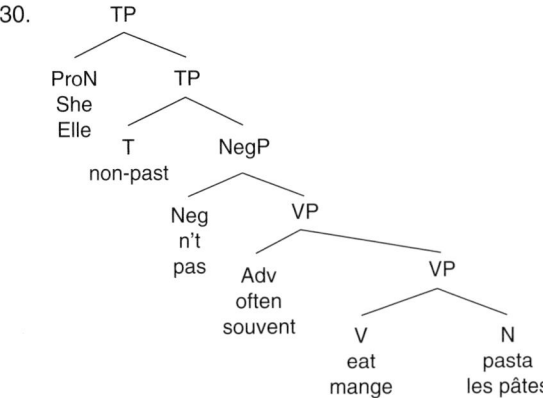

T, Neg and V are all heads of their phrases. When V moves to T in French, it has to move first to Neg. When T and V need to merge in English, it is Neg that blocks that merger. VP adverbs, however, are not heads but modifiers of the VP and do not block the movement of T to V. One possibility is that although L2 learners initially transfer the movement properties of their L1 into the L2, the information they get from input in relation to movement involving heads is more salient than information about movement involving modifiers. They quickly identify the feature of Neg that attracts the lexical verb (in French) or blocks the lowering of T to V (in English). However, it takes them longer to identify the feature of T that attracts the lexical verb when Neg is absent (in French) or requires T to lower when Neg is absent (in English), although they recognise that such raising/lowering is possible and allow it sometimes. On this scenario, both the L1 and input from the L2 play a role in forming the movement rules that L2 learners construct. In section 4.6 an example will be given of input playing a stronger role than L1 influence.

Section 4.4.2 in a Nutshell

L1 French-speaking early-stage learners of English rapidly establish that English lexical verbs do not move to T over negation (as in *Marie likes not pasta*) or to T and then C in questions (*Likes she pasta?*). However, they continue to allow lexical verbs to move to T over VP-modifying adverbs (as in *Marie eats often pasta*). L1 English-speaking early-stage learners of French rapidly establish that French lexical verbs move to T over negation (as in *Marie aime pas les pâtes* 'Marie likes not pasta') but continue to allow lexical verbs not to move to T over VP-modifying adverbs, which is ungrammatical in French (*Marie souvent mange les pâtes*). One account for this behaviour exploits the linguistic distinction between heads of phrases and modifiers. L2 learners quickly identify the property of the Neg head that attracts lexical verbs (French) or blocks the movement of T to V (English) but take longer to identify the relevant property of T, because evidence from movement or lack of movement across modifiers is less salient.

4.5 The Influence of Already-Acquired Languages on the Acquisition of Movement

From the description in sections 4.1–4.3 of how L2 learners acquire sentential negation in English, it is clear that there are developmental processes that are shared by L2 learners. Learners who have quite different L1s (Punjabi, German, Spanish, Japanese) initially use *no* as a sentential negator in English and construct clauses consisting of forms associated with lexical morphemes. Subsequently they introduce forms that are associated with functional morphemes like T (finite forms of *be* and *do*).

In the description of how French-speaking learners of English and English-speaking learners of French develop knowledge of T and V movement in the L2, some evidence began to emerge to suggest a learner's L1 might also play a role in guiding development. French speakers continue to allow lexical verbs to move to T over VP adverbs in English, and English speakers continue not to move lexical verbs to T over VP adverbs in French. This is consistent with the language-specific L1 rules for movement influencing the language-specific rules for movement in the L2. In this section further evidence will be presented that suggests that knowledge of already-acquired languages can be an important factor, alongside linguistic predispositions and knowledge learned from input, in shaping the way further languages are acquired.

4.5.1 Verb Movement to C

When people know a second language already and learn a third language, it appears that movement properties in that second language can influence acquisition of movement in the third language. A study by Bohnacker (2006) was interested in testing whether L1 speakers of Swedish who had learned English as their first L2 and were now learning German as an L3 would treat verb movement differently from L1 speakers of Swedish who were learning German as their first L2.

German declarative sentence structure differs from English in that in main clauses the finite verb (the verb that is marked for tense and agreement with the subject) must always occur in second position in the clause. By contrast, in English the finite verb typically always follows the subject, whether the subject is first, second or third in the sentence. Compare the following examples:

31 a. [₁ John] [₂ **works**] in a café at weekends to earn extra money.
    b. [₁ Johann] [₂ **arbeitet**] am Wochenende in einem Café um extra Geld zu verdienen.

32 a. [₁ At weekends] [₂ John] [₃ **works**] in a café to earn extra money.
    b. [₁ Am Wochenende] [₂ **arbeitet**] [₃ Johann] in einem Café um extra Geld zu verdienen.

33 a. [₁ To earn extra money] [₂ John] [₃ **works**] in a café at weekends.
    b. [₁ Um extra Geld zu verdienen] [₂ **arbeitet**] [₃ Johann] am Wochenende in einem Café.

The verb-second property of German can be understood as the movement of the lexical verb to T and then to C, accompanied by the movement of another phrase to the front of the sentence that merges with CP, as illustrated in (34). (Note that in (34) it is assumed that in German the head T of TP Merges with VP to its left (unlike English), and V also Merges with its complement to the left. This is to account for the fact that in embedded ('subordinate') clauses in German the finite verb is at the end of the clause: *Ich glaube [dass Johann am Wochenende in einem Café **arbeitet**]*, literally 'I think that Johann at the weekend in a café **works**'.)

34.

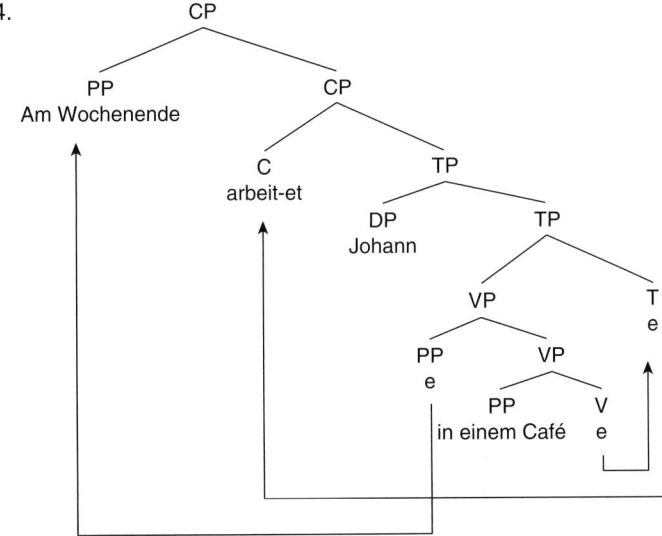

Swedish is a verb-second language like German, and is assumed to have similar movement properties. To investigate whether having learned English before learning German would affect early development of knowledge of the verb-second property in German, Bohnacker recruited four informants. For two of the informants (Märta and Algot) German was the first language other than Swedish that they had learned; the other two informants (Rune and Gun) had already learned English as an L2 (so German was a third language for them). Data were collected four months after informants had started *ab initio* German classes, and again after nine months, from a task where they had to speak in German about 'what I do or would like to do in my spare time'.

The four learners were participating in the same German language programme, and were tested at the same intervals, so it can be assumed that proficiency levels are roughly equivalent. Although all four participants have native knowledge of the verb-second property in Swedish, which is similar in German, two of them also have knowledge of a language which does not require the verb always to be in second position: English. Bohnacker also looked at word orders that are impossible in any of the languages (in order to check that the participants were not responding randomly).

The frequency of word orders produced by the participants in utterances that contained a finite verb (V), an overt subject (S), and some other constituent (object or adverbial, represented by an X) are presented in table 4.4. The key case is XSV, sentences like *Am Wochenende Johann arbeitet in einem Café*, which is the German equivalent of *At weekends John works in a café*, and is ungrammatical in German. If Rune and Gun transfer their knowledge of English into their L3 German, we would expect to see them producing sentences like these, in contrast to Märta and Algot.

The speakers for whom German is an L3 show optionality: they allow both V2 and V3, whereas the speakers for whom German is the first non-primary language they have learned categorically produce verb-second main clauses. At the same time no participant produces verb-initial main clauses, indicating that they are not randomly producing strings of words in German. This suggests that Rune's and Gun's knowledge of German has been influenced by their knowledge of English.

TABLE 4.4 Verb position in the German utterances of four Swedish speakers (based on Bohnacker, 2006: 461)

		SVX	XVS	XSV	VSX
German L2	Märta	58/82	24/82	0	0
	Algot	43/62	19/62	0	0
German L3	Rune	35/64	16/64	13/64 (20%)	0
	Gun	58/78	11/78	9/78 (12%)	0

4.5.2 DP Movement in Information Questions

Example (26) illustrated the movement of T to C in yes–no questions in English. It was noted that because the lexical verb does not move to T, the 'support' verb *do* is inserted to act as host for T's tense inflection. 'Information questions' like *What man did she see?*, *Which boy did the cat bite?* not only involve T-to-C movement, but also movement of a determiner phrase (DP) to merge with CP.

35.

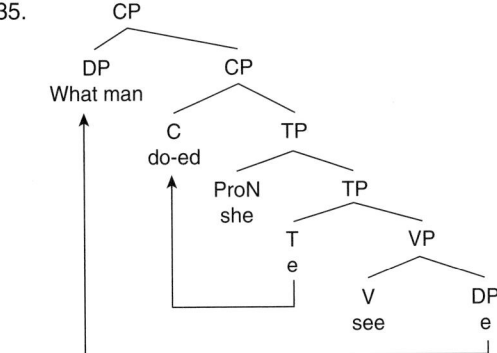

The NP part of the questioned DP need not be specified, so that information questions involving just *What?*, *Which?*, *Who(m)?*, *When?* are produced: *What did she see? Whom did the cat bite? When did the guests leave?* In this case it is assumed that there is a null (unspecified) NP.

The questions illustrated in the previous paragraph involve questioning an object or a time adverbial: *She saw what? The cat bit who? The guests left when?*. When the subject is questioned there appears to be no T-to-C movement: *Who saw the man? What bit the guest?* It is usually assumed that the questioned subject still moves to merge with CP, and that the head C is null:

36.

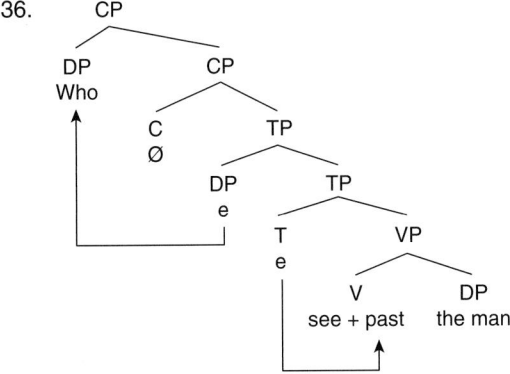

German forms information questions in a similar way. However, because it is a verb-second language, information questions are potentially ambiguous between an interpretation where the questioned DP is a subject or an object:

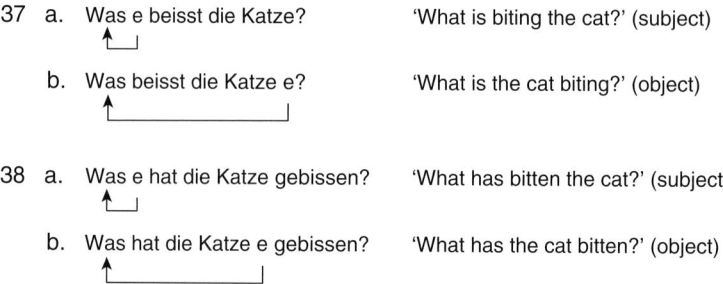

37 a. Was e beisst die Katze?   'What is biting the cat?' (subject)

    b. Was beisst die Katze e?   'What is the cat biting?' (object)

38 a. Was e hat die Katze gebissen?   'What has bitten the cat?' (subject)

    b. Was hat die Katze e gebissen?   'What has the cat bitten?' (object)

Grüter and Conradie (2006) have shown that speakers of English who are very early learners of German assume that DP movement in German questions has the same properties as English, and do not detect the ambiguity of sentences like those in (37–38). They assume that (37) questions the subject because *die Katze* is in the typical position of an object in English. And they assume that (38) questions the object because *die Katze* is in the typical position of a subject in English.

Grüter and Conradie compared seventeen English-speaking learners of German (aged 18–30) with seventeen Afrikaans-speaking learners of German (aged 18–27) and fifteen native speaker control participants.

The L2 learners were beginners with just thirty hours of exposure to German in the classroom. They were asked to interpret the possible answers to questions accompanying pictures. For example, they would be shown a cartoon picture of four animals in a row with a dog biting a cow's tail, the cow biting a cat's tail, and the cat biting a tortoise's tail. This picture was accompanied by the question *Was beisst die Katze?* and two possible answers: 'the cow is biting the cat' (where *cat* is the object of *bite*, as it would be in the equivalent English sentence) and 'the cat is biting the tortoise' (where *cat* is the subject of the sentence). This second interpretation is only possible in German.

In the case of the same picture accompanied by the question *Was hat die Katze gebissen?* the two possible answers are: 'the cow has bitten the cat' (which is not a possible answer in English to *What has the cat bitten?*) and 'the cat has bitten the tortoise' (which is a possible answer to the English equivalent sentence).

Participants were 'made familiar' with the relevant vocabulary before the test started and had to choose answers to ten picture–question pairs in total. Results are presented in table 4.5 for sentences in the present tense (*Was beisst die Katze?*) and compound past (*Was hat die Katze gebissen?*).

TABLE 4.5 Picture–question interpretation results in % (based on Grüter and Conradie, 2006: 107–8, Figures 2–4)

	Present Tense			Compound Past		
	was-subject	*was*-object	both	*was*-subject	*was*-object	both
NS control	16	43	41	7	47	45
L1 Afrikaans	32	60	8	20	68	12
L1 English	71	29	0	2	97	0

The *was*-as-subject answer in the present tense context corresponds to the possible answer in English, the *was*-as-object answer in the compound past context corresponds to the possible answer in English.

While the native speaker participants show that they are aware of the potential ambiguity of the questions in around 40–45 per cent of cases, the L2 speakers have a strong preference for just one of the interpretations. Strikingly, the Afrikaans speakers have a strong preference for the *was*-object interpretation in both contexts, consistent with the verb-second rule in their native language. By contrast, the English speakers show a preference for the *was*-subject interpretation in present tense contexts and a preference for the *was*-object interpretation in compound past contexts, consistent with the absence of the verb-second rule in their native language.

Section 4.5 in a Nutshell

The property of German and Swedish that requires finite verbs to come second in main clauses (the V2 property) results from the movement of the first verb in the VP to T and then C, accompanied by the movement of another phrase that merges with CP. English does not have the V2 property, so that finite verbs can appear in third or later positions in the clause. L1 speakers of Swedish who have acquired English as an L2 and then acquire German as an L3 appear to transfer the English possibility to their mental grammars for German. L1 speakers of Swedish who learn German directly as an L2 treat German only as a V2 language.

Because of the German V2 property, the merger of question DPs like *Was?* 'What?' with CP produces ambiguous clauses. For example, *Was beisst die Katze?* can mean either 'What is biting the cat?' or 'What is the cat biting?' A study by Grüter and Conradie (2006) comparing the early acquisition of L2 German by L1 speakers of English and L1 speakers of Afrikaans (another V2 language) found that the English speakers interpreted the German questions unambiguously as having the meanings of their English counterparts. The Afrikaans speakers, however, favoured interpretations consistent with the German V2 property, as in their L1.

4.6 L1 Influence and Input in the Acquisition of Movement Properties in an L2

There appears to be a trade-off between a learner transferring the movement properties of categories in the L1 to the L2, and a learner identifying the movement properties of L2 categories from encounters with samples of the language ('input'). In the case of French learners of English and English learners of French, it was observed in section 4.4.2 that the possibility of movement through the Neg category is recognised very early in development. French speakers recognise that lexical verbs do not move through Neg in English (making examples like *The boys like not the girls* ungrammatical), and English speakers recognise that lexical verbs do move through Neg in French (making examples like *Les garçons pas aiment les filles* (lit. 'The boys not like the girls') ungrammatical). But both groups continued to allow the L1 movement property where VP-modifying adverbs were involved: *Linda takes often the metro, *Linda souvent prend le métro*. However, studies of the acquisition of other L2s suggest that the input that learners encounter may be an important factor in determining how quickly they acquire target-language movement properties.

4.6.1 The Effect of Input on L2 Speakers' Knowledge of Lexical Verb Movement

Yuan (2001) has shown that when there is clear evidence from input for non-movement of lexical verbs over VP-modifying adverbs, early L2 learners recognise this, and recognition of movement possibilities in the L2 overrides transfer of L1 properties. Yuan used an oral production task and a grammaticality judgement task to investigate the awareness of L1 speakers of French, German and English of lack of lexical verb movement in Mandarin Chinese. French and German move lexical verbs to T, while English does not. Mandarin Chinese is a fairly rigid Subject-Neg-V and Subject-Adv-V language. Lexical verbs never appear to the left of sentential negators or VP-modifying adverbs:

39 a. Ta   bu   he   pijiu.
       He   not   drink   beer
       'He doesn't drink beer.'

    b. Ta   changchang   chi   miantiao.
       She   often   eat   noodle
       'She often eats noodles.'

Additionally, forms that are equivalent to English copula, auxiliary and modal verbs do not appear to the left of sentential negators or VP-modifying adverbs:

40 a. Ta   bu   shi   wo   pengyou.
       He   not   is   my   friend
       'He isn't my friend.'

    b. Ta   xianran   hen   gaoxing.
       She   obviously very   happy
       'She is obviously happy.'

Forty-eight L1 speakers of French, fifty-one L1 speakers of German, sixty-seven L1 speakers of English and ten native speakers of Mandarin Chinese participated.

For the production task, participants were asked to describe the daily activities of a number of imagined Chinese people, based on information they were given that included whether a person did or did not do an activity and how frequently they undertook the activity. For example, participants were prompted to produce (in Mandarin) sentences like 'Mr Zhang often buys an English newspaper', 'Miss Yu isn't going to a Chinese restaurant'. In the judgement task, participants were asked to judge pairs of sentences where VP-modifying adverbs and sentential negators appeared in different positions, some of which were grammatical and some not.

In both tasks, all of the participants, including the speakers of the verb-movement L1s, placed adverbs to the left of the lexical verb in at least 88 per cent of cases, with the majority being placed to the left of the verb in 95 per cent or more of cases. This contrasts with the findings with French-speaking L2 learners of English studied by White, who continued to assume that English verb movement is the same as French where adverbs are involved.

Why do the French and German learners in Yuan's study not move the verb over VP-modifying adverbs, as they would in their L1s? It seems that the Mandarin Chinese input that learners encounter provides sufficiently clear evidence that no verb appears to the left of adverbs for them to recognise that Chinese does not allow lexical verbs to move out of the VP. By contrast, the evidence that French speakers get from English input is somewhat ambiguous. Although lexical finite verbs do not appear to the left of VP-modifying adverbs, modals, finite copula *be*, auxiliary *be*, and auxiliary *have* all do: *He sometimes **walks** to work, She **must** often regret her decision, She **is** usually on time, They **have** barely started*. These different possibilities may delay the French learner's ability to identify the appropriate movement property of English T, with the result of continuing influence from the L1.

More generally, the more salient the evidence is in input for syntactic properties in the L2 that differ from the L1, the more likely a learner is to identify those properties, overriding transferred properties from the L1.

4.6.2 The Effect of Input on L2 Speakers' Treatment of Movement in Relative Clauses

The development of knowledge of relative clauses by L2 speakers appears to be another area where the effect of input can be detected. **Relative clauses** are clauses that modify a noun. In (41), *who passed the exam* is a relative clause that says something about the noun *student*:

41. The student [relative clause who passed the exam] is delighted.

Structurally, (41) is constructed from two clauses that share the noun *student*:

42 a. The student is delighted.
    b. The student passed the exam.

When (42b) is merged with *student* in (42a), the repeated DP becomes *who*. One way of describing this is to say that *who* is a relative pronoun that replaces the DP *the student*, and moves to the front of the clause to Merge with the CP. This CP then Merges with *student* in (42a):

43.

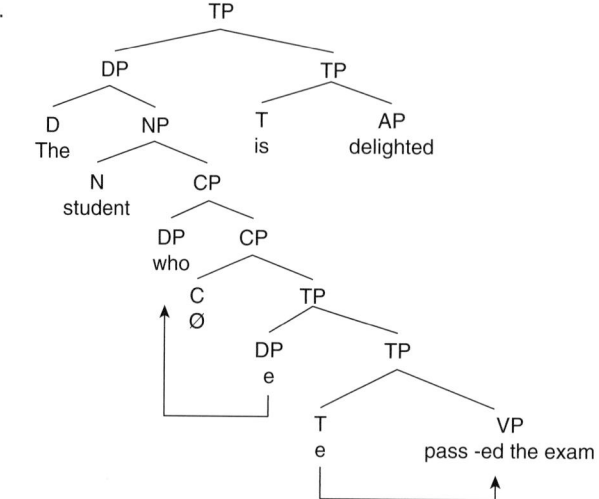

The relative clause illustrated in (43) is a 'subject' relative clause, because the DP that becomes a relative pronoun is in subject position in the clause. In English, relative clauses can also be created from other positions in the clause: direct object, object of a preposition and even the object of the comparative conjunction *than*, as illustrated in (44):

44 a. The student [_{CP} who Ø [_{TP} the professor criticised e]] …

     b. The student [_{CP} who Ø [_{TP} the professor talked with e]] …

     c. The student [_{CP} who Ø [_{TP} the professor is taller than e]] …v

It has been observed in a number of studies that when L2 learners of English begin to acquire relative clauses, they appear to find subject relative clauses easier to produce than object relative clauses. For example, Pavesi (1986) asked eighty-six Italian speakers learning English – forty-eight high school students learning English in the classroom, and thirty-eight adults acquiring English incidentally as part of their jobs in Edinburgh – to describe pictures designed to elicit relative clause constructions. For example, they were shown a picture of a numbered character who is running (e.g. No. 6) and were asked: 'Who is No. 6?' The expected answer was 'No. 6 is the man who is running', a sentence involving a subject relative clause. Or they might be shown a picture of a boy character, who is No. 5, being bitten by a dog and asked the question: 'Who is No. 5?', the expected answer being 'No. 5 is the boy whom the dog is biting', a sentence involving an object relative clause.

Participants in Pavesi's study were asked to respond to five questions where the expected response was a subject relative clause, and five questions where the expected response was an object relative clause. Results were then analysed in terms of the number of participants who produced 4/5 (80%) or more target-like relative clauses. The results are presented in table 4.6.

TABLE 4.6 Percentages of participants who produced target-like relative clauses in 80% or more of cases

	Subject relative clause	Object relative clause
Classroom learners	96%	67%
Immersion learners	100%	61%

The results suggest that the Italian speakers studied find subject relative clauses in English easier to produce than object relative clauses, regardless of whether they are learning English in the classroom or through immersion.

One possible reason for this, if the formation of relative clauses involves the movement of a relative pronoun from its original position to merge with the CP, is the 'structural distance' involved. While a subject relative pronoun only has to cross a TP boundary, an object relative pronoun has to cross a VP boundary as well as a TP boundary, as illustrated in (45). Sentences where movement of a constituent in a relative clause crosses two structural boundaries may be more difficult than sentences where movement only crosses one boundary.

45 a.   The man [CP who Ø [TP e is running]]

b.   The boy [CP who Ø [TP the dog is [VP biting e]]]

Another possibility is that the difficulty results from simple 'linear distance'; *who(m)* is simply closer to the position from which it moves in subject relative clauses than in object relative clauses, and there is no need to invoke 'structure' and crossing structural boundaries at all.

These two possibilities can be distinguished by looking at the use of relative clauses by L2 speakers of languages in which the head noun that the relative clause modifies (i.e. *man* and *boy* in (45)) is to the right of the relative clause, rather than to the left as in English. One such language is Korean (examples from O'Grady, Lee and Choo, 2003). In Korean, there is no overt relative pronoun like English *who*. Instead, a morpheme attaches to the verb to indicate that the clause is a relative clause. The position in the clause which is interpreted as co-referential with the head noun is null, as in English:

46 a.   [CP [TP   e   [VP namca-lul   cohaha   -nun]]]   yeca
                 e-subj   man-obj   like-RC morph. pres tense   woman
         'The woman who likes the man'

b.   [CP [TP namca-ka   [VP e   cohaha   -nun]]]   yeca
              man-subj   e-obj like-RC morph. pres tense   woman
         'The woman whom the man likes'

It can be seen from (46) that in subject relative clauses the null subject position is linearly further away from the head noun *yeca* 'woman' than the null object position. However, structurally the null subject is only separated from the head noun by the TP boundary (as in English) whereas the null object is separated from the head noun by a VP and a TP boundary. If L2 learners have difficulty with relative clauses where there is more linear distance between the head and the position with which it is co-referential, then they should find sentences involving structures like (46a) more difficult than sentences involving structures like (46b). If structural distance is at stake they should find sentences involving structures like (46b) more difficult than (46a).

O'Grady et al. (2003) report a study of fifty-three adult classroom learners of Korean at US universities. Participants were asked to listen to Korean sentences and decide which character in a picture is being described. For example, a participant is shown two pictures, one showing a man who visibly likes a woman (there is a thought bubble full of hearts coming out of his head) and the other showing a woman who visibly likes a man. Hearing a sentence containing a relative clause like (46a), participants have to decide which of the pictures it describes. In the case of (46a) it would be the picture showing a woman who visibly likes a man.

The results show that participants made the correct identifications in 73% of cases when they heard subject relative clauses, but only in 23% of cases when they heard object relative clauses. It appears that object relative clauses in Korean are more difficult for L2 learners to comprehend than subject relative clauses. This finding is similar to Pavesi's for production in English, and suggests that it is 'structural distance' that determines difficulty rather than 'linear distance'.

There have been a number of studies, however, that have looked at the treatment of relative clauses in Mandarin Chinese by speakers of various L1s and found different results. Sung et al. (2016) conducted an eye-tracking study with a group of Japanese L2 learners of Mandarin and a group of native speakers. In Mandarin, the head noun appears to the right of the relative clause as in Korean. Unlike Korean, however, the verb is typically not at the right edge of the clause but precedes its object, as in English:

47 a. [CP [TP e   [VP xihuan   laoshi]   de]   xuesheng
         e-subj   like   teacher-obj   RC-morph.   student
      'The student who likes the teacher'

   b. [CP [TP laoshi   [VP xihuan   e]   de]   xuesheng
         teacher-subj   like   e-obj   RC-morph.   student
      'The student whom the teacher likes'

Sung et al. found that both L2 and native speaker participants spent less time looking at the head noun of object relative clauses than subject relative clauses, suggesting a preference for object over subject relative clauses for both L2 learners and native speakers. In this case, 'linear distance' appears to be what determines how difficult relative clauses are for L2 learners rather than structural distance.

How can the results from O'Grady et al.'s study of learners of Korean and Sung et al.'s study of learners of Mandarin be reconciled? There are two important differences between the form of clauses in Korean and Mandarin Chinese that might be playing a role here. As noted above, whereas the verb in Korean is at the right edge of the clause, following its object, in Chinese the verb precedes its object. Secondly, Korean nouns merge with affixal morphemes that indicate the noun's function in the sentence, subject or object: *namca-ka* 'man-subject', *namca-lul* 'man-object'. These are known as Case markers. Mandarin Chinese does not have Case markers, but like English relies on word order to indicate whether a noun phrase is a subject or an object. It appears that when L2 learners are acquiring relative clauses in a language where the interpretation of noun phrases as subjects or objects is determined by word order alone, clauses with the least linear distance between the head noun and the co-referring position in the clause are the easiest. However, where a language has Case markers indicating the difference between subject and object relative clauses, and word order provides no cue, clauses with the least structural distance between the head noun and the co-referring position are the easiest. This again is an example where input from the target language can be an important determinant of L2 development.

Section 4.6 in a Nutshell

L1 influence on the acquisition of movement properties in an L2 can be overridden by evidence from input. Yuan (2001) found that L1 speakers of French and German, where finite lexical verbs move above Neg and VP adverbs, do not transfer this property when learning L2 Mandarin Chinese. In Mandarin Neg and VP adverbs always appear to the left of lexical verbs, copula, auxiliary and modal verbs. Input from Mandarin appears to provide sufficient evidence to block L1 transfer. Input also seems to influence the acquisition of movement in relative clauses. While input from English and Korean leads L2 learners to find subject relative clauses easier than object relative clauses, input from Mandarin Chinese leads L2 learners to find object relative clauses easier than subject relative clauses.

4.7 L2 Learning of Agreement

Alongside Merge and Move, there is a third syntactic rule that determines dependencies between constituents in phrase structure. In some work this rule is referred to simply as Agree (Chomsky, 2000; Boeckx, 2008, part II). Subject–verb agreement in English is a case of such a dependency. Consider the tree from example (24) (repeated here as (48)):

48.

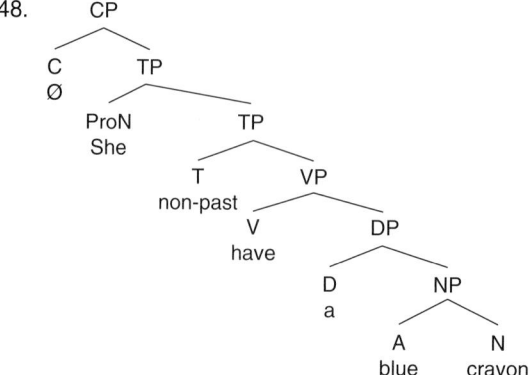

Before Move lowers T to V, T must somehow take on the third person and singular values of the subject so that the V + T constituent that results from Move is realised as *has* and not *have: She has/*have a blue crayon*. Similarly, if the subject were third person and plural, or first/second person and singular, T would have to take on these values to ensure that V + T is realised as *have* and not *has: They/I/You have/*has a blue crayon.*

One way in which T can 'take on' the person and number values of the subject is to have, in addition to its [past/non-past] tense feature, unvalued person and number features:

T [past/non-past, *u*person, *u*number] (where '*u*' means 'unvalued')

The syntactic rule Agree then looks for the person and number features of the subject and copies them onto the unvalued person and number features of T. For example, if T in a clause is finite and non-past, and the subject is third person and singular, Agree will ensure that T is valued as [non-past, person: 3, number: singular]. As in the case of Merge and Move, Agree is assumed to be a rule that learners unconsciously know as part of their linguistic predispositions. However, whether unvalued features for person and number are associated with T is language-specific and has to be learned. Mandarin Chinese, arguably, does not have an abstract T morpheme and therefore does not have [*u*person] and [*u*number] features (verbs in Mandarin do not have special forms determined by the person and number of the subject). English T lacks a [*u*gender] feature, whereas Arabic T has it (it has different verb forms for second and third person subjects that are masculine or feminine – see the next section for discussion of grammatical gender).

4.7.1 Gender Agreement

As discussed in chapters 1 and 2, L2 learners typically take time to show evidence of using forms in the target language determined by Agree (dependency-marking forms). Often they appear to use those forms optionally, and this optionality can be persistent. An example of such optionality can be found in the way that L2 learners treat gender agreement within the DP.

Unlike English, in some languages the category noun is subdivided into classes referred to as genders. In these languages, determiners and adjectives often take on different forms depending on the gender of the noun with which they co-occur. Such cases involve the rule Agree. Determiner and adjective morphemes have an unvalued gender feature that Agree values by copying the gender feature of the noun onto them. The determiner or adjective morpheme with the valued gender feature is then associated with an appropriate form.

To illustrate, in Dutch there are two genders, common and neuter. The definite article takes different forms depending on whether the noun is common or neuter:

49   a. *de appel* 'the apple', *de brief* 'the letter' common gender
    b. *het huis* 'the house', *het paard* 'the horse' neuter gender

This distribution can be accounted for by proposing that when the D category in Dutch is definite it has the feature [*u*gender] and nouns either have the feature [common] or the feature [neuter]. Agree copies the gender feature of the N onto the unvalued gender feature of the definite D, and the D is realised by the appropriate form, for example:

50.

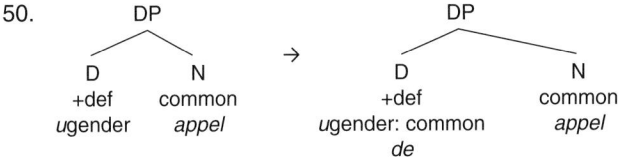

Adjectives that precede N in Dutch like *groen* 'green', *groot* 'big' not only mark a dependency with the N, but also with the D. When the D is a definite article, adjectives end in *-e: de groene appel* 'the green apple', *het groote paard* 'the big horse'. But when the D is an indefinite article, if the N is neuter the adjective has no affix: *een groot paard* 'a big horse'. With an indefinite article and a common noun, adjectives end in *-e: een groene appel* 'a green apple'. The phrase structure of the indefinite examples, once Agree has applied, is illustrated in (51):

51   a.

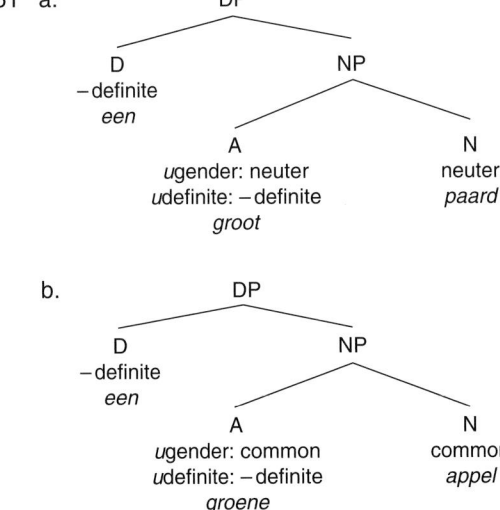

As discussed in section 3.2.3, the forms that realise morphemes are stored in a Vocabulary and are specified for the morphemes with which they are associated. The specification is the one minimally required to ensure that the form is linked to the right morpheme. In the case of adjectives preceding the noun in Dutch, the form that lacks the -e ending appears to be more specified than the form with the -e ending. It is selected when the noun is indefinite and neuter. The form with the -e ending appears in all other contexts preceding the noun: with definite common and neuter nouns, with indefinite common nouns. A representation of this in the Vocabulary might look something like:

52 a. Adj + Ø   ↔   {Adj, −definite, neuter}
    b. Adj + e   ↔   {Adj}

When forms are matched to morphemes, (52a) must apply first. This is because Adj + e is underspecified and could realise any Dutch adjective morpheme. The selection of (52a) before (52b) blocks that possibility. One question then is: how do L2 learners of Dutch acquire knowledge of the agreement properties of adjectives that precede nouns?

A study by Blom et al. (2008) compared the acquisition of Dutch adjective forms by first and second language learners. Participants were three-year-old L1 learners, seven-year-old L2 learners (with a similar length of exposure to Dutch as the L1 learners) and a group of adult L2 learners who were divided into a lower proficiency group and a higher proficiency group. The L1s of the L2 groups were Moroccan Arabic and Berber. All participants were living in the Netherlands. The task used to elicit DPs involved a series of pictures and sentence prompts that participants had to complete orally. The pictures/prompts were designed to elicit both common and neuter nouns, definite and indefinite articles, and adjectives. All participants in the study overgeneralised adjective forms to the wrong context, but the child and adult learners differed in the nature of the overgeneralisation. Table 4.7 shows proportions of overgeneralisation of Adj + Ø forms to contexts where Adj + e is required, and proportions of overgeneralisation of Adj + e forms to contexts where Adj + Ø is required.

TABLE 4.7 Overgeneralisation in percentages and tokens of Adjective + Ø and Adjective + e forms in pre-noun position by L1 and L2 learners of Dutch (based on Blom et al., 2008: 315, Table 4)

Group	Adjective Overgeneralisation	
	Adj + Ø for Adj + e (e.g. *de *groen appel*) in % (tokens)	Adj + e for Adj + Ø (e.g. *een *groote paard*) in % (tokens)
Child L1 (n = 7)	0 (0/16)	84 (16/19)
Child L2 (n = 16)	7 (24/340)	81 (251/322)
Adult (low prof) (n = 10)	77 (34/44)	20 (9/44)
Adult (high prof) (n = 10)	71 (49/69)	44 (34/77)

The child L1 and child L2 results are consistent with the Missing Surface Inflection Hypothesis. You will recall from section 3.2.3 that this account proposes that when learners are using forms productively they have acquired the abstract morphemes with which they are associated and the specification of the forms. However, limitations on the learner's working memory capacity mean that when the demands of constructing a meaningful message are high, less specified elsewhere forms may be accessed rather than more highly specified (but appropriate for the target language) forms. Child learners of Dutch appear to be accessing the less specified elsewhere Adj + e form in contexts where the Adj + Ø form is required.

By contrast, the adult learners are more random in their selection of adjective form, although there is a strong tendency for them to overgeneralise the Adj + Ø form. This is consistent with them not having established [*u*gender] and [*u*definite] features on the adjective morpheme. According to the Morphological Deficit Hypothesis, this pattern of use is the result of the adult learners having both Adj + Ø and Adj + e forms in their Vocabularies with information about the contexts in which they are used. The Adj + Ø form appears to be the default form, and this may be because although it is *morphologically* more specified, it is more frequent in the input that learners are exposed to than the Adj + e form. The reason is that when adjectives appear in predicative contexts like *De deur is groen* 'The door is green', they take the Adj + Ø form. Blom et al. (2008: 304) counted the number of Adj + Ø and Adj + e forms in a corpus of adult speech directed to children. They found that 77 per cent of adjectives used were in the Adj + Ø form, and only 23 per cent in the Adj + e form. It is worth noting, then, that despite the high frequency of the Adj + Ø form in the input they are exposed to, children identify the Adj + e form as the morphological elsewhere form in pre-noun position and tend to overgeneralise this form, whereas adults appear to be more sensitive to the token frequency of forms in input, and build their morphological knowledge on that basis.

It is not clear what the Feature Re-Assembly Hypothesis would say about the different pattern of production between the child and adult L2 learners in this study. Perhaps it could be argued that the child learners have acquired the [*u*gender] feature that Agree values, and this is what leads them to use the Adj + e form. But they have not yet acquired the [*u*definite] feature that would lead to the exclusion of the Adj + e form from indefinite neuter contexts. For the adults perhaps it could be argued that they have yet to acquire either feature [*u*gender] or [*u*definite] and are relying on information based on frequency in the input, as the 'morphological deficit' account also suggests.

Absence of unvalued features on morphemes (or problems of feature re-assembly) may only be a temporary phase of development, however. Given more exposure to Dutch, the adult learners in Blom et al.'s study might identify the feature specification of Adj+Ø so that Adj+e becomes the elsewhere form. A study by McCarthy (2008) of the treatment of adjective agreement with nouns in Spanish by intermediate and advanced proficiency speakers whose L1 is English suggests that this might be the case.

Spanish divides nouns into two genders, masculine and feminine, and accompanying adjectives (which follow the noun) agree with the noun's gender. The form the adjective takes typically alternates between ending in *-o* for masculine nouns and *-a* for feminine nouns (although there are a number of irregular adjective forms):

53 a. un   vino   rojo   'a red wine'
       a-masc   wine-masc   red-masc

    b. una   manzana   roja   'a red apple'
       an-fem   apple-fem   red-fem

McCarthy elicited noun–adjective combinations from fifteen intermediate proficiency learners and nine advanced proficiency learners in interviews where participants and a native Spanish speaker discussed twenty photos. Counting only those noun–adjective pairs involving nouns whose gender participants had correctly guessed in an independent test of gender assignment, McCarthy found the pattern of production accuracy shown in table 4.8.

These results suggest that the intermediate learners were overgeneralising the masculine forms of adjectives to feminine nouns in over a third of cases (34/93), while there were only two cases of overgeneralisation of the feminine forms of adjectives to masculine nouns. This tendency had largely disappeared by the stage of advanced proficiency.

In a similar vein, a study by Hopp (2013) provides evidence that very advanced native-English-speaking L2 speakers of German have established an unvalued [*u*gender] feature on German determiners. German nouns divide into three genders traditionally referred to as masculine, feminine and neuter. This influences the form that the determiner takes. The examples in (54) illustrate the effect in the case of the definite article:

54 a. der   Knopf   'the button'
       the-masc   button-masc
    b. die   Karte   'the card'
       the-fem   card-fem
    c. das   Auto   'the car'
       the-neut   car-neut

TABLE 4.8 Accuracy in gender agreement between adjective and noun (based on McCarthy, 2008: 475, Table 3)

	Intermediate proficiency	Advanced proficiency
Masculine	71/73 (97%)	44/46 (96%)
Feminine	59/93 (63%)	53/61 (87%)

Using the property of German that allows nouns to be null in contexts like the one illustrated in (55), Hopp asked his twenty participants to listen to such questions and look at displays on a computer screen depicting four objects, for example a dress, a button, a playing card and a car.

55. Wo   ist   die   gelbe?
    where   is   the-fem yellow-fem?
    'Where is the yellow one?'

Three of these four objects were of the same colour, but the nouns that refer to them were of different genders. For example, *die Karte* (feminine) 'the card' (the target answer), *das Auto* (neuter) 'the car' and *der Knopf* (masculine) 'the button' were all yellow. The fourth item was of a different colour and different gender from the target answer. For example, *das Kleid* 'the dress' was blue. So the question in (55) uniquely refers to the playing card, which is the only yellow object described by a feminine noun in the display.

Hopp then compared the time it took participants to look at the appropriate object after hearing the question, with the time it took them to look at similar displays where the three objects of the same colour were also of the same gender. In this case the question does not have a unique answer. Hopp reasoned that if the L2 speakers have established that the determiner has a [*u*gender] feature that is valued by the gender of an accompanying noun, they will use this to predict the appropriate object, and they should be faster when there is a unique referent than when there are three possible referents. He found that the L2 participants who had correctly assigned gender to the nouns in an independent production task (eleven out of the twenty) were significantly different in their reaction times when the object was uniquely identifiable from the gender of the determiner than when there were three potential referents, suggesting that those speakers are using the valued gender feature of the determiner to predict the following noun.

4.7.2 Licensing Agreement

'Licensing' describes a situation where the presence of one constituent in a clause is only grammatical if another constituent is present. The presence of this second constituent licenses the presence of the first. One example is the licensing in English of the quantifier *any* by negation or an interrogative C. The sentence **She bought any grapes* is ungrammatical. The grammatical equivalent is *She bought some grapes*. But *She didn't buy any grapes* and *Did she buy any grapes?* are perfectly grammatical because of the presence of negation or an interrogative C. A similar licensing requirement involves English count singular nouns. Count nouns have singular and plural forms, for example *storm/storms, roof/roofs, house/houses*. This contrasts with mass nouns, which do not typically have a plural form unless they are being treated as count nouns: *honey/*honeys, salt/*salts, mud/*muds*. Count singular nouns are ungrammatical if used on their own in sentences, for example:

56. *Storm damaged roof of house

They must be accompanied by a licensing morpheme. This can be a demonstrative (**this** *house*), a numeral (**one** *roof*), a quantifying expression (**some** *house*), a plural marker (*storms*), or one of the articles (**a** *storm,* **the** *house*). Count noun licensing is a type of agreement dependency, similar to subject–verb agreement and gender agreement within the DP. Count nouns have an unvalued feature that will be referred to as [$u$individuation], that needs to be valued by one of the licensing morphemes.

L2 learners of English, particularly if they speak L1s that lack articles (like Chinese, Japanese, Russian – see section 5.3 for discussion), go through a developmental stage where they license count singular nouns in English optionally. That is, they produce sentences like (56) as well as other utterances where demonstratives, articles, numerals etc. are present. And it appears that failure to recognise that count singular nouns in English require licensing can persist for speakers with otherwise quite advanced proficiency in English, who have established perfectly the meaning of articles. White (2003b) reports a study of the use of articles in free conversation by SD, an L1 speaker of Turkish who was recorded at the age of fifty after ten years of residence in Canada. Turkish has no definite article, and linguists disagree about whether it has an indefinite article. Some argue that the numeral *bir* 'one' can be interpreted in this way, while others suggest that Turkish is a language that fully lacks articles. On a general 'proficiency in English' test, SD performed at a level described as 'advanced'. In terms of meaning, White reports that there were no cases where she wrongly used *the* in indefinite contexts, or *a* in definite contexts. She continued, however, to produce unlicensed count singular nouns in around a quarter of cases in her speech, as shown in table 4.9, where a comparison is made between the number of appropriate articles produced and the number of unlicensed nouns in definite and indefinite contexts.

Thus, while SD knows the meaning of the English articles *the/a* and has a mental grammar which leads her to use them in the majority of contexts where they are required, she does not have the requirement present in the grammars of native speakers of English for the licensing of count singular nouns.

TABLE 4.9 Use of articles and unlicensed count singular nouns in definite and indefinite contexts by SD (based on White, 2003b: 136, Table 8).

	Definite Article Contexts	Indefinite Article Contexts
Appropriate article produced	603/765 (79%)	750/1048 (72%)
Unlicensed noun produced	162/765 (21%)	298/1048 (28%)

Section 4.7 in a Nutshell

The syntactic rule Agree copies valued features like [singular], [3 person], [definite] from one morpheme category (e.g. a noun) to another that has unvalued features like [*u*number], [*u*person], [*u*definite] (e.g. an adjective or a determiner). Agree is by hypothesis part of human linguistic predispositions, but the assignment of features to morpheme categories is language-specific and has to be learned from exposure to input. This may take time, with L2 learners having transitional grammars that have morpheme categories with different feature specifications from the target language. Blom et al. (2008) found that child L1 and L2 learners of Dutch overgeneralised Adj + e forms to indefinite neuter noun contexts, but hardly ever overgeneralised Adj + Ø forms to other noun contexts. This is either consistent with them having established the [*u*definite, *u*gender] features of Dutch adjectives and then failing to access the more highly specified Adj + Ø form on occasion (consistent with the Missing Surface Inflection Hypothesis) or having only established the [*u*gender] feature of Dutch adjectives (consistent with the Feature Re-Assembly Hypothesis). Adult L2 learners of Dutch were more random in their use of adjective forms, but with a strong tendency to overgeneralise the Adj + Ø form. This is consistent with them having established neither the [*u*definite] nor [*u*gender] features of Dutch adjectives but storing adjective forms in their Vocabularies with information about contexts of insertion (consistent with the Morphological Deficit Hypothesis).

The non-establishment of unvalued features may be a transitory phase of development in the case of some features. Studies of English-speaking learners of Spanish (McCarthy, 2008) and German (Hopp, 2013) show that high-proficiency L2 speakers make target-like agreement between nouns and adjectives/determiners. But in the case of other unvalued features, non-establishment may be persistent. The acquisition of the [*u*individuation] feature of English count nouns may be difficult to acquire for speakers of L1s that lack such a licensing requirement.

4.8 Concluding Remarks

This chapter has considered the role that the syntactic rules Merge, Move and Agree play in the development of L2 learners' knowledge of the syntax of the target language. The syntax of early-stage L2 learners' utterances can appear very different from that of proficient speakers of the target language, with verbs being optional and 'unanalysed chunks' of the target language being used as single morphemes (Myles, 2005; Myles et al., 1999). It was proposed that L2 learners know how Merge, Move and Agree work as part of their linguistic predispositions. They know that individual morphemes are assigned to a small number of morpheme categories like N, V, A, P, Adv, D among others, and they also know that there are unvalued features corresponding to valued features like person, number, tense and gender. The learning task facing them is to acquire language-specific morphemes, the language-specific ordering of constituents within phrases, the categories that allow or block the movement of constituents, and the cases where agreement between constituents is required. Two hypotheses about the phrase structure of early-stage L2 speakers' utterances were briefly described. The Minimal Trees Hypothesis proposes that the only morpheme categories that are present in early phrase structure are those that have overt exponents. By contrast, the Full Access (to Universal Grammar) Hypothesis proposes that learners know the complete phrase structure of clauses (CPs) as part of their linguistic predispositions. In early L2 grammars, morpheme categories may have null exponents.

The role of the L1 and input in shaping the development of L2 learners' syntactic knowledge were discussed, with evidence coming from the acquisition of sentential negation and verb movement possibilities in English, French, German and Mandarin Chinese and from the acquisition of gender and licensing agreement. It was suggested that there is a trade-off between the transfer of L1 movement properties into the L2 grammar and the evidence for movement that comes from input. Where cues in input are unambiguous, this appears to override L1 transfer. Evidence for this came from a study by Yuan (2001) of French- and German-speaking L2 learners of Mandarin Chinese. Differences in the difficulty of producing/comprehending relative clauses by L2 learners of English, Korean and Mandarin Chinese also suggested that input plays a shaping role in L2 development. The presence of Case markers in Korean appears to lead L2 learners to find subject relative clauses easier than object relative clauses. The absence of such markers in Mandarin appears to lead L2 learners to find object relative clauses easier than subject relative clauses, perhaps because the null object is linearly closer to the head of the relative clause than the subject. In the case of agreement, adult L2 learners of Dutch were argued to have grammatical representations for gender agreement between nouns, adjectives and determiners that were determined by the frequency of forms in input, while child L1 and L2 learners of Dutch had grammatical representations that were target-like, but showed overuse of the elsewhere form of adjectives either because of limitations on language processing capacity, consistent with the Missing Surface Inflection Hypothesis, or because they had not yet acquired the [$u$definite] feature of adjectives that would exclude the Adj + e form from indefinite neuter contexts, consistent with the Feature Re-Assembly Hypothesis.

Linguistic predispositions have figured in a number of the phenomena discussed in this chapter. What these might be is discussed in more detail in Chapter 5.

ACTIVITIES

1. TEST YOURSELF

(i) What are the typical syntactic characteristics of L2 speakers' utterances in the early stages of acquiring an L2?

(ii) What aspects of syntactic knowledge are arguably part of our 'linguistic predispositions' and what aspects have to be learned?

(iii) What are the typical stages that L2 learners go through in acquiring English sentential negation?

(iv) What is the difference between a Minimal Trees view and a Full Access (to Universal Grammar) view of the phrase structure of early L2 grammars?

(v) What evidence suggests that unambiguous cues in the input that L2 learners encounter might override L1 influence in the acquisition of syntactic properties?

(vi) What are the gender agreement forms of Dutch prenominal adjectives? How do child and adult L2 learners of Dutch differ in the way they acquire these forms, according to the study by Blom et al. (2008)? Which of the accounts of L2 optionality are consistent with the findings?

(vii) What method did Hopp (2013) use to show that advanced-proficiency L2 speakers of German had acquired the unvalued [$u$gender] feature of German determiners?

(viii) What is the difference between the meaning of English definite/indefinite articles and their licensing function?

2. PHRASE STRUCTURE TREES

Draw phrase structure trees for the following expressions:

   i. the blue lamp
   ii. a book
   iii. You can't see the blue lamp
   iv. I didn't read a book

3. DOUBLE AGREEMENT

Haegeman (1985) observes that Dutch-speaking classroom L2 learners of English produce sentences like those in (i) in a test that required them to turn affirmative declarative sentences like *She misses the bus, Mary studies French* into negatives:

i   a. *She doesn't misses the bus
    b. *Mary doesn't studies French

What kind of syntactic structure might underlie sentences like these? There is likely to be more than one possible answer to this question. Consider the possibility that the Dutch speakers have not yet analysed *doesn't* into *do* + *s* + *n't* and are treating it as an unanalysed negator.

4. ACQUIRING ENGLISH POSSESSIVE CONSTRUCTIONS

English has two ways of realising a possessive relationship within a DP:

i   a. John's book
    b. The cover of the book

In (ia) the 'possessor' appears to the left of the possessed entity (the 'possessum'). In (ib) the possessor follows the possessum. Some languages allow only one of these orders. In Persian the possessor follows the possessum, in Mazandarani (a northern Iranian language) the possessor precedes the possessum (examples from Fallah et al., 2016):

ii a. Ketab-e   Ali   'Ali's book' (Persian)
       book-Poss Ali

    b. Ali-e   ketab   'Ali's book' (Mazandarani)
       Ali-Poss   book

Fallah et al. tested the willingness of three groups of Mazandarani/Persian bilinguals to accept English sentences involving grammatical possessives like *Ali's father is old* and ungrammatical possessives like **Taxi's John is over there*. The participants in the study were aged thirteen to fourteen, had only been exposed to English in the classroom for between twenty-two and twenty-six hours, and had received no instruction on English possessives. The three groups differed in language dominance. Group A acquired Mazandarani before Persian, and used Mazandarani predominantly in their daily lives. Group B also acquired Mazandarani before Persian, but used Persian predominantly in their daily lives. Group C acquired Persian before Mazandarani, and used Persian predominantly in their daily lives.

Participants were given a grammaticality judgement task that contained both grammatical and ungrammatical possessives, and a constituent re-arrangement task (e.g. organise *Ali/is/pen/'s/over there* into a grammatical sentence). The results are given in table (i).

What conclusions do you draw from these results about the effect that speaking two L1s has on the acquisition of an L2?

TABLE (i). Grammaticality Judgement Task (GJT) and Constituent Re-Arrangement (CR) accuracy scores (%) (based on Fallah et al., 2016: 239, table 5)

Group	GJT	CR
A (n = 11)	80	85
B (n = 13)	17	13
C (n = 7)	18	13

Compare these results with those of Grüter and Conradie (2006) in section 4.5.2. Is this a genuine case of L1 influence on L2 mental grammars? (Bear in mind that the participants had only had 22–26 hours of classroom exposure to English.)

5. ACQUIRING GERMAN WORD ORDER

As discussed in section 4.5.1, German has the following word order properties:

(i) Finite verbs in main clauses always appear as the second constituent, whatever appears as the first constituent:

a. Sie   schreibt   einen   Aufsatz
     She   write-s   an-Accusative   essay   'She is writing an essay'

b. Heute   schreibt   sie   einen   Aufsatz
     Today   write-s   she   an-Acc   essay   'Today she is writing an essay'

(ii) Non-finite verbs that accompany finite verbs appear at the end of the clause:

Sie   hat   einen   Aufsatz   geschrieben
She   has   an-Acc   essay   written
'She has written an essay'

(iii) Finite verbs appear at the end of embedded clauses:

Ich   denke,   dass   sie   einen   Aufsatz   geschrieben   hat
I   think   that   she   an-Acc   essay   written   has
'I think that she has written an essay'

According to Clahsen and Muysken (1986), duPlessis et al. (1987) and Tomaselli and Schwartz (1990), English- and Romance-speaking learners of German go through the stages of development illustrated by representative examples below. (Note that the stages are not discrete – an individual L2 speaker might continue to produce stage 1-type utterances when they are also producing stage 2- or stage 3-type utterances):

Stage 1: Sie hat geschrieben einen Aufsatz
          Heute sie hat geschrieben einen Aufsatz
          Ich denke, dass sie hat geschrieben einen Aufsatz

Stage 2: Sie hat einen Aufsatz geschrieben
          Heute sie hat einen Aufsatz geschrieben
          Ich denke, dass sie hat einen Aufsatz geschrieben

Stage 3: Sie hat einen Aufsatz geschrieben
          Heute hat sie einen Aufsatz geschrieben
          Ich denke, dass sie hat einen Aufsatz geschrieben

Stage 4: Sie hat einen Aufsatz geschrieben
          Heute hat sie einen Aufsatz geschrieben
          Ich denke, dass sie einen Aufsatz geschrieben hat

What kind of initial syntactic structure underlies the utterances in stage 1? How does this structure change in stages 2 to 4?

FURTHER READING

For more on the rules Merge, Move and Agree see:

Koeneman, O. and Zeijlstra, H. 2017. *Introducing syntax*. Cambridge: Cambridge University Press.

For a critical review of the Minimal Trees and Full Access hypotheses about early stages of L2 development see:

White, L. 2003a. *Second language acquisition and Universal Grammar*. Cambridge: Cambridge University Press, chapter 3: The initial state.

For a more advanced discussion of second language syntax see:

Slabakova, R. 2016. *Second language acquisition*. Oxford: Oxford University Press, chapter 8: Acquisition of syntax.

5 Second Language Learning and Universal Grammar

5.1 What is Universal Grammar?

At a number of points in the discussion so far, evidence from the behaviour of L2 learners has led to the conclusion that they have certain 'predispositions' that guide their learning. These predispositions can be linked to a theory known as **Universal Grammar** (UG) (Chomsky, 1986). UG is a set of principles of linguistic organisation, together with categories, features and rules that those principles apply to, that is by hypothesis innate to human beings. UG is often described as a 'genetic blueprint' (White, 2003a: 2) that determines what are and what are not possible grammatical structures, and therefore provides the infant first language learner with information that guides how s/he constructs a mental grammar for any language s/he is exposed to, rapidly and successfully, on the basis of exposure to samples of that language. UG is part of the human 'language faculty' that gives human beings the capacity to acquire human languages. What the principles, categories, features and rules of UG might be is considered in section 5.2. The role that UG might play in L2 learning is discussed in section 5.3. In this section the evidence that linguists have used to argue for UG is briefly reviewed.

One of the main arguments to support UG comes from what is known as the **poverty of the stimulus**. Speakers of a language know more about its grammatical properties than they could plausibly have worked out from exposure to the random samples of language they have encountered and their ability to infer patterns from those samples. Consider the following example. Speakers of English know that in (1a) *who* and *she* can refer to the same person, say *Mary*. (*She* can also refer to a different person from *who*; the sentence is ambiguous). By contrast, in (1b) *who* and *she* cannot refer to the same person. If *she* is *Mary*, then a possible answer to *who* must be someone other than *Mary*, say *Sue*. In other words, *who* and *she* can be co-referential in (1a), but they must be disjoint in reference (refer to different people) in (1b), as indicated by the subscript indices.

1 a. Who$_i$ said she$_i$ would come to the party?   Answer: Mary.
   b. Who$_i$ did she$_j$ say would come to the party?   Answer: Sue.

What is it that speakers know that allows them to recognise the difference in meaning between the two sentences?

The answer runs as follows. Speakers of English know that pronouns like *she* can only be co-referential with DPs, including the interrogative DP *who*, that they are not structurally higher than in the sentence. The notion of 'structurally higher in the sentence' can be defined more specifically as c(onstituent)-command. Informally, c-command is the following:

> A category A c-commands (is structurally higher in the sentence than) another category B if the first branching category dominating A also dominates B.[1]

To illustrate, in (2) *Mary* is category A and c-commands *she* (category B) because the first branching category that dominates *Mary* is TP, and TP also dominates *she* in the lower clause. Therefore *Mary* and *she* can be co-referential.

2. Mary$_i$ said she$_i$ would come to the party

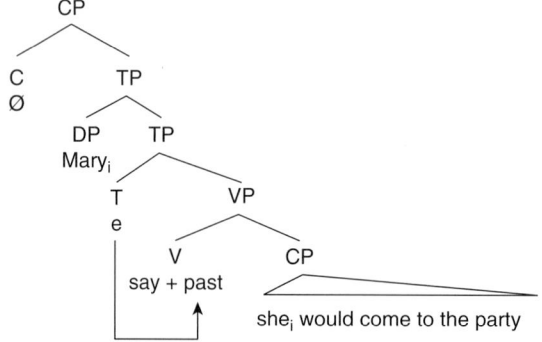

Given this definition of 'structurally higher in the sentence' as c-command, *who* in both (1a) and (1b) would appear to c-command *she*, as shown in (3). So how does this help to distinguish the two meanings?.

3 a. Who$_i$ said she$_i$ would come to the party?

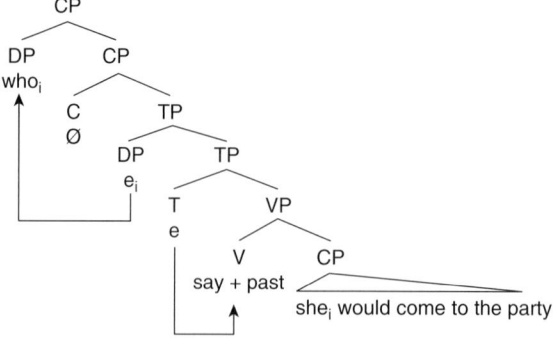

---

[1] See Koeneman and Zeijlstra (2017), section 5.3, or Radford (2009), section 2.6 for discussion of c-command. The discovery of c-command is due to Reinhart (1976).

b. Who$_i$ did she$_j$ say would come to the party?

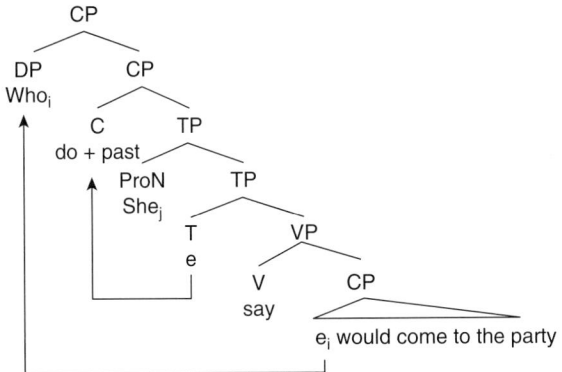

Crucially, co-reference possibilities between pronouns and DPs are determined at the point where they are *first merged* in the phrase structure, not on positions that categories might have been moved to by Move. *Who* in (3a) is first merged with TP in the upper clause, while *she* is first merged with TP in the lower clause; *she* does not c-command *who* in this structure and so the two can be co-referential. By contrast, in (3b), *who* is first merged with TP in the lower clause, and *she* is first merged with TP in the upper clause. Before *who* moves to merge with the upper CP, *she* c-commands *who* and therefore the two cannot be co-referential.

It is difficult to see how speakers of English could work out this pattern of co-reference, requiring that pronouns not co-refer with DPs that they c-command in their first merged position, just on the basis of experience and their ability to infer patterns from the samples of language they encounter. They may hear sentences like (1a) used both with a co-referential interpretation (*who* = *she* = *Mary*) and a disjoint referential interpretation (*who* = *Sue, she* = *Mary*). And they may hear sentences like (1b) used with a disjoint referential interpretation. But there is nothing to tell them that a co-referential interpretation between *she* and *who* in (1b) is impossible. It could be that they just happen not to have heard such a use in the random samples of language they have encountered. And taking the presence of *do* as a cue that co-reference is not possible will not work because there are sentences like *I wonder who$_i$ she$_j$ said would come to the party* where *do* is absent but it is just as impossible for *she* to be co-referential with *who*. It appears that knowledge of c-command and the referential properties of pronouns are under-determined by the evidence available from input (the stimulus is impoverished). A plausible inference to draw is that speakers must therefore know these properties in advance of exposure to any specific language through UG.

A second argument supporting the claim that UG is part of human genetic endowment comes from child language acquisition. All infants (excluding those suffering from certain brain disorders) acquire the language(s) they are exposed to successfully, regardless of intelligence or other personality factors. They do so quickly; by the age of five or six years they are understanding and using complex sentence structures. All children tend to follow a similar developmental trajectory from babbling at around six months onwards to typically producing single word utterances between twelve and eighteen months, two word utterances between eighteen and twenty-four months (like *all broke, more walk, no down* ('don't put me down') – Braine, 1963) to multi-word utterances from twenty-four months onwards.[2] Children need no instruction to acquire language and they typically are not responsive to having their utterances corrected by mature speakers. There are a number of examples in the acquisition literature recording parents who try to correct without success (see Fromkin and Rodman, 1998, chapter 8, for several examples of this kind). All of this, it is argued, is consistent with children having an innate language faculty with UG at its heart helping the child select the appropriate grammatical representations for the language s/he is exposed to.

If UG is indeed guiding the child's acquisition of language, one might expect to see evidence for properties like pronouns not co-referring with DPs that they c-command as soon as children are at a stage where they are using pronouns and multi-clause sentences. Crain and Thornton (1991) conducted a clever experiment with twelve children ranging in age from 3 years 7 months to 4 years 8 months that shows precisely this. They presented the children with short scenes acted out with dolls and a puppet. For example, in one scene the Joker (a character from *Batman*) judges a smiling contest in which there are three participants: Grover (from *Sesame Street*), a Teenage Mutant Ninja Turtle and Yogi Bear. The Joker says to the Ninja Turtle that he has the best smile. Grover and Yogi Bear each complain saying 'Joker, you're wrong. I have the best smile.' Watching the scene unfold are the child and the puppet Kermit the Frog (from the *Muppets*). Kermit comments on what has happened, and the child's role is to reward Kermit, if what he says is correct, with a slice of pizza, his favourite food. If Kermit gets it wrong the child has to help him pay better attention by making him do push-ups, or feeding him food which is not his favourite. In relation to the scene described, Kermit might say either (4a) or (4b).

4   a. I know who he said has the best smile. Grover and Yogi Bear.
    b. I know who said he has the best smile. Grover and Yogi Bear.

Statement (4a) is an inappropriate comment on the scene. Because *he* c-commands *who*, *he* cannot be co-referential with either Grover or Yogi Bear, the characters who said 'I have the best smile.' *He* must refer to the Joker. In (4b), however, *who* and *he* can be co-referential at the point of first merger. A plausible interpretation is that *he* refers either to Grover or to Yogi Bear, since both

---

[2] See Guasti (2002) for an overview of the time course of child language acquisition.

said 'I have the best smile.' Crain and Thornton found that the children made the correct decision about disjoint reference in cases like (4a), making Kermit do push-ups, or feeding him his non-favourite food, in over 90 per cent of cases. This suggests that the children studied have access to this particular property of UG even though they are only three to four years old.

A third argument that has been used in support of UG is the ability of speakers of a language to produce and understand sentences they have never heard before, and to determine whether those sentences are grammatical or not. Human languages are **generative**: from a finite set of syntactic operations and a finite set of morphemes a potentially infinite set of grammatical sentences can be generated. This generative capacity of language offers a tremendous advantage in the transmission of knowledge from one person to another. We can acquire new knowledge through understanding the propositions expressed by novel sentences. Consider the following sentence (from Penrose, 2004: 9):

> Although mathematical truths of various kinds had been surmised since ancient Egyptian and Babylonian times, it was not until the great Greek philosophers Thales of Miletus (c625–547 BC) and Pythagoras of Samos (c572–497 BC) began to introduce the notion of *mathematical proof* that the first firm foundation stone of mathematical understanding – and therefore of science itself – was laid.

Unless you have read Penrose's book the chances are that you have never encountered this sentence before, and yet you can determine that it is a possible grammatical sentence of English, and what it means. Furthermore, if you are paying attention to its propositional content, and did not know this already, you have learned something about the history of mathematics.

The novel combination of known morphemes is one way in which language is generative. Another way is through the potentially infinite merger of phrases and clauses in the same sentence, known as recursion. An illustration is given in (5) where the dots (...) indicate where other clauses could be added ad infinitum.

5. This is the student who wrote the essay that dealt with a topic that is controversial that appealed to the judges who ... that won the prize.

In reality we do not normally produce so many recursively merged clauses, but our mental grammars for English (and the grammars of every language) offer that possibility.

Both types of generativity, it is argued, derive from UG, which provides the tools that enable language learners to construct language-specific grammars that go beyond the random samples of language they are exposed to.

Section 5.1 in a Nutshell

Three arguments were presented to support the claim that humans have a language faculty at the heart of which is Universal Grammar (UG). UG is a 'genetic blueprint' for the form that human language takes that guides the language learner when s/he constructs a mental grammar from the random samples of language s/he is exposed to.

The first argument is that random samples of language that the learner is exposed to provide insufficient information to explain the range of grammatical knowledge that a speaker of any language possesses. This is an argument for UG from the poverty of the stimulus. An example illustrating the poverty of the stimulus is the difference in the co-reference possibilities between *she* and *who* in sentences like *I wonder who$_i$ said she$_i$ would come to the party* (where co-reference is possible) and *I wonder who$_i$ she$_j$ said would come to the party* (where there must be disjoint reference). It is implausible that a speaker of English could work out this difference just from exposure to samples of English.

The second argument is the uniformity, speed and success of child language acquisition and children's awareness of properties of language that are underdetermined by input. Crain and Thornton (1991) have shown that children between the ages of three and five years are aware of the constraint that pronouns like *she* cannot be co-referential with DPs like *who* that they c-command.

The third argument is the generativity of language: the ability of speakers to produce and understand a potentially infinite range of novel sentences, and to determine whether those sentences are grammatical or not. This, it is argued, is a result of the linguistic constructs and procedures that UG makes available.

5.2 The Content of UG: Categories, Features, Rules, Principles and Parameters

In its classical form (Chomsky, 1981; 1986) UG consists of a set of categories (N, V, A, P, C, T, D and possibly others) to which language-specific morphemes learned from experience are assigned, a set of features like [past], [non-past], [singular], [plural], [1, 2, 3 person], among others, that can be encoded in the categories, a small number of syntactic rules that compute expressions involving the categories (Merge, Move and Agree), some invariant principles that constrain the form that computations and their output can take, like c-command, and a number of parameters of variation that account for divergence between languages. Research into the properties of UG is often referred to as the 'principles and parameters' approach, but the categories to which language learners assign the many thousands of morphemes they learn from experience, the features they encode and the operations that Merge, Move and Agree perform are just as important.

What counts as a linguistically-relevant category, feature, rule, principle or parameter and the extent to which they are specific to UG or can be derived from more general learning mechanisms is an empirical question to be decided through the investigation of the world's languages and the acquisition of those languages. It is not surprising, therefore, that over the decades there have been significant developments in what is viewed as the proper content of UG as new evidence and insights come to light. A snapshot is presented here of some classic proposals. Some examples of claims about the role of UG in second language learning are given in section 5.3.

The binarity of Merge is a good candidate for a principle constraining the building of phrase structure. Recall that binary Merge immediately provides the basis for interpreting ambiguous phrases like *American football coach*, as discussed in section 4.2. On one interpretation this refers to someone who coaches American football. The adjective *American* has merged with the noun *football* to form an NP that then merges with the noun *coach* to form a larger NP: [$_{NP}$ [$_{NP}$ American football] coach]; on the other interpretation it refers to someone who coaches football and happens to be American. The nouns *football* and *coach* merge first to form an NP that then merges with the adjective *American* to form another NP: [$_{NP}$[$_A$ American] [$_{NP}$ football coach]].

Other classic examples of hypothesised principles of UG are the Coordinate Structure Constraint and the Adjunct Island Constraint. The Coordinate Structure Constraint blocks movement of a constituent from a coordinated phrase (one involving *and* in English). So while the whole coordinated phrase in (6a) can be questioned to form (6b), one of its constituent DPs cannot (e marks the empty position left behind when a constituent is moved):

6   a. Sue read [the book and the accompanying notes]
    b. What$_i$ did Sue read e$_i$?
    c. *What$_i$ did Sue read [the book and e$_i$]?
    d. *What$_i$ did Sue read [e$_i$ and the accompanying notes]?

The Adjunct Island Constraint blocks movement out of an adverbial clause or phrase ('adjuncts' to the clause). Adverbials seem to form 'islands' from which sub-phrases cannot escape:

7   a. Sue had dinner [after she finished reading the book]
    b. *What$_i$ did Sue have dinner [after she finished reading e$_i$]?
    c. Sue read the book [after dinner]
    d. *What$_i$ did Sue read the book [after e$_i$]

Another principle that was proposed early in the development of a theory of UG is structure dependence: Merge, Move and Agree operate on constituents that are defined by their location in phrase structure and not in any other way, for example by counting how far a constituent is from the beginning or end of the clause, or by choosing the first example of constituent X in a linear string.

Structure dependence can be illustrated by *yes–no* question formation in English, although it applies to all syntactic operations in all languages. For example, taking the declaratives in (8), *yes–no* questions are formed by moving *is* and *can* to the front as in (9).

8 a. The woman is our new teacher
   b. She can play the piano

9 a. Is$_i$ the woman e$_i$ our new teacher?
   b. Can$_i$ she e$_i$ play the piano?

   Given encounters with examples like these, the child learner of English could potentially hypothesise rules that are erroneous. For example, form *yes–no* questions by taking the fourth word from the end of the sentence and moving it to the front. This works in the case of (8), but it soon becomes clear that this makes the wrong prediction, e.g. *She can play the piano and the guitar* would become **Piano$_i$ she can play the e$_i$ and the guitar?* (this also violates the Coordinate Structure Constraint). Or more plausibly the child could hypothesise that the first tensed copula, modal or auxilary verb is moved to the front. This would work for many clauses in English, but it still makes the wrong prediction in cases like those in (10):

10 a. The woman who can play the piano is our new teacher
   b. *Can$_i$ the woman who e$_i$ play the piano is our new teacher?
   c. Is$_i$ the woman who can play the piano e$_i$ our new teacher?

   When (10a) is turned into a *yes–no* question it is the second instance of a tensed copula that is moved to the front. Moving the modal that comes first produces an ungrammatical sentence.

   The correct generalisation is that *yes–no* question formation takes the finite T in the *main clause* of a sentence, wherever it is located and whatever it contains (a copula, modal, auxiliary or just Tense, giving rise to the insertion of *do*), and moves it to the main clause C. The main clause finite T in (10) contains *is* (and not *can*, which is in a finite T in a relative clause) and this is moved into the main clause C. In other words, movement in the formation of *yes–no* questions in English must refer to the phrase structure of the clause. It is a structure-dependent operation.

   Crain and Nakayama (1987) have shown that children as young as three to five years have grammars that do not violate structure dependence. They played a game with thirty English-speaking children where the child was prompted to ask questions of a Jabba the Hutt doll (a *Star Wars* character). The prompts were of the form: 'Ask Jabba if … ' followed by statements like 'the man who is beating a donkey is mean':

11. Ask Jabba if the man who is beating a donkey is mean

The child then produces a *yes–no* question. If young children have reached a stage of development where they are moving a tensed copula/modal/auxiliary to the front in *yes–no* questions, they should do so in a structure-dependent fashion and not produce ungrammatical sentences like (10b). Crain and Nakayama found that no child produced such ungrammatical sentences. They either produced target sentences or sentences where they copied the tensed copula/modal/auxiliary at the front of the sentence: *Is the man who is beating a donkey is mean?* The results are consistent with children having grammars that are constrained by the UG-derived principle of structure dependence.

An example of a parameter that interacts with the principle of c-command is the domain within which reflexive pronouns (forms like *myself, yourself, herself* etc. in English) must be co-referential with a DP. Reflexives, like pronouns, are subject to the constraint that they must not c-command a potential co-referring DP. But they are more restricted in co-reference possibilities than pronouns in that they must be c-commanded by a co-referring DP within a certain structural domain. That structural domain can vary depending on the language. This is illustrated from English and Mandarin Chinese in the following example. (This case is discussed in more detail in section 6.2.2). In (12) the reflexive pronoun *herself* can be co-referential with *Kate*, but not with *Sue* (as the subscript co-indexing indicates).

12. Sue$_i$ thinks that Kate$_j$ likes those photos of herself$_j$

The domain within which reflexives can co-refer with DPs in English is, broadly, limited to the immediate finite clause containing the reflexive. However, in Mandarin Chinese the *-self* equivalent form *ziji* can co-refer with DPs that are not within the immediate finite clause. Both *Kate* and *Sue* are possible targets of co-reference in (13):

13. | Sue$_i$ | xiang | Kate$_i$ | xihuan | ziji$_i$ | de | zhaopian |
    |---------|-------|----------|--------|----------|-----|----------|
    | Sue | think | Kate | like | self | 's | photo |

    'Sue thinks that Kate likes those photos of herself'

So English and Mandarin differ in the domain over which co-reference is possible. English is more restrictive than Mandarin.

The c-command constraint is universal: an invariant principle of UG. But differences in the domain of co-reference of reflexives between languages is a possible example of a parameter of variation allowed by UG. While reflexive pronouns must take their reference from another DP that they do not c-command, where that other DP is located in phrase structure can vary from one language to another (within limits).

When parameters of variation were first proposed (Chomsky, 1981) they typically had two values, with languages selecting one or other of these values. Furthermore, the value selected gave rise to a cluster of syntactic effects. The movement of T-to-V and V-to-T discussed in section 4.4.1 illustrates a parameter of this type, which has been called the Verb Raising Parameter. This has two values:

raise the lexical verb out of the verb phrase to finite T (as in French) or do not raise the lexical verb out of the verb phrase to finite T (as in English). A cluster of syntactic consequences appears to follow when a language chooses one or other of these values. For example, in French finite lexical verbs appear to the left of negation (14a), verb phrase adverbs can appear between a finite transitive lexical verb and its object (14b), finite lexical verbs can move to C in interrogatives (14c), and subject quantifiers (e.g. *toutes* 'all' in *toutes ses amies* 'all her friends') can move to a position between a finite lexical transitive verb and its object (14d). None of these are possible in English, as illustrated in (14). The cluster of properties in English that follow from selecting the non-raising value of the Verb Raising Parameter are illustrated in (15).

14 a. Elle lit pas de romans   *She reads not novels
    b. Elle lit souvent des romans   *She reads often novels
    c. Lit-elle des romans?   *Reads she novels?
    d. Ses amies lisent toutes des romans *Her friends read all novels

15 a. She doesn't read novels
    b. She often reads novels
    c. Does she read novels?
    d. Her friends all read novels

Subsequent work investigating the extent to which parameters hold cross-linguistically has uncovered some problems with their early formulation. Some languages do not display the same clustering of properties associated with a particular parameter. Some parameters are not binary, having several values. For an overview of the classic parameters and their possible limitations, see Ayoun (2003), chapter 4.

Nevertheless, the notion of UG providing language learners with parameters of variation with limited options that are 'set' from exposure to samples of specific languages encountered has intuitive appeal. And as discussed in chapter 4, proposed parameters like the Verb Raising Parameter have been of some interest in the investigation of second language learning. The question has typically been: can L2 learners reset the value of an L1 parameter that has a different value in the L2? And how do they go about doing that? The answer seems to be that they can, and section 4.4.2 discussed how French learners of English and English learners of French go about resetting the Verb Raising Parameter.

UG-derived parameters of variation can be viewed as the consequence of alternative choices that languages make in the selection of linguistic features. It has often been suggested that the Verb Raising Parameter is a result of a distinction between languages that have a richly inflected T, like French and Spanish, or a T that is poor in inflection, like English or Mandarin Chinese. In languages with a lot of feature distinctions realised in the T category the verb moves to T out of the verb phrase, while in languages with few or no feature distinctions realised in the T category the verb stays in the verb phrase (Holmberg and Roberts, 2013).

We saw in chapters 2 to 4 that linguistic features like [past], [non-past], [singular], [plural], [common], [neuter], [1, 2, 3 person] are an important element in some of the analyses of L2 learning that were considered. Where do these features come from? As in the case of all other aspects of UG it is an empirical question whether they come directly from UG or whether they are derived from more general cognitive distinctions that the human mind is programmed to make and have been co-opted by the language faculty. For example, the contrast between [singular] and [plural] might reflect a basic human perceptual distinction made between one of something and more than one of something. However, it is interesting to note that all languages tend to draw from the same limited set of features (like those cited above), even though there is a potentially limitless number of perceptual distinctions that humans can make. Distinctions like the size of an object (big vs small), its shape (round vs square), its texture (soft vs hard), its hue (light vs dark), and so on, appear not to play a major role in the syntactic or morphological operations of the world's languages, in contrast to number, tense, person, gender. This suggests that there are some features that are particularly salient for language that the language learner is alerted to if they are part of UG. An argument based on L2 learning that the features [definite]/[indefinite] and [specific]/[non-specific] derive from UG is presented in the next section.

Section 5.2 in a Nutshell

UG consists of a set of categories (N, V, C, T, D among others); a set of features ([past], [singular], [1 person], [feminine], among others) from which specific languages select and which they encode in the categories; the syntactic rules Merge, Move and Agree, invariant principles that constrain the form that grammatical representations can take; and a number of parameters of variation that account for divergence between languages. Determining what the categories, features, rules, principles and parameters are is an empirical question. They must be justified on the basis of evidence from the comparative investigation of the world's languages and through the study of language acquisition. Examples of hypothesised principles are binary Merge, c-command, the structure dependence of rules, the Coordinate Structure Constraint and the Adjunct Island Constraint. Examples of hypothesised parameters are differences in the structural domain within which reflexive pronouns must co-refer with c-commanding DPs and the Verb Raising Parameter. Parameters can be viewed as alternative choices that languages make in the encoding of linguistic features in morpheme categories. Such features may derive from general perceptual distinctions the human mind is programmed to make, but it is noteworthy that the world's languages tend to select features from the same limited set (number, tense, person, gender, for example) and ignore the many other perceptual distinctions humans can make, suggesting that they may be specific to UG.

5.3 Universal Grammar and Second Language Learning

Most researchers investigating second language learning would agree that learners have biologically-determined mental capacities that are necessary prerequisites for language learning. There is an ongoing debate, however, about whether any of these capacities come from UG, or whether language is a by-product of more general mental processes that underlie our ability to acquire and use other kinds of knowledge, for example, learning and using the rules of games, learning where objects are located in space and using that knowledge to find your way around, learning how to bake a cake, and so on – domain-general capacities.[3]

Looking at the kinds of predisposition that have been identified so far in studies of L2 learning, the question is: can any of them plausibly be considered specific to language, or are they more likely to be applications of general mental processes to the particular case of learning an L2? In chapter 1 it was reported that children and adults unconsciously tally the frequency with which sounds/syllables co-occur in the input they hear (Saffran et al. 1996a, 1996b). Since recurrent strings of sounds are potentially paired with specific meanings, frequency-tallying is an important step in solving the segmentation problem. But the ability to identify recurrent patterns may not be specific to language. It is probably also fundamental to learning about objects in the physical world around us. Indeed, Saffran et al. (2007) showed seven-month-old children a series of pictures each depicting two dogs from the same breed and a third from a different breed. They were in the order A B A, for example Husky – German Shepherd – Husky, or Dachshund – Labrador – Dachshund. After a period of looking at these sequences, the stimulus changed to the order A A B, i.e. Husky – Husky – German Shepherd. Saffran et al. found that when this happened the children spent more time looking at the novel pattern, suggesting that they had identified the recurrent A B A pattern in the pictures, and were surprised when it changed. Commenting on this finding, Traxler (2012: 341) observes that 'the existence of statistical learning for both language and non-language visual stimuli could indicate that general-purpose learning mechanisms, rather than innate, genetically-determined, language-specific learning mechanisms, are responsible for speech segmentation and word learning'.

Generativity is also a key feature of language and, as discussed in section 5.1, is one of the arguments that has been used to justify the postulation of UG. However, generativity may not be specifically linguistic. It also appears in other domains of thinking. We can create infinitely new sequences of numbers (and this capacity is what allows the creation of new phone numbers, and underlies all digital communication), infinitely new melodies in music, infinite ways of arranging flowers in our gardens. Some, though, have argued that generativity is specific to language, and that generativity in other domains is a by-product of generativity in language (Chomsky, 1988: 169; Bloom, 1994).

---

[3] For some discussion of this question see the special issue of *Lingua*, vol. 118 (4), April 2008.

One area where there is prima facie evidence for innate, language-specific pre-dispositions is the poverty of the stimulus, where L2 speakers know something implicitly about the target language that they could not plausibly have inferred from input, from their L1 or from domain-general learning capacities. Here is an example that suggests that L2 learners have mental grammars that are constrained by a principle of UG.

A principle of UG that was proposed early on in the development of the theory and has been explored by L2 researchers is the Overt Pronoun Constraint (OPC) (Montalbetti, 1984). The OPC holds in languages that allow an alternation between overt and null pronouns, like Spanish. To illustrate, in the following sentence the subject of the embedded clause can either be an overt (*él* 'he') or a null pronoun (examples from Pérez-Leroux and Glass, 1997):

16. Juan$_i$ cree   que   él$_i$/Ø$_i$ ganará   el   premio
    Juan   thinks   that   he/Ø   win-will   the   prize
    'Juan thinks that he will win the prize'

Both overt and null pronouns in Spanish can co-refer with DPs that have specific, identifiable referents like *Juan* (referential DPs). This possibility is indicated by the subscript indices in (16). Both *él* and Ø can co-refer with *Juan*.

The OPC specifies that where a language allows an alternation between overt and null pronouns, as Spanish does, the overt pronoun cannot co-refer with a quantified expression. Quantified expressions are those like *someone, nobody, which student?* that do not have fixed referents: *someone* refers to an unspecified member of the class of people; *nobody* refers to no member of the class of people; *which student?* asks for information about an unspecified member of the class of students. This means that in a sentence differing from (16) only in having a quantified expression as the main subject, the overt pronoun must refer to someone outside the sentence (*Pedro, Miguel* or some other referential DP identifiable from the discourse or context):

17. Nadie$_i$ cree   que   él$_{*i}$/Ø$_i$ ganará   el   premio
    Nobody   thinks   that   he/Ø   win-will   the   prize
    'Nobody thinks that he will win the prize'

(The asterisk indicates that *él* and *nadie* are not co-referential.)

The OPC is a proposed universal constraint that applies to all languages that allow an overt pronoun/null pronoun alternation. It is not instantiated in languages where there is no such alternation, like English. In English overt pronouns can co-refer equally with quantified and referential expressions: *Nobody$_i$ thinks that he$_i$ will win the prize.*

It is not clear that English speakers, for whom the OPC is not instantiated in their L1, who learn L2 Spanish could arrive at the OPC from exposure to input. They will encounter examples where overt pronouns in Spanish can co-refer with referential noun phrases, and they will encounter examples where null pronouns can co-refer with both referential noun phrases and quantified expressions. But there is nothing to tell them that overt pronouns cannot co-refer with quantified expressions. Furthermore, the topic is not referred to in standard Spanish language textbooks or taught in language classrooms. Given its linguistic specificity, it seems implausible that the OPC could be arrived at through domain-general learning mechanisms. It looks like a candidate principle of UG. If L2 speakers' mental grammars are constrained by the principles of UG, it is expected that they would observe the OPC in languages where there is an overt/null pronoun alternation.

Pérez-Leroux and Glass (1999) presented a group of eighteen L1-English advanced-proficiency speakers of Spanish and twenty native Spanish controls with a translation task.[4] Participants read short scenarios like those illustrated in (18), and were then asked to translate a sentence into Spanish. Scenarios like (18a) favour co-reference between the pronoun *he* in the sentence to be translated and a referential DP. Scenarios like (18b) favour co-reference between the pronoun *he* in the sentence to be translated and a quantified expression (Pérez-Leroux and Glass, 1999: 232–3).

18 a. *Referential DP favoured as co-referent*
       In the OJ Simpson trial, it is clear that the press has a negative bias against the defendant in their reporting. Some journalists said he was a wife-beater.
       Sentence to translate:
       But no journalist said that he is guilty. (Co-reference between *he* and *OJ Simpson* favoured)
    b. *Quantified expression favoured as co-referent*
       The court charged that some journalists had been in contact with the jurors. Several of them were questioned by the judge.
       Sentence to translate:
       No journalist admitted that he had talked to the jurors. (Co-reference between *he* and *no journalist* favoured)

If participants' grammars are constrained by the OPC, it is expected that they would allow both overt and null pronouns in scenarios like (18a), but strongly prefer the null pronoun in scenarios like (18b). Results are presented in table 5.1.

Both groups show a clear difference in their use of overt pronouns in contexts where the DP with which the pronoun co-refers is referential and where it is quantified. The

TABLE 5.1 Proportion of overt and null pronouns used (based on Pérez-Leroux and Glass, 1999: 234, Table 1)

Co-referent	Pronoun	L2 Spanish (n = 18)	Native Spanish (n = 20)
Referential	él	32%	68%
	Ø	58%	31%
Quantified	él	0%	14%
	Ø	93%	85%

[4] They also tested elementary and intermediate-proficiency speakers of Spanish. These results are not considered here.

L2 speakers only use a null pronoun where the DP with which it co-refers is a quantified expression, but allow both overt and null pronouns where the DP with which it co-refers is referential. The native speakers allow a small proportion of overt pronouns to co-refer with quantified expressions, but far fewer than with referential expressions. Both these findings are consistent with the idea that a principle of UG – the OPC – constrains the mental grammars that speakers construct. (Pérez-Leroux and Glass suggest (1999: 231) that the unexpected use of overt pronouns with co-referential quantified expressions by the native speakers may be the result of including speakers of Caribbean Spanish in their sample. Caribbean Spanish is 'a dialect noted for having higher rates of use of overt subject pronouns than most varieties of Spanish').

The feature-based approach to parameter variation between languages assumes that there is a set of linguistic features made available by UG that guides the hypotheses that language learners make about properties in the samples of the specific language they are exposed to. As already discussed, which features form this universal set is an empirical question. An illustration of how L2 researchers have gone about identifying candidate universal features is provided by the acquisition of English definite and indefinite articles. Two features appear to be relevant to the meaning of articles in those languages that have them (not every language does): [±definite] and [±specific].

Informally, the [±definite] distinction expresses a speaker's assumption that the listener can identify a referent from the set of referents described by a noun. If I say 'Would you pass me the mug?' I am assuming that my listener can identify the mug I have in mind: *the* signals a definite reference. If I say 'Would you pass me a mug?' I am assuming that my listener knows what *mug* refers to, but I do not expect him/her to identify a particular mug: *a* signals indefinite reference.

The [±specific] distinction concerns whether the referent of a noun currently exists, or has yet to come into existence. Consider the following examples from Lyons (1999: 167):

19 a. Joan wants to present the prize to the winner
   b. Peter intends to marry a merchant banker

Example (19a) is ambiguous between an interpretation where 'the winner' is already in existence (because the race has finished) – a specific interpretation – and one where the race has not yet been run, so a specific winner does not yet exist: Joan will present the prize to the winner once it is known who that person is. Similarly, in (19b) Peter may already know the merchant banker he intends to marry; she exists and he has been dating her for several months (a specific interpretation). Or his plan is to become wealthy through marrying a merchant banker, but he hasn't met one yet (a non-specific interpretation). English articles do not encode specificity, as can be seen from the sentences in (19). Both the definite and indefinite articles can be interpreted as specific or non-specific. Context, rather than morphology, determines which interpretation is appropriate.

There are languages, however, where articles appear to encode specificity rather than definiteness. Samoan, for example, uses different articles in contexts like (20a) (an indefinite noun phrase with specific reference) and (20b) (an indefinite noun phrase with non-specific reference) (examples from Fuli, 2007, discussed in Ionin, Zubizarreta and Philippov 2009: 340):

20 a. I want to see a movie (but it's sold out) (specific)

Ou	te	fia	matamata	i	le	ata …
I	particle	want	watch	particle	a	movie …

   b. I want to see a movie (but I don't know which one) (non-specific)

Ou	te	fia	matamata	i	se	ata …
I	particle	want	watch	particle	a	movie …

The article *le* is used to indicate the existence of the movie that I want to see, while the article *se* indicates that there is no movie that I can specify as the one I want to see.

A number of the world's languages have no article system at all: Russian, Serbian, Korean, Mandarin Chinese, Thai, among others. When speakers of these languages acquire English they typically select *the* not only with nouns that have definite reference, but also with nouns that have indefinite but specific reference. They tend to select *a* not only with nouns that have indefinite reference, but also with nouns that have definite but non-specific reference. Ionin, Ko and Wexler (2004) asked twenty-six native speakers of Russian and thirty-nine native speakers of Korean, of intermediate to advanced proficiency in English, to select appropriate articles in a multiple-choice test involving contexts like the following:

21 *Meeting on a street*
   a. Roberta: Hi, William! It's nice to see you again. I didn't know that you were in Boston.
      William: I'm here for a week. I am visiting **(a, the, –)** friend from college. His name is Sam Brown, and he lives in Cambridge now.
      (The context favours selection of "a" with a [–definite, +specific] meaning)
   b. Ruby: It's already 4pm. Why isn't your little brother home from school?
      Angela: He just called and told me that he got in trouble! He is talking to **(a, the, –)** principal of his school! I don't know who that is. I hope my brother comes home soon.
      (The context favours selection of "the" with a [+definite, –specific] meaning)

There were also contexts favouring selection of *the* with a [+definite, +specific] meaning and selection of *a* with a [–definite, –specific] meaning in the test. The results are presented in table 5.2, in the form of percentage selections of *the* and

TABLE 5.2 Selection of *the* and *a* by L2 speakers in various contexts (based on Ionin et al., 2004: 33, Tables 16 and 17)

	–def, +spec	+def, –spec	+def, +spec	–def, –spec
L1 Russian (n = 26)	the (36%)	a (33%)	a (8%)	the (7%)
L1 Korean (n = 39)	the (22%)	a (14%)	a (4%)	the (4%)

a in these contexts. In none of these cases would native speakers be expected to select the article in question.

The participants overuse *the* and *a* asymmetrically: *the* is overused in indefinite contexts when the meaning is specific, not non-specific; *a* is overused in definite contexts when the meaning is non-specific, not specific. Furthermore, the pattern of non-target-like use is common to both groups of learners, who speak L1s that are linguistically quite different, apart from the absence of article forms.

What might give rise to commonality in L2 article use by speakers of L1s that lack articles? Ionin, Zubizaretta and Bautista Maldonado (2008: 572) propose that 'innate linguistic knowledge supplies the learners with *possible* specifications of article use'. That is, learners know in advance from UG that if a language has an article system just two binary features are possible candidates for identifying the reference of nouns: [±definite] or [±specific]. So when speakers of L1s that lack articles encounter an L2 that has them, there is a large number of potential hypotheses about their function that learners do not entertain: ' "*the* is used only at the start/end of the sentence"; "*the* is used only with singular/plural nouns"; "*the* is used only when the noun is preceded (or not preceded) by an adjective" ... ' and so on (Ionin et al. 2008: 571).

The reason why learners of English do not immediately identify just the feature [±definite] as relevant to the meaning of *the/a* may be because of the ambiguity of some of the samples of language they encounter. Where nouns are mentioned for the first time as a unique part of the meaning of another noun, they require *the*: *A storm damaged **the** roof of a house*. Here *the roof* could equally well be interpreted as definite or as indefinite but specific. To rule out the use of *the* in contexts with an indefinite specific meaning (in cases like *A storm damaged a/*the roof in the village*), learners will have to 'pay attention to the use of *a*, and note that in contexts which are [+specific] but [−definite], *the* is never used by native English speakers' (Ionin et al. 2008: 573).

Section 5.3 in a Nutshell

The properties that are given by UG need to be distinguished from innately-determined domain-general learning capacities that may also be involved in second language learning. The ability to track the co-occurrence probabilities of sounds/syllables and the generativity of language may not be properties specific to language but the result of the application of general learning mechanisms. However, poverty of the stimulus cases provide prima facie evidence for language-specific properties. The Overt Pronoun Constraint was cited as an example of a poverty of the stimulus case. This determines possible co-referential possibilities for overt and null pronouns in languages that allow such an alternation, like Spanish. Only null pronouns can be co-referential with c-commanding quantified expressions. The L2 learners of Spanish studied by Pérez-Leroux and Glass (1999) were aware of this constraint.

Ionin et al. (2004, 2008) argue that the features [±definite] and [±specific] are made available to language learners through UG and are involved in parametric variation between languages that have articles. Some languages have selected [±definite] to determine article meaning (like English, Spanish, Greek) while others have selected [±specific] (like Samoan). When speakers of languages that lack articles (like Russian, Korean, Japanese) learn English as an L2, they go through a developmental stage where they fluctuate between assigning the features [±definite] and [±specific] to articles. Because they only fluctuate between these two features and do not appear to consider a large range of other potential hypotheses about article meaning/use, Ionin et al. (2008: 572) conclude that 'innate linguistic knowledge supplies the learners with *possible* specifications of article use'.

5.4 Concluding Remarks

Clearly, exposure to a significant sample of sentences from a specific language is necessary in order to learn it. And many aspects of language can only be learned from experience. For example, only exposure to samples of English will allow a learner to establish that round, tennis-ball-sized crunchy fruits are called *apples*. This must be something that can only be learned from experience because the same concept is associated with different forms in other languages (*pommes* in French, *pingguo* in Mandarin Chinese, for example). Experience is required to learn all such sound–meaning correspondences that a speaker needs to understand and produce the language effectively. This is no small task. Similarly, exposure to a sample of sentences is needed to learn some of a language's syntactic properties, for example the order of adjectives and nouns. In English, adjectives typically precede nouns (*red apples, ripe bananas*) but in French they typically follow (*pommes rouges, bananes mûres*). This has to be learned from experience.

However, there are other aspects of linguistic knowledge that speakers possess that are under-determined by the samples of language they are exposed to. The input is too poor to provide relevant evidence for this knowledge. In such cases it seems necessary to propose that humans have innate knowledge about how language works. It is then a question of whether this knowledge is specific to language and derives from a dedicated language faculty with UG at its heart, or whether it results from applying domain-general learning capacities to the specific task of language learning.

It was suggested in this chapter that the ability of children and adults to track the frequency with which sounds/syllables occur in samples of language, an important element in solving the segmentation problem, may not be specific to UG, as the generative capacity of mental grammars may also not be a domain-specific property of UG. At the same time it was suggested that the morpheme categories, linguistic features, the rules Merge, Move and Agree, universal principles that constrain grammatical representations and some variation between the grammars of languages are specific to UG, although this remains an empirical question. Chapter 11 explores more fully competing theories that have been proposed about the general role of UG in L2 learning. In the next chapter attention turns to how L2 learners establish meanings assigned to phrases, clauses and sentences that go beyond the meanings of the individual morphemes that constitute them: the 'semantics' problem.

ACTIVITIES

1. TEST YOURSELF

(i) What do you understand by the 'poverty of the stimulus' argument for Universal Grammar?

(ii) Which of the proposed principles of UG described in section 5.2 are responsible for the following ungrammatical sentences in English?

    (a) *What did the bride and groom leave the church while the organist played?

    (b) *Has the company has appointed a new CEO who worked in Africa?

    (c) *It was strawberries that I forgot to buy and cream at the market

(iii) Explain the Overt Pronoun Constraint (OPC). What was the design of the study undertaken by Pérez-Leroux and Glass (1999) to test whether L2 speakers of Spanish were sensitive to the OPC?

(iv) Give an example of a proposed UG parameter of variation.

(v) What features appear to be relevant in the acquisition of the meaning of English articles by speakers of L1s that lack articles?

2. USE OF ENGLISH ARTICLES BY L2 SPEAKERS

Thomas (1989) asked thirty L2 speakers of English of low to high proficiency (the L1s of twenty-three of whom lacked articles) to describe pictures. Participants worked in pairs, sitting back-to-back. One member of the pair was asked to 'tell your partner everything you see in the picture' (1989: 344). The partner subsequently was shown two pictures and had to identify the one that had been described. Each participant took a turn as a speaker and a listener.

The results presented in table (i) show the use (and overuse) of *a* and *the* with count singular nouns only by all participants in [–definite, –specific], [–definite, +specific] and [+definite, +specific] contexts. Table (ii) shows article use (and overuse) with all types of noun in obligatory contexts for *the* and *a* by the speakers of L1s that lack articles and speakers of L1s that have articles.

Question (i): Consider the distribution of the 'wrong' article forms in table (i). Can use of articles in the three contexts be compared on the basis of the raw scores? If not, what needs to be done to make scores comparable?

TABLE (i) Use and overuse of articles in three count singular noun contexts by all participants (based on Thomas, 1989)

	Forms Produced	
Contexts	a	the
–definite, –specific	105	7
e.g. I guess I should buy *a new car*		
–definite, +specific	517	124
e.g. Chris approached me carrying *a dog*		
+definite, +specific	17	620
e.g. *The dog* jumped down		
She heard *the engine* of a car in the distance		

TABLE (ii) Use and overuse of articles in obligatory contexts for *the* and *a* by speakers of L1s with and without articles (based on Thomas, 1989)

	Form produced		
Participants with L1s that have no article (n = 23)	a	the	Ø
the contexts	18	585	120
a contexts	419	110	181
Participants with L1s that have articles (n = 7)			
the contexts	1	287	9
a contexts	212	23	37

Question (ii): Is the pattern of use displayed in table (i) similar to that found in the studies discussed in this section?

Question (iii): Consider the overuse of Ø in table (ii). Taking a difference in scores of at least 10% to be of significance, what differences are there between the participants with L1s that lack articles and participants with L1s that have articles?

What conclusions do you draw from these findings about the mental grammars that these speakers have for the use of *a, the* and Ø?

3. ACQUISITION OF CONSTRAINTS ON *WH*-MOVEMENT IN ENGLISH BY L1 GERMAN SPEAKERS

The following sentences involving embedded questions are discussed in Felix and Weigl (1991: 176):

i   a. John can't remember who bought which car
    b. *John can't remember which car who bought

As the asterisk indicates, the second sentence is ungrammatical in English. This is because a *wh*-object cannot cross a *wh*-subject to appear in C in English. The German counterpart of sentence (ib) is, however, grammatical. On the basis of the description of German syntax and English question formation in sections 4.5.1 and 4.5.2, can you explain why this is possible?

Felix and Weigl gave three groups of L1 German-speaking classroom learners of English a grammaticality judgement task that involved sentences like (ib). The average age of the groups was 12, 14.2 and 17.3 years. Their exposure to English in the classroom was 1.8 years, 3.8 years and 6.8 years respectively. Their mean accuracy in judging sentences like (ia) as grammatical and sentences like (ib) as ungrammatical is given in table (i).

TABLE (i) Mean percentage group accuracy in judging grammatical and ungrammatical sentences

	Group 1 (n = 24)	Group 2 (n = 26)	Group 3 (n = 27)
Grammatical	83%	100%	56%
Ungrammatical	29%	38%	59%

How do you interpret these findings, and in particular the apparent drop in accuracy in the group with the most exposure to English (who are performing at around chance in judging both grammatical and ungrammatical sentences)? (NB. Participants are very unlikely to have been explicitly taught about the difference between German and English on type (ib) sentences.)

4. TEXTUAL, SITUATIONAL AND CULTURAL USES OF 'THE'

Chrabaszcz and Jiang (2014) gave three groups of L2 learners of English an elicited imitation task involving the definite article *the*: a group of L1 Russian speakers (n = 16), a group of L1 Spanish speakers (n = 16) and a control group of native English speakers (n = 16). Participants saw a relevant picture on a computer screen, read a context-setting sentence and then heard a test sentence that they were asked to repeat orally. The sentences for imitation contained three uses of *the* on which the study focused (terminology and examples from Chrabaszcz and Jiang):

(i) 'Textual' – *the* is used with a noun phrase that has already been encountered in the preceding discourse (the context-setting sentence read on the computer screen), for example:

Robinson Crusoe was cast away on a remote tropical **island**.
He had to live on **the** island for many years.

(ii) 'Situational' – *the* is used with a noun phrase that describes a referent present in the non-linguistic context (in this case the picture on the computer screen), but has not been mentioned in the preceding linguistic discourse, for example:

(In the hairdresser's) This woman seems to be very happy with her new haircut. She should give **the** hairdresser a generous tip.

(iii) 'Cultural' – *the* is always used with a noun phrase, whatever the context, for example:

The US Congress consists of **the** Senate and **the** House of Representatives.
   The Congress meets in **the** Capitol in Washington, D. C.

Both L2 groups had had between eight and ten years of formal instruction in English, had been resident in the US for at least three years, and were matched for general proficiency.

Some of the sentences that participants were asked to imitate were fully grammatical, others were ungrammatical in that *the* had been omitted. The assumption underlying elicited imitation is that speakers do not repeat heard sentences parrot-fashion, but pass them through their mental grammars. If they have acquired the distribution of definite articles in English they will unconsciously correct the ungrammatical sentences by inserting definite articles. Mean accuracy scores by group for the production of the grammatical sentences and the correction of the ungrammatical sentences are presented in table (i). The maximum possible score for fully correct production of the sentence is 5.0; 0 is failure to produce *the* in every required context.

The Russian group were statistically significantly less accurate than the Spanish group on every condition. The Spanish group were only statistically significantly different from the native control group in imitating the ungrammatical 'cultural' uses of *the*.

Question (i): Are the results surprising? Give reasons for your answer.
Question (ii): Was this study a test of knowledge of the meaning of the English definite article or of the licensing of count nouns?
Question (iii): The Russian speakers are more accurate in producing *the* in textual uses than in situational or cultural uses. Why might that be?

TABLE (i) Accuracy in supplying *the* in obligatory contexts (based on Chrabaszcz and Jiang, 2014: 370, Table 7)

	Grammatical Stimulus Sentences			Ungrammatical Stimulus Sentences		
	Textual	Situational	Cultural	Textual	Situational	Cultural
L1 Russian	3.94	3.25	3.25	1.88	1.63	1.50
L1 Spanish	4.81	4.63	4.25	3.56	4.13	2.94
Native English	4.81	4.81	4.88	4.38	3.94	4.38

5. ARTICLES AS ADJECTIVES

Trenkic (2007) observes that L1 speakers of Serbian, a language that lacks articles, are more likely to omit articles in L2 English when nouns are preceded by adjectives than when they are not. The following example is taken from her study (2007: 306):

You come to **wooden bridge** ... and you go over **the bridge**

In an elicited oral production task based on information sharing between L2 speakers discussing directions on a map she found that out of 325 article + N contexts, articles were omitted in 86 cases (23%), whereas out of 152 article + adjective + N contexts, articles were omitted in 69 cases (45%).

Trenkic claims that 'the Missing Surface Inflection Hypothesis cannot predict the asymmetry at all' (2007: 289).

Question (i): What do you think is the basis for this claim? Can you offer a defence of the Missing Surface Inflection Hypothesis in this case?

Trenkic's own proposal is that her participants have not acquired articles as members of the category D, but have misanalysed them as adjectives, with 'identifiability of the referent' as a possible lexical interpretation. As adjectives, they can be used optionally like all other adjectives. When they are omitted preceding other adjectives it is because the other adjective is more informative. To use her example, if there are two mugs on the table, one green and one red, saying 'Pass me red mug' conveys all the information that is necessary to achieve one's wishes. If, however, there is a blue cup and a red mug on the table, 'Pass me the mug' is sufficient to achieve the desired result; it is unnecessary to specify its colour.

Question (ii): Think of an experiment that might determine whether L2 speakers with L1s that lack articles treat English articles as members of the category A or the category D?

FURTHER READING

For a collection of recent articles on the history of Universal Grammar, its component parts and its role in language acquisition, see:

Roberts, I. (ed.) 2017. *The Oxford handbook of Universal Grammar*. Oxford: Oxford University Press.

For a general discussion of the role of Universal Grammar in second language learning, see:

White, L. 2007. Linguistic theory, Universal Grammar and second language acquisition. In B. VanPatten and J. Williams (eds) *Theories in second language acquisition: an introduction*. Mahwah, NJ: Lawrence Erlbaum Associates, pp. 37–55.

Mitchell, R., Myles, F. and Marsden, E. 2013. *Second language learning theories*. Third Edition. Abingdon: Routledge, chapter 3: Linguistics and language learning: the Universal Grammar approach.

For discussion of an early principles and parameters of Universal Grammar approach to explaining second language acquisition, see:

White, L. 2003a. *Second language acquisition and Universal Grammar*. Cambridge: Cambridge University Press, chapter 1: Universal Grammar and language acquisition; and chapter 2: Principles of Universal Grammar in L2 acquisition.

6 How Phrasal and Sentential Meaning are Learned

6.1 Semantic Ambiguity

Sentences like (1) are ambiguous:

1. Some people in the room speak two languages.

On one interpretation, the people in question speak the same two languages, for example English and Chinese. On the other interpretation, not everyone in the room speaks the same two languages. For example, Amy speaks English and Chinese, Tom speaks English and German, Alice speaks German and Spanish, and so on.

The ambiguity arises because the expressions *some people* and *two languages* do not have a fixed reference in the way that, say, the expressions *Joanne Smith* and *French* do. *Some people* can refer to different sets of individuals, and who those people are depends on the context; *two languages* can refer to any pair of the (roughly) 6,500 to 7,000 languages spoken around the world. *Some* and *two* give an estimate of the quantity of the thing(s) referred to by the following noun phrase. They are known as quantifiers (*each, every, all* are also quantifiers). As speakers of English, we know that the quantified expressions in (1) can be understood to interact in two ways that give two distinct interpretations for a single sentence. In one case, the sentence is making an assertion about *two languages*:

2 a. Two languages are such that some people in the room speak them.

In the other case, the sentence is making an assertion about *some people*:

  b. Some people in the room are such that they speak two (unspecified) languages.

This interaction is known as 'quantifier scope'. In (2a) *two languages* is outside the scope of *some people*, giving the 'two specified languages' interpretation. In (2b) *two languages* is within the scope of *some people*, giving the 'unspecified languages' interpretation.

One of the tasks facing the L2 learner is to identify the range of interpretations that might be assigned to phrases and larger syntactic structures in the target language (the 'semantics problem' referred to in section 1.5). As in the case of syntax itself, some of this knowledge about interpretation is arguably part of what humans already know about language before the learning task begins. It is part of Universal Grammar. Some of this knowledge is attributable to the learner's experience with samples of the target language (input). And some may be transferred from a speaker's L1.

6.2 Knowledge of Meaning that Derives from Universal Grammar

6.2.1 L2 Knowledge of Meaning Differences Associated with Quantifier Scope

Knowledge of the effects of quantifier scope on interpretation is the kind of knowledge that might reasonably be attributed to UG. One illustration is provided by a study of 'object scrambling' in Dutch undertaken by Unsworth (2005: 298 – examples taken from that study). Dutch has two ways of translating 'The girl has twice tickled a monkey'. In (3a) *een aap* 'a monkey' is in the normal position for objects. In (3b) it has moved above the adverb *twee keer* 'twice'. This is known as 'scrambling'. (3b) is the case where the object has scrambled. (Note that in Dutch, as in German, in compound tenses non-finite forms of the verb appear at the end of the clause.)

3 a. Het   meisje   heft   twee keer   een   aap   gekieteld
      The   girl   has   two   times   a   monkey   tickled

   b. Het   meisje   heft   een   aap$_i$ twee keer   e$_i$ gekieteld
      The   girl   has   a   monkey$_i$ two   times   e$_i$ tickled

Twee keer is a quantified noun phrase functioning as an adverb, and scrambling the object *een aap* to take it outside its scope has an effect on the interpretation of the sentence. The unscrambled sentence (3a) has two possible interpretations: the girl might have tickled two different monkeys or the same monkey twice. The scrambled sentence (3b) only has the interpretation that the girl tickled the same monkey twice.

It is not clear that this difference in interpretation between sentences with and without scrambled objects can be learned from experience. Learners of Dutch will encounter unscrambled sentences with both interpretations, and they will encounter scrambled sentences with just the 'same object affected twice' interpretation. But there is nothing they encounter that could tell them that scrambled sentences cannot have a 'different objects affected' interpretation as well. Given the generative nature of linguistic knowledge (see section 5.1), it would be a reasonable assumption to make that the scrambled version also has both interpretations, contrary to fact.

Unsworth tested knowledge of the interpretive effects of Dutch object scrambling in a group of thirteen native speakers of English who had first been exposed to Dutch between the ages of eight and thirty-two. At the time of testing they were aged between twenty-two and fifty, and had been resident in the Netherlands between three months and twenty-seven years. Participants were presented with a series of four pictures which told a story about a girl or a boy. There were also three animals of the same type in the pictures, but differentiated from each other by colour, for example three monkeys: a black one, a grey one and a white one. In the course of the story, the girl or boy carried out an action on one or two of the three objects, for example tickling two monkeys, kissing two rabbits, etc., or tickling the same monkey twice, kissing the same rabbit twice. A puppet then produced an utterance describing the tickling, kissing, etc., event either with an unscrambled or scrambled object. The participant helped the puppet by saying whether the puppet's utterance was true or false.

Results are presented in table 6.1. The participants were divided by general proficiency in Dutch into two groups: mid-level proficiency and high-level proficiency.

In the 'no scrambling' condition both interpretations are possible. For example, for a sentence like *Het meisje heeft twee keer een aap gekieteld* both a picture of a girl tickling a black monkey and a white monkey, and a picture of a girl tickling the black monkey twice would be true. It is the scrambled condition that is relevant for testing whether the L2 participants know about the effects of scope on interpretation in Dutch. Only a picture of a girl tickling the same monkey twice would be true. Notice that the mid-level proficiency speakers are poor in judging this condition. In 76 per cent of cases they allow both interpretations where the object has been scrambled. However, the high-level proficiency learners are 78 per cent accurate. That is higher than chance and suggests that they know the effects of scope on interpretation.

If knowledge of the effects of scope on interpretation is given by UG, why are the less proficient speakers not also more accurate? Possibly because they have not yet acquired the syntactic rule that moves objects upwards over the adverbial. Note that these are not sentences that participants have produced themselves. They are presented with them by the researcher. It is possible that they are just guessing what their interpretation is. Once speakers have acquired the scrambling rule, the interpretation determined by scope relations becomes automatically available.

TABLE 6.1 Target-like accuracy (%) in determining the truth of non-scrambled and scrambled statements in Dutch by L2 speakers with L1 English (based on Unsworth, 2005: 319–20, Tables 53 and 54)

Proficiency	Target-Like Responses (No Scrambling)	Target-Like Responses (Scrambling)
Mid	88%	24%
High	88%	78%

Another case of the effects of scope on interpretation is provided by examples like the following in French. (The verb takes an imperfect form in French which translates into English as a simple past tense).

4 a. [Qui de célèbre]$_i$ fumait   e$_i$ au bistrot dans les années soixante?
      Who of famous   smoke-past-imp   in bars   in   the 1960s?

   b. Qui$_i$ fumait   e$_i$ de célèbre au bistrot dans les années soixante?
      Who smoke-past-imp   of famous in bars in   the 1960s?
      'Which famous people smoked in bars in the 1960s?'

The question phrase *qui de célèbre* 'which famous people' can take two forms when it appears at the front of the clause. Either the whole phrase appears at the front, or *qui* 'who' alone appears there, leaving its complement *de célèbre* 'of famous' below the verb.

Dekydtspotter and Sprouse (2001) have observed that there is a scope effect on interpretation between these two constructions. In the case of (4a), there are two possible answers to the question: people who are famous now, and who used to smoke in bars in the 1960s, and people who were famous in the 1960s who used to smoke in bars. In the case of (4b), only the second interpretation is possible. On the assumption that past tense is a kind of quantifier of time, they argue that this is because *célèbre* 'famous' is within the scope of the past tense in (4b), but not in the case of (4a), and this affects possible interpretations. Because English does not have similar constructions, there is no equivalent scope effect.

Dekydtspotter and Sprouse asked forty-seven intermediate-proficiency and eleven advanced-proficiency speakers of French (with L1 English) to determine the accuracy of answers to questions like (4) given contexts which favoured either a reference to a person who was famous, rich, etc., in the past or is famous, rich, etc. now. Answers to questions like (4b) would only be true if the context suggested the person was famous, rich, etc., in the past. The accuracy of the participants in judging the appropriateness of answers is given in table 6.2.

Both groups accept the 'famous then' interpretation for both non-separated and separated constructions. In the case of the 'famous now' interpretation, both groups are more willing to accept this interpretation with the non-separated construction than with the separated construction. The differences were statistically significant.

TABLE 6.2 Acceptance of 'famous now' and 'famous then' interpretations (based on Dekydtspotter and Sprouse, 2001)

	Intermediate		Advanced	
	now	then	now	then
Qui de Adj V	41%	91%	47%	80%
Qui V de Adj	25%	91%	16%	91%

This means that even the intermediate-proficiency speakers are aware of the effect of the adjective being within or outside the scope of past tense. Since the separated construction is not possible in their L1, and there is nothing in the samples of French they encounter to tell them that a 'famous now' interpretation is disfavoured with the separated construction, a plausible assumption is that this knowledge comes from UG.

6.2.2 L2 Knowledge of the Interpretation of Anaphors

The way that speakers interpret forms like *myself, yourself, himself, herself, itself, ourselves, themselves* appears to derive from UG. Although these reflexive pronouns have features for person, number and gender (for example, *herself* is third person, singular and feminine; *ourselves* is first person and plural), their reference is determined by another DP in the sentence. To illustrate, in (5) *herself* has the same reference as *Kate*:

5. Kate likes those photos of herself

Kate and *herself* co-refer, identifying the same individual. Forms that take their reference from another DP elsewhere in the sentence are traditionally known as anaphors. The category includes pronouns, reflexive pronouns and reciprocal expressions like *each other*.

A property of English reflexive pronouns is that they cannot be co-referential with just any DP in the sentence with which they share the same person, number and gender features. In (6), *herself* can only be co-referential with *Kate*, not with *Sue*. (Possible co-referring antecedent DPs are followed by a tick ✓; impossible co-referring DPs are followed by an asterisk *):

6. Sue* thinks that Kate✓ likes those photos of herself

To refer to *Sue* in (6) a different kind of anaphor would need to be used, the pronoun *her*, which conversely cannot refer to *Kate: Sue✓ knows that Kate* likes those pictures of her.*

In contrast to English, the Mandarin Chinese reflexive anaphor *ziji* 'self' can refer both to *Kate* and to *Sue* in sentences equivalent to (6):

7. Sue✓   xiang   Kate✓   xihuan   ziji   de   zhaopian
   Sue   think   Kate   like   self   's   photo
   'Sue thinks that Kate likes those photos of herself'

In (7) *Kate* can either like photos of *Kate*, or photos of *Sue*. Because of these possibilities, *ziji* is said to be a long-distance anaphor. It can not only be co-referential with a DP within its own (embedded) clause (*Kate* in (7)), but also with a DP in the main clause (*Sue* in (7)). In English, by contrast, reflexive pronouns are local anaphors; they can only be co-referential with a DP within their own clause.

There are restrictions, however, on which noun phrases are possible antecedents for long-distance anaphors like *ziji*. One is that they can only co-refer with subjects. Thus while in English both subject *Sue* and object *Kate* are possible co-referents for *herself* in (8a), only *Sue* is a possible co-referent in the Mandarin equivalent sentence (8b):

8 a. Sue✓ gave Kate✓ those photos of herself

   b. Sue˅   song   Kate*   ziji   de   zhaopian
      Sue   present   Kate   self   's   photo

Ying (1999) also points out that while the subject of the embedded clause in (7) is a possible target for co-reference, if the *ziji* phrase (a DP) is moved to the front of the embedded clause (a grammatical possibility in Mandarin), the embedded clause subject can no longer be co-referential:

9. Sue˅   xiang   ziji   de   zhaopian   Kate*   xihuan
   Sue   thinks   self   's   photos   Kate   like
   'Sue thinks that those photos of herself Kate likes'

However, if the verb phrase containing the *ziji* phrase is moved to the front of the embedded clause when a modal verb like *hui* 'will' is present, the subject of the subordinate clause becomes a possible target for co-reference again (this is a grammatical possibility in Mandarin, but is much less natural in English):

10. Sue˅ xiang xihuan   ziji   de   zhaopian   Kate˅   yiding   hui
    Sue   think like   self   's   photos   Kate   definitely   will
    'Sue thinks that like those photos of herself Kate definitely will'

A standard explanation of why English reflexive pronouns and Mandarin *ziji* differ in their potential for co-reference has to do with their morphology. English reflexive pronouns each consist of two morphemes, pronoun + *self*: *her-self, my-self* and so on. They are polymorphemic. Mandarin *ziji* is a single morpheme; it is monomorphemic. Some linguists have suggested that the association between polymorphemic status and local co-reference, and monomorphemic status and long-distance co-reference with the restrictions illustrated above, is part of our innate knowledge of Universal Grammar (Progovac, 1992; Bennett and Progovac, 1998). Once learners have identified from input that a reflexive anaphor is monomorphemic or polymorphemic, knowledge of its co-referential possibilities is given by UG. Ying (1999) observes that the subtlety of the possibilities for co-referential interpretations of *ziji* mean that it is unlikely that a language learner could work them out from positive evidence from input, and goes on to suggest that 'if English-speaking learners of Chinese can be shown to know the properties of *ziji* … this would serve as important evidence of underdetermination [of knowledge by input]' (1999: 56), i.e. that L2 learners' knowledge in this domain is guided by UG.

To test whether English-speaking L2 learners of Mandarin are aware of the subtle co-referential possibilities of *ziji*, Ying (1999) presented twenty-seven L2 learners of Mandarin Chinese, twenty of intermediate proficiency and seven of advanced proficiency (all L1 English speakers), and a control group of twenty native speakers of Mandarin with a randomised set of forty-eight Mandarin sentences. Sixteen of them were two-clause sentences like (11) with no movement of the *ziji* phrase. Both *nainai* 'grandma' and *mama* 'mother' here are possible co-referents for *ziji*:

11. Nainai˅   xiang   mama˅ xihuan   ziji   de   zhaopian
    Grandma think   mother like   self   's   photos
    'Grandma thinks that mother likes those photos of herself'

Sixteen were two-clause sentences where the DP *ziji de X* had moved to the front of the embedded clause. Here only *nainai* is a possible co-referent for *ziji*:

12. Nainai˅   xiang   ziji   de   zhaopian   mama* xihuan
    Grandma think   self   's   photos   mother like
    'Grandma thinks that those photos of herself mother likes'

Sixteen of them were two-clause sentences where a VP containing the *ziji* phrase had moved to the front of the clause. Here both *nainai* and *mama* are possible co-referents for *ziji*:

13. Nainai˅ xiang piping ziji   de   zhaopian mama˅ jue   bu   hui
    Grandma think criticise self 's   photos   mother definitely not   will
    'Grandma thinks that criticise those photos of herself mother definitely won't'

The participants were asked to decide, for each sentence, whether they agreed or disagreed that *ziji* could be the same person as *nainai* and *mama*. The results are presented in table 6.3 as percentages of agreeing responses to *nainai, mama* or both.

TABLE 6.3 Responses accepting co-reference with *ziji* in three syntactic contexts (based on Ying, 1999: 59–60, Tables 2–4)

	Co-Referent	Intermed.	Advanced	NS control
No movement	Mama˅	94	91	20
	Nainai˅	0	2	3
	Both˅	6	7	77
DP movement	Mama*	4	7	2
	Nainai˅	77	76	82
	Both*	19	17	16
VP movement	Mama˅	31	18	4
	Nainai˅	3	4	8
	Both˅	66	78	88

The performance of both L2 groups on the DP movement and VP movement sentences suggests that even the intermediate-proficiency learners are aware of the co-reference possibilities of *ziji* as a monomorpheme. In particular, both L2 groups' acceptance of *mama* as a possible co-referent with VP movement (97% for the intermediates, 96% for the advanced-proficiency speakers) contrasts with their much lower acceptance of *mama* as a co-referent with DP movement (23% and 24% respectively). Ying attributes their apparent lack of acceptance of *nainai* as a long-distance co-referent when there is no movement to L1 influence. He suggests that L1 influence affects structures that resemble each other in the two languages, whereas the new structures required learners to observe the options offered by UG (1999: 63). In other words, despite appearances in the case of the no-movement sentences, the learners studied had identified *ziji* as a monomorpheme, in contrast to the polymorphemic English reflexives, but the influence of their L1 biased their responses to prefer a local co-referent.

Sections 6.1 and 6.2 in a Nutshell

Quantified expressions like *some people, two languages* have scope. The interpretation of sentences may change depending on whether a sentence constituent is within or outside the scope of a quantified expression. Knowledge of such changes appears to come from UG. If L2 speakers' grammars are shaped by UG they should be aware of the different interpretations associated with quantifier scope. Unsworth (2005) found that English-speaking advanced-proficiency L2 speakers of Dutch were aware of the interpretive effects of object scrambling over a quantified adverb. Intermediate-proficiency speakers were not aware of these effects, but this may be because they had not yet acquired the scrambling property of Dutch. English-speaking L2 learners of French at both intermediate and advanced proficiency levels were aware of the interpretive effects of moving an adjectival expression outside the scope of T(ense).

The interpretation of reflexive anaphors also derives from UG. Language learners know innately the interpretive properties of polymorphemic and monomorphemic anaphors. Ying (1999) has shown that English-speaking L2 learners of Mandarin Chinese are aware that monomorphemic *ziji* 'self' cannot co-refer with its local subject when it is moved to the front of its own clause, but can when it is part of a VP that is moved to the front of its own clause.

6.3 Knowledge of Meaning that Derives from Input

Consider the meaning of the verb phrase in the following sentence:

14. Suzie danced into the room

The verb expresses the idea of a particular manner of motion, 'dancing' (as opposed to walking, running, skipping, ambling, and so on), and its prepositional phrase complement the idea of a path along which the motion occurs, 'from out-side to inside' the room. A number of the world's languages cannot express 'man-ner of motion along a path' in this way. In French and Spanish, for example, the verb rather than a PP complement expresses the notion of path, and the manner of motion has to be expressed by a present participle adjunct to the clause, as the following French example shows:

15. Suzie   est   entrée   dans   la   salle   dansant
     Suzie   is   entered in   the   room   dancing
    'Suzie entered the room dancing'

While *Suzie entered the room dancing* is also grammatical in English, it is much less natural than *Suzie danced into the room*. However, the equivalent construction in French – *Suzie a dansé dans la salle* – simply cannot have a 'manner of motion along a path' interpretation. It means 'Suzie was in the room and danced', equiv-alent to English *Suzie danced in the room*. Talmy (1985, 2000) has identified the contrast in this domain between languages like English on the one hand and French and Spanish on the other as a major typological distinction in the world's languages. He describes English-type languages as 'satellite-framed' (because they express the path of motion in a phrase that is a complement to the verb, a 'satel-lite' phrase), and French-type languages as 'verb-framed' (because they express the path of motion in the verb).

One explanation of the difference between satellite- and verb-framed languages is that while in both types of language spatial prepositions that are complements to the verb can encode reference to a place where a manner of motion event occurs, only satellite-framed languages allow spatial prepositions to encode ref-erence to a path. For example, while English and French have the equivalent prepositions *in/dans, on/sur* expressing place, French has no equivalent to the path-expressing prepositions *into, onto*. It also has no equivalent path interpre-tation for prepositions equivalent to English *under, over, behind*. These are ambig-uous in English: *swim under the bridge* can mean either 'be under the bridge and swim there' (the place interpretation) or 'swim from outside the bridge to under it' (the path interpretation). The French *nager sous le pont* can only mean 'be under the bridge and swim there'. To get the manner-of-motion-along-a-path interpre-tation a path verb has to be used, for example: *passer sous le pont en nageant* 'go under the bridge by swimming'.

Speakers of verb-framed L1s acquiring satellite-framed L2s like English will encounter positive evidence from input that spatial prepositions encode path as part of their meaning. Hearing sentences like *Suzie danced into the room* in contexts where a manner-of-motion-along-a-path interpretation is appropriate should pro-vide such positive evidence. Will this allow them to assign appropriate interpre-tations to VPs consisting of manner-of-motion verbs with path PP complements? And if they do acquire such interpretations, will this pre-empt their use in the L2 of the typical pattern for expressing manner of motion along a path in their L1s, i.e. sentences like *Suzie entered the room dancing*?

Bautista Maldonado (2011) showed three groups of L1 Spanish learners of English (of low-intermediate, intermediate and advanced proficiency in English) and a control group of native English speakers pictures of manner-of-motion events where an object either moved along a path (indicated by a directional arrow) or remained in place (indicated by an arrow going around in a circle on one spot). For example, a picture of a football outside a goal and an arrow showing a path of movement into the goal, or a picture of a football already in the goal with a circular arrow showing movement on the spot. Participants were asked to rate the naturalness of sentences like *The football rolled into the goal*, *The football entered the goal rolling* and *The football rolled in the goal* accompanying each of these pictures on a scale from +2 (very natural) to –2 (very unnatural). The mean naturalness ratings of sentences accompanying pictures depicting manner of motion along a path by each group are presented in table 6.4a, and the naturalness ratings of sentences accompanying a picture depicting manner of motion on the spot are presented in table 6.4b. The closer the mean is to 2, the more natural participants felt the sentence to be as a description of the event shown in the picture. A negative mean rating indicates that participants did not find the sentence a natural description of the event.

While all the L2 speakers find motion verbs with spatial PP complements expressing place natural as descriptions of motion on the spot (e.g. *Suzie danced in the room*) from early stages of learning English, they do not initially find manner-of-motion verbs with spatial PP complements expressing path very natural. The lower-intermediate proficiency speakers prefer the Spanish construction where path is expressed by the verb. However, with more exposure to English input the intermediate and advanced proficiency speakers come to find the latter construction more natural. Their awareness of the English pattern does not, however, completely pre-empt the Spanish version. It seems that the advanced-proficiency

TABLE 6.4a Mean ratings of sentences accompanying pictures depicting manner-of-motion-along-a-path events (based on Bautista Maldonado, 2011, Table 4.1)

	Low	Intermed.	Advanced	NS control
Motion verb + path PP (e.g. example 14)	.23	.73	.94	1.67
Path verb + manner-of-motion present participle (e.g. example 15)	.75	.43	.65	−1.07

TABLE 6.4b Mean ratings of sentences accompanying pictures depicting manner-of-motion-on-the-spot events (based on Bautista Maldonado, 2011, Table 4.1)

	Low	Intermed.	Advanced	NS control
Motion verb + place PP (e.g. *The ball rolled in the goal*)	1.34	1.50	1.27	1.61

speakers allow both English and Spanish possibilities, although the Spanish possibility is clearly quite unnatural for the native English-speaking control group.

Inagaki (2001) investigated the same phenomenon involving Japanese. Japanese, like Spanish, is a verb-framed language. Sentences equivalent to *John ran into the house* are ungrammatical (16a); the grammatical form is *John entered the house by running* (16b) (examples from Inagaki 2001: 154–5). (In Japanese, finite verbs always appear at the end of the clause.)

16 a. *John-ga   ie-no   naka-ni

     John-Nom   house-of   inside-at

     'John ran into the house'

   b. John-ga   ie-no   naka-ni   hasitte

     John-Nom   house-of   inside-at   running

     'John entered the house by running'

Interestingly, Inagaki investigated both L1 Japanese speakers acquiring L2 English and L1 English speakers acquiring L2 Japanese. He used the same picture–sentence naturalness matching design that Bautista Maldonado used, but restricted to the interpretation of manner of motion along a path pictures, and the same rating scale from –2 (completely unnatural) to +2 (completely natural). The participants were forty-two L1 Japanese speakers of intermediate proficiency in English and twenty-one L1 English speakers of advanced proficiency in Japanese. The L1 English speakers acted as control participants in the L2 English study, and the Japanese participants as control participants in the L2 Japanese study. The results are presented in table 6.5. Positive scores indicate that participants find the sentences natural, negative scores indicate that participants find the sentences unnatural.

Both Japanese learners of L2 English and English learners of L2 Japanese rate the appropriate construction for expressing manner of motion along a path in the target L2 as natural, i.e. manner of motion verb + path PP in English, and present participle + path verb in Japanese. However, in neither case does this pre-empt acceptance of the L1 construction. This contrasts with native speaker negative ratings for the inappropriate constructions. Exposure to target language input

TABLE 6.5 Mean ratings of sentences accompanying pictures depicting manner-of-motion-along-a-path events (based on Inagaki, 2001: 160–1, Tables 2 and 4)

	Participants	
English Task	L1 Japanese (n = 42)	L1 English (n = 21)
Manner of motion V + path PP e.g. example 14	1.24	1.92
Path V + by motion V-ing e.g. example 15	1.13	–.51
Japanese Task		
*Path PP + Manner of motion V e.g. example 16a	–.80	.78
Present participle + Path V e.g. example 16b	1.47	1.32

has allowed learners to identify the appropriate target language phrase structure for expressing manner of motion along a path, but this has not replaced the L1 option.

Gabriele (2009) found a similar pattern of acquisition of target phrasal interpretations, but absence of pre-emption of the L1 pattern, in the case of the acquisition of English progressive *be + V-ing* with certain types of verbs by L1 speakers of Japanese. The English progressive, as its name suggests, expresses the idea that an event is in progress. It is perfectly natural with verbs that have a dynamic and durative meaning like *run, play, bake* (*Tom is running, playing, baking*). However, it is typically much less natural with verbs that are dynamic and punctual, like *glimpse, recognise, notice: ?*Tom is glimpsing a man in the bushes, ?*is recognising him, ?*is noticing that he has a moustache* versus *Tom glimpses a man in the bushes, recognises him, notices that he has a moustache*. (For discussion of the aspectual terms dynamic, durative and punctual, see section 3.2.2.) However, some of the dynamic, punctual class of verbs appear to be able to shift their punctual interpretation to durative when they co-occur with the progressive. *Arrive* has a basic dynamic, punctual interpretation, but when it co-occurs with the progressive it is interpreted as durative: *The train is arriving* means 'the train is close to its destination and on the point of arrival'. *Die* has a dynamic, punctual interpretation but in *Tom is dying* it has shifted to mean 'Tom's health is so poor that he will inevitably die.'

Japanese has an equivalent form to English *be + V-ing* with a very similar semantic function: *te-iru*. When it co-occurs with dynamic durative verbs it also expresses the idea of an event in progress (examples from Gabriele, 2009: 376):

17. Taroo-ga   hashitte-iru
    Taroo-nom   run te-iru
    'Taroo is running'

However, when *te-iru* co-occurs with the equivalent of English dynamic, punctual verbs like *arrive, die*, their meaning does not shift to durative. Instead, *V + te-iru* gives rise to a resultative meaning: *has arrived, has died*:

18. Hikoki-ga   kuko-ni   tuite-iru
    Plane-nom   airport-at   arrive te-iru
    'The plane has arrived and is at the airport'

Gabriele gave 110 L1 Japanese speakers of L2 English, ranging in proficiency from low to near-native, and a control group of twenty-three native English speakers a story compatibility task. This required them to listen to three- or four-sentence-long stories narrated by a native English speaker that depicted either incomplete or complete events. The stories were accompanied by pictures of the event. After each story participants were presented with a sentence and were asked to rate the compatibility of the sentence with the story on a scale from 1 (not compatible at all) to 5 (fully compatible). All of the test sentences involved the progressive. Half of them contained dynamic, durative verb phrases like *make a cake, paint a portrait*, and half of them contained dynamic, punctual verbs that can shift their meaning to durative when they co-occur with the progressive, like *arrive, die*. An example of a story involving an incomplete event and the accompanying test sentence is the following (Gabriele, 2009: 384):

19. This is the plane to Tokyo. At 4pm the plane is near the airport. There is a lot of wind. At 4.30pm the plane is still in the air.
    Test sentence: The plane is arriving at the airport.

The expectation is that the native speaker control group would rate the test sentence close to 5, as fully compatible with the meaning of the story. If the Japanese speakers, as a result of exposure to English input, have acquired the shift in interpretation of *arrive* from punctual to durative with the progressive, they should also rate this sentence close to 5.

An example of a story involving a complete event and the accompanying test sentence is given in (20).

20. This is the plane to Tokyo. At 4pm the plane is near the airport. At 5pm the passengers are at the airport.
    Test sentence: The plane is arriving at the airport.

The expectation is that the native speakers will rate this close to 1 because *arrive* in the progressive is not compatible with the resultative interpretation of the story. If the acquisition of the shifted interpretation of *arrive* and similar verbs has pre-empted the Japanese resultative interpretation, the Japanese participants should also rate this sentence close to 1.

Results show that all the L2 participants, from low proficiency to near native, and the native speaker controls, rate sentences involving dynamic, durative verbs (like *run, play, bake*) as compatible with incomplete story scenarios like (19). Ratings range from 3.5 to 5. And they reject the same verbs in the be+V-ing construction with complete story scenarios like (20), with ratings below 3.

The results of performance on sentences where the progressive co-occurs with dynamic, punctual verbs (like *arrive, die*) suggest initial competition between the English durative interpretation and the resultative interpretation of Japanese *te-iru*. Low- and intermediate-proficiency learners rate the compatibility of the test sentences with both incomplete and complete story scenarios at around 3. The high-proficiency and near-native speaker participants rate the English durative interpretation at around 4, but they still also rate the Japanese resultative interpretation at around 3. The native speakers by contrast rate the durative interpretation at 4, but the resultative interpretation close to 1 (incompatible with resultative events).

With longer exposure to English input, then, Japanese learners acquire the shift of dynamic, punctual verbs like *arrive, die* co-occurring with the progressive to a durative interpretation. However, this does not pre-empt the resultative interpretation, which they continue to allow. These Japanese speakers are showing optionality in their interpretation of this particular example of phrasal meaning.

These findings might suggest a more general prediction for L2 development that 'the acquisition of a new semantic representation is easier than the pre-emption of the existing L1 representation' (Gabriele, 2009: 378). However, in a parallel study that Gabriele conducted with English learners of Japanese, using the same method, she found that they performed like the Japanese native speaker control group. That is, they rated the resultative interpretation of sentences like *Hikoki-ga kuko-ni tuite-iru*, the literal equivalent of *The plane is arriving at the airport*, but with the interpretation 'The plane has arrived at the airport', as compatible with complete story scenarios and not compatible with incomplete story scenarios – they would be expected to treat such sentences as compatible with incomplete story scenarios if they were transferring the English interpretation.

Gabriele argues that input is key here to explaining the difference between the performance of the Japanese learners of L2 English and the English learners of L2 Japanese. Firstly, she assumes that learning about the shift in interpretation of dynamic, punctual verbs to durative in English is a complexity that English speakers do not face in learning Japanese. In other words, while Japanese learners have to move from a less complex semantic representation to a more complex one, English speakers move from a more complex semantic representation to a simpler one, the default interpretation of dynamic, punctual verbs, and acquisitionally the latter is easier than the former. Then, she proposes that English learners of L2 Japanese get very clear positive evidence from input that sentences like *Hikoki-ga kuko-ni tuite-iru* have a resultative interpretation. They will hear such sentences in contexts where it is clear that the plane has arrived and is standing on the tarmac – and this may pre-empt the durative meaning of the English equivalent sentence. By contrast, the cues available from English for Japanese speakers that *be + ing* with verbs like *arrive, die* cannot have a resultative interpretation are less clear. A plane that is taxi-ing along the tarmac can be described by saying *The plane is arriving*, but this is also consistent with the plane having arrived.

Section 6.3 in a Nutshell

English expresses the meaning 'manner of motion along a path' through verbs that describe a manner of motion (like *walk, dance*) with prepositional phrase (PP) complements that encode a path. A number of languages, including French, Spanish and Japanese, disallow this construction. Instead they use verbs that describe a path (like *enter, cross*) with a manner-of-motion adjunct, such as a present participle. Languages like English have been referred to as satellite-framed and languages like Spanish as verb-framed (Talmy, 2000). L1 speakers of one of these types of languages learning an L2 of the other type take time to acquire the appropriate L2 construction for manner of motion along a path, but do so successfully. However, this does not 'pre-empt' the L1 construction from their L2 grammars. Exploring a related case, the acquisition of the 'event in progress' meaning of dynamic, punctual verbs like *arrive* used with *be + ing* by Japanese-speaking L2 learners, and the acquisition of the 'resultative' meaning of the Japanese counterpart by English-speaking L2 learners, Gabriele (2009) found that while the Japanese learners of English optionally allowed both the event-in-progress and resultative interpretations of *be arriving*, the English learners of Japanese only allowed the resultative interpretation of *tuite-iru*. She attributes pre-emption of the English option to input. The cues provided by Japanese for the resultative interpretation are unambiguous, whereas it is less clear that the cues provided by English rule out a resultative interpretation.

6.4 L1 Influence on the Acquisition of Phrasal and Sentential Meaning

In the previous section it was already becoming clear that the L1 might play a role in the way that L2 speakers deal with the challenge of acquiring phrasal and sentential meaning in the target L2. Spanish and Japanese learners of English allow verb-framed clause structures to express manner of motion along a path, for example *Suzie entered the room dancing*, a possibility that exists in their L1, but is quite unnatural in English. Japanese speakers continue to interpret dynamic, punctual verbs like *arrive* as resultative when they co-occur with *be + ing*, interpreting *The plane is arriving at the airport* as 'The plane has arrived at the airport', the interpretation that would be given to the equivalent sentence in Japanese.

Methodologically, however, one needs to be careful in making claims about the effects of a speaker's L1 on their knowledge of an L2 simply on the basis of similarity between the properties of the L1 and what they accept/produce in the L2. Allowing verb-framed sentence structures to express manner of motion along a path may be something that all L2 learners do, regardless of their L1, as part of L2 development. To be certain that L1 influence is involved, L2 learners from different L1 backgrounds need to be compared, where the L1 of one group has a property that is similar to the L2, and the L1 of the other group is different on that property. If such learners, at the same stage of general development of knowledge of the target L2, show clearly different behaviour, then there are good grounds for thinking that the L1 is playing a role in guiding development. In this section two representative studies of such cases are considered.

In English, when dynamic, durative verbs like *read, drink, bake* are followed by objects that lack articles, the whole event described is interpreted as having no specific endpoint (is atelic – see section 3.2.2) and can be interpreted as a habitual event:

21 a. Antonia baked cakes
    b. Georgia drank whisky

When objects have determiners, the event is interpreted as telic and specific:

22 a. Antonia baked a cake
    b. Georgia drank a whisky

In the Slavic languages, this contrast in interpretations is realised by imperfective or perfective forms of the verb. The following are examples from Russian (Slabakova, 2008: 146):

23 a. Maša   jela   tort
       Masha   Imperf-eat-past cake
       'Masha ate cake'
    b. Maša   s- jela   tort
       Masha   Perf-eat-past   cake
       'Masha ate the cake'

Slabakova (2000, 2001) gave L1 speakers of Spanish who were of low intermediate proficiency in English, L1 speakers of Bulgarian (a Slavic language) of low intermediate and advanced proficiency in English, and a control group of native speakers of American and British English an interpretation task. They had to rate sentences like the following as natural or unnatural:

24 a. Antonia worked in a bakery and made a cake.
    b. Antonia worked in a bakery and made cakes.

For native speakers of English, sentences like (24a) are less natural because there is a clash between the habitual interpretation of the first clause 'worked in a bakery' and the telicity of the second clause induced by the presence of the determiner *a*.

Participants were asked to rate such sentences on a scale from −3 (very unnatural) to +3 (very natural). The results are presented in table 6.6.

The low-intermediate proficiency Bulgarian speakers are not distinguishing the difference in naturalness between telic and atelic clauses following clauses

TABLE 6.6 Mean ratings of naturalness of sentences like (24a–b) (based on Slabakova, 2000; 2001)

	and made a cake (telic)	and made cakes (atelic)
NS-American	0.19	2.09
NS-British	0.81	2.41
L1 Spanish (low intermed)	0.55	2.04
L1 Bulgarian (low intermed)	1.44	1.95
L1 Bulgarian (advanced)	0.41	2.0

that describe habitual events. This suggests that they have not yet established the effect on phrasal meaning produced by the presence versus absence of an overt indefinite article heading the object DP. By contrast, Spanish speakers at the same general level of proficiency have. Since Spanish, like English, determines the telicity of VPs through the use of articles while Bulgarian distinguishes the telicity of VPs through a contrast involving the presence (telic) versus absence (atelic) of a pre-verbal affix, it is likely that the difference in performance is the result of L1 influence. The low-intermediate proficiency Bulgarian speakers are treating both types of example in the test as atelic because the verb lacks a telicity-inducing pre-fix. It is clear that this L1 effect is not persistent. With longer exposure to English, Bulgarian native speakers come to make a distinction between the naturalness of the two types of sentence, as the performance of the advanced proficiency speakers indicates.

The study of the acquisition of the Mandarin Chinese reflexive anaphor *ziji* 'self' reported by Ying (1999) (see section 6.2.2) found that learners were sensitive to subtle restrictions on possible co-referring subject noun phrases when *ziji* was within a moved DP and when it was within a moved VP. However, they did not choose a long-distance (main clause) co-referential subject like *nainai* 'grandma' in simple sentences not involving movement like *Nainai xiang mama xihuan ziji de zhaopian* 'Grandma thinks that mother likes those pictures of herself'. Ying attributed this to the learners' L1 English biasing them to prefer a local co-referent, even though they knew that *ziji* is a monomorpheme that allows long-distance co-reference.

Without comparing L1 English speakers with speakers of an L1 that has similar co-referential properties to Mandarin, though, we cannot be certain that this pattern is not a feature of L2 development generally. A study by Yuan (1998) comparing English-speaking learners of Mandarin with Japanese learners of Mandarin provides evidence bearing on this question. Japanese has a monomorphemic reflexive anaphor – *zibun* 'self' – that allows both local and long-distance subjects to be co-referential (example from Yuan, 1998: 325):

25. Naoki ́-wa   Mamoru ́-ga   zibun-o   sinyoshite-iru   to   omotteiru
    Naoki-Top   Mamoru-Nom   self-Acc   trust te-iru   that   think
    'Naoki thinks that Mamoru trusts himself'

Yuan asked twenty-four Japanese speakers with intermediate proficiency in Mandarin, thirty-two English speakers with intermediate proficiency, twenty-five English speakers with advanced proficiency and twenty-four native speakers of Mandarin to decide which subject noun phrases *ziji* could be interpreted as co-referential with in two-clause sentences like:

26. Gaolin   zhidao   Lidong   feichang   xiangxin   ziji
    Gaolin   know   Lidong   very much   trust   self
    'Gaolin knows that Lidong trusts himself very much'

This sentence is pragmatically neutral with respect to the subject with which *ziji* might be co-referential. *Gaolin* and *Lidong* are equally plausible. However, some of the test sentences were constructed to strongly favour co-reference with the main clause subject, as in (27):

27. Wangming   bu   gaoxing   de   shuo   Lidong   jingchang   bu   xiangxin   ziji
    Wangming   not   happy   -ly   say   Lidong   often   not   trust   self
    'Wangming said unhappily that Lidong often does not trust himself'

The presence of the adverb *bu gaoxing de* 'unhappily' in the main clause favours an interpretation where *ziji* 'self' is co-referential with *Wangming*. Other sentences were constructed to favour co-reference with the local subject:

28. Lidong   jide   Wang   laoshi   diyi   ci   lai   shangke
    Lidong   remember   Wang   teacher   first   time   come   class
    deshihou   meiyou   jieshao   ziji
    when   not   introduce self
    'Lidong remembers that teacher Wang didn't introduce himself the first time he came to teach the class'

Here the reference to *teach the class* in the embedded clause favours an interpretation where *teacher Wang* is the co-referent of *ziji*.

The results from the study are presented in table 6.7. The key comparison is between responses where participants choose, on the one hand, long-distance or long-distance together with local co-referents (LD + LD/Loc), i.e. the possibilities that exist in Mandarin and Japanese, but not English, and, on the other hand, local-only co-referents (Loc) (the situation that exists in English). Responses are presented as percentages.

As far as responses to co-reference in the neutral sentences are concerned – that is, where both the embedded clause subject and main clause subject are equally plausible as co-referents for *ziji* – both the native speaker and Japanese groups have a preference for the long-distance main clause subject. Neither of the English groups shows this preference, selecting both long-distance and local co-referents

TABLE 6.7 Choice of co-referents for *ziji* in three types of sentences (based on Yuan, 1998: 332, Table 3)

	Neutral		Long-distance favoured		Local favoured	
	LD + LD/Loc	Loc	LD + LD/Loc	Loc	LD + LD/Loc	Loc
Japanese (n = 24)	75	25	91	8	26	74
English Interm. (n = 32)	48	52	53	47	27	73
English Adv. (n = 25)	40	60	71	29	17	83
Native speakers (n = 24)	81	19	94	6	33	67

about equally. This suggests that the English speakers are aware that *ziji* has the possibility for long-distance co-reference, even when they are of intermediate proficiency. However, the contrast in choices with the Japanese speakers is striking. The Japanese speakers, who have the same general intermediate proficiency in Mandarin as the English intermediate group, favour long-distance co-reference. This difference suggests L1 influence since Japanese has a monomorphemic reflexive anaphor (*zibun*) similar to Mandarin *ziji*.

Responses on sentences where the long-distance main clause subject is favoured as a co-referent are consistent with this view. While the Japanese learners are strongly aware of the bias, 91 per cent of them choosing the long-distance co-referent, the intermediate-proficiency English group is still choosing both long-distance and local co-referents about equally. The advanced-proficiency group, however, appear to be more sensitive to the pragmatic bias that favours the long-distance co-referent. This suggests that the requirement from English for local co-reference with reflexive anaphors is still influential for the intermediate-proficiency L2 learners of Mandarin, in contrast to the Japanese intermediate-proficiency L2 learners, but that with longer exposure to Mandarin, the influence of English becomes weaker. In the case of the sentences that favour the local subordinate clause subject as co-referent, as expected, all groups show a strong tendency to select the local co-referent, although all groups, including the English speakers, still allow the long-distance possibility for co-reference to a certain extent.

Section 6.4 in a Nutshell

Convincing evidence for L1 influence on the development of L2 knowledge comes from comparing two groups of learners, one whose L1 has a property similar to that in the L2 and one whose L1 does not. For example, Spanish determines the (a)telicity of dynamic, durative transitive verbs like *make* through the presence or absence of an overt determiner in the accompanying object: *made a cake* (telic) vs *made cakes* (atelic). The Slavic languages determine (a)telicity in such cases through the presence of a verbal prefix: *s-jela tort* 'ate the cake' (telic) vs *jela tort* 'ate cake' (atelic). Slabakova (2000, 2001) compared Spanish- and Bulgarian-speaking low-intermediate proficiency L2 learners of English and found that while the Spanish speakers were sensitive in a sentence naturalness interpretation task to the role of the determiner in producing (a)telic interpretations, the Bulgarian speakers were not. This suggests L1 influence in the acquisition of this interpretive property of English VPs. With proficiency, Bulgarian speakers do acquire the English property. Similarly, Yuan (1998) has shown that Japanese-speaking L2 learners of intermediate proficiency in Mandarin Chinese are more sensitive to the possibility of the reflexive anaphor *ziji* 'self' co-referring with a long-distance subject noun phrase than English-speaking L2 learners of Mandarin, suggesting L1 influence.

6.5 Concluding Remarks

Quantifier scope effects, anaphor co-reference possibilities and differences in the structures that languages use to express the same meaning, as in the expression of 'manner of motion along a path' or the expression of (a)telicity of dynamic, durative events, are representative examples of how the meaning of phrases and sentences goes beyond the meanings of the individual morphemes of which they are constituted. While some aspects of these phenomena come from Universal Grammar (the effects of quantifier scope on interpretation and the co-referential possibilities of polymorphemic and monomorphemic reflexive anaphors), others are language-specific (the choice of structure for expressing 'manner of motion along a path' and the (a)telicity of dynamic, durative VPs). L2 learners appear to take time to acquire target-language properties of phrasal and sentential meaning. Even where meanings derive from UG, it may take L2 learners time to acquire the syntactic structure from which the UG-derived meaning is computed (as in the case of L2 learners of Dutch who may need to acquire the language-specific object-scrambling property before they are aware of its effects when an object is scrambled over a quantified adverb).

Properties of the L1 are also influential, as in the case of the acquisition of co-reference between monomorphemic anaphors and long-distance subjects in Mandarin Chinese or the continued availability to Spanish- and Japanese-speaking L2 learners of English of the verb-framed option for expressing 'manner of motion along a path', even though the satellite-framed option has been acquired. The presence of unambiguous cues in L2 input appears to play an important role in overriding L1 influence, for example in the case of English learners of Japanese whose acquisition of the 'resultative' interpretation of Japanese *te-iru* with dynamic, punctual verbs pre-empted the 'event in progress' interpretation associated with the English *be* + *ing* counterpart.

The three factors UG, L1 influence and input are also involved in shaping the way that L2 learners deal with the challenge of acquiring a language's sound system, the topic of the next chapter.

ACTIVITIES

1. TEST YOURSELF

(i)   What effect does the 'scrambling' of an indefinite object over a quantified adverb in Dutch have on the interpretation of sentences? Are L2 speakers of Dutch aware of this effect?

(ii) What is the difference between the interpretation of reflexive anaphors (-*self* forms) in English and in Mandarin Chinese?

(iii) What did Ying's (1999) study of English-speaking learners of Mandarin Chinese show?

(iv) What is the difference between 'satellite-framed' and 'verb-framed' languages? What did Bautista Maldonado and Inagaki find in their studies of speakers of verb-framed languages acquiring satellite-framed English?

(v) What is the difference between English and Slavic languages like Bulgarian in the way they realise telicity in their verb phrases? What did Slabakova (2000, 2001) find when she investigated how Bulgarian and Spanish speakers acquire the English property?

2. POSITIONAL EFFECTS ON THE INTERPRETATION OF ADJECTIVES

Spanish, like French, allows some adjectives to appear before and after the noun. This can sometimes change the interpretation of the DP. Rothman et al. (2010) observe that with some adjective–noun pairings, the difference is between 'restrict[ing] the set to which the [noun] refers' (postnominal position) and 'applying to all possible members of the set referred to by the noun' (prenominal position) (2010: 55). They illustrate this with the following example:

(i) a. *los incas valientes* 'the brave Incas', as in 'while the brave Incas stayed behind to defend the village, the less brave ones took to the hills' (postnominal set-restricting interpretation)
   b. *los valientes incas* 'the brave Incas', as in 'the brave incas (i.e. all of them) held out for many months against the Spanish invaders' (prenominal, referring to all members of the set)

The English DP *the brave Incas* is inherently ambiguous between these two meanings, the relevant one being determined by context.

Rothman et al. gave two groups of adult L2 speakers of Spanish (speaking non-Romance L1s, mostly English), of intermediate and advanced proficiency, and a group of native Spanish speakers a sentence interpretation task. Participants read a sentence (as in (ii)) and had to choose one of the two interpretations offered underneath the sentence:

(ii) Los valientes incas resistieron a los conquistadores
   'The brave incas held off the invaders'
   a. Only the brave Incas (i.e. not the cowardly ones) resisted the invaders
   b. The Incas, who are all brave, resisted the invaders

The correct choice here is (b). The results from the study are presented in table (i) as mean accuracy scores (out of 10).

The advanced-proficiency group were not statistically significantly different from the native speakers. The intermediate-proficiency group were significantly less accurate than the other two groups, but their performance was above chance.

Compare these findings with those of Anderson (2008) reported in section 1.5. What conclusions do you draw?

TABLE (i) Mean accuracy in choosing appropriate interpretations for pre- and postnominal adjectives (based on Rothman et al., 2010: 63, figure 1)

	Prenominal	Postnominal
Intermediate proficiency L2 group (n = 21)	8.14	8.48
Advanced proficiency L2 group (n = 24)	9.38	9.33
Native speakers (n = 15)	9.60	9.40

3. THE INTERPRETATION OF *WH*-QUESTIONS WITH QUANTIFIED SUBJECTS

English sentences with a questioned direct object (e.g. *what?*) and a quantified subject (e.g. *everyone*) like (i) can be answered in two ways:

(i)   What did everyone buy?

One answer is that everyone bought the same thing, e.g. *John bought eggs, Sue bought eggs* and *Jan bought eggs*. This is known as an individual interpretation of the question. A second answer is that each person referred to bought something different: *John bought eggs, Sue bought milk* and *Jan bought fruit*. This is known as a pair-list interpretation of the question.

Marsden (2008) observes that while sentences like (i) in English and equivalent sentences in Mandarin Chinese give rise to individual and pair-list answers, equivalent sentences in Japanese only give rise to individual answers; the pair-list interpretation of the question is not available in Japanese. One account for this difference (Saito, 1999) is that the feature composition of the Japanese quantified expression *daremo*, equivalent to English *everyone* and Mandarin *meigeren*, is different. It contains the *wh*-element *dare* 'who' and a conjunction *mo*. The presence of the *wh*-element blocks the pair-list interpretation. By contrast, English *everyone* and Mandarin *meigeren* do not contain a *wh*-element and the pair-list interpretation is available (Marsden, 2008: 195).

Marsden gave L1 English and L1 Mandarin Chinese learners of L2 Japanese (of intermediate and advanced proficiency) a picture–sentence rating task where they saw cartoon characters holding items that they had drawn, bought, etc. They were presented with possible answers to questions like *What did everyone draw?*, *What did everyone buy?* etc. (both in Japanese), and had to rate the answers on a scale going from –2 (definitely not a possible answer) to +2 (a perfect answer). Answers were either consistent with individual or with pair-list interpretations. She also gave native speakers of Japanese, English and Mandarin the same test in their native languages (as a point of comparison).

Marsden took scores of +1 and +2 to indicate 'acceptance' of the answer, and scores of –1 and –2 to indicate 'rejection' of the answer. The mean percentage acceptance of each interpretation, individual and pair-list, by each group is presented in table (i)

TABLE (i) Mean acceptance (%) of individual and pair-list interpretations (based on Marsden, 2008: 207 and 210, figures 3 and 4)

	Individual interpret.	Pair-list interpret.
Native Japanese (n = 18)	94	37
Native English (n = 21)	90	99
Native Mandarin (n = 14)	36	87
L1 English intermediate L2 Japanese (n = 21)	87	86
L1 Mandarin intermediate L2 Japanese (n = 7)	60	69
L1 English advanced L2 Japanese (n = 12)	90	58
L1 Mandarin advanced L2 Japanese (n = 10)	92	62

As expected, the Japanese native speakers favour individual interpretations over pair-list interpretations, and this was statistically significant. The native English and Mandarin speakers favour pair-list over individual interpretations, strikingly so in the case of the Mandarin speakers.

How do you interpret the development of knowledge of the meanings of this construction in Japanese by the L2 participants?

4. TELICITY IN A LANGUAGE THAT LACKS ARTICLES

Japanese is a language that lacks articles. Verb phrases with 'bare' direct objects can be interpreted either as atelic or telic. For example, in (i) *kaado-o* 'card-Accusative' can be interpreted either as 'cards' (atelic) or 'the cards' (telic), depending on the context (example from Gabriele, 2010: 387):

(i) Ken-wa   tanjoobi-ni   kaado-o   kakimashita
     Ken-Top   birthday-on   card-Acc   write-past
     'Ken wrote cards/the cards on his birthday'

Gabriele gave two groups of English-speaking learners of Japanese (of intermediate and advanced proficiency) and a control group of native speakers of Japanese an interpretation task. They saw pictures and heard accompanying narratives that favoured either an atelic or telic interpretation of the verb phrase. An example of one such narrative is given in (ii) (Gabriele, 2010: 387):

(ii) Today is Ken's birthday. He received four presents. He wants to write thank you
      cards to his friends. Ken writes three cards. Then he starts to write the last card.

The final sentences of the narrative suggested either an atelic interpretation ('But Ken has to go to school. He cannot finish the fourth card.') or a telic interpretation ('He finishes the last card. Then he gives the cards to his friends.').

Following the narratives, participants were presented with a sentence in Japanese that they had to rate for compatibility with the story, e.g. a sentence like (i). This sentence is compatible both with an atelic and a telic interpretation.

The rating scale went from 1 'I definitely cannot say this sentence in the context of the story' to 5 'I definitely can say this sentence in the context of the story'. There were four items in Gabriele's test design that involved narratives like the one in (ii) where the test sentence to be interpreted involved a count noun in direct object position. Full acceptance of th   appropriateness of all four test sentences by a participant would therefore giv ₐ total rating of 20. Full rejection of the appropriateness of the four test sentences would give a total rating of 4.

Table (i) presents the results in the form of the number of participants whose total ratings fell in the ranges 16–20, 12–15, 8–11 and 4–7 in atelic and telic contexts.

TABLE (i) Number of participants who fall into different rating bands for the interpretation of Japanese VPs with bare count noun direct objects in atelic and telic contexts (based on Gabriele, 2010: 392, Table 1)

	Atelic Context			Telic Context		
Rating	Intermediate (n = 38)	Advanced (n = 7)	Native (n = 17)	Intermediate (n = 38)	Advanced (n = 7)	Native (n = 17)
16–20	6 (16%)	3 (43%)	17 (100%)	32 (84%)	7 (100%)	17 (100%)
12–15	17 (45%)	3 (43%)		4 (11%)		
8–11	10 (26%)	1 (14%)		2 (5%)		
4–7	5 (13%)					

Question: Compare these results with Slabakova's (section 6.4) on the acquisition of telicity in English by Bulgarian speakers. Are there differences between learners going from an L1 that lacks articles to an L2 that has them and learners going from an L1 with articles to an L2 that does not? What implications do you draw from your comparison of the findings?

Read Gabriele's article to learn about how her participants rated mass nouns (like *juice* in *John drank the juice*) and count nouns modified by a numeral (as in *Ken wrote four cards on his birthday.*)

FURTHER READING

For discussion of other examples of the 'semantics problem' facing L2 learners see:

Slabakova, R. 2008. *Meaning in the second language*. Berlin: Mouton de Gruyter.
Slabakova, R. 2014. *Second language acquisition*. Oxford: Oxford University Press, chapter 10: Acquisition of the syntax-semantics interface.

7 How Sound Systems are Learned

7.1 Sounding Like a Native (or Not)

Joseph Conrad, author of *Lord Jim*, *The Secret Agent* and other novels, is regarded as one of the great writers in English of the early twentieth century. One of the remarkable things about him was that English was not his first language – Polish was. He only acquired English when he joined the English merchant navy in his late teens. Nevertheless, while his knowledge of English syntax and the English lexicon was on a par with that of native speakers, he apparently retained a very strong Polish accent throughout his life. His friend and collaborator, Ford Madox Ford, wrote of him (1924: 35):

> He spoke English with great fluency and distinction, with correctitude in his syntax, his words absolutely exact as to meaning, but his accentuation so faulty that he was at times difficult to understand …

By 'accentuation' Madox Ford means 'pronunciation'. Approximating native-like pronunciation of an L2 appears to be a challenge for most L2 learners, even for those who are motivated to sound like native speakers. And the challenge can be persistent. There are numerous examples of L2 learners who, like Conrad, spend many years in a community where the target L2 is spoken who nevertheless retain a strong 'foreign accent'. Yet there are others who manage to sound almost like native speakers. Why is this the case?

To understand how L2 learners acquire the sound system of a target language, where they are successful and where they diverge persistently, it is necessary to look at three levels at which linguistic sounds are organised: (a) the individual segments of sound that each language draws on to create the forms that are associated with morphemes (such as the [b] [a] and [n] that make up *ban*); (b) the organisation of sound segments into **syllables** – morphemes may be realised by one, two, or more syllables, for example *ban* (one syllable), *bangle* (two syllables: ban-gle), *banister* (three syllables: ba-ni-ster); and (c) prosody, the processes that affect syllables when they are organised into words, phrases and clauses. This covers (i) word stress: in ʹbanister the first syllable is stressed (is audibly more prominent than the other two), in baʹnana the second syllable is stressed; (ii) lexical tones in languages like Mandarin Chinese, where, for example, the morpheme *ma* can mean four different things depending on whether it is spoken with a high level pitch, a rising pitch, a falling and rising pitch, or a falling pitch: 'mother', 'hemp', 'horse', 'curse', respectively; and (iii) intonation, which can, for example, distinguish statements like *She eats pizza* (said with falling pitch towards the end of the sentence) from questions like *She eats pizza?* (said with rising pitch towards the end of the sentence).

As in the development of other L2 linguistic knowledge, three key factors play a role: the L1, input and processes that appear to apply universally in acquisition.

This chapter discusses in turn the L2 acquisition of segments, syllable structure and prosody. The discussion presupposes some knowledge of how linguistic sounds are produced. For readers unfamiliar with this topic, a brief outline is given in an appendix to the chapter.

7.2 Segments

The number of linguistic sounds available to the world's languages for forming language-specific sound systems has been estimated at 200–300 (Ashby and Maidment, 2005: 2). However, each individual language selects a relatively small number of possibilities from this universal set. For example, while English, depending on the variety, uses 20–24 consonant sounds (sounds like [b], [p], [s], [z] and so on), Russian uses 32 and Japanese 19 (Larson-Hall, 2004).

Some of the linguistic sounds that are used in a language distinguish the meanings of different morphemes. For example, *goal* and *coal* are not the same thing. The sound structure of these morphemes differs minimally in the first segment: 'g' and 'k' are both stop sounds that are formed by making a closure between the main body of the tongue and a part of the palate at the back of the mouth known as the velum, followed by the release of air. The difference between them is one of voicing: 'g' is a voiced velar stop, 'k' is a voiceless velar stop. Segments that distinguish the meaning of morphemes in a language are known as **phonemes**; 'g' and 'k' are phonemes of English. Every language has its own particular phonological system (the set of phonemes it has selected to distinguish morphemes from each other).

But not all of the physical properties of sounds that are found as part of a language's sound system are relevant to distinguishing word meanings. Compare the following:

1 a. Where did you put the keys?
   b. Where did you put the skis?

Speakers of standard educated British English produce two different 'k' sounds here. In *key*, where 'k' is the initial consonant in the word, an audible release of air follows the closure made by the tongue with the velum. If you speak English with a British accent you might be able to feel this if you hold the palm of your hand close to your mouth and say *key* vigorously. Now do the same thing with the word *ski*. You should find that there is little or no puff of air. The puff of air that follows the release of the closure made by the tongue with the velum in *key* is known as 'aspiration'. It is represented in phonetic transcription by a small ʰ following k: [kʰi]. Aspiration is absent in *ski*: [ski].

The phonetic distinction between aspirated and unaspirated [k] is not relevant to word meaning in English. It does not matter whether *key* is pronounced as [kʰi] or [ki] – it still has the same meaning. But in some languages the aspirated/non-aspirated contrast is relevant to meaning. In Hindi the following two words are distinct (examples from Graddol et al., 1994: 50):

2. kʰana   'to eat'
   kana   'one-eyed'

So a distinction needs to be made between **phones**, which are actual speech sounds, and **phonemes**, which are categories of sound that are relevant for distinguishing one morpheme from another. Linguists have adopted the convention of representing phones in square brackets [ ], and phonemes between slant brackets / /. [kʰ] and [k] are phones realising the English phoneme /k/ that appear in contextually-determined positions (word-initial vs other contexts). But they are separate phonemes /kʰ/ and /k/ in Hindi.

7.2.1 Identifying and Learning Phones and Phonemes

At birth, children appear to be sensitive to the full range of linguistic sounds that might be relevant to the sound system of any language. This is highly desirable because infants cannot know in advance which language(s) they might be exposed to. But as they get more exposure to the language(s) spoken around them, they focus on just those sounds that are relevant to distinguishing the meaning of morphemes, and ignore others. Again, this is highly desirable. Being able to ignore irrelevant linguistic noise helps the child identify new morphemes more quickly.

Werker and Tees (1984) were able to show this pattern of development by using a 'head turn' procedure. In this procedure the infant sits on the parent or carer's lap facing someone from the research team. There is a loudspeaker to one side of the researcher. The loudspeaker plays a continuous background stimulus of syllables (like *tatatatatatabababababa* …). Initially, children are interested in the sounds and look at the loudspeaker. If the same sound continues, however, as in the case of *tatatatatata*, they lose interest and look at other more interesting things. It has been found, though, that if they detect a change in the stimulus, for example a change from *tatatatatata* to *bababa*, this arouses their interest, and they tend to look at the loudspeaker again. By measuring the child's head turn in these cases one can determine whether he or she has detected a change or not.

Werker and Tees were interested in testing children for two specific consonant contrasts that do not distinguish word meaning in English, but do in Hindi and Salish (a native Canadian language). The first is a contrast between a voiceless alveolar/dental stop [t], found in both English and Hindi, and a voiceless alveolar retroflex flap [ɽ] (produced by curling the tip of the tongue behind the crescent of bone located just behind the upper front teeth – the alveolar ridge – and then flapping it forwards) found only in Hindi. The second is a contrast between a voiceless velar stop [k], found in both English and Salish, and a voiceless stop produced a bit further back in the mouth by a closure between the tongue and uvula, the voiceless uvular stop [q], found only in Salish.

They tested children who were learning each of the three languages natively. The English children ranged in age from six to twelve months. They were compared with native Hindi and Salish speakers who were twelve months old. The results from the study show that at six to eight months, children being exposed to English are almost as good at detecting the contrast between syllables like [ta] and [ɽa] (over 90% responses to a change from [ta] to [ɽa]) as twelve-month-old children being exposed to Hindi (100% response to the change). The same children are nearly as good at detecting a [ki]–[qi] contrast (over 80% responses to the change) as twelve-month-old children being exposed to Salish (100% response to the change). However, by eight to ten months the responses of the English-acquiring infants drop to 70% for the [ta]–[ɽa] contrast and just over 50% for the [ki]-[qi] contrast. And by ten to twelve months the responses of English-learning children drop to 20% or less to both contrasts. At a similar age the Hindi-acquiring and Salish-acquiring children are showing 100% responses to the contrast that distinguishes meanings in their language. These results suggest that although infants initially have the ability to identify all of the linguistic sounds that can be found in languages, they quickly select those relevant for the phonological system of the ambient language, and ignore those that are not.

In the context of L2 learning, the sound system of another language may contain phones and phonemes that are the same as those in a learner's L1, are similar (but differ in certain ways) to those in a learner's L1, or that are not found in the L1 at all. Given the picture of L1 acquisition presented above, where sensitivity to sounds not relevant to distinguishing meaning in a speaker's L1(s) decreases with experience with the L1(s), it is not surprising that the selection of phones and phonemes made during L1 acquisition has a strong influence on the perception and production of phones and phonemes in the L2. When the sounds are the same, L2 learners may have little difficulty perceiving or producing them. However, where sounds in the L2 are similar to those in the L1, but differ along certain dimensions, or have no counterpart in the L1, learners may not perceive these differences initially, and sometimes may fail to do so over long periods, leading to persistent 'foreign accent', as in the case of Joseph Conrad. The effects of these differences will be considered first in the case of phones that do not distinguish morphemes, and then in the case of phonemes.

Sections 7.1 to 7.2.1 in a Nutshell

To explain why some L2 learners retain strong foreign accents while others might sound almost like native speakers, the acquisition of three dimensions of sound systems needs to be considered: the acquisition of segments, the acquisition of syllables and the acquisition of prosody. Although there are 200–300 potential sound segments available to the world's languages, each language selects only a small number of these to create its individual sound system. Infants appear to be sensitive to the full range of universally available sounds at birth, but over the first year of life become sensitive only to those sounds that are relevant for the L1. Sounds that distinguish the meanings of morphemes in a language are called phonemes. /k/ is a phoneme of English because it distinguishes words like *cat* from *hat* and *mat*. Aspirated [kʰ] and unaspirated [k] are found in English, and are phonetically distinct, but they are contextually determined, [k] being used after [s]. [kʰ] and [k] are phones that are exponents of the phoneme /k/. Given that part of acquiring an L1 sound system is learning to ignore linguistic sounds that are not relevant to that system, L2 learners are likely to have initial difficulty perceiving L2 sounds that do not occur in their L1.

7.2.2 Learning L2 Sounds at the Sub-Phoneme Level

The sub-phonemic contrast in English between aspirated and unaspirated stop sounds described above ([pʰ]–[p], [tʰ]–[t], [kʰ]–[k]) does not exist in Italian. Italian word-initial stops sound very similar to the stops in English that follow [s] in words like *ski, spy, stop*. Another way of looking at this contrast is in terms of the time it takes the voicing of the following vowel to begin after the release of air following the closure made for the stop. This is known as **voice onset time** (VOT). The VOTs following English word-initial [pʰ] and [tʰ] are typically 57 and 60 milliseconds (ms), whereas the typical VOTs for Italian word-initial [p] and [t] are 12ms and 17ms respectively (Flege et al., 1996: 58). When Italian speakers learn English as an L2, how do they treat this contrast between L2 and L1 sounds that does not affect meaning distinctions?

Flege et al. (1996) looked at the pronunciation of English word-initial [pʰ] and [tʰ] by 240 native speakers of Italian who had lived in English-speaking Ottawa for over thirty years. Some of these had arrived in Canada when they were children, others when they were teenagers or in their early 20s. Participants in the study were asked to produce twenty-five one-syllable words like *pick, tack* in a 'carrier phrase', 'Now I say …' (e.g. *Now I say pick, Now I say tack*), so that the words were not produced in isolation. It was found that participants who had arrived at or after the age of fifteen produced these words with significantly shorter VOTs than native English-speaking control participants and those Italian speakers who had arrived before the age of fifteen.

It appears, then, that the extent to which L2 learners can produce L2 sounds that differ from those in the L1 at the sub-phoneme level (at least in the case of VOT), is affected by the age at which they are first exposed to the L2. Those L2 learners exposed to English in their middle teens or later appear to assimilate word-initial English stops to the representation they already have for such sounds in their L1, and continue to do so despite long exposure to the L2 (more than thirty years). Those exposed to L2 English before the age of fifteen appear more likely to establish VOTs that are closer to the target language norm.

Nevertheless, even for the older starters, exposure to English had some effect on those representations. Although the VOTs of the post-fifteen learners were significantly shorter than those of native speakers, they were not as short as the typical VOTs of monolingual speakers of Italian. The L2 learners appear to have noticed at some level that English word-initial stops give rise to longer VOTs than Italian stops, and have partially re-adjusted their mental representations for these sounds. The level at which 'noticing' occurs is below conscious awareness. Speakers are generally not aware of phonetic differences that are not phonemic. Speakers of Italian are not consciously aware of VOTs with stop consonants in their native language or of the fact that VOTs in English are different. They have an unconscious set of rules for articulating sounds in their native language that includes a specification for the VOT following the release of stops. The input they get from English leads to an unconscious modification of that specification.

7.2.3 Learning that a Sub-Phonemic Contrast in the L1 is Phonemic in the L2

It was observed above that the contrast between aspirated and unaspirated stops (those giving rise to long or short voice onset times for the following vowel) is not phonemic in English. It does not matter whether one pronounces the word *pit* as [pʰɪt] or [pɪt], it is still the same word. It was also noted that speakers of English and Italian are not consciously aware of such systematic differences in the form of phones when they do not contribute to distinguishing morphemes.

In other languages, however, the contrast between aspirated and unaspirated stops is phonemic. And speakers are consciously aware of the difference because it distinguishes word meaning. This is the case in Thai, where different pronunciations of 'pit' have different meanings (examples from Curtin et al., 1998):

3. /pɪt/   'cake'
   /pʰɪt/   'flower'

How easy is it for L2 learners to recognise that a sub-phonemic distinction in their L1 serves to distinguish word meanings in an L2? That is, how easy is it to turn unconscious awareness of a contrast between phones into conscious awareness of a contrast between phonemes?

TABLE 7.1 Accuracy in matching heard Thai words to pictures (based on Curtin et al., 1998: 367, Table 1)

	pʰ vs p / tʰ vs t	pʰ vs b / tʰ vs d	p vs b / t vs d
Day 4	63%	95%	77%
Day 11	68%	95%	82%

Curtin et al. taught nine English speakers (in their 20s), who had never encountered Thai before, eighteen one-syllable Thai words over a three-day period. Teaching involved pairing aurally presented words with pictures (e.g. hearing the Thai word /pʰɪt/ while looking at a picture of a flower). The words all began with stop consonants, but either differed in aspiration (e.g. /tʰak/ 'shoe' – /tak/ 'cat') a contrast that does not exist in English, or in voicing (e.g. /tʰak/ 'shoe' – /dak/ 'bucket') a contrast that does. At the end of the teaching period participants were given a test where they were shown pairs of pictures and simultaneously heard a Thai word. The task was to select the picture that corresponded to the heard word. For example, if one picture depicted a cat and the other a shoe, and the word heard was /tak/, a correct answer would be the picture depicting the cat. Participants were tested on the day after the teaching sessions (day 4) and seven days later (day 11). Accuracy results are presented in table 7.1.

Table 7.1 shows that participants were most successful in identifying Thai words distinguished by phonemes that also distinguish meaning in English – those beginning with voiceless aspirated stops versus those beginning with voiced stops (column 2). They were least successful in identifying Thai words beginning with voiceless stops that differed only in VOT, a contrast that exists in English but is not phonemic (column 1). And they had intermediate success in identifying Thai words beginning with stops that differed in voicing, but where the voiceless stop had a short VOT (column 3). This difference in performance on the contrasts in columns 3 and 2 is not surprising given that voiceless stops with short VOTs are much closer acoustically to voiced stops (where voicing begins before the release of the stop), and a difference between them is more difficult to perceive than a contrast between voiceless stops with long VOTs and voiced stops.

The results suggest that in the early stages of learning an L2 phonemic contrast that is sub-phonemic in the L1, learners are not immediately able to convert distinctions they are making unconsciously in their L1 into phonemically relevant categories.

A similar shift from a sub-phonemic to a phonemic mental representation is required of Spanish speakers learning the contrast in English between /d/ and /ð/, as in the pair *day–they*. In Spanish, [ð] is a phonetic realisation of the phoneme /d/ when it follows a vowel, as in *nada* [naðə] 'nothing'. Just as in the case of English speakers learning Thai, Spanish speakers have to become aware that a sub-phonemic contrast in their L1 distinguishes meaning in the L2 in cases like *day–they, breathe–breed, other–udder*.

Eckman et al. (2003) looked at awareness of the phonemic contrast /d/–/ð/ in a group of seven Spanish speakers aged between seventeen and thirty-one who were enrolled on an intensive English programme in the US. By asking participants to describe pictures that elicit words like *cloudy, bathing, ladder, leather*, Eckman et al. established that the participants were producing the /d/–/ð/ contrast with less than 80 per cent accuracy. Participants were then trained on invented words showing the distinction, like *goudy* [gudi], *gouthy* [guði] . As the result of training, all the participants came to produce the contrast following a vowel accurately in over 80 per cent of cases, suggesting that with exposure to examples of the relevant target-language phonemic contrast, L2 learners can bring the unconscious knowledge they have in the L1 to conscious awareness.

7.2.4 Learning New Phonemes in the L2

English has the vowel phonemes /u/ as in *two, soon* and /i/ as in *tea, see*. French not only has /u/ and /i/ in words like *tous* 'all', *si* 'if', but also the phoneme /y/ in words like *tu* 'you', *su* 'known'. The /y/ phoneme is realised by a tongue shape that is similar to the tongue shape for [i] accompanied by rounding of the lips; /y/ does not exist in English. So when L1 English speakers acquire French they have to acquire a new phoneme that will contrast with /u/ and /i/. Furthermore, the quality of the [u] phone that realises /u/ in French is different from the phone that realises /u/ in English. Roughly speaking, the English [u] is more lax and the tongue is more central in the vocal tract (O'Connor, 1973: 162) than French [u].

Flege (1987) studied how successful English speakers were at acquiring the new phoneme /y/ in French and also the extent to which they were able to acquire the sub-phonemic difference in the quality of French [u] compared with English [u]. Participants in his study were all adults. There were three groups who had started learning French as an L2 in late adolescence or early adulthood: a low-proficiency group, an advanced-proficiency group and a very advanced-proficiency group (who had been living in France for an average of 11.7 years). There was also a group of monolingual English speakers and a group of monolingual French speakers. Flege asked his monolingual English speakers to read a set of phrases like *two little boys* containing the phoneme /u/ and then use those phrases to make up sentences. This provided baseline information about the quality of the [u] phone in English. He asked the monolingual French speakers to do the same with French phrases like *tous les soldats* 'all the soldiers', *tu les regardes* 'you watch them', containing the phonemes /u/ and /y/. This was to provide baseline information about the vowel quality of French [u] and [y]. The three groups of L2 learners then performed the same task in both languages.

Results show that all the L2 learners of French produced [y] in a way that was acoustically closely parallel to the production of [y] by the monolingual French speakers. Only the low-proficiency group were statistically different from the monolingual French group. This suggests that completely new phoneme contrasts in an L2 are acquirable, and that they may be acquired quite quickly.

By contrast, all three L2 groups failed to approximate to the vowel quality of French [u] produced by the French monolingual group. Even the very advanced speakers who had lived in France for many years continued to produce an [u] that was closer to the [u] produced by the monolingual English group than the French monolinguals. This is consistent with the findings of Flege et al. (1996) discussed in section 7.2.2 that Italian-speaking L2 learners of English over the age of fifteen did not fully acquire the voice onset time of the English stop consonants [pʰ], [tʰ], [kʰ], even after long exposure to English. However, like the L2 speakers in that study, as proficiency in French increased, speakers produced an [u] sound that was intermediate between the English and French vowel sounds.

French does not use the consonant sounds represented by the English orthography 'th' in words like *think, this*. These are fricative sounds, produced by placing the tip of the tongue on the upper teeth and allowing air to pass over the tongue. The voiced segment [ð] appears in words like ***this, bathe***, the voiceless segment [θ] appears in words like ***think, both***. When native speakers of French initially learn English, it has been suggested that they often assimilate the 'th' sounds of English to sounds that do exist in French, are also fricatives, and are produced at a position in the mouth that is close to the upper teeth: the [s] and [z] sounds. So they pronounce *think* as *sink*, and *this* as *zis*.

Weinberger (1997) has observed that speakers of languages that lack [θ] and [ð] do not all assimilate these sounds to [s] and [z] when they learn English, even though [s] and [z] exist in their native languages. Speakers of Russian pronounce *think* and *this* as *tink* and *dis*. These sounds are similar to [θ] and [ð] in being dental (produced at the upper teeth) but they are different in being stop sounds. So French learners of English identify the fricative nature of 'th' but move the tongue position from the teeth to the alveolar ridge, whereas Russian speakers identify the dental nature of 'th' and change the manner of articulation from fricative to stop.

Weinberger argues that these cases of 'differential substitution' arise because within the overall sound system of French, [s]/[z] are specified for fewer articulatory/acoustic features than [t]/[d], whereas within the overall sound system of Russian, [t]/[d] are specified for fewer features than [s]/[z]. When speakers of these languages learn English and encounter the 'th' sounds, they initially replace them with sounds from the L1 that share some of the features of 'th' sounds. Where there are potential competitors the L1 sounds with the fewest specified articulatory/acoustic features are chosen as the default.

Wenk (1979) provides evidence that suggests that French speakers' substitutions for /θ, ð/ are somewhat more variable than Weinberger assumes, but that there is a developmental pattern whose endpoint is a good approximation to the dental fricatives of English native speakers. He gave thirteen French-speaking learners of

English at the University of Strasbourg, of different proficiency levels in English, a test that included free speech, imitation and reading. This produced 650 contexts where /θ, ð/ could be produced. He found a tendency for the least proficient speakers to substitute /f, v/ for /θ, ð/, maintaining the fricative manner of articulation, but changing the active articulator from the tongue to the lower lip. (Both /f, v/ are phonemes in French.) More proficient speakers tended to substitute not only /s, z/ for /θ, ð/, but also /t, d/. The most proficient speakers were producing target-like dental fricatives. It appears then that a completely new phoneme in a target L2 may initially be equated with a phoneme in the L1 that is phonologically similar along some dimension, but with longer exposure to the target language the new phoneme will be acquired.

Sections 7.2.2 to 7.2.4 in a Nutshell

Adolescent and adult L2 learners typically show persistent L1 influence in producing L2 sounds that differ from the L1 at the sub-phoneme level. L1 Italian speakers who had long experience of living in English-speaking Ottawa, but who had arrived when they were fifteen or older, were significantly different from native English speakers in voice onset time (VOT) of their word-initial English stops – [pʰ], [tʰ], [kʰ]. They unconsciously adopted VOTs intermediate between those of Italian and English word-initial stops. Italian speakers who had arrived in the same environment before the age of fifteen acquired the English VOT values (Flege et al., 1996). English speakers acquiring French showed a similar failure to acquire the sub-phonemic difference between the realisation of English /u/ and French /u/ (Flege, 1987).

However, sub-phonemic contrasts in the L1 that have a phonemic value in the L2 appear to be acquirable, although this may only occur at higher levels of proficiency. English speakers initially learning the phonemic contrast in Thai between aspirated and unaspirated /pʰ, p/, /tʰ, t/ are less successful at distinguishing them than they are at distinguishing the voiceless/voiced contrast /pʰ, b/ that exists in English (Curtin et al., 1998). But Eckman et al. (2003) found that Spanish speakers were able to produce the English /d, ð/ phoneme contrast with over 80 per cent accuracy after training, even though the distinction is sub-phonemic in Spanish.

Entirely new phonemes appear to be acquirable. English speakers of advanced proficiency in L2 French produce the phoneme /y/ in a way that is acoustically close to the production of native speakers (Flege, 1987). French speakers of advanced proficiency in L2 English can approximate the acoustic quality of /θ, ð/, despite this contrast not existing in French (Wenk, 1979).

7.2.5 Learning a Phonemic Contrast in the L2 that Conflates onto a Single Phoneme in the L1

A Japanese-speaking student who had been learning English for many years, and was undertaking doctoral studies in an English-speaking university, wanted to sell a lamp she no longer needed. She knew that a good place to advertise was the noticeboard in the Student Union building. So she put up a postcard with the headline 'Ramp for Sale'. Fortunately, one of her friends spotted the card and changed the 'R' to an 'L'.

This example is representative. Native speakers of Japanese are persistently variable in perceiving and producing the phonemic contrast that exists in English between /l/ and /r/ in initial and medial position in words like *lamp/ramp, collect/correct*. Phonetically, these segments are produced at or just behind the alveolar ridge. In the case of [l], the tongue tip makes a complete closure with the ridge, and air is released down the sides of the tongue. (You can feel this by making the tongue position for [l] and sucking air in. You should feel the air passing down the underside of your tongue). [r] is produced by making a partial closure between the tongue tip and a position just behind the alveolar ridge and pushing air over the top of the tongue between the gap. Because in the production of both [l] and [r] there is less frication ('hissing') than in the case of fricative consonants like [z] and [v], [l] and [r] are known as approximants.

The closest phoneme that Japanese has to English /l/ and /r/ is an alveolar flap /ɾ/ where the tongue tip is retracted to behind the alveolar ridge and then flapped forward. Like English /l/ and /r/, /ɾ/ is voiced and produced around the alveolar ridge. It differs in being a flap rather than an approximant.

Perceiving and producing a phonemic contrast between /l/ and /r/ is not inherently difficult for L2 speakers. A study by Iverson et al. (2003) shows that native speakers of German have no difficulty with it. They compared twenty-four Japanese-speaking learners of English with twelve German-speaking learners of English. Both groups had been exposed to English for the same length of time (7.5 years of classroom instruction). German has an /l/–/r/ phoneme contrast, although the phone realising German /r/ is produced by bringing the back of the tongue close to the tip of the velum (known as the 'uvula'), so phonetically the German realisation of /r/ is quite different from the realisation of English /r/. Using a discrimination task where participants were asked to decide whether pairs of syllables like [la]–[ra], [la]–[la], [ra]–[ra] were similar or different, Iverson et al. found that the German speakers had no difficulty deciding whether pairs were similar or different, whereas the Japanese learners did.

Nor is perceiving other phonemic contrasts in an L2 that conflate onto a single phoneme in the L1 inherently difficult for Japanese speakers. Japanese has a voiceless bilabial fricative phoneme /ɸ/ (produced by rounding the lips and blowing through them), but no /f/–/v/ contrast. /f/ and /v/ are like /ɸ/ in being fricatives and involving the lips (more specifically a partial closure between the lower lip and the

TABLE 7.2 Percentage group accuracy in identifying phoneme contrasts in Russian (adapted from Larson-Hall, 2004: 57, Table 9)

Contrast	Beginner (n = 11)	Intermediate (n = 12)	Advanced (n = 10)	Native Speakers (n = 8)
/l/ vs /r/	71	78	82	98
/f/ vs /v/	100	100	98	100

upper front teeth). Larson-Hall (2004) has shown that Japanese speakers are much less variable in the perception of this contrast than in the perception of the /l/–/r/ contrast. Her study looked at thirty-three Japanese-speaking university learners who were learning Russian, divided into three groups: beginner (n = 11), intermediate (n = 12) and advanced (n = 10), compared with eight native speakers. Russian has both an /l/–/r/ and /f/–/v/ contrast, like English. The task for the participants was to listen to pairs of invented (but plausibly Russian-sounding) one-syllable words, like those in (4), and to indicate which of the pairs contained different 'words':

4. (i) laf, raf   (ii) raf, raf
   (i) faf, faf   (ii) faf, vaf

While her study tested the perception of sixteen different phoneme contrasts, the results just from the /l/–/r/ and /f/–/v/ pairs are shown in table 7.2.

It can be seen that while the Japanese speakers improve in distinguishing Russian /l/ and /r/ as they become more proficient, their perception of the contrast remains variable. By contrast even from the beginner level their perception of the /f/–/v/ contrast is effectively categorical.

Larson-Hall argues that to understand this pattern of behaviour it is necessary to go beyond the specific phones and phonemes to look at the articulatory/acoustic features that define them, just as we needed to look at the role of abstract morpho-syntactic features to understand L2 speakers' acquisition of morphology and syntax (see chapters 3 to 5). She suggests that one of the features needed in English and Russian to distinguish /l/ from /r/ is [lateral]. The one major difference between /l/ and /r/ is that in the case of /l/ air passes laterally down the sides of the tongue, whereas it passes over the top of the tongue in the case of /r/. Japanese does not need the feature [lateral] because it has no /l/–/r/ contrast. In the early months after birth, children growing up in a Japanese-speaking environment are capable of distinguishing /l/ and /r/, because they have access to the universal set of features required to distinguish segments in any language. But as they grow older and become more proficient in their native language, features that are not relevant to their native language drop out of the inventory of active features. Later, when Japanese speakers encounter the /l/–/r/ contrast, they are unable initially to establish it successfully in their mental grammars because they have no way of representing the contrast. However, with longer exposure to a language that has this phonemic contrast they may be able to bring [lateral] back into the set of active features that they use for perceiving and producing phonemic contrasts.

In the case of the /f/–/v/ contrast, the features involved are already active in distinguishing other contrasts in Japanese: [voice] is required in contrasts like /t/–/d/, [labial] is required in contrasts like /p/–/t/, and [continuant] is a feature needed to distinguish fricatives like /s/ from stops like /t/. So, even though /f/–/v/ is a new contrast for Japanese learners of English or Russian, they can perceive the contrast very early because they can identify the features that determine the contrast using their L1 grammar.

Section 7.2.5 in a Nutshell

Where a phoneme contrast in the L2 conflates onto a single phoneme in the L1, for example English/Russian /l/–/r/ conflating onto Japanese /ɾ/ and /f/–/v/ conflating onto Japanese /ɸ/, difficulty in establishing the L2 contrast is related to whether the L1 has instantiated the relevant abstract articulatory/acoustic features. Larson-Hall (2004) argues that Japanese does not instantiate the feature [lateral] which is necessary for distinguishing the /l/–/r/ contrast, but it has instantiated the features [voice], [labial] and [continuant] that are necessary for distinguishing the /f/–/v/ contrast. Japanese-speaking L2 learners of Russian acquire the /f/–/v/ contrast even from early levels of proficiency, but acquiring the /l/–/r/ contrast takes them much longer.

7.3 Syllables

7.3.1 Syllable Structure Differences between Languages and their Effect on Pronunciation

To be usable in speech production and perception, segments are organised into **syllables**. These are the minimal pronounceable units. They usually consist of a core vowel (referred to as the nucleus of the syllable) that may or may not be accompanied by preceding segments (known as the onset) and following segments (known as the coda). The nucleus and the coda together form a unit known as the rhyme.

Syllables are the basis of the forms that realise morphemes. Morphemes can be realised by single syllables, as in the case of *bed, egg, shoe* etc., or by more than one syllable: *kit-chen, ba-sket, con-fi-dent, or-gan-ise* and so on.

All languages organise their segments into syllables for production and perception. They differ in the segments they select from the universal set available (see section 7.2) to populate syllables, and in the number and type of segments they allow in onset and coda position. In English, onsets can be null or consist of up to three consonants:

5 a. are   /ɑː/[1]

   car   /kɑː/

   scar   /skɑː/

   screw   /skru/

Codas can also be null or consist of up to three consonants:

   b. egg   /ɛg/

   elk   /ɛlk/

   text   /tɛkst/

Some languages allow even more segments in onset or coda position. Others are more restrictive than English.

Where an L2 learner's L1 has more restrictions on syllable structure than the L2, this appears to exert a persistent influence on that learner's pronunciation of the L2. For example, while English allows onset clusters of two or three segments where the first one is an [s], Spanish does not. Spanish allows a maximum of two segments in syllable onset position (for example *pl, tr, gl, fr*), but the first segment cannot be an [s]. An effect of this is that Spanish-speaking learners of English are often heard adding a vowel at the beginning of words like *scar, splash, screech*: *escar* [ɪskɑː], *esplash* [ɪsplaʃ], *escreech* [ɪskriːʧ]. Carlisle (1997) asked eleven Spanish speakers of intermediate proficiency in English to read a series of sentences like *The soup spilled, Jeff sprinted down the track*, and found that they added a vowel in front of *sp-, spr-* about half the time. Why do they do this?

The answer is that because Spanish onsets are restricted to clusters that do not involve an initial [s], Spanish-speaking learners of English cannot fit the [s] into the syllable. They are forced to create an additional preceding syllable by inserting a vowel with [s] as its coda. Effectively they are turning monosyllabic morphemes like *scar, splash, screech* into bisyllabic morphemes. The insertion of a vowel to create a new syllable is known as **epenthesis** (an epenthetic vowel is added to the syllable structure).

A similar pattern holds in coda position for speakers of L1s with more restrictions on codas than the target L2. Mandarin Chinese only allows a single nasal consonant [n, ŋ] or a single approximant [j, r] in coda position. Broselow et al. (1998) asked ten Mandarin speakers of intermediate proficiency in English to listen to and memorise invented (but plausibly English) words that were provided with definitions. The invented words had codas that consisted of a voiceless or voiced stop (one of p/b, t/d or k/g), e.g. *vig*. None of these are possible codas in Mandarin, so *vig* is not a plausible Mandarin word. Participants were subsequently given the definitions with a choice of three possible forms and asked to read the one that matched the definition.

---

[1] This is British English. In some varieties of American English *are* is realised with an [r] in coda position: [ɑːr])

Broselow et al. found that of the 180 words produced by the participants, few were pronounced in a target-like way. Participants mostly either simply omitted the final consonant, pronouncing *vig* as [vɪ], or inserted an epenthetic vowel to create an additional syllable: [vɪ.gə]. Again, L1 syllable constraints show persistent influence on the development of L2 pronunciation. L2 speakers appear to filter L2 forms through their mental representations for L1 syllables, creating morphemes that conform to those representations.

An example of the strength of L1 syllable structure constraints on the way that L2 speakers treat target-language morphemes is provided by Broselow (1983, 1988), who noticed an interesting difference in the use of epenthetic vowels in L2 English by L1 speakers of two varieties of Arabic: Eqyptian and Iraqi. Speakers of these varieties insert an epenthetic vowel differently in consonant clusters in words like: *children, **plastic**, **Fred**, **translate**:

6. *Egyptian*   *Iraqi*
   chi**ldir**en   chi**lidr**en
   bilastic   **ibl**astic   (= 'plastic')
   Fired   **iFr**ed
   tiransi**l**ate   **itr**ani**sl**ate

Both Egyptian and Iraqi Arabic have the same syllable structure: CVC (Consonant–Vowel–Consonant) is the maximal allowable syllable, so you can have constructions like:

7 a. katablu 'he wrote to him' (Egyptian Arabic)
   b. ka-tab-lu (CV-CVC-CV)

but not constructions like:

8 a. *katabtlu 'I wrote to him'
   b. *ka-tab-t-lu (CV-CVC-C-CV)

because the 't' cannot be assigned to the syllable to its left or right. This would yield a *CVCC or *CCV structure, which is impossible in both varieties of Arabic. In this case Egyptian Arabic inserts an epenthetic vowel to the right of the problematic consonant:

9 a. katabtilu
   b. ka-tab-ti-lu

Iraqi Arabic, however, inserts an epenthetic vowel to the left of the problematic consonant:

10 a. *ki-tab-t-la 'I wrote to him'
    b. ki-ta-bit-la

The properties of syllable structure in Arabic and the strategy for rescuing problematic consonant clusters appear to be transferred into English in the speakers Broselow studied. If the behaviour displayed in the English samples were the result of general L2 development rather than L1 influence, we would not expect to see a difference in the placement of the epenthetic vowel between the two groups of speakers.

Broselow and Park (1995) also observed an interesting property in the L2 English **phonology** of native speakers of Korean. Sometimes these speakers add an extra vowel at the end of English monosyllabic words, and sometimes they do not, for example:

11. *Extra vowel added* *No extra vowel*
    beat-i   bit
    cheap-i   tip
    peak-i   pick
    coat-i   book

Broselow and Park argue that the vowels in the words of the first column are double-weighted (are equivalent in duration to two short vowels of the kind illustrated in the second column). Korean does not allow syllables whose rhymes consist of double-weighted vowels followed by a consonant. Only a single-weighted vowel with a following consonant is possible. The English words in the second column are unproblematic for the Korean speakers because they conform to Korean syllable constraints (a single-weighted vowel followed by a consonant). Broselow and Park suggest that in the case of the first set of words these speakers recognise that the vowel is double-weighted in English, but because this conflicts with the constraint on syllable structure in their L1, they shift half of the weight to after the following consonant, creating two-syllabled words where each nucleus is single-weighted: [bɪ-tɪ], [ko-tɪ] etc., rather than the native [bi:t], [kout]. This is a rather subtle case of interaction between awareness of the phonological properties of the L2 and the influence of the L1.

7.3.2 A Syllable-Based Account of L2 Optionality

In chapter 3 possible explanations were considered for the observation that L2 learners of English optionally produce both bare and inflected verb forms like *walk/walks, swim/swam* in contexts where the inflected form is obligatory for native speakers. In that chapter the explanations were morpho-syntactic or lexical in nature. Goad, White and Steele (2003) have proposed a different account of such optionality based on the different ways in which languages organise syllables into larger units. Where an L1 and L2 differ in such organisation, Goad et al. propose that the L1 inhibits acquisition of the L2 organisation, just as was seen in the case of Spanish-, Arabic- and Korean-speaking L2 learners' acquisition of English onsets, codas and rhymes, and this gives rise to the kind of optionality observed.

Goad et al.'s account assumes two universal principles that constrain syllable organisation.[2] The first is that syllable rhymes (the nucleus + coda of a syllable)

---

[2] These principles are justified within the particular model of phonology assumed by Goad et al. One has to accept them for their account to go through.

maximally consist of two segments. Words like *ban* [bæn], *try* [traj] conform to this constraint. However, *bank* [bæŋk] and *arrive* [ərajv] do not, because their rhymes consist of three segments: [æ – ŋ – k] and [a – j – v] respectively. This requires that the final constituent becomes the onset of a new final syllable with its own null nucleus: [bæŋ.kØ], [ə.raj.vØ]. This means that *bank* is a two-syllable morpheme and *arrive* a three-syllable morpheme, although on the surface we only perceive them as monosyllabic and disyllabic respectively. They each form what Goad et al. call a prosodic word (PWd). When inflectional suffixes realising past tense (*arrive -d*) or third person non-past tense subject–verb agreement (*arrive -s*) merge with these PWds they add a further syllable: [ə.raj.vØ.dØ], [ə.raj.vØ.zØ]. Now the second universal principle comes into play: a prohibition on adjacent empty nuclei within the same PWd. The realisations of past tense and third person non-past tense subject–verb agreement therefore cannot be incorporated into the verb's PWd, but must be adjoined to it to form an extended PWd:

(12).

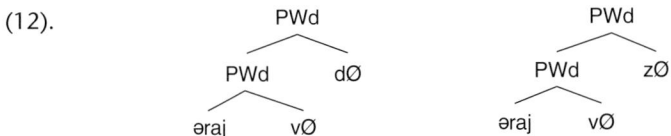

Given these assumptions, there is a syllable-based difference in English between regular past tense verb forms like *arrived* and irregular past tense verb forms like *slept*. Although *sleep* is a two-syllabled PWd, [_PWd slij.pØ], in its irregular past tense form the [ij] diphthong is shortened to a single segment [ɛ], allowing the past tense [t] to be incorporated into the PWd without adjunction: [_PWd slɛp.tØ]. Regular past tense verbs therefore typically involve the creation of an extended PWd through adjunction [_PWd [_PWd ...]] while irregular past tense verbs typically do not.

Goad et al. observe that some languages do not allow the creation of extended PWds through adjunction. Mandarin Chinese is one of them. Although Mandarin has suffixal morphemes, like the aspectual morpheme *-le* that signals completion, these incorporate into the host morpheme's PWd. For example *mai-le* (lit. 'buy-completion') 'bought' has the syllable structure [_PWd maj.lə].

Goad et al. then argue that when Mandarin-speaking L2 learners of English optionally use bare English verb forms in contexts where an inflected verb form is required, they fail to pronounce the inflection if it cannot be incorporated into the PWd. That is, syllable-structure organisation in their L1 inhibits their pronunciation of inflectional morphemes in the L2. This Prosodic Transfer Hypothesis (PTH) is a variation on the Missing Surface Inflection Hypothesis. Learners have fully represented abstract morphemes like past tense and third person singular non-past tense subject–verb agreement in their mental grammars for English. The absence of the forms of these morphemes from the learner's speech results from the filtering effect of the organisation of syllables into larger groupings in their L1.

Evidence to support the PTH comes from a study that Goad et al. conducted of the use of third person non-past tense subject–verb agreement with twelve

Mandarin-speaking learners of English of high-intermediate to low-advanced proficiency who had been living in Canada for between six months and five years.
Oral data were elicited by asking participants to describe a sequence of pictures
illustrating a typical day in a woman's life. Overall this produced fifty-seven tokens
of verb + third person singular subject–verb agreement in 201 obligatory contexts
for the use of that form. That is, participants were producing verbs without the
inflection in 72 per cent of cases.

Looking more closely at individual performance, Goad et al. found that six of
the participants were supplying the third person singular subject–verb agreement
inflection in only 10 per cent of cases. They refer to these as the across-the-board
deletion group; these participants simply were unable to accommodate English
inflection within the restrictions imposed by their L1 on adjunction to the PWd.
The other six participants are more interesting for the PTH. This group supplied
the third person singular subject–verb agreement inflection in 49 per cent of obligatory contexts. But the contexts in which the inflection was produced were those
where it is possible to incorporate inflection into the verb's PWd. These are cases
like *fills*, where the inflection forms the second syllable of the PWd: [$_{PWd}$ fɪl.zØ].
Production of the inflection in such contexts was 75 per cent. Similarly, where the
inflection was followed by a word beginning with a vowel to which the inflection
could attach as an onset, production was high (68 per cent). These are cases like
builds on: [$_{PWd}$ bɪl.dØ] [$_{PWd}$ zɑn]. However, in cases where the inflection must be
adjoined to the host verb's PWd, as in cases like *builds them* [$_{PWd}$ [$_{PWd}$ bɪl.dØ].zØ]
[$_{PWd}$ ðəm], production drops to 9 per cent. And this suggests that the Mandarin
constraint on non-adjunction to a PWd forces the learners not to pronounce the
inflection attached to *builds*.

The performance of this second group of Mandarin speakers in supplying the
third person non-past tense subject–verb agreement inflection is consistent with
the claim of the PTH that L1 constraints on syllable organisation are transferred
to the L2 and determine what can and cannot be pronounced. Where the L2
forms can be accommodated within the L1 structure, they are pronounceable,
but when they cannot be accommodated they are deleted. One of the strengths
of the account is that it explains why L2 learners show much less optionality in
supplying target third person forms of copula and auxiliary *be* than they do in the
case of forms of inflected lexical verbs – copula and auxiliary *is, am, are* are monosyllabic PWds unaffected by possible constraints in the learner's L1 on possible
syllable combinations. Similarly it offers an account of why L2 learners of English
are typically more accurate in producing irregular past tense verb forms than regular ones – irregulars generally do not require adjunction to the host verb's PWd.

However, Goad et al. acknowledge that not all cases of missing inflection can
be explained by the PTH. Even the second group of six participants in their study
who accommodated the third person singular inflection still failed to supply it in
around a quarter of required contexts. And it is not clear why the across-the-board
deletion group do not accommodate inflection where there is the possibility of

doing so. Furthermore, as Goad et al. note, it appears that L2 speakers of English, including those with L1 Mandarin Chinese, are less likely to use the regular plural inflection with nouns optionally than they are to use the third person singular non-past tense subject–verb agreement inflection optionally, although phonologically the two inflections have the same properties.

Section 7.3 in a Nutshell

Syllables are the minimal pronounceable units and consist of an onset, nucleus and coda (the nucleus and coda together forming a rhyme). Languages differ both in the segments they choose to populate syllables and in the number of segments allowed in the onset and coda. Where an L2 learner's L1 is more restrictive in the number of segments allowed in onset or coda position, this exerts persistent influence on pronunciation. Spanish-speaking learners of English add an epenthetic [ɪ] to onset clusters beginning with [s], e.g. [ɪsplaʃ], because Spanish disallows [s] in onset clusters. Mandarin Chinese-speaking learners of English omit coda segments that are not [n, ŋ, j, r] (or add an epenthetic vowel). Speakers of different varieties of Arabic (Egyptian and Iraqi) insert epenthetic vowels in English words to avoid consonant clusters, but do so in different ways determined by their L1 syllable structure. Korean-speaking L2 learners of English are aware that English can 'double weight' vowels in syllable rhymes, but their L1 leads them to restructure such rhymes to create two single-weighted syllables (Broselow and Park, 1995).

Goad et al. (2003) argue that optionality in the use of affixal morphology in English by L2 speakers is (at least partly) the result of difficulty pronouncing syllables because of the constraints imposed by L1 syllable structure. Their Prosodic Transfer Hypothesis accounts for observed production and omission of the English third person non-past tense subject–verb agreement form -*s* by Mandarin Chinese speakers and also explains why L2 learners of English show much less optionality in the production of forms of copula and auxiliary *be* than in the production of affixal verb morphology: forms of *be* conform to the constraints on syllable structure in Mandarin.

7.4 Prosody

Prosody is a term that refers to the acoustic properties of syllables when they are organised into words, phrases and clauses. It can cover (a) the assignment of word stress (where one syllable is louder, of higher pitch and longer than other syllables in the word); (b) the assignment of tone in languages like Mandarin Chinese (where changes in pitch on the same syllable signal different meanings);

(c) changes to the prominence of stress on individual words when they combine into phrases and clauses (the rhythm of phrases/clauses); and (d) intonation (the pitch contour over sentences that can signal differences between statements, questions and orders, or signal speaker perspectives like anger, irony and uncertainty). This section focuses on the L2 acquisition of word stress and tone.

Languages differ in whether and how they assign word stress. English and Spanish, for example, have variable word stress that is largely unpredictable. Some two-syllable words have stress on the first syllable (*'anger, 'exit*), others on the second syllable (*re'ply, ex'pect*); three-syllable words can be stressed on the first, second or third syllable: *'underground, re'payment, guaran'tee*. But there is no categorical rule for deciding where a word is stressed. For L2 learners of English and Spanish, where word stress is located largely has to be learned on a case by case basis. Other languages have fixed word stress. For example, in Welsh stress always falls on the penultimate syllable. This means that in a two-syllable word like *'ysgol* 'school' the stress shifts when the plural affix *-ion* is added making it a three-syllable word: *ys'golion* 'schools' (Ashby and Maidment, 2005: 157). In such cases, once language learners identify the pattern they can assign stress by rule and do not need to learn the pattern for every individual word.

In French, when words are uttered in isolation they are stressed on the final syllable: *ache'té* 'bought', *ba'teau* 'boat'. But when they are used in combination, only the final syllable of a phrase is stressed, the stress of the other words being reduced: *J'ai acheté un ba'teau* 'I bought a boat'. Stress in French serves to demarcate where one phrase ends and another begins. In English and Spanish, stress serves to demarcate words, and can sometimes even distinguish words that are otherwise phonologically identical, as in English *'conflict* (noun) versus *con'flict* (verb) or Spanish *'bebe* 'she drinks' versus *be'be* 'baby' (Dupoux et al., 2008).

When the L1 and L2 differ in word stress assignment patterns, does the L1 affect how the L2 pattern is acquired, as it appears to do in other areas of the sound system? Dupoux et al. (2008) conducted two experiments to determine how successfully L1 speakers of French (a language with phrase-final stress as described above) can identify the variable and potentially meaning-distinguishing word stress patterns of Spanish. Their starting assumption was that native speakers of French do not encode stress with words in their mental lexicons (strictly speaking they do not encode stress with word forms in their Vocabularies) and are therefore faced with the challenge of establishing such lexical representations for Spanish words.

In their first experiment they gave a stress sequence recall task to fourteen beginning, fourteen intermediate and eleven advanced-proficiency learners of Spanish along with two control groups: twenty native speakers of Spanish and twenty monolingual speakers of French who had never learned Spanish. The task required participants to listen to sets of four invented, but plausibly Spanish or French, words. Each set of four consisted of two pairs of words that were minimally distinct, like those illustrated in (13):

TABLE 7.3 Percent incorrect responses to word sequences involving a phoneme contrast and a stress contrast (based on Dupoux et al., 2008: 693, Table 5)

	Phoneme Contrast	Stress Contrast
L2 Spanish beginners (n = 14)	22	66
L2 Spanish intermediate (n = 14)	21	79
L2 Spanish advanced (n = 11)	25	74
French monolinguals (n = 20)	27	79
Spanish native speakers (n = 20)	25	20

13　a.　fiku – fitu – fitu – fiku

　　b.　'numi – 'numi – nu'mi – nu'mi

In (13a) the words are distinguished by a phoneme contrast between /k/ and /t/ (a contrast that exists in both French and Spanish). In (13b) the words are distinguished by location of stress alone, either on the first or the second syllable. Participants were presented with twenty-eight such sets and had to type the sequence they heard in each set using the numbers 1 and 2. For example, the sequence of words in (13a) is 1–2–2–1, and the sequence in (13b) is 1–1–2–2. Dupoux et al. counted every response that was not 100 per cent correct as incorrect. The results for incorrect responses are presented in table 7.3.

While all the groups, including the French monolinguals, perform in a similar way in identifying the sets of invented words that have phoneme contrasts, making errors in around a quarter of cases, there is a striking difference between the Spanish native speakers and all the French groups in identifying the sets of invented words that have stress contrasts. None of the L2 speakers of Spanish, including the advanced-proficiency group, are significantly different from the monolingual French group who have had no exposure to Spanish. This 'stress deafness', as Dupoux et al. call it (2008: 695), appears to be persistent.

In a second experiment involving just the L2 learners and the Spanish native speaker control group, Dupoux et al. tested the ability of participants to distinguish real words from invented words. The real words were forms like *blanco* 'white', *gorro* 'hat'. These were changed into invented, but possible, words either by substituting one of the phonemes, e.g. *blanco* → **blanto*, or shifting the position of the stress, e.g. *'gorro* → **gor'ro*. Participants heard 152 of these items one by one, half real words and half invented words, and had to decide, yes or no, whether the word they were hearing was real. Table 7.4 presents the percentage incorrect decisions both for real words and for the invented words involving a phoneme change or a stress shift.

These results suggest that whereas the L2 Spanish speakers make few errors in identifying invented words on the basis of a phoneme change, and get better at this the more proficient they are in Spanish, they have greater difficulty in

TABLE 7.4 Percentage of incorrect choices in a lexical decision task (word or invented word) (based on Dupoux et al., 2008: 697, Table 6)

	Phoneme Change		stress shift	
	Word	Invented **Word**	Word	Invented **Word**
L2 Spanish beginners (n = 14)	11	18	32	56
L2 Spanish intermediate (n = 14)	5	16	23	62
L2 Spanish advanced (n = 11)	1	11	16	56
Spanish native speakers (n = 20)	1	3	4	5

identifying non-words that have been created through stress misplacement. This did not improve with proficiency. This is in contrast to the native Spanish control group who make few errors in identifying invented words, whether they result from a phoneme change or stress misplacement. Dupoux et al. conclude that this reflects a problem for the L2 learners in encoding stress as part of the representation of words in the mental lexicon, even for those of advanced proficiency in Spanish (2008: 699).

Lexical tones also fall under the heading of prosody. Lexical tones are changes in pitch on syllable nuclei that distinguish meanings. Mandarin Chinese has four distinct tones that can be applied to any syllable, with the potential to distinguish meaning. These are shown as diacritics in the following example:

14. mā (a high level pitch)   'mother' (first tone: T1)
    má (pitch rising from mid to high)   'hemp' (second tone: T2)
    mǎ (pitch falling from mid to low, then rising to high)   'horse' (third tone: T3)
    mà (pitch starting high and falling to low)   'curse' (fourth tone: T4)

Cantonese is also a tone language that has six lexical tones (Hao, 2012: 271), not all of which are directly comparable to the Mandarin tones. While Cantonese has tones comparable to Mandarin T1 and T2, it also has (i) a mid, level tone; (ii) a low, level tone; (iii) a low to mid rising tone; and (iv) a mid to low falling tone.

Hao (2012) compared two groups of L2 learners of Mandarin in their ability to identify and mimic tones accurately: a group of ten L1 speakers of English (a language without lexical tones) and a group of nine L1 speakers of Cantonese (a language with lexical tones). The English speakers had been learning Mandarin on average for two and a half years, and the Cantonese speakers on average for four years. Their task was first to listen to a set of sixty-four words created from the four syllables *you* [jo], *ma* [ma], *wang* [waŋ] and *yi* [ji] (all real words in Mandarin). Each of these syllables was read by a native Mandarin speaker with all four of the tones, and in thirty-two of the items the syllables were combined into two-syllable words like *youma*, *wangyi* and so on. The participants were asked to mark the tone(s) of every item they heard using the diacritics – ′ v ˋ on a sheet that provided the written forms (the 'identification task'). Two native speakers of Mandarin performed the task and were 100% and 98% accurate, indicating that the stimuli provided clear cues to the tones. In a second task participants were asked to listen to the same items presented in a different order and imitate each syllable they heard (the 'mimicry task').

The results show that overall the participants were less accurate on the identification task than the native speakers, but on the whole quite accurate, with no mean accuracy scores on any of the tones falling below 60 per cent. In the mimicry task both groups were over 90 per cent accurate on T1 and T4.

The English and Cantonese speakers were not statistically significantly different from each other overall. Both groups were more accurate on imitating tones than on identifying which of the four categories a tone represented. Both were more accurate in identifying tones T1 and T4 than tones T2 and T3.

These results suggest that speaking an L1 with lexical tones confers no particular advantage in acquiring another L2 with lexical tones over speakers of an L1 that lacks such tones, despite the Cantonese speakers also having longer exposure to Mandarin than the English speakers. Hao concludes that 'for speakers of tonal L1s, attuning their attention to the different relevant dimensions of the L2 tonal categories may not be easier than establishing new tonal categories' (2012: 276).

Hao suggests that the better performance on the mimicry task than the identification task implies that the problem is not one of accurately hearing or articulating the pitch contour of the syllable nuclei, but in identifying which of the four tone categories the pitch belongs to. In other words, an L2 learner could hear, for example, a pitch contour that falls and rises, and even be able to imitate it, but cannot determine whether it is a T3 or a T2. And this, of course, is important for distinguishing the meaning of the syllable.

Section 7.4 in a Nutshell

The section looked at the L2 acquisition of two aspects of prosody: word stress and lexical tone. Some languages (English, Spanish) have variable word stress, which must be learned by L2 speakers on a case-by-case basis and stored with each word in the mental lexicon (strictly speaking with word forms in the Vocabulary). Other languages have predictable word stress (Welsh, for example) or stress at the phrase, rather than word, level (French). In the latter two cases stress may not be encoded with words in the mental lexicon. Dupoux et al. (2008) found that French-speaking L2 learners of Spanish, even of advanced proficiency, were inaccurate in recalling sequences of words distinguished only by word stress and in deciding whether invented words that differed from real words only in stress location were in fact real or invented (unlike native speakers of Spanish). They conclude that this persistent 'stress deafness' results from French speakers failing to encode stress with Spanish morphemes in their mental lexicons.

Lexical tones are changes in pitch on syllable nuclei that distinguish the meanings of words. The Mandarin Chinese *ma*, for example, can mean 'mother', 'hemp', 'horse' or 'curse' depending on the tone. Hao (2012) compared the acquisition of lexical tone in Mandarin by two groups of intermediate-proficiency L2 learners, one speaking an L1 with lexical tones (Cantonese), the other speaking an L1 without lexical tones (English). Using a tone imitation and a tone identification task, Hao found no significant differences in the performance of the two groups, suggesting that speaking an L1 with lexical tones conveys no particular advantage in learning an L2 with lexical tones. Both groups were highly accurate in imitating tones but less accurate in identifying the category to which a tone belongs. Identification of tone category is important for determining the meaning of the word.

7.5 Concluding Remarks

A speaker's L1 appears to be persistently influential in determining which aspects of an L2 sound system can and cannot be acquired, and whether a speaker will come to sound more or less like a native speaker of the target language. Sub-phonemic contrasts, such as a difference in the voice onset time of syllable-initial stops between the L1 and the L2, are not fully acquired by learners who started learning the L2 in later adolescence or beyond (Flege et al., 1996). Sub-phonemic contrasts in the L1 that are phonemic in the L2 are acquirable, but acquisition may only occur in later stages of development. Learning completely new phonemes in the L2 is possible. English speakers acquire French /y/ successfully and quickly (Flege, 1987). French speakers can acquire English /θ, ð/, although initially they map these phonemes onto phonemes in the L1 like /f/–/v/ or /s/–/z/ (Wenk, 1979). Where a contrast between two phonemes in an L2 maps onto a single phoneme in the L1, the L2 contrast is successfully acquired if the L1 instantiates the abstract articulatory/acoustic features that identify the contrast. Japanese speakers acquire the /f/–/v/ contrast of Russian despite having only a /ɸ/ phoneme in Japanese. However, they are persistently inaccurate with the /l/–/r/ contrast, which maps onto the single /r/ phoneme in Japanese. Larson-Hall (2004) attributes this difference to the fact that Japanese instantiates the features [voice], [labial], [continuant] that are required to distinguish /f/ from /v/, but does not have the feature [lateral] which is necessary for distinguishing /l/ from /r/ and appears to be persistently difficult for Japanese speakers to access.

L1 syllable structure imposes persistent constraints on L2 learners' ability to pronounce L2 syllables that fall outside those constraints. Spanish speakers insert epenthetic vowels into English onset clusters that begin with [s], Mandarin Chinese speakers introduce epenthetic vowels into English codas that are not one of the segments [n, ŋ, j, r] (or omit them), Arabic speakers introduce epenthetic vowels into English consonant clusters. In each case L2 learners are restructuring English input to make it consistent with L1 syllable structure.

Goad et al. (2003) offer an L1-syllable-based account of optionality in the production of English affixal morphemes by L2 speakers of languages like Mandarin Chinese. Their Prosodic Transfer Hypothesis proposes that Mandarin speakers fail to pronounce affixal morphemes when they involve syllable structure that is not licensed by their L1. Specifically, Mandarin disallows adjunction of the forms of inflectional morphemes to prosodic words. While Goad et al. acknowledge that this account does not extend to all cases of missing inflection, it has the advantage of explaining why L2 learners of English are less likely to omit forms of copula and auxiliary *be* than affixes attached to lexical verbs.

L2 word stress appears to be persistently difficult to acquire if a speaker's L1 does not encode stress with words in the mental lexicon. Dupoux et al. (2008) showed that French-speaking L2 learners of Spanish, even of advanced proficiency, appear not to be sensitive to word stress contrasts. Lexical tone, by contrast, does appear to be acquirable, although speakers may have ongoing difficulty identifying the category to which a tone belongs, which is an important cue to distinguishing word meanings.

UG plays a role in the acquisition of sound systems at the very beginning of life, when infant language learners have available to them all the abstract articulatory/acoustic features needed to identify any linguistic segment that might occur in human language. But the range of options available is narrowed over the first twelve months of life to just those required by the L1(s) being acquired. In later adolescence access to those UG-provided features that have not been instantiated in the L1(s) becomes more difficult, as shown by the persistent inaccuracy in discriminating the /l/–/r/ contrast by Japanese speakers (based on the feature [lateral] according to Larson-Hall (2004)) or the persistent inaccuracy in the identification of words distinguished by stress by French speakers uncovered by Dupoux et al. (2008). In the domain of sound, UG, the L1 and input interact in individual mental grammars to produce a filter for pronunciation. Some parts of the L1 system can be restructured, but other parts remain persistently resistant to change.

ACTIVITIES

1. TEST YOURSELF

(i) What is the difference between a phone and a phoneme? Give an example of a sub-phonemic contrast between sounds in English.

(ii) What did Flege et al. (1996) find in their study of voice onset times in the L2 English of Italian speakers with over thirty years' residence in Ottawa?

(iii) Can L2 speakers learn that a sub-phonemic contrast in their L1 is phonemic in the L2?

(iv) Can L2 speakers learn phonemes that are completely new to them in the L2?

(v) Why do Japanese speakers find the /l/–/r/ phoneme contrast in English diffi-cult to acquire?

(vi) Why do Spanish speakers often pronounce English words like *splash* as [ɪsplaʃ]?

(vii) How do Goad et al. (2003) explain optionality in the use of English third person singular non-past tense subject–verb agreement -*s* by L2 learners with L1 Mandarin Chinese?

(viii) Why do Dupoux et al. (2008) claim that L1 French speakers who are L2 speakers of Spanish have 'stress deafness'?

2. PREDICTING THE PRONUNCIATION OF WORDS

Major (1986) observes that Brazilian Portuguese only allows [s], [r] and [l] (or no consonant) as syllable codas. What do you predict Brazilian Portuguese-speaking early-stage L2 learners of English might do when they pronounce the words below? Give reasons for your predictions.

a. aspect
b. lost
c. pub
d. community
e. middle

3. THE RELATIONSHIP BETWEEN PHONES AND WORD STRESS

The Spanish phonemes /b/, /d/ and /g/ are realised by different phones, depend-ing on their position in the word. In the onset position of stressed initial syllables, they are pronounced as stops, e.g.:

'**b**año [b] 'bath' (voiced bilabial stop)
'**d**onde [d] 'where' (voiced dental stop)
'**g**allo [g] 'rooster' (voiced velar stop)

In the word-internal onset position of unstressed syllables they are pronounced as the corresponding fricatives, e.g.:

'na**b**o [β] 'turnip' (voiced bilabial fricative)
'na**d**a [ð] 'nothing' (voiced dental fricative)
'a**g**ua [ɣ] 'water' (voiced velar fricative)

In two-syllable words in Spanish, stress typically falls on the first syllable.

Shea and Curtin (2010) conducted an experiment where they asked L2 and L1 speakers of Spanish to identify the stressed syllable in invented two-syllable words with the following structures (V = vowel):

stop V fricative V   e.g. baβa, daða, gaɣa

fricative V stop V   e.g. βaba, ðada, ɣaga

Participants were fifteen low-intermediate proficiency L2 speakers, fourteen high-intermediate proficiency L2 speakers (all with L1 English) and fifteen native speakers of Spanish.

Crucially, there was no stressed syllable. Both vowels were of equal pitch, length and loudness. If participants did identify one syllable as more stressed than the other it was not because of the quality of the vowel.

Question (i). What do you think the aim of this study was?

TABLE (i) Number of first syllables identified as stressed and number of first syllables beginning with a stop identified as stressed: % (tokens) (based on Shea and Curtin, 2010: 597, Table 3)

	Low-Intermediate	High-Intermediate	Native Spanish Speakers
Stressed first syllables out of all syllables	56% (444/792)	53% (397/747)	48% (380/785)
Stressed first syllables beginning with a stop	52% (229/444)	54% (215/397)	60% (229/380)

Table (i) gives two pieces of information. The first row is the number of words where participants identified the first syllable as stressed out of the total number of words they heard. The second row is the number of words which begin with a stop where participants identified the first syllable as being stressed out of the total number of first syllables identified as stressed.

The native Spanish group were statistically significantly more likely than the two L2 groups to identify stress on the first syllable when it began with [b], [d] or [g] than when it began with [β], [ð] or [ɣ]. The two L2 groups were not different from each other.

Question (ii). What conclusions do you draw from these results?

4. USING PHONETIC CUES TO IDENTIFY WORD BOUNDARIES

Potentially ambiguous word boundaries in English in cases like *keep stalking/keeps talking, see Mabel/seem able* provide an opportunity to test whether L2 speakers can make use of the phonetic features that native speakers use to decide where the word boundary resides. In the case of *keep stalking/keeps talking* aspiration or non-aspiration of [t] is an important clue. If [t] is aspirated – [tʰ] – then the boundary comes between [s] and [t] because [tʰ] only occurs in syllable-initial position, not when it follows [s]. In the case of *see Mabel/seem able* a glottal stop before words that begin with a vowel provides an important clue to where the word boundary comes.

TABLE (i) Accuracy (%) in choosing the correct word division in response to an auditory stimulus (based on Altenberg, 2005: 341, Table 3)

Clue		Native speakers	L2 speakers
Aspiration	*keep stalking/keeps talking*	97%	59%
Glottal stop	*seem able/see Mabel*	97%	88%

Altenberg (2005) gave twenty-nine L1 speakers of Spanish, who were of intermediate or advanced proficiency in L2 English, and twenty native speakers of American English a word boundary discrimination task. Participants listened to someone reading expressions like *keepstalking* and had to choose whether they had heard *keep stalking* or *keeps talking*. There were eighty-four items in the test. The mean correct responses of participants are shown in table (i).

There was no statistically significant difference in the native speakers' discrimination of word boundaries based on aspiration or the presence of a glottal stop. The L2 speakers found it significantly more difficult to discriminate word boundaries when aspiration was the clue than when a glottal stop was the clue.

How do you interpret these results? Are they consistent with findings discussed in this chapter about sub-phonemic contrasts made in L1s and L2s?

FURTHER READING

For a general introduction to linguistic sounds see:

Ashby, M. and Maidment, J. 2005. *Introducing phonetic science*. Cambridge: Cambridge University Press.

Zsiga, E. C. 2013. *The sounds of language: an introduction to phonetics and phonology*. Oxford: Wiley Blackwell.

For a comprehensive review of studies of the acquisition of L2 sound systems see:

Colantoni, L., Steele, J. and Escudero, P. 2015. *Second language speech: theory and practice*. Cambridge: Cambridge University Press.

APPENDIX

A BRIEF DESCRIPTION OF HOW LINGUISTIC SOUNDS ARE PRODUCED

As background to the topics discussed in this chapter, this section briefly illustrates those parts of the throat, mouth and nose that are involved in the production of linguistic sounds, collectively known as the vocal tract (see figure 7.1).

For the production of most sounds, air is expelled from the lungs through the vocal tract, although some rare sounds in some languages are produced by sucking air in (for example, in the production of clicks). Differences between sounds are the result of different configurations of the vocal tract. For example, the uvula (the tip of the velum, also known as the soft palate) can make a complete closure

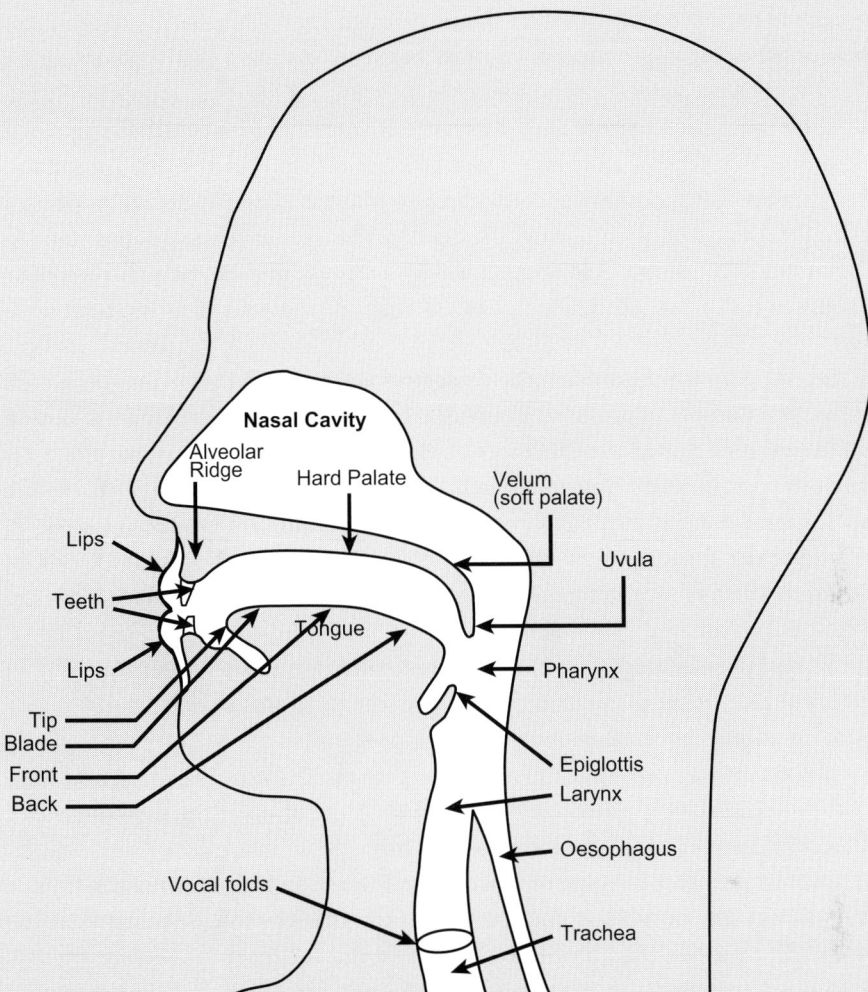

Figure 7.1 Parts of the vocal tract involved in producing linguistic sounds (from Wells and Colson, 1971)

with the wall of the nasal cavity, or it can be open to allow air to pass through the nose. When air passes through the nose, nasal sounds like [m], [n], or [ŋ] (the final sound in *sing*) are produced. When the nasal cavity is closed, oral sounds like [b], [d] and [g] can be produced. Changes to the shape of the tongue in the oral cavity give rise to different sounds. When the tongue leaves a large gap between it and the palate, various vowel sounds can be produced, like [i] (as in *beat*), [u] (as in *boot*), [ɛ] (as in *egg*). When it is brought into close approximation with the palate or the alveolar ridge (a crescent of bone behind the upper front teeth), or the teeth themselves, audible friction is produced when air passes through, giving rise to fricative sounds like [s] (as in *sea*) or [θ] (the *th* sound in *think*).

When air leaves the lungs it first encounters the vocal cords, also called vocal folds. These bands of cartilage can allow air to pass freely through, or they can be brought together so that when air passes through they vibrate. This difference – open or vibrating – produces a contrast between voiceless and voiced sounds. When sounds are voiced, there is audible 'buzzing'. Try saying the sound [f] followed by the sound [v] repeatedly: [fvfvfv ...]. You should hear a buzzing when you pronounce [v] that stops when you pronounce [f]: [v] is a voiced consonant, [f] is a voiceless one. The vocal cords can also make a complete closure to stop air passing through and then release it suddenly. This is known as a glottal stop [ʔ]. Glottal stops tend to occur in English between vowels, and can be a characteristic of some non-standard varieties, e.g. where *butter* is pronounced as *bu'er, sitting* as *si'ing*.

Proceeding up the vocal tract, the passage of air is shaped by the tongue, which can adopt a number of positions in the oral cavity. It can make a complete closure at different points with the soft palate (velum), hard palate, or alveolar ridge. Or there can be a complete closure of the lips. When air builds up behind the closure and is then released 'stop' (also called 'plosive') sounds are produced like [k, g] (closure at the soft palate, or velum), [t, d] (closure at the alveolar ridge), [p, b] (closure at the lips). If the tongue or lips do not make a complete closure but are in close approximation, a fricative sound is produced like [s, z] (close approximation to the alveolar ridge), [θ, ð] (close approximation to the upper teeth), [ʃ, ʒ] (close approximation to the hard palate – the sounds in **sh**ip, mea**s**ure), [f, v] (close approximation between the lower lip and top teeth).

When the uvula is lowered and air passes through the nose, a complete closure at the velum produces [ŋ]; a complete closure at the alveolar ridge produces [n]; and a complete closure at the lips produces [m].

Three factors affect the type of vowel sound that is produced when the tongue leaves a large gap between it and the palate: whether the tongue bunches at the front or the back of the mouth, the height of the tongue and whether the lips are rounded or spread. [i], as in *beat*, is produced when the tongue bunches high towards the front of the mouth and the lips are spread. French [y] is like [i] but with rounded lips. [ɑ], the sound in *father, cart*, is produced when the tongue bunches low at the back of the mouth and the lips are spread. The [ɛ] of *egg* is produced when the tongue bunches at the front of the mouth but is lower in height than [i] (and the lips are spread). The [u] of *boot* is produced when the tongue bunches high at the back of the mouth and the lips are rounded. And so on. For full treatments of the production of linguistic sounds see the further reading section above.

8 Real-Time and Contextual Use of Language by Second Language Speakers

8.1 Not All Grammatical Knowledge is Made Available in Real-Time Language Use

Even a full description of the grammatical properties of a speaker's mental grammar is not enough to explain how that speaker uses such knowledge in the real-time comprehension and production of utterances. For example, do you find the following sentence grammatical or ungrammatical?

1. The woman sold the house emigrated to Australia

Many people encountering sentences like (1) for the first time find that there is something funny about them. They might think, for example, that there is a missing conjunction: *The woman sold the house **and** emigrated to Australia*. In fact, there is nothing ungrammatical about (1), if the sentence is interpreted in the following way: *Sold* is not a finite transitive verb where *the house* is the object of an act of selling (*The woman sold the house*) but a **passive** participle in a relative clause. Part of this clause has been omitted. The main finite verb in the sentence is *emigrated*, not *sold*:

1'. The woman (who was) sold the house emigrated to Australia

The structure of this sentence would have been much clearer from the start if the verb involved had been unambiguously interpreted as a participle. This is the case for any verb that has an *-en* inflection: *giv-en, writt-en, brok-en* etc. The sentence in (2) feels fully grammatical from a first reading:

2. The woman given the house emigrated to Australia

Examples like (1) suggest that although speakers of English know that *The woman sold the house* is structurally ambiguous (between a transitive verb with an object, and a passive participle in a 'reduced' relative clause), in real-time comprehension they favour the transitive verb interpretation. It can be shown more generally that when speakers unconsciously analyse sentences they hear or read (this is referred to as parsing) which potentially have more than one grammatical analysis, they often have a preference for one of those analyses over the other(s).

Sentences like (1) have come to be known as 'garden path' sentences in the psycholinguistic literature because the tendency for speakers to interpret the first verb as a transitive leads them 'up the garden path' (i.e. misleads them). It is a robust effect that can be found with any verb whose simple past tense form can also be interpreted as a passive participle:

3 a. The ball rolled down the hill stopped
   b. The horse raced past the barn fell
   c. The boat floated down the river sank

Because speech and efficient reading are fast, parsing has to be fast too. It seems that to achieve the necessary speed, not all the information that is present in a speaker's mental grammar can be made available during on-line analysis. The 'parser' has its own principles of operation where some grammatical properties take precedence over others in the initial analysis.

8.2 Use of Grammatical Knowledge by L2 Speakers During Comprehension

How do L2 learners deal with the challenge of using their grammatical knowledge in real time? Many L2 speakers who learned the target language beyond childhood, even when they are of quite high proficiency in 'off-line' measurements of their grammatical and lexical knowledge (such as gap-filling tests or multiple-choice tasks), find comprehension of fast native speech, or the efficient reading of L2 texts, difficult. Two different explanations have been offered for this. One is that L2 speakers have the same parsing procedures as those used by native speakers of the target language, but they are just slower in using them. The other is that L2 speakers use different parsing procedures from native speakers, and it is this that makes comprehension more difficult. A lively debate has been under way in the recent literature on this topic, with some evidence consistent with the first possibility and other evidence consistent with the second.

8.2.1 L2 Speakers' Comprehension of Garden-Path Sentences

A study reported by Juffs (2004) of the way that L2 speakers parse garden-path sentences is consistent with the 'same procedures, slower implementation' view. Juffs used an on-line, self-paced reading task which required participants to read sentences one word at a time on a computer screen. In this task participants press a key to call up the first word of the sentence. When they have read the word, they press the key again. The word disappears and the second word of the sentence appears, and so on. In this way, the participant controls the speed at which he/she reads the sentence. Crucially, the time it takes to press the key can be calculated, and this can be used as a way of measuring how fast or how slowly a participant is reading each word in the sentence. It is assumed that parts of sentences that are read more slowly than others are where parsing is more difficult.

Juffs asked participants to read 162 sentences among which were randomly distributed six tokens of three types of experimental sentence (making a total of eighteen). The first type were 'strong garden-path' sentences created from an introductory adverbial clause ending with a verb that can be either **transitive** or **intransitive**, as in (4a). Native readers have a strong tendency to interpret the determiner phrase following that verb as its object, and subsequently have to re-analyse it as the subject of the following clause. The second type were 'weak garden-path' sentences created from main clauses where the verb can in principle take either a direct object or a clause as its complement, as in (4b). In this case native readers have a slight preference for interpreting the determiner phrase following the verb as its object, but this tendency is not as strong as in the case of the strong garden-path sentences. The third type of sentence had the same structure as the sentence in (4a), but the verb at the end of the adverbial clause was obligatorily intransitive, hence the following determiner phrase is unambiguously the subject of the following clause (4c), and there is no garden-path effect. In the experiment, performance on sentences of type (4c) provided a point of comparison with performance on the garden-path sentences.

4 a. After the children cleaned the house looked very neat and tidy   (strong GP)
   b. The doctor knew the nurses liked the man from England   (weak GP)
   c. When the student arrived the professor asked her about her trip (no GP)

Participants were twenty-eight L1 speakers of Japanese, thirty L1 speakers of Chinese, forty-six L1 speakers of Spanish and a control group of twenty-one native speakers of English. The English proficiency of the L2 groups was probably intermediate to advanced. with the Japanese speakers the least proficient. (Although Juffs gave them a proficiency test, he does not offer descriptive labels for their performance.)

Juffs predicted that if participants are indeed 'garden pathed' by sentences like (4a–b) as the result of applying a parsing procedure that favours an interpretation of the first finite verb as a transitive with a following object, this should show up in a slowdown in reading time when the second verb (*looked, liked*) is encountered. This is because it becomes clear at this point that the second verb lacks a subject, which is impossible in English, and that the sentence has been wrongly analysed. By contrast, there should be less of a slowdown when the second verb (*asked*) in sentences like (4c) is encountered because it will already have been established that the preceding determiner phrase cannot be the object of the obligatorily intransitive first verb.

Juffs found that the L2 participants were typically 100–400 milliseconds slower than the natives in reading the second verb in these sentences. Crucially, when he measured the difference between the reading times of the second determiner phrase (*the house, the nurses, the professor*) and the reading times of the second verb, he found that the native and non-native speakers performed in similar ways: a statistically significant slowdown in going from *house* to *looked* in the strong garden-path sentences (4a) by comparison with the non-garden-path sentences of (4c), and a weaker, but marked, slowdown in going from *nurses* to *liked* in the weak garden-path sentences. This suggests that despite reading sentences more slowly than the native speakers, the non-native speakers were using syntactic information (the difference between optionally transitive and obligatorily intransitive verbs) and a parsing procedure (treat determiner phrases that follow optionally transitive verbs as objects of those verbs) in a qualitatively similar way. This is particularly striking given that the L2 participants all speak L1s that allow null subjects. In null subject languages, sentences like (4a) potentially have a non-garden-path reading: 'After the children cleaned the house it looked very neat and tidy'. The 'it' in this kind of sentence would be null in null subject languages, with the result that *house* could be interpreted as the object of *cleaned*. The reading times of the participants in Juffs' study suggest that they do not analyse these sentences as containing a null subject but are comprehending them in a way that is consistent with the grammar of English.

Roberts and Felser (2011) also examined the parsing of garden-path sentences by L2 speakers and natives, but from a perspective that suggests that L2 speakers may use slightly different parsing procedures from natives: they are more influenced by meaning in determining the structure of a sentence. Roberts and Felser used strong and weak garden-path sentences similar to those used by Juffs (see example (4)), but manipulated the plausibility of the determiner phrase following the first finite verb as a possible object. Consider the examples in (5–6):

5 a. While the band played the song pleased all the customers   (strong GP)
   b. While the band played the beer pleased all the customers

6 a. The inspector warned the boss would destroy very many lives   (weak GP)
   b. The inspector warned crimes would destroy very many lives

While *song* is a plausible object for *played* in (5) (*played the song*), *beer* is much less so (*??played the beer*). Similarly, in (6) *boss* is a more plausible object of *warn* than *crimes* (*warned the boss, ??warned crimes*).

The task used was a self-paced reading task, as in the Juffs study. Participants were twenty-five advanced-proficiency L2 speakers of English with L1 Greek and a control group of twenty-four native speakers of English. Both groups showed a slowdown in reading when they encountered the second finite verb (suggesting that they have been garden-pathed by misanalysing the preceding determiner phrase as an object of the preceding verb). The effect was stronger for the strong garden path sentences, as Juffs had found. However, there was a difference between the groups in relation to the plausibility of the preceding determiner phrase as an object of the first verb. This had no effect on the reading times of the native speakers. The L2 speakers were slower in reading the second finite verb when the preceding determiner phrase was a plausible object of the first verb (5a, 6a) than when it was not. Roberts and Felser argue that 'non-native comprehenders may be influenced more strongly than native ones by pragmatic plausibility information' when they parse sentences (2011: 322).

8.2.2 L2 Speakers' Comprehension of Structurally Ambiguous Sentences

Felser et al. (2003) collected evidence from the parsing of a different type of construction that is consistent with the view that late-learning L2 speakers do not parse sentences in the same way as natives. They investigated the preferences of native and non-native speakers of English in resolving the ambiguity inherent in sentences like (7):

7 a. The dean liked the secretary of the professor who was reading a letter
   b. The dean liked the secretary with the professor who was reading a letter

Grammatically, the ambiguity arises because the relative clause *who was reading the letter* can be interpreted either as modifying *the professor* or *the secretary*. However, in existing studies of how native speakers of English parse these sentences in real time, it has been shown that they prefer the closest noun as the target of modification (*professor* in (7)) (Carreiras and Clifton 1993). A different preference has been found for native speakers of German and Greek for equivalent constructions (Papadopoulou and Clahsen 2003). Although speakers of these languages prefer modification of the closest noun when the preposition is the equivalent of *with*, when the preposition is the equivalent of *of* the preference is for the relative clause to modify the noun that is further away, i.e. *secretary*.

According to Gibson et al. (1996), the reason why this cross-linguistic difference is found is that there are two potential choices the parser could make: interpret the relative clause as modifying the most recently parsed phrase, i.e. *the professor*. English speakers have adopted 'recency' for both types of sentence in (7). The other choice is to interpret the relative clause as modifying the whole object phrase *the secretary of/with the professor*. Since *secretary* is the head noun in this complex phrase, the interpretation is that *the secretary* was reading the letter. Native speakers of German and Greek choose the most recent phrase for the case where the preposition linking *professor* and *secretary* is the equivalent of *with*, but the whole object phrase where the preposition is the equivalent of *of*.

Felser et al. (2003) tested whether L1 speakers of German and Greek who were advanced-proficiency speakers of English (as measured by an off-line proficiency test) had acquired the English parsing preference for interpreting relative clauses as modifying the most recent phrase when the preposition *of* was involved, had transferred the preference for interpreting relative clauses as modifying the whole object from their L1s, or were parsing these sentences in some other way. To do

TABLE 8.1 Response latencies (in milliseconds) at the segments *were* vs *was* (based on Felser et al., 2003: 466–73, Tables 3, 6 and 8)

Participants		Response Latency	Significant?
NS controls (n = 45)	*were* (closest N)	495 ms	Yes
	was (higher N)	581 ms	
L1 German (n = 28)	*were* (closest N)	439 ms	No
	was (higher N)	435 ms	
L1 Greek (n = 39)	*were* (closest N)	533 ms	No
	was (higher N)	508 ms	

this they used a self-paced reading task where the segments that participants saw were words or phrases, as illustrated by the '/' in (8):

8. The dean liked / the secretary of the professor / who / was / reading a letter

While the interpretation of the relative clause in (8) remains potentially ambiguous even when all the sentence has been read, in (9) the sentence is disambiguated as soon as a reader encounters the verbs *was* or *were*.

9 a. The dean liked / the secretary of the professors / who / was / reading a letter
   b. The dean liked / the secretary of the professors / who / were / reading a letter

This is because the second of the nouns in the object phrase *the secretary of the professors* is plural. *Was* in (9a) means that the relative clause can only modify the whole phrase, where *secretary* is the main noun, and *were* in (9b) means that the relative clause can only modify *professors*. If participants' parsing preference is for modification of the most recent noun, the speed at which they press the key to advance the sentence after they have encountered *were* should be faster than when they encounter *was*. This is because with a preference for 'recency' they should be expecting *were*, which agrees with *professors*. *Was*, which agrees with *secretary*, would be unexpected. Results are presented in table 8.1. They show that the speed of key-pressing – described more technically as 'response latencies', measured in milliseconds – is significantly faster statistically after *were* has been read than after *was* has been read for the native speaker control participants, as expected, but not for either group of advanced-proficiency non-native speakers.

Felser et al. also included similar sentences in their study where the preposition linking the two nouns preceding the relative clause was *with* rather than *of*: *The dean liked the professors with the secretary who was/were reading a letter*. Their assumption was that *with* encodes more specific lexical information than *of*, and that this might affect participants' parsing preferences. Recall that native speakers of German and Greek prefer the interpretation where the relative clause modifies the whole of the object phrase when the linking preposition is the equivalent of *of*, but the interpretation where the relative clause modifies the second noun

TABLE 8.2 Response latencies (in milliseconds) to *was* and *were* when the linking preposition was *with* (based on Felser et al., 2003: 466–73, Tables 3, 6 and 8)

	was	were	Significant difference
NS controls (n = 45)	512	648	Yes
L1 German (n = 28)	428	502	Yes
L1 Greek (n = 39)	532	661	Yes

('recency') when the preposition is the equivalent of *with*. If participants opt for 'recency' when the preposition is *with*, they should be expecting a verb that agrees with *secretary* rather than *professors*, and hence be quicker in pressing the key to advance the sentence after they have read *was* than after they have read *were*. The mean response latencies are presented in table 8.2.

The conclusions that Felser and her colleagues draw from these findings are firstly that they cannot be explained by simple transfer of parsing procedures from the participants' L1s. If simple transfer had been involved, the German and Greek speakers should have preferred an interpretation where relative clauses modify the whole object phrase when the linking preposition was *of*. This is the preference found for equivalent constructions in their L1s. In fact they showed no preference for one interpretation over the other in their treatment of English. Secondly, the results suggest that because the L2 participants show a clear preference for interpreting relative clauses as modifying the most recent phrase when the preposition is *with*, they 'can access and make use of lexical-semantic information during on-line sentence comprehension' (2003: 474), this information being provided by *with*. This suggests to Felser et al. that the L2 participants in their study do not use information about syntactic phrase structure during parsing (and that is why they have no preference for either a recent-phrase-modifying or a whole-object-modifying interpretation of the relative clause when the preposition is *of*), unlike the native speakers. But they make use of lexical-semantic information, possibly to a greater extent than native speakers do, as suggested in the Roberts and Felser (2011) study.

Sections 8.1 and 8.2 in a Nutshell

The first verb in garden-path sentences like *The woman sold the house emigrated to Australia* is ambiguous: *sold* can be interpreted either as the past tense form of a transitive verb or as a passive participle. In parsing, speakers have a preference for the transitive verb interpretation. Juffs (2004), using a self-paced reading task, has shown that L2 speakers of English display the same parsing preference as native speakers, although generally they were slower readers overall.

When Roberts and Felser (2011) manipulated the plausibility of the determiner phrase following garden-path verbs (e.g. *While the band played the song pleased ...* versus *While the band played the beer pleased ...*) they found that this had no effect on native-speaker parsing, but L2 speakers (with L1 Greek) were slower when the determiner phrase following the garden-path verb was a plausible direct object than when it was not. This is consistent with the claim that the parsing of sentences by native speakers is fundamentally determined by syntactic properties, while L2 speakers may rely more on semantic or pragmatic information. This was further supported in a study by Felser et al. (2003) of the preference for modification of complex DPs like *the secretary of/with the professor* by a relative clause complement like *who was reading a letter*. Native speakers of English have a parsing preference for the closest DP as the subject of the relative clause. Native speakers of German and Greek have a preference for the closest DP when equivalent sentences in German and Greek have the preposition *with*, but for the whole object phrase when the preposition is *of*. This is because *with* encodes specific lexical information that blocks modification of a more distant DP, while *of* does not. Greek and German speakers with advanced L2 proficiency in English also have a 'closest DP' preference when the preposition in English is *with*, but no preference when the preposition is *of*. Felser et al. interpret this to mean that the L2 speakers are using lexical-semantic information during parsing (hence the preference for the most recent DP when the preposition is *with*) but are not using syntactic/phrase structure information when the preposition is *of* (hence the absence of a preference).

8.3 The Interface between Grammatical Knowledge and Discourse Information

The preference for treating the determiner phrase following a transitive verb as its object (leading to garden-path sentences), and for allowing a relative clause to modify one noun rather than another in a complex determiner phrase (in instances like *the secretary of the professor who was reading the letter*) are cases where the listener/reader knows more about the grammar of the language than they actually use in real-time comprehension. There are also things that a listener/reader needs to know in real-time comprehension that go beyond the strictly grammatical. One such type of knowledge is understanding how information is organised across sentences and how this links to grammatical knowledge.

8.3.1 The Marking of 'Topic' and 'Focus' in Languages

Sentences do not normally occur in isolation. They combine with other sentences in conversations, talks, narratives, reports and so on, to create extended stretches of meaning. The term **discourse** is often used to refer to such cases of multiple sentence use. Discourse imposes its own constraints both on the choice of lexical items used and on the grammatical form of individual sentences. These constraints relate to cohesion in the presentation of old and new information. To illustrate, the following narrative is distinctly odd, not because there is anything wrong with the grammaticality of the individual sentences, but because there are too many repetitions of *coach driver*.

10a. The coach driver reported to the police that the coach driver's coach had been stolen. The coach driver said the coach driver's coach was parked behind the hotel overnight.

A more normal-sounding narrative is produced if some of the occurrences of *coach driver* and *coach* are replaced by pronouns:

10b. The coach driver reported to the police that **his** coach had been stolen. **He** said that **it** was parked behind the hotel overnight.

After the introduction of *coach driver* as new information, the discourse constraints of English determine that subsequent references to this now 'old' information be in less specified forms: pronouns.

There are similar discourse constraints on the choice of word order patterns. The following dialogues are odd not because of the choice of lexical items or the grammaticality of individual sentences, but because sentences with the wrong information structure have been chosen for the answers to the questions. (The answers in these examples should be read so that the main stress falls on the last word, as indicated by capital letters).

11 a. Q: Whom did the letter offend?
       A: Jim was offended by the LETTER.
    b. Q: What offended Jim?
       A: The letter offended JIM.

If the answers are reversed in (11a–b) the two dialogues sound completely normal:

12 a. Q: Whom did the letter offend?
       A: The letter offended JIM
    b. Q: What offended Jim?
       A: Jim was offended by the LETTER.

The two fundamental constructs relevant to information cohesion in discourse are **topic** (old information that the speaker/writer assumes his/her hearer/reader shares) and **focus** (new information that the speaker/writer assumes is not shared by his/her hearer/reader). While the marking of topic and focus in discourse is a universal of all languages (Erteshik-Shir, 2007: 43–7), they vary in the mechanisms they use to implement the distinction. English can use contrastive stress to signal focus. So while *The letter offended JIM* is a discourse-inappropriate response to the question in (11b), if the main stress is shifted to *LETTER*, the answer becomes appropriate:

11 b'. Q: What offended Jim?
            A: The LETTER offended Jim.

This is because, in English, focus information can either appear at the end of a clause, or in an earlier position in a clause if it receives contrastive stress.

Spanish does not have a rule that shifts main stress to mark focus information. Instead, the syntactic rule Move shifts topic information to the left, leaving the focus in a clause-final position where it receives main stress (Zubizarreta and Nava, 2011: 659–660). In (13a), in the answer to the question *What did Maria buy?*, the object of the verb is the focus, and the word order is the same as in English. But in (13b) the focus in the answer to the question *Who bought an old stamp?* is the subject. In English, *Maria* can be contrastively stressed to signal that it is the focus, but in Spanish the verb and its complement have shifted to the left:

13 a. Q: ¿Que   compró María?
             What   bought Maria?
             'What did Maria buy?'
        A: María   compró un   sello viejo
             Maria   bought a   stamp old
             'Maria bought an old stamp'

    b. Q: ¿Quién   compró un   sello   viejo?
             Who   bought a   stamp   old?
             'Who bought an old stamp?'
        A: Compró un   sello   viejo   María
             Bought a   stamp   old   Maria
             'MARIA bought an old stamp'

Because languages vary in the linguistic devices they use to establish information cohesion in discourse, L2 learners need to identify those devices that are appropriate for the language in question. How successful are L2 learners in acquiring this knowledge?

8.3.2 The Acquisition of Topic and Focus Marking by L2 Learners

In German, like Spanish, Move shifts topic information to the left to allow a focused constituent to appear towards the end of a clause. The following examples are from Hopp (2007: 277). They concern word order in an embedded clause. Example (14a) is the non-moved word order where the subject, *der Lehrling* 'the apprentice', precedes the direct object, *den Arbeiter* 'the worker'. In (14b) the direct object has moved to the left leaving the subject as the last determiner phrase in the clause. (As noted in section 4.5.1, in German embedded clauses the finite verb and any non-finite verb forms occur at the end):

14 a. Ich glaube, dass **der Lehrling** am Montag den **Arbeiter** abgelenkt
        I   think   that   the apprentice   on Monday the worker   distracted
        'I think that the apprentice distracted the worker last Monday'

    b. Ich glaube, dass **den Arbeiter** am Montag **der Lehrling** abgelenkt hat
        I   think   that   the worker   on Monday the apprentice   distracted has
        'I think that the apprentice distracted the worker last Monday'

The roles of subject and direct object in these sentences are clearly marked by the Nominative Case form of the definite article *der*, and the Accusative Case form of the definite article *den*. Version (14a) occurs most naturally in contexts where all the information given is in focus (i.e. new) – all-focus contexts – for example, in response to a question like 'What happened?' It also occurs naturally in a context where only the direct object is focused, for example in response to a question like 'Whom do you think the apprentice distracted last Monday?' Version (14b) by contrast is most natural in a context where the subject is focused and the direct object is part of the topic information, for example in response to a question like 'Who do you think distracted the worker last Monday?'

Hopp (2007) investigated how native and L2 speakers of German parse sentences like those in (14) in three different discourse contexts: one where most of the sentence is new information (the all-focus context), one where the direct object of the embedded clause is the focus, and one where the subject of the embedded clause is the focus. Examples of the kinds of context he used are illustrated in (15):

15. All-focus: In the factory the machines ground to a standstill last Monday.
                   What had happened?
    Object-focus: In the factory, the apprentice distracted someone last Monday.
                   Whom did the apprentice distract?
    Subject-focus: In the factory the worker was distracted by someone last
                   Monday. Who distracted the worker?

Participants in the study were advanced-proficiency and near-native speakers of German with L1 English or L1 Russian,[1] and a control group of native German speakers to provide baseline information. The self-paced reading task required participants first to read contexts like those in (15) on a computer screen, and then to read a test sentence broken up into seven reading segments, for example:

16.   1   2   3   4   5   6   7
    Ich glaube | dass | der Lehrling | am Montag | den Arbeiter | abgelenkt | hat

---

[1] Hopp also included L1 speakers of Dutch in his study. These are not considered here.

Participants pressed a key on the computer keyboard to see the first segment, pressed the key again to see the next segment, which replaced the first segment, and so on to the end of the sentence. The time it took participants to read each segment was recorded in milliseconds. Hopp then summed the reading times from segment 3 to segment 5, covering the subject and direct object phrases. The prediction was that if participants had acquired the link between word order and discourse information (topic and focus), this would be reflected in their reading times. Where a word order focuses a part of the clause that is in conflict with the information provided by the context there should be a slowdown in reading time as participants attempt to re-analyse a structure which they have mis-parsed (just like in the case of the garden-path sentences). Importantly, in Russian Move shifts topic information to put subjects syntactically into focus position, just like German. This is not the case in English. The design therefore allowed Hopp to test for potential influence from the L1 on the acquisition of the link between word order and topic and focus information. English speakers might be expected to have more difficulty acquiring the link than Russian speakers because such linking is absent from English.

The reading time results (mean sum of each group's reading times for segments 3 to 5 of the test sentences) are presented in table 8.3. SO refers to the non-moved subject–direct object word order; OS refers to the shifted direct object–subject word order that puts the subject in focus position. Statistically significant differences in reading times between the SO and OS word orders are signalled by an asterisk.

The native speaker responses are as expected. They are significantly slower in reading segments 3 to 5 in sentences with shifted OS word order in all-focus and

TABLE 8.3 Mean reading times for segments 3 to 5 in test sentences like (16) (based on Hopp, 2007: 296, Tables 7.15 and 7.16)

	All-Focus			Object-Focus			Subject-Focus		
	SO	OS	diff	SO	OS	diff	SO	OS	diff
Native speakers (n = 16)	2005	2285	280*	1782	2227	445*	1832	1984	152
Eng near-natives (n = 11)	2700	2994	294*	2265	2720	455*	2405	2680	275
Eng advanced (n = 9)	2946	3196	250	2496	2968	472*	2611	2625	14
Russ near-natives (n = 10)	3181	3557	376*	2732	3043	311*	2579	2778	199
Russ advanced (n = 12)	3108	3291	183	2572	3323	751*	2694	2956	262

object-focus contexts by comparison with SO word order. This is because the word order specifically identifies the subject as new information, but either this information has already been supplied by the context or more new information than just the subject is required. The slowdown in reading time is consistent with native speakers' expectations about topic and focus not being met. Their reading times do not slow down when they read OS sentences in contexts that favour the subject as new information. They are not significantly different from the reading times for the non-shifted SO word order. Furthermore, their reading times are significantly faster for OS order in subject-focus contexts than in direct object-focus contexts (1984 ms versus 2227 ms). These results suggest that native speakers clearly link shifted and non-shifted word order with topic and focus information determined by the discourse.

The near-native-proficiency Russian speakers perform just like the native speakers, suggesting that they have also fully established the relevance of topic and focus to shifted and non-shifted word order. The near-native English speakers are almost like the natives. They find OS word order statistically significantly less natural than SO word order in all-focus and direct object-focus contexts. They also do not slow down significantly when OS word order is encountered in a subject-focus context, by comparison with SO word order. However, their reading times for OS word order are not significantly faster in the subject-focus context than in the direct object-focus context (2680 versus 2720), as they are for the native speakers (1984 versus 2227) and Russian near-native speakers (2778 versus 3043). This leads Hopp to suggest that this shows an element of L1 influence: 'the context effect attained for the L1 English group can be considered to be somewhat weaker than for the native and the L1 Russian group. This may be related to facilitatory effects of analogous L1 properties for the L1 Russian group' (2007: 299).

The performance of the advanced-proficiency English and Russian groups suggests that the acquisition of knowledge of the link between syntactic structure and topic and focus may come relatively late in development. Neither advanced-proficiency group is like the native-speaker control group or the near-native speakers, even though Russian has a similar link between word order and topic/focus to German. Although both advanced groups recognise the unnaturalness of OS word order in object-focus contexts, by comparison with SO order, there is no significant difference in their reading times for SO and OS order in all-focus contexts and their reading times for OS order in subject-focus contexts are not significantly faster than in direct object-focus contexts.

In conclusion, L2 speakers appear able to establish a link between word order properties and topic/focus information, even when no such link exists in their L1. But this occurs very late in development.

Another domain in which there is a link between topic/focus and grammatical knowledge involves two subclasses of intransitive verbs (verbs that do not have direct objects) known as **unaccusative** and **unergative**. Unaccusative intransitive verbs are those that describe a change of state, like *open, close, die, arrive, sink, melt* (Levin and Rappaport Hovav, 2005: 12–13). For example, *Tom arrived* describes a change from a state where *Tom* was not at a particular place to a state where he was. Unergative intransitive verbs do not describe a change of state: *shout, laugh, run, walk*. Because the subjects of unaccusative verbs are typically affected by the change of state, rather than being instigators of it, some linguists have argued that unaccusative clauses are derived from a phrase structure where the subject is first merged with the verb as its object (Perlmutter, 1978), e.g. *e arrive Tom*. In English, Move then moves *Tom* to the empty subject position. By contrast, the subject of unergatives is first merged directly in the subject position.

Unlike English, in some languages the subjects of unaccusatives can surface in their first-merged post-verbal position, as well as in pre-verbal position. In these languages this difference in word order is linked to topic and focus. Spanish is one such language. Hertel (2003) observes that where Spanish unaccusative intransitive verbs (e.g. *llegar* 'to arrive', *entrar* 'to enter', *venir* 'to come', *desaparecar* 'to disappear', etc.) appear in sentences that express all-focus information for the hearer/reader (as in response to a question like *¿Qué pasó?* 'What happened?'), those sentences typically have verb–subject (VS) word order, as in (17) (examples from Hertel):

17 a. Q: ¿Qué   pasó?
            What   happened?
        A: Llegó   mi   nieto
            Arrived my   my grandson
            My grandson arrived'

In contrast, all-focus sentences containing unergative intransitive verbs (e.g. *gritar* 'to shout', *llorar* 'to cry', *bailar* 'to dance', *dormir* 'to sleep', etc.) typically have subject–verb (SV) word order:

17 b. Q: ¿Qué   pasó?
            What   happened?
        A: Mi   nieto   gritó
            My   grandson   shouted
            'My grandson shouted'

However, when the information expressed by the verb is assumed to be known to the hearer/reader, for example, in response to questions like *Who arrived? Who shouted?*, the word order is typically VS for both unaccusative and unergative intransitives. This is because Spanish has a syntactic rule for moving non-focused information to the left (see the discussion in section 8.3.1), in this case the unergative verb.

18 a. Q: ¿ Quién   llegó?
            Who   arrived?
        A: Llegó   mi   nieto
            arrived   my   grandson
            'My grandson arrived'
    b. Q: ¿ Quién   gritó?
            Who   shouted?
        A: Gritó   mi   nieto
            shouted   my   grandson
            'My grandson shouted'

It can be seen from these examples that L2 learners of Spanish need to learn (a) that Spanish has a syntactic rule that moves the verb (and any complement it might have) to the left of the subject; (b) that the decision about when to use this rule is conditioned by discourse information (i.e. what the focus and the topic in the sentence are).

Hertel tested knowledge of these properties in four groups of L2 speakers of Spanish (all with L1 English) ranging in proficiency from beginner to advanced, and compared them with a control group of native speakers. Participants read contexts like the one in (19) (Hertel's example (12)) followed either by a question that required an all-focus answer or a question that required a subject-focus answer.

19. You and your friend Sergio are at a party. Sergio leaves to use the bathroom. While he is in the bathroom, Sara, the life of every party, arrives. When Sergio returns he notices that everyone seems much more festive.

Sergio asks you: ¿Qué pasó?   (all-focus)
What do you answer?   _____
Sergio asks you: ¿Quién llegó?   (subject-focus)
What do you answer?   _____

There were six contexts requiring an answer to an all-focus question and six contexts requiring an answer to a subject-focus question, as well as six distractor contexts where the question was a *why?*-question. Results are presented in table 8.4 as mean percentages of VS answers (all other answers were SV). If the L2 speakers have acquired the discourse-information function expressed by word order in Spanish, they should produce VS answers with unaccusatives but not unergatives in response to all-focus questions, and VS answers with both types of verbs in response to subject-focus questions.

It is evident from the native-speaker results that the use of VS order to ensure discourse information cohesion is a tendency rather than a categorical requirement.

TABLE 8.4 Mean percentage VS answers to all-focus and subject-focus questions (based on Hertel, 2003: 290–1, Tables 3 and 4)

	All-Focus		Subject-Focus	
	Unacc	Unerg	Unacc	Unerg
Beginners (n=24)	0	0	0	0
Lower Intermed (n=15)	6	0	5	0
High Intermed (n=18)	9	1	15	13
Advanced (n=24)	56	33	54	36
Native controls (n=18)	39	7	36	33

In all cases the native-speaker responses involved more examples of SV order than VS order. Nevertheless, the native speakers make a clear distinction in their use of VS order when all information in a sentence is in focus and when the subject only is in focus. In the all-focus context, the use of VS with unaccusative verbs is considerably higher than with unergatives, and this was statistically significant. In the subject-focus contexts the native-speaker control participants use VS word order with unergatives, as well as with unaccusatives. This is because they use the syntactic rule Move to shift non-focused information to the left in a context where the verb is the topic and the subject is the focus.

Although the advanced-proficiency English speakers also use VS word order with unergative verbs, it may not be because they have acquired the topic shift rule of Spanish. Their use of VS word order with unergatives is the same in subject-focus and all-focus contexts, suggesting that they optionally allow both unaccusatives and unergatives to appear in SV and VS word orders without a specific link to topic and focus. The less proficient L2 speakers have recognised that Spanish allows VS word order only to a limited extent.

As in the case of the link between word order and topic/focus in German, the results from Hertel's study suggest that the acquisition of such a link in Spanish may also come very late in development. Advanced-proficiency speakers have not yet acquired it.

Lozano (2006) looked at the same phenomenon in Spanish using a different methodology, and comparing advanced-proficiency L2 speakers of Spanish with L1 English and L1 Greek. Interestingly, Greek, like Spanish, allows unaccusative intransitive sentences to have VS word order in all-focus contexts, but like English does not have a rule that shifts the verb and its complement to the left when the subject is in focus. That is, it uses the same pattern of word order as Spanish in examples like (18a) but does not have the word order pattern shown in (18b). Like Hertel, Lozano presented participants with contexts followed either by all-focus questions (*¿Qué pasó?* 'What happened?') or subject-focus questions (*¿Quién llegó?* 'Who arrived?'), but were then given two possible answers to that question, and a scale on which to rate those answers going from −2 (completely unacceptable) to +2 (completely acceptable), as illustrated in (20).

20. a. La policía llegó   −2 −1 0 +1 +2 (The police arrived)
    b. Llegó la policía   −2 −1 0 +1 +2 (Arrived the police)

The mean scores for participants were converted into mean percentages of acceptance. Results are presented in table 8.5 in a format similar to that of Hertel for the purpose of comparison.

The native speakers in this study are accepting more VS word order with unergative verbs in all-focus contexts than might be expected, but they are doing this significantly less than in subject-focus contexts. This is consistent with the expectation that VS word order is more natural with unaccusative verbs in all-focus contexts than with unergative verbs.

The English and Greek participants are using VS word order with unergative verbs to just about the same extent in all-focus and subject-focus contexts, suggesting that they may not have acquired the topic shift rule of Spanish but are optionally allowing SV and VS word order with unergative verbs. The fact that they are using VS word order more with unaccusatives than unergatives might suggest nevertheless that they are aware that these are distinct verb classes (as in the case of Hertel's advanced-proficiency participants).

Again, if the link between word order and topic/focus is acquirable by L2 speakers, that knowledge must come very late in development because advanced-proficiency speakers have not yet established it.

Going in the other L1–L2 direction, Zubizarreta and Nava (2011) examined whether native speakers of Spanish who are L2 learners of English are sensitive to the use of main stress assignment in English clauses to signal focus. They first observe that the location of main stress in English distinguishes unaccusative from unergative verbs in all-focus contexts. The most natural main stress assignment with unaccusative verbs is the subject determiner phrase and not the verb (examples from Zubizarreta and Nava, 2011: 654):

21 a. Why are you so happy?   My FRIEND arrived
   b. What was that crashing sound?   A WINDOW broke

However, with unergatives in all-focus contexts main stress is possible both on the subject determiner phrase and the verb:

22 a. How did the party end?   A GUEST sang
   b.   A guest SANG

TABLE 8.5 Mean percentage ratings of VS answers to all-focus and subject-focus questions (based on Lozano, 2006: 187, Appendix 2)

	All-Focus Question		Subject-Focus Question	
	Unacc	Unerg	Unacc	Unerg
L1 English (n=17)	87	70	85	77
L1 Greek (n=18)	91	69	82	75
Native speakers (n=14)	84	46	87	84

TABLE 8.6 Percentage location of main stress in all-focus and subject-focus contexts (based on Zubizarreta and Nava, 2011: 661–2, Tables 2 and 4)

	All-Focus Contexts				Subject-Focus contexts
	Unaccusative		Unergative		Unacc + Unerg
	S̲V	SV̲	S̲V	SV̲	S̲V
Natives (n = 34)	97	3	42	58	98
High proficiency (n = 27)	36	64	39	61	96
Intermediate prof. (n = 19)	4	96	16	84	68

In subject-focus contexts, main stress in English would naturally fall only on the subject determiner phrase:

23 a. Who arrived?   My FRIEND arrived
    b. Who sang?   A GUEST sang

As described above, Spanish does not allow main stress to shift from the end of the clause to the subject determiner phrase to signal focus.

Zubizarreta and Nava (2011) asked nineteen Spanish speakers of intermediate proficiency in English, twenty-seven of high proficiency and thirty-four native English speakers to participate in a task involving scripted question and answer dialogues. Participants worked in pairs. Each read a script that represented one half of a dialogue, the other half of which was read by the co-conversationalist. Participants were asked to read their part 'as if they were engaged in a natural conversation' (2011: 660). Embedded in the conversations were twelve unaccusative and twelve unergative verbs in all-focus contexts. Four verbs (two unaccusatives and two unergatives) were in subject-focus contexts. Results are presented in table 8.6 as percentages of main stress assignment on the subject or the verb, indicated by underlining: S̲V (stress on the subject), SV̲ (stress on the verb).

In all-focus contexts the native speakers produce utterances with main stress location as expected: on the subject determiner phrase with unaccusatives, but either on the subject or the verb in the case of unergatives. The intermediate-proficiency L2 speakers predominantly locate main stress on the verb, which is where it would be located in Spanish. The high-proficiency L2 speakers have recognised that English allows main stress to fall on the subject, but they are not distinguishing unaccusatives from unergative verbs in all-focus contexts. They are optionally allowing stress to fall on the subject in both cases. However, their performance in subject-focus contexts is a bit surprising. It appears that here they have established the link between stress on the subject and focus since they are placing stress appropriately in 96% of cases.

This requires a rethinking of the results in the other studies described. In all four studies (Hopp, Hertel, Lozano and Zubizarreta and Nava) advanced-proficiency L2 speakers perform in a target-like way in subject-focus contexts, recognising that syntactic movement or stress assignment are ways of ensuring that the subject of a clause is the focus (provides new information in the discourse). Their non-target performance occurs in all-focus contexts, where they optionally move or optionally assign main stress to subject or verb where only one of these is appropriate. Thus it may be easier for learners to identify the target-language mechanism for focusing the subject in clauses than to identify how syntax or stress assignment is involved in focusing all of the information in a clause.

Sections 8.3.1 and 8.3.2 in a Nutshell

L2 speakers need to learn how discourse-determined topic (old information) and focus (new information) link to syntax, lexicon and/or phrasal stress assignment in the target language. In the default case, topic information appears early in the clause and focus information at the end. But where the subject is focused, English can signal this through contrastive stress (*The LETTER offended Jim*). Spanish and German use Move to shift topic information to early in the clause so that the subject can be focused (for example, *Compró un sello viejo María* lit. 'Bought an old stamp Maria'). English-, Russian- and Greek-speaking L2 learners of Spanish and German can acquire the link between topic and focus information and syntactic topic shift, but only at very high levels of proficiency. Spanish-speaking L2 learners of English with high proficiency are moving towards establishing the link between shifted main stress and identification of the focused constituent. During development, L2 learners appear to identify the grammatical mechanism for indicating a focused subject more quickly than the mechanism for indicating that all information in a clause is new.

8.3.3 The Acquisition of Pronoun Reference Resolution by L2 Speakers

Like the reflexive anaphors discussed in section 6.2.2, pronouns (forms like English *he, she, they, I, you*) are dependent for their reference on a determiner phrase elsewhere in the current sentence, or outside the sentence in an earlier part of the discourse, or an entity in the non-linguistic context in which the discourse occurs. When they assign interpretations to sentences, speakers need to identify the appropriate co-referents for pronouns. This is not always a straightforward task. There may be several potential DPs in the discourse or entities in the non-linguistic context that could act as co-referents. Imagine the following scenario (taken from Sorace and Filiaci, 2006): a grandmother, a mother and her daughter are all present in a room. One of them is putting a coat on and the mother is giving her daughter a kiss. In the context of this scenario you hear the following sentence:

24. While **she** is putting her coat on, the mother gives her daughter a kiss.

In English, the pronoun *she* is triply ambiguous, given the scenario. It could be co-referential with one of the two DPs within the sentence: *mother* or *daughter*; i.e. the mother could be putting her coat on or the daughter could be putting her coat on. It could also be co-referential with the other person in the scenario, but who is not mentioned in the sentence: the grandmother.

In contrast to English, some languages allow an alternation between null and overt pronouns. Italian and Mandarin Chinese are two such languages. In these languages it would be normal to use a null pronoun where it represents expected known (topic) information. For example, in a discourse like the following the null pronoun is expected to be co-referential with *Mr Li: Mr Li went shopping for his father. Ø bought some eggs.* Overt pronouns in null subject languages shift the topic reference from the expected co-referential DP to another entity. In this case the reference shifts to the father.

In sentences equivalent to (24) in Italian and Mandarin Chinese, the use of a null pronoun appears to favour the closest DP within the sentence as the co-referent, i.e. *the mother is putting her coat on.* The use of the overt pronoun shifts the topic and strongly favours a referent external to the sentence, i.e. *the grandmother is putting her coat on.* Sorace and Filiaci (2006) investigated the co-reference choices for null and overt pronouns made by advanced-proficiency and near-native L2 speakers of Italian (with L1 English) compared with native speakers. The Italian equivalent of (24) is given in (25):

25. Mentre lei/Ø si mette   il   cappotto, la   mamma dà   un baciò alla   figlia
　　While   she/Ø is wearing the coat   the mother gives a   kiss   to-the daughter

Twenty participants saw sentences like these in the context of three pictures, where each picture differed in the person putting the coat on. Participants had to indicate which of the pictures corresponded to the meaning of the sentence. Results for the near-native speakers (n = 14) are reported in table 8.7 as percentage choices of the picture depicting one of the characters putting her coat on where the pronoun is null and where it is overt.

TABLE 8.7 Native and near-native Italian speaker choices of co-referents for pronouns (based on Sorace and Filiaci, 2006: 354, Table 1)

		grandmother	mother	daughter
Native Italian (n = 20)	Ø	4	85	11
	lei	64	12	24
Near-native Italian (n = 14)	Ø	6	85	9
	lei	28	47	25

Both groups strongly favour the subject of the main clause – *mother* – when the pronoun is null. This is the expected topic and both the native speakers and the near-native L2 group assume the null pronoun refers to it. In the case of the overt pronoun, the native speakers in the majority of cases shift the co-reference to a different topic: *grandmother*. The majority of responses from the near-native speakers continue to identify *mother* as the co-referent, although the shift in topic effected by the choice of an overt pronoun is recognised to some extent. It appears that the L2 speakers, despite being of near-native proficiency, have not fully established the link between pronoun choice and discourse-determined topic information.

Zhao (2008) investigated co-reference choices for pronouns by advanced proficiency L2 speakers of Mandarin Chinese (with L1 English) in similar sentences and scenarios to those of Sorace and Filiaci. Zhao presented her participants with pictures showing, for example, a character called *Lao Lu* climbing a tree and another character watching him. Accompanying sentences were like the one in (26):

26. Ta/Ø   pa   shu   shihou Lao   Lu   meiyou chuan   xiezi
    He/Ø   climb tree   when, Lao   Lu   not-have wear   shoe
    'When he climbs the tree, Lao Lu is not wearing shoes'

Zhao asked sixteen native speakers of Mandarin Chinese and thirteen advanced-proficiency L2 speakers (with L1 English) to rate the sentences as possible descriptions of the pictures on a scale from –2 (completely untrue to the picture) to +2 (completely true to the picture). In the case of (26), the sentence with the null pronoun would be completely true to the picture since the co-referent is Lao Lu. However, the sentence with the overt pronoun is not true to the picture because the overt pronoun most naturally shifts the topic to the other, non-tree-climbing character, who becomes the co-referent. The mean ratings for co-reference between the null pronoun (Ø) and the main clause subject (true to the picture) and overt pronoun (*ta*) and main clause subject (not true to the picture) are given in table 8.8.

While the native speakers' ratings are as expected (they rate the sentence with a null subject as true to the picture, but reject the sentence with the overt pronoun because it identifies (incorrectly) the bystander as the person climbing the tree), the L2 speakers rate both Ø and *ta* as natural descriptions of the picture. That is, they allow both Ø and *ta* to have the same co-referent.

TABLE 8.8 Mean rating of the main clause subject as a co-referent for null and overt third person singular pronouns in Mandarin Chinese (based on Zhao, 2008)

	Ø	ta
Native speakers (n = 16)	+1.88	−1.44
Advanced proficiency L2 speakers	+1.88	+1.00

What the results of these two studies appear to suggest is that while the L2 speakers have established the reference resolution properties of null subjects (performing like native speakers), they are persistently divergent in their treatment of the reference resolution properties of overt pronominals. Since pronoun resolution in this case is discourse-determined, a conclusion that could be drawn is that English-speaking learners of Italian and Chinese are having difficulty matching up the morphological realisation of pronouns with their co-referents in discourse.

Sorace and Filiaci (2006) consider two ways in which this might be understood:

(i) as a grammatical problem
(ii) as a problem to do with integrating grammatical and discourse information in real time – a 'processing' problem

As a grammatical problem, they propose that in languages that have a null/overt pronoun alternation, the overt pronoun has the feature [+topic shift]. Returning to sentence (25), if the pronoun is interpreted as co-referential with the matrix subject *mother* it represents a 'continued topic', hence a pronoun form realising the feature [+topic shift] is ruled out. On this interpretation, the L2 speakers have failed to make the link between overt pronouns and the feature [+topic shift]. They allow overt pronouns to take 'continued topics' as antecedents, a possibility allowed in English.

As a processing problem, the account favoured by Sorace and Filiaci (2006), the idea is that L2 speakers 'may not consistently hav[e] the computational resources necessary to coordinate the use of an overt pronoun with the introduction of a new or contrastive topic' (Sorace, 2005: 71). This assumes that L2 speakers know that the use of overt pronouns in null-subject languages signals topic shift, but because of limitations in their ability to integrate discourse information while they are parsing grammatical information, they allow overt pronouns to have sentence-internal reference (Sorace, 2005: 73). This is exacerbated by L1 influence in the case of L1 English speakers since in English pronouns are 'not conditioned by discourse factors' (2005: 70), so that English speakers are not used to taking discourse information into account in pronoun reference resolution.

There is evidence from other studies that is potentially problematic for the 'processing problem' interpretation. This evidence relates to L2 speakers persistently allowing discourse to 'condition' syntactic computations where it is inappropriate to do so, and suggests that L1 transfer is a major player in determining whether there is divergence between L2 speakers and L1 speakers where syntax and discourse interface. It is not the interface per se that is problematic, but whether L2 speakers can restructure from the transferred L1 properties of syntax–discourse mapping to those of the L2.

Roberts et al. (2008) studied pronoun reference resolution in L2 speakers and native speakers of Dutch, a non-null subject language. Fourteen L1 Turkish speakers (Turkish a null-subject language), sixteen L1 German speakers (German normally regarded as a non-null-subject language) and thirty native speakers participated

TABLE 8.9 Choices of closest topic in a comprehension task

	'Peter' chosen
Dutch NS	100%
L1 German	91%
L1 Turkish	55%

in a co-referent resolution task.[2] Both L2 groups were highly proficient in Dutch. Participants were presented with sentences of three different types, one of which was the following (in English gloss form):

27a. Peter and Hans are in the office. While Peter working is, eats **he** a sandwich. It is a quiet day.

Note here that there are two potential co-referents for *he*: Peter and Hans. Having heard sentences like this, participants answered a comprehension question, which determined their preferred co-referent:

27b. A sandwich is eaten by _____ .

Results from this task, presented as percentage choices of *Peter*, the closest topic, are presented in table 8.9:

On the assumption that overt pronouns in null subject languages have the feature [+topic shift], what we seem to see in these results is the Turkish speakers continuing to assume that overt pronouns in Dutch shift the topic, just as they do in their L1. In around half of their choices they prefer to shift the topic rather than continue with *Peter* as the topic. The German speakers do not do this. Although Dutch does not have an overt pronoun/null pronoun alternation, and therefore Turkish speakers have to use overt pronouns where null forms would be required in Turkish (in sentence-internal continued topic contexts), where there is an option to select a shifted topic as the antecedent, the Turkish speakers opt for it. If processing limitations affect the ability of L2 speakers to integrate discourse information into syntactic representations, the Turkish speakers might have been expected to select the sentence-internal topic, which does not require integration of sentence-external discourse information. The contrast between the Turkish speakers and the German speakers is striking. The German speakers do not look outside the current sentence for a potential antecedent, as they would not in their L1. The asymmetry here between the German and the Turkish speakers suggests L1 influence on discourse–syntax mapping, rather than a processing problem.

A second example comes from an eye-tracking study of the reference resolution of reflexives by Bertenshaw (2009). Bertenshaw measured the eye movements of thirty-seven native speakers of English and thirty-two advanced-proficiency L2 speakers with L1 Japanese. In English, reflexives do not co-refer with determiner

---

[2] Roberts et al. also conducted an eye-tracking study and gave participants a comprehension questionnaire. The results of these are not considered here.

phrases outside their immediate clause, whereas the Japanese reflexive *zibun* 'self' does (see section 6.4). In an initial task requiring participants to decide possible co-referents for reflexives in sentences, the Japanese speakers performed like the natives in only selecting local co-referents. The on-line eye-tracking study looked at eye movements when participants read sentences like those in (28) and (29):

28. John/Jane and Richard were very worried in the kitchen of the expensive restaurant. **John/Jane** noticed that **Richard** had cut **himself** with a very sharp knife. Kitchens can be dangerous places.

29. John/Jane and Richard were very worried in the kitchen of the expensive restaurant. It was clear to **John/Jane** that **Richard** had cut **himself** with a very sharp knife. Kitchens can be dangerous places.

The critical constituents for the experiment are in bold typeface. *John* matches *himself* in gender, while *Jane* clashes. Both *John* and *Jane* are 'inaccessible' co-referents for *himself* in English, only *Richard* is possible. Example (28) differs from (29) in that in (28) *John/Jane* is the subject of the main clause – a possible co-referent in Japanese. In (29) *John/Jane* is the object of a preposition, which is not a possible co-referent even in Japanese.

Bertenshaw found that the Japanese speakers looked significantly longer than the native speakers at *himself* in sentences where the inaccessible co-referent matched in gender (*John* but not *Jane*), but only where it was the subject of the main clause. In the other case there was no significant difference between the Japanese participants and the natives in the time spent looking at *himself*. Thus, although in an off-line task the Japanese speakers showed that they preferred a local co-referent for English reflexives (where in Japanese a long-distance co-referent would also be possible), the eye-tracking results seem to suggest that they are still evaluating discourse information for a potential long-distance co-referent. That this behaviour is not random or indeterminate is signalled by the fact that such information is only relevant for the Japanese speakers when the inaccessible co-referent matches the reflexive in gender and is in main clause subject position. When the potential co-referent clashes in gender or is in a non-subject position, Japanese speakers do not keep track of it. They are keeping track of syntactically-conditioned discourse information just in case it is relevant to subsequent reference resolution, as they would in Japanese.

Section 8.3.3 in a Nutshell

In languages that allow a null pronoun/overt pronoun alternation in subject position (null-subject languages) the null pronoun typically co-refers with the most recent topic in the discourse and the overt pronoun shifts co-reference to another topic. Sorace and Filiaci (2006) found that while near-native speakers of Italian with a non-null-subject L1 (English) establish co-reference for the null pronoun like native speakers, they had not fully acquired the 'topic shift' function of the overt pronoun. Zhao (2008) found a similar pattern in the acquisition of Mandarin Chinese by L1 English speakers. Sorace and Filiaci offer two potential explanations for this: (a) overt pronouns in null-subject languages have a [+topic shift] feature that has not been fully acquired by the L2 speakers (a 'morphological deficit' or 'feature re-assembly' explanation; see sections 3.2.4 and 3.2.5); (b) L2 speakers have acquired the [+topic shift] feature of overt pronouns, but sometimes fail to access it when demands on their working memory capacity are high (a variant of the Missing Surface Inflection Hypothesis (section 3.2.3) but where a feature rather than a form is not accessed when working memory is under pressure). Sorace and Filiaci favour the (b) account: L2 speakers have difficulty integrating discourse information with grammatical structure when real-time language processing demands are high. A problem for this account is evidence that L2 learners transfer L1 discourse-grammar links that are inappropriate to the L2. If learners were having difficulty integrating discourse information with grammatical knowledge it would not be expected that they would continue to scan discourse for properties that are not relevant to the L2.

8.4 Language Choices Conditioned by the Context of Language Use

In section 1.6.2 it was observed that English-speaking L2 learners of Canadian French, in a classroom immersion setting where they were interacting with native speakers, had not yet acquired the context-sensitive use of the pronouns *on* and *nous*, both meaning 'we', although they were using both forms. *On* predominates in spoken Canadian French and *nous* in written French. The L2 learners were using *nous* predominantly in both contexts (Rehner et al., 2003).

Spoken versus written use of a language is just one dimension in which there may be variation in its forms, morphemes or constructions. Linguistic variation may also correlate with different speech styles (formal vs casual), with differences in membership of socio-economic or regional groups (standard vs non-standard or regional varieties), with age differences (younger vs older speakers) and with sex differences (male vs female). On the whole, L2 speakers can acquire the varying properties of the target L2 but typically do not become aware of the correlation with context of use until they are of advanced proficiency.

Regan (1996) found that while a group of (Irish) English-speaking L2 learners of French were aware that the French sentential negator has two forms – *ne V pas* or *Ø V pas*, for example *Je ne déjeune pas à la maison, Je déjeune pas à la maison*, both meaning 'I don't have lunch at home' – their use of the forms in formal and casual speech only approximated that of native speakers after a nine-month period of residence in a French-speaking community (1996: 189). Native speakers use Ø *V pas* just under half the time in formal speech and just over half the time in casual speech. By comparison, the L2 learners were under-using Ø *V pas* in formal speech and over-using it in casual speech, before their nine months of immersion.

The verbal affix *-ing* (*reading, walking, leaving* etc.) has two pronunciations in a number of varieties of English: [ŋ] with a velar nasal coda and [n] with a dental nasal coda. [n] is found more in casual speech than in formal speech. Adamson and Regan (1991) compared thirty-one adult native speakers of English, most of whom lived in Philadelphia, and a group of fourteen adult L2 speakers with L1 Vietnamese and Cambodian (Khmer), most of whom also lived in Philadelphia, on this linguistic alternation. The task used was an interview that allowed for shifts in formality of style. As expected, the native speakers used more [n] forms in casual speech (65%) than in formal speech (28%). However, there was an interesting difference by sex. Female speakers used [n] only 8% of the time in formal speech (versus 42% in casual speech) but male speakers used [n] 51% of the time in formal speech (and 95% of the time in casual speech). The female L2 participants' use of [n] in formal speech was similar to that of the female native speakers (9%). They used [n] more in casual speech, but not as much as the female native speakers (20%). The male L2 participants showed a reverse pattern of use; they used [n] 38% of the time in formal speech but only 14% of the time in casual speech. While both female and male L2 speakers have acquired the distinct ways of pronouncing *-ing* in American English, only the female speakers showed sensitivity to the stylistic significance of that distinction.

A correlation with sex and proficiency was found in a study of L2 speakers' sensitivity to a specific speech style in Taiwanese by Hardeman (2013). Taiwanese is similar to Mandarin Chinese. In both varieties there is a style of speech characterised by higher pitch than in normal speech that is referred to as *sajiao*. A person using the *sajiao* style is perceived by native speakers as being 'cute, friendly and pleasant' (Hardeman, 2013: 156). Hardeman found that the majority of her L1 American English-speaking L2 speakers of Taiwanese were aware of the linguistic properties of *sajiao* and the correlation with sex (it was used more by the female L2 speakers than the male speakers). However, they were not aware of the correlation with the perception of the speaker as 'cute, friendly and pleasant'. They interpreted its effect as signalling submissiveness. Only two of the L2 participants with long residence in Taiwan interpreted *sajiao* in the same way as native speakers. Hardeman concludes that 'it seems likely that the Americans' lack of association of *sajiao* with friendliness, and being pleasant-sounding was due to incomplete acquisition' (2013: 162).

These representative studies of how L2 speakers acquire the contextual correlates of variation in linguistic forms, morphemes and constructions suggest that acquisition of the variable forms themselves precedes acquisition of their contextual significance. The acquisition of contextual significance may not come until speakers have had long exposure to the target language.

8.5 Concluding Remarks

The observations made in this chapter are consistent with the view that mental grammars are independent of the uses to which they are put. Mental grammars can assign more than one grammatical description to the same form or construction: *sold* can be both a finite past tense transitive verb and a passive participle; relative clauses attached to complex DPs can have merged either with the closest noun or with the whole object DP. But in comprehending incoming speech or writing there is an independent parser that can only handle one grammatical description at a time and must therefore prioritise just one of the descriptions that the mental grammar offers up.

Mental grammars can include two forms or constructions that have the same linguistic meaning or function: overt and null pronoun alternations, or different word orders where the subject precedes or follows a verb phrase or a direct object DP and the meaning is the same. But each member of the pair is linked with a particular external function: signalling topic or focus in the discourse, or differences in speech style, group membership, sex.

L2 speakers can acquire some of these grammar-independent uses, but may differ from native speakers on others. While L2 speakers of English broadly use the same parsing procedures as native speakers (Juffs, 2004) they may rely more on lexical-semantic properties than native speakers (Roberts and Felser, 2011; Felser et al., 2003). In other cases L2 speakers show more optionality than native speakers, for example in the choice of morphemes, word order and contrastive stress to mark cohesion with the information in preceding discourse (Sorace and Filiaci, 2006; Hertel, 2003; Lozano, 2006; Zubizarreta and Nava, 2011).

In most cases it appears that the links between properties of the mental grammar and the contextual use of language are acquired only when L2 speakers have had long exposure to the target language.

ACTIVITIES

1. TEST YOURSELF

(i)   What are the structural characteristics of 'garden path' sentences? Are L2 speakers 'garden-pathed' in the same way as native speakers?

(ii) What led Felser et al. (2003) to conclude that L2 speakers do not make use of syntactic phrase structure during the parsing of complex DPs with relative clause complements?

(iii) At what stage of development did Hopp (2007) find that L2 learners of German were aware that the syntactic movement of direct objects was linked to discourse information? What method did he use to show this?

(iv) How do English unaccusative and unergative clauses differ in main stress assignment in all-focus contexts? Can Spanish speakers acquire the difference? (Refer to the study by Zubizarreta and Nava (2011) in answering this question).

(v)   What appears to be the function of overt pronouns in languages that allow an overt pronoun/null pronoun alternation, like Italian and Mandarin Chinese? Can L2 speakers of languages that do not have such an alternation (like English) acquire that function?

(vi)   What evidence is there that L2 speakers transfer syntax–discourse information links from their L1 into their L2 grammars?

(vii) Can L2 speakers become aware of the contextual significance of linguistic distinctions (like the different forms of sentential negation in French (*ne V pas* versus *Ø V pas*), different pronunciations of English *-ing*, and the use of a speech style known as *sajiao* in Taiwanese/Mandarin Chinese)?

2. ACQUISITION OF OBLIGATORY SUBJECTS IN ENGLISH BY L1 SPEAKERS OF MANDARIN CHINESE AND SPANISH

Both Mandarin Chinese and Spanish are null-subject languages. In Mandarin, null subjects are licensed by context. They are possible when the reference of the subject is known from preceding discourse or from the non-linguistic context. In Spanish, null subjects are uniquely identified by the person and number affixes of the verb, e.g. *habl-o* 'I speak', *habl-as* 'you (singular) speak', *habl-a* 's/he speaks', *habl-amas* 'we speak', *habl-áis* 'you (plural) speak', *habl-an* 'they speak'.

When L1 speakers of Mandarin and Spanish acquire English, they have to establish that English disallows null subjects. Roebuck et al. (1999) gave thirteen Mandarin speakers and fifteen Spanish speakers of matched proficiency in English an elicited imitation task. Participants were asked to listen to sentences spoken by a native speaker and then repeat them. Some of the sentences contained ungrammatical null subjects in *wh*-questions, for example: *I saw the mailman come this morning. What did bring me?* Others contained grammatical overt pronouns, for example: *I am going to the party tomorrow night. What can I bring?* The rationale for elicited imitation tasks is that they permit 'access to the speaker's grammar without drawing his or her attention to it … the speaker is obliged to process and repeat the sentence in terms of his or her own grammar in an unconscious fashion' (Roebuck et al., 1999: 268). That is, if the participant's mental grammar disallows null subjects that will be reflected in the repeated sentences they produce.

The findings of the study were that the Mandarin speakers produced overt subjects in 90 per cent (47/52) of the sentences they heard which had null subjects. The Spanish speakers produced overt subjects in 69 per cent (43/62) of the same sentences. This difference was statistically significant.

Why might the Mandarin speakers, who were at the same general proficiency level in English as the Spanish speakers, be more likely to supply overt subjects?

(For some discussion of the differences between speakers of Chinese-type null-subject languages and Spanish-type null-subject languages in the acquisition of overt subjects, see Hawkins, 2001: chapter 5.7.2, pp. 214–20.)

3. ACQUIRING DISCOURSE-LINKED MOVEMENT IN MANDARIN CHINESE

In Mandarin Chinese, the expressions equivalent to *who(m)?* and *whose N?* normally appear in the position in a clause where they are interpreted – in situ *wh-*expressions. They are not moved to the front of the clause, as they are in English (Mandarin examples from Dugarova, 2014):

i. Ta   bu   xiang jian   shei?
    She   not   want   see   who?
    'Whom does she not want to see?'

ii. Ta   xihuan kan   sheide xiaoshuo?
    She   like   read   whose novel?
    'Whose novels does she like to read?'

In fact, moving *shei/sheide* to the front of the clause is ungrammatical:

iii a. *Shei ta bu xiang jian?
     b. *Sheide xiaoshuo ta xihuan kan?

However, when sentences like these are part of a discourse where *shei* and *sheide* pick up information that has already been introduced (the discourse topic), they can grammatically move to the front of the clause, the typical position for topics in Mandarin. (In the examples below, DE is a linking particle, and CL stands for 'classifier'):

iv. Jintian renshi de   ji   ge   nanhai dangzhong **shei** ta   bu   xiang **jian?**
    Today   meet   DE   few   CL   boy   among   who   she   not   want   see?
    'Of the boys she met today, whom does she not want to see?'
    (*shei* refers to the already-introduced *nanhai* 'boy(s)')

v. Zhongguo zuojia   dangzhong **sheide xiaoshuo** ta   xihuan kan?
    Chinese writer   among   whose novel   she   like   read?
    'Of Chinese writers, whose novels does she like to read?'
    (*sheide* refers to the already-introduced *zuojia* 'writer(s)')

Dugarova asked twenty-eight L1 Russian speakers who were of advanced proficiency in Mandarin and twenty native speakers to rate sentences like (i–v) on a scale from –2 (completely unacceptable) to +2 (completely acceptable). The results are presented in table (i).

> Question (i): What conclusions do you draw from these results about L2 speakers' ability to make links between grammatical knowledge and discourse information?
>
> Question (ii): Do you have any explanation for the difference in performance of the Russian group on sentence types (5) and (6)? (Compare your answer with Dugarova's, 2014: 429.)

TABLE (i). Mean ratings of in situ and moved *wh*-expressions in Mandarin (based on Dugarova, 2014: 426–7, Figures 4 and 5)

	Native speakers (n= 20)	L1 Russian (n = 28)
1. *shei?* (who?) in situ	1.97	1.96
2. *sheide? N* (whose N?) in situ	1.93	1.85
3. *Discourse-independent fronted *shei?*	−1.69	−1.49
4. *Discourse independent fronted *sheide N?*	−1.75	−1.64
5. Discourse-linked fronted *shei?*	1.57	0.59
6. Discourse-linked fronted *sheide N?*	1.59	1.48

4. DISCOURSE INFORMATION AND PRONOUN REFERENCE RESOLUTION

The claim that L2 learners have difficulty linking grammatical properties with discourse information because of processing limitations (section 8.3.3) implies that they are likely to perform at chance where such links are involved in real-time parsing.

Jegerski et al. (2011) examined pronoun reference resolution in mini discourse situations involving two clauses among native speakers of English, native speakers of Spanish and L2 learners of Spanish (of intermediate and advanced proficiency). They observe that in English an embedded-clause subject pronoun is more likely to refer to a subject in the main clause (the topic) when the embedded clause describes an event that is simultaneous with the main clause event than when the embedded clause describes an event that precedes or follows the event described in the main clause (i.e. the two events are sequential):

i   a. Jeffrey saw Ricky while he was hunting for coins in the fountain
       (the two events are simultaneous)
    b. Anita talked to her sister after she had the baby (sequential: one event occurs
       before the other)[3]

This suggests that information about the simultaneity or sequentiality of events in the discourse is influential in determining which DP a pronoun subject co-refers with.

This is not true of Spanish, where subject pronouns can be overt or null. Null subjects of embedded clauses tend to refer to the subject of the main clause, whereas overt subjects are equally likely to refer to the subject or the object of

---

[3] Jegerski et al. refer to the discourse type in (ia) as 'coordination' and that in (ib) as 'subordination'. Because of the potential confusion with the syntactic terms 'coordination' (two main clauses merged together) and 'subordination' (a main clause with a dependent embedded clause), the description in terms of simultaneous versus sequential events is preferred here.

TABLE (i). Selection of the main clause subject (%) as the co-referent for the embedded clause pronoun where discourse events are simultaneous or sequential (based on Jegerski et al., 2011: 502, Figure 6)

	Simultaneous	Sequential	Significant?
Native English (n = 43)	64	53	Yes
Native Spanish (n = 26)	64	61	No
Intermediate L2 Spanish (n = 23)	63	53	Yes
Advanced L2 Spanish (n = 21)	63	54	Yes

the main clause, according to Jegerski et al. (2011: 487). Whether the two events are simultaneous or sequential is not a factor in determining the reference of the embedded-clause subject pronoun.

Results from an interpretation task where participants had to decide who the pronoun in sentences like (i) referred to (*Jeffrey* or *Ricky, Anita* or *her sister*) are presented in table (i) as mean percentage selections of the main clause subject as the co-referent for the pronoun. (The results for the Spanish-speaking groups combine selections for both null and overt pronouns.)

How do you interpret these results in relation to the L2 acquisition of grammar–discourse links, and the claim that L2 learners have difficulty linking grammatical properties with discourse information because of 'processing' (working memory) limitations?

FURTHER READING

For overviews of the ways that L2 speakers parse sentences in the L2 see:

Dussias, P. E. and Piñar, P. 2009. Sentence parsing in L2 learners: linguistic and experience-based factors. In W. C. Ritchie and T. K. Bhatia (eds) *The new handbook of second language acquisition*. Bingley: Emerald Group Publishing, pp. 295–317.

Slabakova, R. 2016. *Second language acquisition*. Oxford: Oxford University Press, chapter 12: L2 processing.

For a general introduction to discourse information structure see:

Erteshik-Shir, N. 2007. *Information structure: the syntax–discourse interface*. Oxford: Oxford University Press.

For a detailed discussion of the acquisition of discourse-grammar links see:

Slabakova, R. 2016. *Second language acquisition. Oxford*: Oxford University Press, chapter 11: Acquisition of the syntax–discourse and semantics–pragmatics interfaces.

For more on the effect of social context on language use by second language speakers see:

Geeslin, K. L. 2014. *Sociolinguistics and second language acquisition: learning to use language in context*. Abingdon: Routledge.

9 The Role of Input in Second Language Learning

9.1 Types of Input

The view that has been emerging so far about second language acquisition is that three factors play a key role in shaping the way that L2 learners deal with the segmentation, categorisation, syntax, semantics and context problems: innate knowledge, a speaker's L1 and input. This chapter focuses on the role that input plays in providing the L2 learner with evidence for properties of the target language.

Input can take a variety of forms; among others: random samples of language encountered in everyday interactions, or **positive evidence**; instruction by a teacher about properties of the target language; correction of a learner's non-target utterances by a more proficient speaker, known as **negative evidence** about the target language (i.e. evidence about what cannot be said); modelling of the target form following a learner's production of a non-target utterance by a more proficient speaker, e.g.:

Learner:	Today I buy new bed.
More proficient speaker:	You bought a new bed?

This kind of reformulation, where the more proficient speaker provides a model of the past tense form of *buy*, is known as a 'recast', and potentially provides a learner with information that they have not used the appropriate target-language form (**indirect negative evidence**).

Given these various types of potential information about the target language, which does the L2 learner use to establish a mental grammar? If different kinds of input are usable by the L2 learner, are some kinds more effective than others in promoting acquisition?

9.2 Effects of Exposure to Positive Evidence

For child first-language learners, simple exposure to positive evidence (random samples of language as they occur in everyday interaction) appears to be sufficient to allow them to acquire the target language successfully. Infants are not given instruction about the properties of the language they are acquiring (how could they understand such instruction?). And even though children might in principle be amenable to being corrected when they produce non-target-like utterances, studies have shown that parents/carers either do not typically correct them, or if they do it has little effect on linguistic development. Guasti (2002: 3–4) summarises the findings as follows:

> Much research has been conducted to establish whether negative evidence is available to children in the form of parents' disapproval or failure to understand, parents' expansion of what children say, and frequency of parents' reactions to children's utterances … Although the question is still much debated, the general conclusion is that negative evidence is not provided to all children on all occasions, is generally noisy [*i.e. does not clearly identify what the correct target form is – RH]* and is not sufficient.

Children's success in establishing mental grammars for their first language(s) on the basis of simple exposure to samples of the language would appear to be because they are equipped, through genetic endowment, with the capacity to segment continuous input into sequences of form–meaning pairings, to use innate knowledge to categorise those form–meaning pairings as morphemes for use in building sentences, and have a particular organisation of memory that allows linguistic information to be stored in ways that are well-designed for rapid access during comprehension and production.

If L2 learners have similar capacities for language acquisition as child L1 learners, again through genetic endowment, is it possible that simple encounters with samples of language in everyday interactions are sufficient to allow them to successfully acquire mental grammars of the target language? This is certainly the claim made by a number of commercial language-learning programmes. Rosetta Stone, for example, suggests that the key to successful language learning is 'your complete immersion in the target language … Through carefully chosen context-based images and words you'll soon develop an intuitive sense of the meaning. It's about learning a new language the way you learned your first' (www.rosettastone.co.uk, accessed 29/3/2017). A similar claim about learning an L2 in the same way that L1s are learned is made in publicity material for the Michel Thomas method: 'Go from absolute beginner to confident speaker – all without books, homework or having to memorise anything … the highly acclaimed Michel Thomas Method lets you pick up a new language naturally – just as you learned your own' (www.michelthomas.com, accessed 29/3/2017). It is also a view that was strongly promoted by Stephen Krashen in the 1980s in the form of an 'Input Hypothesis' (Krashen, 1985). This 'claims that humans acquire language in only one way – by understanding messages, or by receiving "comprehensible input" … If input is understood, and there is enough of it, the necessary grammar is automatically provided' (1985: 2).

There are three kinds of evidence that Krashen uses to support this view. Firstly, where classroom language learners are engaged in 'immersion' language programmes (that is, where the normal school curriculum is taught through the medium of the foreign language) language learning is successful. In discussing language immersion programmes in Canada, one of the countries that pioneered this approach to foreign language learning, he notes 'they have all succeeded in encouraging very high levels of second language proficiency' (1985: 16). Secondly, where traditional classroom instruction has been supplemented with or replaced by 'Pleasure Reading' (where learners choose what they want to read and are not tested or graded on the outcome) results produce higher proficiency in the L2 than more traditional instructional classrooms. Thirdly, evidence from classroom language programmes described as 'Just Listen' (Lightbown and Spada, 1993: 88), where learners either respond to instructions in the target language to act (e.g. 'stand up', 'sit down', 'pick up the pencil') or listen to recordings of their own choice, but in both cases just listen to the target language without any requirement to speak. Having compared the results of 'Just Listen' programmes offered to eight- to ten-year-olds in Canadian classrooms with the results of regular, instruction-based and teacher-led classrooms, Lightbown and Spada (1993: 89), reporting work by Lightbown (1992), observe that the 'Just Listen' learners perform 'as well as (and in some cases better than) learners in the regular programme' . Remarkably, the success is not just in comprehension skills but also in speaking skills, despite the learners never having spoken in the L2 in the classroom. These findings appear to be consistent with the claim that simple exposure to samples of the target language is sufficient for L2 acquisition to occur.

However, unlike child L1 learners who achieve high levels of success on the basis of simple exposure to the target language, becoming native speakers, there appear to be limitations to the levels of success that L2 learners achieve. Students in the Canadian immersion programmes achieve high levels of ability to comprehend the target language and produce communicatively coherent utterances, but in production continue to diverge from native speakers on a number of morphological, syntactic, lexical and contextually-determined properties. For example, Harley and Swain (1984) report that students in grade 10 of an early French immersion programme (that is, after seven to eight years of immersion) differ from grade-matched native speakers in the use of the French imperfect to express habitual events, in continuing to use manner verb + path PP to express manner of motion events like *Mary ran into the room* (in French the construction is the equivalent of *Mary entered the room running* – see section 6.3) and in using the polite second person plural form *vous* when addressing strangers. 'Pleasure Reading' and 'Just Listen' programmes are successful in promoting the development of linguistic knowledge in early stages, but are less effective once learners need to go beyond basic knowledge. Lightbown and Spada (1999) report that a follow-up study of the children involved in the 'Just Listen' programme when they were thirteen years old found that they were performing less well than learners in a more traditional classroom where there was teacher feedback on speaking and writing, and classroom interaction activities.

Furthermore, the starting point for L2 learners is different from the starting point for L1 learners. L2 learners have already acquired one or more primary languages and have maturing (or matured) cognitive capacities (hearing, vision, working memory capacity, thinking), whereas child L1 learners have no prior knowledge of a particular language, and acquisition of an L1 goes hand-in-hand with the development of cognitive capacities. And for many L2 learners, exposure to samples of the target language is limited to a few hours a week at best, often in classrooms where the dynamics of interaction are different from those experienced by child L1 learners. While it can still be maintained that the *mechanism* for acquiring language is the same in L1 and L2 learners, requiring exposure to samples of the target language, the conditions under which L2 learners experience that exposure are different from those of L1 learners. In view of this, many language teachers and researchers have wondered what kinds of input might lead to faster and more successful development of mental grammars in L2 learners. Many studies comparing a variety of input types have been conducted in an attempt to identify those that are most effective.

Since the evidence that has accumulated from a large number of these studies is often conflicting, we will proceed by asking a series of questions about different input types, then look at representative studies that have addressed those questions. The questions are:

- How effective is instruction in promoting learning gain?
- How effective is explicit correction of learner errors in promoting learning gain?
- How effective is indirect negative evidence about the target language (provided, for example, through recasts) in promoting learning gain?

Sections 9.1 and 9.2 in a Nutshell

L2 learners can encounter the target language in various ways: through simple exposure to samples of the language; through being instructed about properties of the language; through being corrected when non-target forms are used; through hearing recasts of their utterances by more proficient speakers. While simple exposure to samples of language is sufficient for child L1 learners to fully acquire their native language, it may be insufficient for L2 learners to achieve high levels of proficiency because of factors that do not affect L1 acquisition: the presence of an already acquired L1, already mature cognitive capacities (hearing, vision, working memory capacity, thinking) and the limited number of contact hours many L2 learners will have with the target language. While there are good grounds for thinking that L2 learners have the same mental capacities for language acquisition as children (innately-determined capacity for segmenting, categorising and storing linguistic information) and acquire language in the same way, the additional factors mean that L2 learners may benefit from being exposed to input that is enhanced through instruction and/or direct and indirect negative evidence (evidence about what cannot be said in the L2).

9.3 How Effective is Instruction?

'Instruction' can cover a variety of ways of presenting facts about the target language, but in essence involves providing learners with statements about properties of that language, known as 'metalinguistic information' (the use of language to describe language itself that can be consciously learned and remembered). Examples of metalinguistic information are statements like 'the pronoun *you* can be used to talk about people in general as well as to refer to the person or people you are talking to, as in *You can book tickets on-line*', 'relative clauses can be introduced by a *wh*-word or *that*, as in *The book which/that she likes*' and so on. Learners have access to such metalinguistic information through media like grammars or oral explanations by more proficient speakers such as teachers.

A typical traditional instructional method for language learning in the classroom involves the teacher providing learners with metalinguistic information about a grammatical property followed by a set of exercises where learners have to produce sentences involving the targeted property. For example, a presentation about the use of English third person subject pronouns (*he/she/it/they*) might be followed by an exercise where full noun phrases are highlighted in sentences and have to be replaced by an appropriate third person pronoun.

Is an instructional method of this kind effective in promoting second language acquisition? Long (1983) was probably the first to look objectively at the possible effects of instruction. He reviewed eleven studies comparing instructed, naturalistic (i.e. simple exposure to the target language), or mixed exposure to L2s and found that six of the studies identified apparently faster development in learners who had received instruction than in learners who had not. Ellis (1990) reviewed fifteen studies comparing instructed classroom learners with naturalistic learners and found that in seven of them instructed learners appeared to perform better in the L2 in the tasks that were used for assessment. Norris and Ortega (2001) reviewed fifty-one studies where input involving metalinguistic information was compared with methods involving exposure to samples of the target language and found that learners who had been given metalinguistic information were generally more accurate in the tasks used to measure their proficiency than learners who had not.

However, many of the studies reviewed measured the effects of instruction immediately after participants had received that instruction and did not look at longer-term effects. Furthermore, the tests used were of a kind that might allow conscious knowledge and general problem-solving skills to be accessed rather than a reflection of unconscious mental grammars for the target language. Krashen (1985) distinguishes consciously established knowledge of an L2 (metalinguistic knowledge), which he refers to as 'learning', from unconsciously established knowledge, which he refers to as 'acquisition'. In his view, these are two separate systems of knowledge, which are fed by different types of experience: instruction about the target language and conscious memorisation in the case of learning, interaction with comprehensible samples of the target language in the case of acquisition. For Krashen, learning can never turn into acquisition, although L2 speakers can sometimes use learned knowledge to 'monitor' the output from their acquired knowledge. While a number of researchers have more recently doubted this view and have suggested that consciously learned knowledge, if practised in comprehension and production tasks, can gradually become unconscious, acquired knowledge (Dörnyei, 2009: 151–77; DeKeyser, 2007), it is nevertheless the case that many studies claiming to have found a beneficial effect of instruction over simple exposure have based their results on tests that do not measure the longer-term effects of instruction and that tend to allow learners to access consciously learned knowledge.

One series of studies that has looked at the longer-term effects of instruction compared explicit instruction with simple exposure to samples of L2 sentences. These involved the interaction between lexical verb movement and the placement of manner and frequency adverbs like *quickly* and *often* in English. The participants were a group of French-speaking eleven- to twelve-year-olds in Canada (White, 1991; Trahey and White, 1993; Trahey, 1996). In French, lexical verbs raise from the verb phrase to a higher Tense category over manner and frequency adverbs (see section 4.4), as illustrated in (1):

1. Suzanne   joue$_i$ souvent   e$_i$ du   piano

    Suzanne   plays$_i$ often   e$_i$ of-the   piano

In English, lexical verbs do not raise, and manner and frequency adverbs appear to the left of the verb:

2 a. Suzanne often plays the piano
   b. *Suzanne plays often the piano

The children in the study had had one or two years of classroom English for only a few hours a week, but at the time of testing were undergoing an intensive five-month programme of communicative English. White and her colleagues used a battery of tests to establish what knowledge their participants had of adverb placement in English before the experiment began (the pre-tests). The results of one of the tests, a preference task, will be taken here as representative of the others. In the preference task participants were presented with pairs of English sentences like those in (2), and were asked to make one of five decisions: only (a) is correct (i.e. *Suzanne often plays the piano*); only (b) is correct (i.e. *Suzanne plays often the piano*); (c) both are correct; (d) neither is correct; or (e) 'don't know'. At the pre-test, results indicated that all of the participants preferred the French location of the adverb, between the lexical verb and its object, as in (2b).

Participants were then divided into subgroups who underwent two weeks of specialised teaching. One group – the instruction group (n = 82) – were given instruction about where adverbs can and cannot be placed in English. Another group (n = 52) were given materials for communicative language practice that contained a lot of examples with manner and frequency adverbs in the English position. This group is referred to in the study as the 'flood group'.

Immediately following the two weeks of different types of exposure, participants were given the same battery of tests, and then were tested again one year later. On the immediate post-test, the instructed group showed a strong preference for the English location of adverbs over the French location. Recall that at the pre-test all participants preferred the French location. The flood group, however, allowed both the French and English locations on the immediate post-test. That is, simple exposure to samples of English containing a high frequency of manner and frequency adverbs in the English location had not enabled the learners to determine categorically that lexical verbs do not raise to Tense in English. By contrast, instruction about the location of adverbs had apparently led learners to identify the non-raising property of lexical verbs in English.

Results one year later are rather different. They are summarised in Table 9.1. The effects of instruction appear not to have persisted over time. Both groups are allowing both possibilities for adverb location in their L2 grammars. A conclusion that could be drawn from this is that instruction has short-term effects, but these effects may not be on learners' unconscious mental grammars. In Krashen's terms, the instructed informants had established learned knowledge of adverb placement which they can use in a task like sentence preference, but this knowledge is short-lived. They had not converted this into acquired knowledge, so in the longer term their mental grammars are developing in the same way as every other French learner of English, including the flood group. For a possible explanation of why French learners of English go through a stage where they allow optional lexical verb raising see section 4.4.

TABLE 9.1 Summary of preferences for manner and frequency adverb location in English of the instruction and flood groups (adapted from Trahey, 1996: 125 and 131)

	French Location	English Location
Instruction group	68.2%	67.3%
Flood group	73.3%	79.1%

TABLE 9.2 Percentage acceptance of sentences like (3a) by a group instructed about adverb location and a group instructed about question formation (based on White, 1991: 149, Table 2)

	Pre-Test	Post-Test
Adverb-instructed group	82%	16%
Question formation-instructed group	71%	75%

An interesting question addressed by White (1991) is what kind of learned knowledge the instruction group might have established from being instructed. Absence of lexical verb raising in English means that manner and frequency adverbs cannot separate transitive verbs from their direct objects. However, when verbs have prepositional complements rather than direct objects, as for example in *John walked along the narrow path*, it is perfectly grammatical for verb phrase adverbs to follow the verb and precede the prepositional phrase, although manner adverbs seem more natural in this position than frequency adverbs:

3 a. John walked carefully along the narrow path.
   b. ?John walked often along the narrow path.

Using the same preference task, White compared the responses of the instruction group to sentences like these on the pre-test and immediate post-test with the responses of a third group of learners who had been undergoing instruction on question formation, but not instruction on adverb placement, in English. Responses to the manner adverb location in (3a) are presented in table 9.2.

The results show that instruction had the negative effect of leading learners to the conclusion that adverbs cannot appear between a verb and any complement, rather than to the conclusion that adverbs cannot appear between transitive verbs and their direct objects.

Thus it looks like instruction may not only give rise to temporarily learned (as opposed to acquired) linguistic knowledge, but may also lead to learners making erroneous assumptions about properties of the target language.

A modification to the typical traditional instructional method has been proposed by VanPatten and colleagues (VanPatten and Cadierno, 1993; Henry et al., 2009, among others) that aims to encourage acquisition rather than learning. VanPatten and Cadierno suggest that the following stages are involved in the successful conversion of L2 input into acquired knowledge that can be used successfully for comprehension and production:

input → intake → developing system → output

Input is the totality of expressions of the target language that the learner is exposed to. Some, but not all, of these will leave memory traces (the intake) that will influence the learner's developing unconscious mental grammar for the target language (the developing system). Output is the learner's ability to produce utterances in the target language.

VanPatten and Cadierno observe that in the traditional instructional classroom, once learners have been exposed to a metalinguistic explanation (the input), they are often given exercises that go straight to focusing on output (using the instructed property immediately in production). The problem with this is that the intake stage is bypassed. Learners use the metalinguistic information they are given to complete the exercises in a conscious, problem-solving way which may have no effect on the unconscious developing system.

As an alternative, they propose that practice following instruction should focus on the intake phase. For them this can be achieved through comprehension (rather than production) tasks that require learners to use metalinguistic information to make semantic or lexical decisions. They refer to this as 'processing instruction'. In their 1993 study they tested the hypothesis that processing instruction would lead to greater gains in learning than traditional instruction with a group of L1 English speakers who were elementary L2 classroom learners of Spanish. The property on which the learners received instruction was the location of Spanish unstressed direct object pronouns. Unstressed direct object pronouns precede the finite verb in Spanish. Spanish also allows subjects to follow the verb under certain conditions (see section 8.3.2). So a sentence like 'The man follows her' has two possible translations in Spanish:

4 a. El   señor   la   sigue
       The   man   her   follows

   b. La   sigue   el   señor
      Her   follows the   man

Previous research had shown that elementary learners of Spanish tend to misinterpret sentences like (4b) as 'She follows the man', where the direct object *la* is misinterpreted as a subject pronoun.

A pre-test in VanPatten and Cadierno's study required participants to: (a) listen to sentences in Spanish and following each sentence choose one of a pair of pictures that best matched the meaning of the sentence; for example, after hearing sentence (4b) participants had to choose the appropriate picture from a pair, one showing a man following a woman and the other showing a woman following a man; (b) complete a sentence on the basis of a picture prompt which encouraged the use of unstressed direct object pronouns. The (a) test was an intended measure of comprehension and the (b) test a measure of production. Following the pre-test, participants were divided into three groups: one that would receive processing instruction (instruction followed by the kinds of semantic decision task involved in choosing a picture appropriate to a heard sentence, or in deciding whether the proposition expressed by a sentence is true or false of the hearer), a second group that would receive traditional instruction plus output practice, and a third group that would receive no instruction but would continue with normal classroom communicative activities.

TABLE 9.3 Accuracy scores for performance on a comprehension and production task involving Spanish unstressed object pronouns (based on VanPatten and Cadierno, 1993: 236–7, Tables 1 and 2)

	Comprehension				Production			
	Pre-t	Post-t 1	Post-t 2	Post-t 3	Pre-t	Post-t 1	Post-t 2	Post-t 3
Traditional Instruction (n = 27)	1.31	3.04	3.42	3.89	2.69	8.54	9.04	8.12
Processing Instruction (n = 26)	1.74	8.07	7.19	7.41	2.19	8.89	8.19	8.11
No instruction (n = 27)	1.11	1.41	2.26	2.22	2.29	3.44	3.85	3.83

The participants in the processing instruction and traditional instruction groups received two days of instruction/practice. Using the same tasks as in the pre-test, all the participants were tested again immediately after the instruction phase (the first post-test), again after one week (the second post-test) and again after one month (the third post-test). The results are presented in table 9.3. These are scores (out of 10) for accuracy on the comprehension task and the production task.

Statistical analysis showed no significant differences between the three groups in the pre-tests. At the first post-test, following the two-day treatment phase, there was a significant gain in the comprehension test by the processing instruction group compared with the other two groups, who were not significantly different from each other. In the production test both the traditional instruction and processing instruction groups made significant gains by comparison with the no instruction group. These patterns continued one week and one month later.

These results suggest that in terms of improving learners' performance in using Spanish unstressed direct object pronouns, metalinguistic knowledge (instruction) helps. However, processing instruction is more effective than traditional instruction in that it promotes both comprehension and production gains, even though the method only involves comprehension activities, whereas traditional instruction promotes gains only in production. Henry et al. (2009: 562), reflecting on these results, suggest that processing instruction 'caused changes in the underlying grammar of learners that could then be accessed for production'. The results of the traditional instruction group are consistent with their claim that the focus on production activities bypasses the intake stage and does not affect the developing mental grammar.

Similar effects of processing instruction have been found in studies that have focused on the Spanish past tense (Cadierno, 1995), the Italian future tense (Benati, 2001), the English simple past tense (Benati, 2005), and the French causative construction, for example *Jean fait promener le chien à Marie* (lit. 'Jean makes to-walk the dog to Marie') 'Jean makes Marie walk the dog', which early-stage L2 learners of French tend to misinterpret as 'John walks the dog for Marie' (VanPatten and Wong, 2004).

An interesting question asked by Henry et al. (2009) is whether the 'instruction' part of processing instruction is needed or whether comprehension-based semantic decision tasks and judgements of whether the proposition expressed by a sentence applies to the hearer are sufficient to promote the kinds of learning gains found. To test this they conducted a study of thirty-eight low-proficiency L2 learners of German at a US university acquiring German Nominative and Accusative Case marking. Determiners accompanying masculine nouns in German differ in form when the DP functions as a subject (Nominative) from when it functions as a direct object (Accusative): *der* is the Nominative form of the definite article 'the', while *den* is its Accusative counterpart:

5. Der   Sohn   ruft   den   Vater
   The-Nom   son   calls   the-Acc   father
   'The son calls the father'

German also has the possibility of putting non-subject DPs in first position in the clause followed by the finite verb (the verb-second property of German – see section 4.5.1). This occurs when a non-subject DP is the topic of conversation and has already been mentioned or is implied elsewhere in the discourse:

6. Den   Vater   ruft   der   Sohn
   The-Acc   father   calls   the-Nom   son
   'The son calls the father'

Knowing the difference between *der* and *den* as Case markers is crucial to interpreting the sentences in (5) and (6) correctly.

At the start of Henry et al.'s study, none of their participants were able to interpret sentences like (6) accurately, interpreting the first DP as a subject. Participants were then divided into two groups of nineteen. One group received explicit instruction about the Case marking of determiners and Object–Verb–Subject word order followed by a picture–sentence decision task (the 'processing instruction' group). The other group were exposed only to the picture–sentence decision task (the 'no instruction' group). The picture–sentence decision task required participants to view pairs of pictures on a computer screen, for example a father calling his son and a son calling his father, while listening to a single sentence, and then select the picture corresponding to the meaning of the sentence. If the right picture was selected, 'correct!' would appear on the screen. If the wrong picture was selected, 'incorrect!' would appear on the screen. There were thirty items in total, ten with Subject–Verb–Object word order and twenty with Object–Verb–Subject word order.

Henry et al. measured learning gain by the number of items a participant had to encounter before s/he selected the correct picture for three Object–Verb–Subject sentences and at least one Subject–Verb–Object sentence in a row. The results were that on average the processing-instruction group achieved the learning gain criterion by item 12 (of the thirty-item test), while the no-instruction group did not do so until item 22. Furthermore, 63 per cent of the no-instruction group had not achieved the learning-gain criterion by the end of the experiment, whereas only 16 per cent of the processing-instruction group had not achieved it. Henry et al. conclude that the 'instruction' part of processing instruction appears to facilitate the initial processing of input (at least for German Case marking) more than semantic decision-making tasks alone.

Processing instruction is a promising method for presenting classroom L2 learners with samples of language that they can unconsciously segment, categorise and store in memory for use in comprehension and production. It is important to be clear, however, that processing instruction itself does not 'cause' L2 acquisition, as Henry et al. (2009: 562) claim. Like the other methods discussed in this chapter for presenting L2 learners with samples of the target language, processing instruction is a way of enhancing those samples so that they become available to a learner's mental processes of segmentation, categorisation and storage. It is the latter that cause acquisition.

It should be noted that there is a limitation on the applicability of processing instruction. Processing instruction can only enhance input where there is the potential for an L2 learner to misconstrue the meaning of an L2 form. In the case of Spanish unstressed object pronouns, learners must initially misconstrue them as subject pronouns to allow the kinds of processing activity (semantic decision taking/judgements of applicability to the hearer) that will lead to segmentation, categorisation and storage in memory. The same applies to the German Case example. It is not clear whether processing instruction could be deployed to enhance the recognition of phenomena as simply ungrammatical, such as the movement of V to T in English over VP adverbs (*She drinks often tea) or the movement of T to V in French (*Elle souvent boit du thé), or gender agreement between determiners, adjectives and nouns, discussed in chapter 4. In these cases no semantic anomaly arises as the result of non-target use.

Another method for enhancing the samples of language that L2 learners encounter that just about falls under the heading of 'instruction' is the use of dual-modality input (simultaneous hearing and reading). Where learners are literate, it has been found that presenting them with audio-visual input from the target L2 with subtitles also in the L2 (the kind of captioning that is used to assist the hearing impaired) enhances recall and retention of the material learners are exposed to. For example, Neumann and Koskinen (1992) compared three groups of advanced-proficiency L2 learners of English over a nine-week period. One group watched nine 5- to 8-minute subtitled science programmes. A second group watched the same programmes, but without subtitles. A third group just listened to the sound track and read a transcript while listening. At the end of the nine weeks all three groups were tested on their ability to distinguish real words encountered in the programmes from non-words, to detect sentence anomalies involving word meaning, and to give the meaning of words in isolation that were encountered in the programmes. The group who had been exposed to dual-modality input outperformed the other two groups.

Holobow et al. (1984) found an advantage for an L2 auditory stimulus paired with an L2 written transcript compared with learners who had only read the transcript, but found an even better effect for what they call 'reversed subtitling': listening to an L1 auditory stimulus (in their case, English) while reading an L2 translation (in their case, French). Their L2 French proficiency-matched participants were grade 5 and 6 students (aged ten to eleven) in early French immersion programmes. They found that over a ten-week training period the reversed-subtitling group significantly outperformed participants who had experienced L2 input accompanied by an L2 transcript on tests of comprehension, the contextual meaning of expressions and recall of the exact phrasing of expressions in the stimulus material. The participants who had experienced L2 input accompanied by L2 transcripts were, however, significantly more successful than a group who had only read the French transcripts.

Again, dual modality input looks like a promising method for enhancing samples of language that L2 learners encounter so that they can segment, categorise and store the linguistic information contained in them. However, a limitation on its effectiveness is that most of the material encountered already needs to be familiar to learners. Where even around 30 per cent of the material is new, learners do not make detectable learning gains (Danan, 2004: 74).

Section 9.3 in a Nutshell

A typical traditional instructional method involves providing learners with metalinguistic information followed by production practice through exercises. Reviews of studies of the effectiveness of traditional instruction in promoting learning gain have found that some, but not all, show an advantage for instruction when compared with simple exposure to samples of the L2. But a number of the studies that have found an advantage only looked at immediate, and not longer-term, effects, and used measures that tested the ability to perform in grammar tests rather than looking at the ability to use language for spontaneous communicative purposes. A series of studies with French-speaking low-proficiency L2 learners of English in Canada (White, 1991; Trahey and White, 1993; Trahey, 1996) not only found no effect for instruction about verb-raising/adverb placement after a year, but found an immediate negative effect in leading learners to assume that English verbs cannot be separated from prepositional phrase complements by intervening manner and frequency adverbs, contrary to fact.

Processing instruction is a modification of the traditional instructional method in that the focus of follow-up exercises is on comprehension. Specifically, learners are required to make semantic or truth decisions about the meaning of utterances. A study by VanPatten and Cadierno (1993) found gains both in comprehension and production in the use of Spanish unstressed object pronouns by using this method. It appears that instruction is an important element of the method. A study by Henry et al. (2009) found that input that included both instruction and comprehension tasks led to more learning gains than input that only involved comprehension tasks. It is not clear whether processing instruction can be used to enhance input for learners on all properties. The properties where the method appears to work are where there is potential for learners to misconstrue meaning.

Dual-modality input (audio-visual input accompanied by written transcripts) has also been shown to enhance input for learners, leading to more gains in recall and retention of L2 material than simply watching/listening or simply reading. A requirement for success using this method appears to be that learners must already be familiar with at least 70 per cent of the material they are watching/listening to.

9.4 How Effective is Explicit Correction?

Teachers of foreign languages around the world spend many hours correcting the writing of their L2 learners. They underline or highlight non-target morphological, syntactic, lexical and orthographic (spelling, punctuation) forms and write in appropriate target alternatives. They assume that the direct negative evidence this provides about what can and cannot be said in the target language will lead to the acquisition of target forms, not just in writing, but also in speaking. But is this the case?

Truscott (2007) has reviewed a number of studies that have compared the effects on performance in authentic writing of giving learners corrective feedback (direct negative evidence) and not giving them such feedback. Authentic writing is writing for a communicative purpose, as opposed to writing in grammar tests. His finding is that in all cases corrective feedback is not effective. For example, a study by Polio, Fleck and Leder (1998) compared a group of L2 English learners in a US university writing course who, over a semester, were given corrections, grammar reviews and training in editing their writing with another group who were given none of these. At the end of the semester the performance of both groups in an in-class essay and an in-class revision of that essay was evaluated. There were no significant differences in the performance of the two groups either in the essay or the revisions to the essay.

In another study, Sheppard (1992) gave two L2 English groups identical instruction over a ten-week period but additionally corrected the work of one group. The other group only received content-oriented comments. In a measure of the accuracy of each group in using verb forms at the end of the ten-week period, the group who had not received correction were more accurate than the correction group, although this was not statistically significant. It suggests, however, that explicit correction of morphological, syntactic and lexical errors had no greater effect on grammatical accuracy than commenting on the content of learners' writing.

In a third study, Fazio (2001) considered the effects of correction on grammatical accuracy in the journal-writing of three groups of adolescent classroom L2 learners of French over a four-month period. One group received corrective feedback, the second were given comments on content, and the third received both corrective feedback and comments on content. There were no statistical differences between the three groups at the end of the four months, although the group who had received comments only on content performed somewhat better than the other two groups. It seems that the feedback the learners were receiving had no effect on their spontaneous use of French in journal entries, which were produced on the basis of the learners' unconscious mental grammars.

It appears from these studies that direct negative evidence has no positive effect on learning gain, at least on authentic L2 writing performance. Truscott is careful to point out that this conclusion does not hold for the effect of direct negative evidence on performance in grammar tests or other kinds of non-spontaneous use of the L2 in writing. Indeed, he points out that the claimed benefits of direct negative evidence have all been found where the measures used to test performance are of the grammar test variety.

9.5 How Effective is Indirect Negative Evidence?

L2 learners are presented with indirect evidence about what cannot be said in the target language when more proficient speakers either fail to understand what has been said and ask for clarification, or reformulate what has been said, replacing a non-target form with a target form. The latter are recasts. An example of a clarification request is given in (7) (from Yang and Lyster, 2010: 244) and a recast in (8) (from Ellis, 1988: 14).

7. Student: Why does he fly to Korea last year?
   Teacher: Pardon?
   Student: Why did he fly to Korea last year?

8. Teacher: Take a look at the next picture
   Student: Box
   Teacher: A box, yes
   Student: A box banana

In (7) the teacher's failure to understand, and request for clarification, leads the student to revise the utterance to include an appropriate past tense. In (8) the teacher understands what the student is saying, but recasts it in a form that is grammatical in English. (Count singular nouns need to be accompanied by a 'licensing' determiner.) The recast is taken up by the student.

There has been considerable debate among L2 researchers about the effectiveness of recasts. Long (2007: 77) proposes that one of the advantages of recasts is that they provide information about the target language in a meaningful context in which a learner is actively engaged and therefore likely to be motivated, conditions that may lead to the learner noticing the discrepancy between their utterance and that of the more proficient speaker. He describes a number of studies that suggest a positive effect of recasts on learning gain. For example, Mackey (1999) investigated the effect of negotiation of meaning in conversations between native and non-native speakers where recasts are likely to be involved. The conversations occurred during teacher-allocated tasks: working out the ending of a story, discovering the correct order of a scrambled picture story, and drawing a picture that one of the participants cannot see but is described by the other participant. The focus of Mackey's study was the ability of the non-native speakers to produce target question forms in English. The allocated tasks were particularly likely to give rise to the use of questions.

It is known that there is a typical sequence of development in the L2 acquisition of English questions. L2 learners start out just by using rising intonation on phrases or clauses (e.g. *Four children? The boys throw the shoes?*). Later they place a question word at the front of the main clause, without moving copula *be* or an auxiliary verb to the front (e.g. *Is the picture has two planets on top? Where the little children are?*). At the next stage copula *be* moves to the front of the clause, or to second position if a *wh*-word is present (*Is there fish in the water? Where is the sun?*). Finally, auxiliaries, modal verbs and *do* move to the front of the clause, or to second position (e.g. *What is the boy doing? Can you tell me? How do you say 'proche'?*) (all examples from Lightbown and Spada, 1993: 63).

Mackey was interested in whether participating in conversations with native speakers, where negotiation of meaning and recasts are likely to be involved, would lead the L2 English learners to move more quickly through the stages of acquiring target English question forms. A group of fourteen learners were given a week of daily fifteen- to twenty-minute interactions with native speakers of the kind described above. A control comparison group of seven learners had no exposure to such interactions. All participants were pre-tested using a task in which the L2 learner was required, by asking questions, to find ten differences between two pictures that could only be seen by the native speaker. They were tested again at the end of the treatment week (first post-test), a week later (second post-test), and three weeks later still (third post-test). Learning gain was measured by counting the number of participants who produced 'at least two different higher level question forms in at least two of the post-tests' (Mackey, 1999: 571). She found that eleven out of fourteen of participants involved in the interactions were producing higher level question forms both at the first and third post-tests while only one out of seven control participants was.

Although we cannot know the extent to which learning gains were the result of recasts in this study, or just the fact of interacting with native speakers, the findings suggest unsurprisingly that intensive interaction with proficient speakers of the target language in communicative tasks leads to more learning gain than not participating in such interactions.

In another study, Révész (2009) used a photo description task to compare the effects of recasts on the development of the use of the English past progressive construction (forms like *were talking, was sitting*) by L2 learners. Her participants were L1 speakers of Hungarian learning English in high school. They were of elementary proficiency in English and at the start of the study were typically using target forms with less than 25 per cent accuracy. They were shown ten photographs and presented with the hypothetical scenario that they were in New York taking these photographs when a bank robbery occurred. They were asked to describe what was happening in the photographs to a police officer. This activity, the 'treatment phase' of the study, which took about fifteen minutes, was repeated three times over a week. Thirty-six participants consistently received recasts when they used non-target past progressive forms; thirty-six participants underwent the same treatment but were not given recasts. There was also a control group of eighteen participants who were not involved in the treatment phase. Performance was tested before and after the treatment began by asking participants to write a description of a photograph and give an oral description of a photograph. There were two post-tests, one immediately after the treatment phase and another four weeks later. Results show that the participants who had received recasts made significant learning gains in the use of target past progressive forms by comparison with the control group. The no-recast participants also made learning gains, but significantly fewer than the recast group.

However, alongside studies like those of Mackey and Révész there are others that suggest that the kind of enhancement of input that indirect negative evidence from recasts provides L2 learners with may not be as effective as direct negative evidence. For example, Lyster and Ranta (1997) looked at a range of indirect and direct negative feedback given by teachers to nine- to ten-year-old pupils in L2 French immersion programmes in Montreal. They analysed eighteen hours of recordings of teacher–student interactions in the classroom and classified the teachers' feedback under six headings: recasts, clarification requests, metalinguistic feedback, corrective feedback, repetition (where the teacher repeats the non-target form but with interrogative intonation) and elicitation (where the teacher encourages the student to provide the target form by asking a question like *What's this called?* or pausing to allow the student to complete the teacher's utterance, for example *It's a ...*). They then looked at the extent to which students took up the form provided in the feedback to repair their non-target utterance.

TABLE 9.4 Teacher feedback on students' non-target forms and student take-up of that feedback to repair their utterances (based on Lyster and Ranta, 1997: 53–4, Tables 2 and 3)

Teacher Feedback Type	No. of Instances of Feedback	Student Take Up and Repair
Recast	375	66 (18%)
Clarification request	73	20 (28%)
Metalinguistic feedback	58	26 (45%)
Corrective feedback	50	18 (36%)
Repetition	36	11 (31%)
Elicitation	94	43 (46%)

The results are summarised in table 9.4. The first column shows the number of times a teacher used a particular kind of feedback in the sample. The second column shows the number of times the students produced a repaired utterance following the feedback. The percentages in this column represent the proportion of take-up given the number of instances of feedback provided (e.g. 66/375 = 18%).

Metalinguistic feedback (direct negative evidence) and elicitation (no feedback at all) produce the highest number of utterances immediately repaired by the students, recasts produce the lowest proportion of take-up. The implication is that although recasts may lead learners to produce target forms, and the teachers in the study used them a lot, they are less effective proportionally than providing learners with metalinguistic information or getting them to draw on their existing L2 knowledge to self-correct through elicitation. Lyster and Ranta are particularly impressed by the effect of elicitation leading to repairs: 'we believe that these student-generated repairs … allow opportunities for learners to automatize the retrieval of target language knowledge that already exists in some form … and thus actively confront errors in ways that may lead to revisions of their hypotheses about the target language' (1997: 57).

Sheen (2010) also examined the effect of different forms of feedback on learning gain in L2 speakers, focusing on the acquisition of English articles. She compared the effects of four kinds of feedback on low-proficiency learners: oral recasts, oral metalinguistic feedback (where the teacher supplies the correct form and offers metalinguistic information), written correction and written metalinguistic feedback (again the teacher both corrects the form and offers metalinguistic information, this time in writing).

The 143 participants (speaking eleven different L1s) were divided into five groups, four receiving one of the four types of feedback described above with the fifth receiving none and acting as a control group. The feedback groups were asked to read a written story. The story was then removed and they were asked to retell the story. This occurred twice over a two-week period. Two groups retold the story orally, one receiving oral recasts and the other oral metalinguistic feedback; two groups retold the story in writing, one receiving written correction and the other written metalinguistic feedback. The control group continued with normal English

TABLE 9.5 Overall percentage gains in target performance on article use in English in speeded dictation, story writing and error correction (based on Sheen, 2010: 220–2, Tables 4 and 6)

Group	Pre-t	Post-t 1	Diff	Post-t 2	Diff
Oral recast	46	53	7	54	8
Oral metalinguistic	50	61	11	63	13
Written correction	44	58	14	58	14
Written metalinguistic	50	65	15	69	19
Control (no feedback)	48	52	4	51	3

language classes. The participants' knowledge of English articles was tested before they retold the stories (the pre-test), immediately after they had retold the stories (the first post-test) and again three to four weeks later (the second post-test). The test consisted of a speeded dictation, writing a story based on four linked pictures and an error correction test. The results are presented in table 9.5, where gains in accuracy are measured as percentage differences between participants' scores on the pre-test and their scores in the post-tests.

Unsurprisingly, there was hardly any gain in the case of the control group, who did not experience the input the other groups received. Of the four groups who read and retold the stories, most gains in performance on the post-tests were by the participants who received written metalinguistic feedback, written correction, or oral metalinguistic feedback, all cases of direct negative evidence. Oral recasts alone produced fewer gains. Sheen concludes that 'where article errors ... are concerned, learners simply do not benefit from implicit corrective feedback [indirect negative evidence], such as that provided by oral recasts' (2010: 225). This is, perhaps, overstating the findings since the oral recasts did lead to some gain in target performance. Furthermore, two of the three tasks used to measure learning gain (speeded dictation and error correction) are of the 'grammar test' type. Truscott (2007) has suggested that we might expect to see learning gains from corrective feedback on such tasks. It is in authentic writing where gains have not been found.

Alongside studies that suggest a positive impact for recasts (Mackey, Révész), then, there are others that suggest that other kinds of enhancement of input are more effective in promoting learning gain (Lyster and Ranta, Sheen). Long (2007) has defended the value of recasts by pointing out several factors that might have affected the results of studies that suggest otherwise. The main elements of this defence are, firstly, that there was no concrete measure of the effectiveness of recasts in the Lyster and Ranta study; no pre-test to establish a baseline level of performance of learners and then post-testing after the learners had experienced the different types of input. (Such measures are present in the Sheen study, which still finds a lesser impact of recasts on learning gain than other types of input enhancement.)

Secondly, the immediate uptake of a recast may not always be possible in an interaction, so using this as a measure of the effectiveness of recasts on learning gain is misleading. Long cites a study by Oliver (1995) of child native-speaker and L2 learner interactions in problem-solving games where immediate take-up of recasts by the L2 learner was impossible because the native speaker continued to speak after the recast or because recasts were in the form of yes–no questions where a response of 'yes' or 'no' was appropriate, precluding the possibility of repeating the recast (Oliver, 1995: 472). The fact that learners are not immediately taking up recasts does not mean that they are not having an effect. (Again, however, the study by Sheen includes a delayed post-test which suggests that oral recasts are having no more effect after three or four weeks than they are immediately after they have been encountered.)

Thirdly, learners may be taking up recasts in their private rehearsal of the samples of language they encounter, in a way that is missed by most observational studies of classroom interactions. A study by Ohta (2000) tracked the private speech of seven classroom L2 learners of Japanese using lapel microphones. Private speech is the language addressed by students to themselves during classes. This revealed that students were taking up more of the recasts that the teacher was using in their own private rehearsal of language than would be obvious from observing interactions between a teacher and a student, as in the case of Lyster and Ranta's study. Again, if this were the case this should show up in delayed post-tests of the kind used by Sheen, where a larger gain might be expected than that found.

Sections 9.4 and 9.5 in a Nutshell

In a review of the effect of explicit correction (direct negative evidence) of L2 learners' authentic writing, Truscott (2007) found no evidence that explicit correction leads to learning gains, although he notes that explicit correction may lead to gains in performance on grammar tests where metalinguistic knowledge gained from corrections might be deployed.

Results from studies comparing the effects of indirect negative evidence (recasts, clarification requests, repetitions) with other kinds of interaction with more proficient speakers (elicitation, correction, metalinguistic feedback) have produced mixed results. Studies like that of Mackey (1999) of the effect of negotiation of meaning between L2 learners and native speakers found learning gains in the use of English question forms, compared with learners who were not involved in the interaction activities. Assuming that interaction involves native speakers providing indirect negative evidence to L2 speakers, it suggests that interaction where L2 learners are directly involved is effective in enhancing input. Other studies, however, have suggested that recasts in particular may be less effective in promoting learning gain than other kinds of interactional strategy like elicitation (Lyster and Ranta, 1997). Lyster and Ranta found that the take-up of oral recasts was lower than the take-up of metalinguistic feedback or elicitation, while Sheen (2010) found that oral recasts produced fewer learning gains than oral metalinguistic feedback. Sheen also found an effect on learning gain from written correction and written metalinguistic feedback. However, two of her three measures (speeded dictation and error correction) are examples of grammar tests. Truscott had suggested that we might expect learning gains from correction on such tasks.

9.6 The Role of Output

VanPatten and Cadierno (1993) criticised the traditional instructional classroom approach to enhancing input because it passed directly from providing L2 learners with metalinguistic information to output practice (production exercises), bypassing a stage where the new information could be assimilated to the developing mental grammar for the L2 (see section 9.3 for discussion). Swain, however, in a series of studies (1985, 1995, 2005) has argued that production practice – output – is an important element in turning already-acquired mental morphological, syntactic and lexical knowledge into a form that can be quickly and accurately accessed for production in normal communicative contexts. Swain (2005: 472) noted from her observation of Canadian French immersion programmes that students did not talk as much in French in the French portion of the day as they did in English in the English portion of the day, and that teachers did not 'push' students to talk in a way that was grammatically accurate or sociolinguistically appropriate. Her output hypothesis 'claims that the act of producing language (speaking or writing) constitutes, under certain circumstances, part of the process of second language learning' (471). She goes on to suggest that output practice enhances fluency in the L2, leads learners to become consciously aware of things that they do not know how to say, forces them to try out different ways of saying something in the L2, and encourages metalinguistic reflection.

The findings of Lyster and Ranta (1997) that elicitation, where an L2 learner is prompted by a more proficient speaker to draw on their existing knowledge to produce a response, produces a lot of take-up and repair are consistent with this claim. The positions of VanPatten and Cadierno and Swain are not incompatible either. Learners must already have unconscious knowledge of the relevant properties of the target language for output practice to be effective in improving performance.

9.7 Concluding Remarks

Instruction (providing learners with metalinguistic information), comprehension practice involving semantic or truth decision-making, dual-modality input, recasting, requesting clarification, and repetition (with interrogative intonation) of L2 learners' non-target utterances by more proficient speakers are all ways in which the samples of language that L2 learners encounter can be enhanced. In this chapter a selection of the large number of studies that have tried to measure the success of these types of enhancement in promoting learning gain has been considered. It should be noted that none of these enhancements can be said to directly cause acquisition. Acquisition occurs as the result of subconscious processes of segmentation, categorisation and storage. All of the examples of enhancement potentially make samples of the target language more accessible to the unconscious mental processes, with some being more successful at doing this than others. Knowing which kind(s) of enhancement work best is of use to teachers and learners in classroom settings where learners have limited contact time with the L2 and where the dynamics of interaction are typically different from the kind of interaction experienced by L1 learners or L2 learners in immersion settings.

It has been found that simple exposure to random samples of the target language can be effective in promoting both comprehension and production in the early stages of learning an L2 (Lightbown and Spada, 1993). It can also lead to high levels of comprehension in more proficient speakers, as evidenced by the success of the Canadian L2 immersion programmes (Swain and Barik, 1977; Harley and Swain, 1984). However, simple exposure appears to have limitations. Beyond the early stages of learning it appears to be less effective in promoting proficiency in production compared with enhancement of input involving metalinguistic feedback (Lightbown and Spada, 1999) or production practice (Swain, 2005).

A number of studies have found that a traditional instructional method that provides learners with metalinguistic information followed by exercises that practise production leads to higher learning gains than simple exposure to the target language through communicative activities. But other studies have not found such an advantage (Norris and Ortega, 2001). The problem with many of the studies that do find an advantage for traditional instruction is that they focus on immediate effects. Longer-term effects, which would indicate that acquisition has occurred, have not always been considered. Furthermore, the measures used to gauge learning gain have often been of the kind that tap learners' ability to use conscious problem-solving skills and do not reflect changes that might have occurred in their unconscious mental grammars. It is the latter that underlie the ability to comprehend and produce the L2 spontaneously in normal communication.

More effective, perhaps, than the typical traditional instructional method is processing instruction, which focuses on follow-up comprehension-based activities involving semantic or truth decision-making. This appears to have longer-term effects both on comprehension and production. A limitation of this type of input enhancement is that it may not be applicable to properties that cannot be presented to learners in a form that leads to binary choices in comprehension tasks (e.g. deciding which of two pictures is consistent with the meaning of a single utterance).

Another promising variant on input enhancement is dual-modality presentation of the target language, that is by reversed subtitling (L1 audio-visual stimulus with L2 subtitling/transcript) or captioning (L2 audio-visual stimulus with L2 subtitling/transcript). Greater learning gains occur in learners who experience dual-modality input than in those who simply see/hear or read the material. A limitation is that learners need already to be familiar with a large proportion of the material, perhaps as much as 70 per cent (Danan, 2004).

Explicit correction of authentic writing (i.e. writing for a communicative purpose) appears to lead to no learning gains by comparison with feedback that involves commenting on the content of the writing (Truscott, 2007).

Indirect negative evidence in the form of oral recasts and clarification requests, when learners are engaged in meaningful interaction with more proficient speakers, does appear to lead to learning gains (Mackey, 1999; Révész, 2009). But these may not be as great as the gains that learners make following provision of oral metalinguistic information (Sheen, 2010).

Finally, Swain's 'output hypothesis' raises an interesting question about the relationship between a learner's mental grammar and the ability to use that knowledge for production. Just as it was argued in chapter 8 that the procedures used for comprehending input (parsing procedures) draw on, but are independent of, the mental grammar, so it seems that production routines may also draw on, but be independent of, the mental grammar if immersion L2 learners can achieve native levels of comprehension but continue to diverge from native norms in speech. The effects that Swain claims output practice has (improving fluency, forcing learners to try out different ways of saying things and raising awareness of what they cannot say) may mean that learners need, through producing the language, to establish a set of procedures through which knowledge from the mental grammar can be deployed in speech.

ACTIVITIES

1. TEST YOURSELF

(i) What kinds of evidence support Krashen's (1985: 2) view that 'humans acquire language in only one way – by understanding messages, or by receiving "comprehensible input" ... if input is understood, and there is enough of it, the necessary grammar is automatically provided'?

(ii) In the studies by White and her colleagues (White, 1991; Trahey and White, 1993; Trahey, 1996) what were the effects of instruction compared with exposure to a flood of examples on the acquisition of verb-phrase adverb placement in English by L1 speakers of French?

(iii) What was the rationale underlying VanPatten and Cadierno's (1993) proposal of the method known as 'processing instruction'? What is the claimed advantage of processing instruction over traditional instruction? What is the limitation on processing instruction?

(iv) What is your assessment of the relative benefits of metalinguistic feedback, recasts and correction in making samples of language more accessible to the mental processes involved in L2 acquisition?

2. EFFECTS OF INSTRUCTION ON THE ACQUISITION OF ENGLISH DATIVE DOUBLE OBJECTS

A number of English verbs allow the following alternation:

i   a. She bought the laptop for her friend   – She bought her friend the laptop
    b. He lent some money to his cousin   – He lent his cousin some money

The V DP DP structure of the second sentences in (ia) and (ib) is known as the 'dative double object' construction. Not all verbs that have a V DP PP structure (where the preposition is *to* or *for*) allow double objects, as the following illustrate:

ii a. She borrowed the laptop for two   – *She borrowed two weeks the
        weeks   laptop
    b. He despatched some money to his   – *He despatched his cousin some
        cousin   money

To allow a dative double object complement, a verb must typically be mono-syllabic, or have main stress on the first syllable (so *lend* and *'offer* allow dative double objects, but *des'patch* does not). Furthermore, it must involve a transfer of possession, whether this involves a physical object, as in lending money, or a more abstract entity such as information, as in telling someone a story (so *for two weeks* is excluded from dative double object constructions because it cannot take possession of anything).

While many languages have V DP PP constructions involving counterparts of the prepositions *to* and *for*, few languages allow dative double objects. Spanish is a language that does not allow dative double objects. In learning English as an L2, one of the challenges facing Spanish speakers is acquiring the constraints on dative double objects. Carroll and Swain (1993) conducted an experiment to find out to what extent direct and indirect negative evidence might promote the acquisition of these constraints.

One hundred L1 Spanish speakers of low intermediate proficiency in English were divided into five groups of twenty. All groups were presented with a number of sentences with a V DP PP structure and were asked 'to think of a different way of saying the same thing' if possible (1993: 364). Some of the sentences allowed a dative double object alternant and some did not. Four of the groups were given different kinds of feedback on their responses:

Group A were told they were wrong whenever they produced an ungrammatical alternation, and were given an explanation about the syllable/stress and transfer-of-possession constraints.

TABLE (i) Mean percentage accuracy in producing grammatical dative double object constructions one week after treatment (based on Carroll and Swain, 1993: 370, Table 6)

	Mean (%)
Group A – told they were wrong, with explanation	63
Group B – told they were wrong, no explanation	52
Group C – incorrect alternations reformulated	55
Group D – asked for confidence about answer when wrong	55
Group Z – no feedback given	34

Group B were told that they were wrong whenever they produced an ungrammatical alternation, but were given no explanation about why.

Whenever participants in **Group C** produced an ungrammatical alternation, it was reformulated by one of the researchers.

Whenever participants in **Group D** produced an ungrammatical alternation they were asked if they were sure of their response.

The fifth group – **Group Z** – received no feedback of any kind.

The participants were given a production test immediately after they had undergone the treatment phases described above, and a delayed production test one week later. Correct responses on the delayed production test are given in table (i). Group A were statistically significantly more accurate than all the other groups. Groups B, C, D were not statistically different from each other. Group Z was statistically significantly less accurate than all the other groups.

> Question (i): How would you classify the kinds of input that each group received in terms of positive, direct negative and indirect negative evidence for the dative alternation?
>
> Question (ii): Carroll and Swain propose that 'our results raise the possibility that claims that learning about the language is useless in promoting learning of the language may be incorrect' (1993: 372). Do you agree with this statement? What other evidence encountered in the chapter is consistent with this?
>
> Question (iii): Are you convinced that the study has shown that changes have taken place in the participants' mental grammars? How would you go about testing this?

3. EFFECTS OF INSTRUCTION ON THE ACQUISITION OF RELATIVE CLAUSES

In section 4.6.2 it was suggested that L2 learners might find relative clauses easier to understand and produce when the noun that heads the clause is co-referential with an empty position in the clause that is either linearly or structurally close than when it is further away from the head. For example, of the following three English sentences, (a) would be easier than (b), and (b) would be easier than (c) because the empty position in (a) is the closest to the head, and the empty position in (b) is the next closest.

i   a. She knows the professor who$_i$ e$_i$ gave a talk (Subject relative)
   b. She knows the professor whom$_i$ the students invited e$_i$ (Direct Object relative)
   c. She knows the professor whom$_i$ the students had dinner with e$_i$ (Object of a
      Preposition relative)

Eckman (1985) reports a study teaching relative clauses to L2 speakers. Four groups of nine participants each were given a pre-test where they had to combine two sentences into one containing a relative clause (e.g. *She knows the professor. The professor gave a talk.* → *She knows the professor who gave a talk*). The targeted relative clauses were the three types illustrated in (i): Subject, Direct Object and Object of a Preposition. Following the pre-test each group experienced a different instructional treatment. One group were instructed on the formation of Subject relatives, a second group on the formation of Direct Object relatives, and a third group on the formation of Object of a Preposition relatives. The fourth group were given instruction on a completely different topic and acted as a control group.

Two days after all four groups experienced the instructional treatment, they were given a post-test, the form of which was identical to the pre-test but involved different sentences. The performance of the four groups in both tests is presented in table (i) in terms of the total number of inaccurate sentence combinations produced by each group.

> Question (i): What conclusions do you draw from this study about the effects of instruction?
>
> Question (ii): What further information about this experiment would it be useful to know?
>
> Question (iii): How might one determine whether the effects of instruction have *really* led to changes in participants' mental grammars for English?

TABLE (i) Inaccurate relative clause formation (tokens) made by four groups of L2 learners of English (based on Eckman, 1985: 301, Table 3)

Instructional group	Pre-Test			Post-Test		
	Subj	Dir Obj	Obj of Prep	Subj	Dir Obj	Obj of Prep
Instructed on Subject	34	36	42	4	25	38
Instructed on Dir Object	32	32	42	10	12	38
Instructed on Obj of Prep	35	39	42	0	4	1
Control group	27	30	42	23	30	42

4. EFFECTS OF PROCESSING INSTRUCTION VERSUS OUTPUT PRACTICE

In French, unstressed direct object pronouns precede the finite verb or, if a modal verb is present, precede the following infinitive, e.g.:

i.   a.   Jean **me** regarde   'John is watching **me**'
       b.   Elle **les** a mangés   'She has eaten **them**'
       c.   Nous pouvons **le** faire   'We can do **it**'

Direct object pronouns also encode person, number and gender features, e.g. *me* 'me' vs *le* 'him, it' (first vs third person), *le* 'him, it' vs *les* 'them' (singular vs plural), *le* 'him, it' vs *la* 'her, it' (masculine vs feminine). English-speaking early-stage L2 learners of French often omit direct object pronouns, mislocate them or are inconsistent in using the appropriate form.

Erlam (2003) tested whether two different methods for enhancing input involving unstressed direct object pronouns would lead to learning gains. The participants in her study were fourteen-year-old classroom learners of French.

One group (n = 23) experienced essentially the 'processing instruction' method used by VanPatten and Cadierno (1993), referred to by Erlam as 'structured input'. They were given explicit instruction about the placement of direct object pronouns and were also taught about the pronoun forms associated with person, the pronoun forms associated with number and the pronoun forms associated with gender separately. Following instruction they were given meaning-based comprehension activities: deciding which of two statements best described a picture, where the direct object was crucial to the interpretation, and deciding whether statements involving direct object pronouns were true for them or not (e.g. *Le professeur, je l'écoute toujours en classe (oui/non)* 'The professor, I always listen to her/him in class (yes/no)'). Additionally, they were asked to identify the correct co-referents for direct object pronouns in short reading comprehension passages and to identify pronoun placement and form errors in written and aural input.

A second group (n = 21) received what Erlam describes as 'output-based instruction' (which looks a lot like the 'traditional instruction' condition in the VanPatten and Cadierno (1993) study). The instruction phase was identical to that for the 'structured input' group (with the exception that the form correlates of person, number and gender were not taught separately but 'all at once' (2003: 568) for reasons that are not made clear in the article). Following instruction, participants were given production exercises that required them to replace full direct object DPs in sentences with pronouns, and to fill gaps in texts with pronouns from a list. Additionally, they were given oral production tasks where they had to supply answers to yes–no and information questions using sentences involving pronouns, e.g. in response to a question like *Comment trouves-tu le français?* 'What do you think of French?' they would answer something like *Je **le** trouve difficile* ' I find it difficult'.

There was a third, same-age control group (n = 26) of participants who were instructed on a different topic.

Erlam used a variety of measures to test the effects of the different treatments in a pre-test/post-test format. The first post-test occurred one week after the treatment

TABLE (i) Mean accuracy scores on direct object pronouns following three instructional treatments (based on Erlam, 2003: 573–4, Tables 3, 5 and 6)

Treatment type	Listening comp. (k = 10)			Written production Pronoun form (k = 20)			Written production Pronoun placement (k = 20)		
	Pre-t	Post 1	Post 2	Pre-t	Post 1	Post 2	Pre-t	Post 1	Post 2
Input (n = 23)	2.7	3.2	3.4	2.0	9.8[b]	7.3	2.0	8.6	6.7
Output (n = 21)	2.9	4.8[a]	3.7	2.8	11.6[b]	9.52[c]	3.0	11.3[a]	8.8[c]
Control (n = 26)	3.1	2.9	2.7	1.7	3.9	4.9	1.7	3.9	4.6

(k = number of tokens)

a– the score is significantly different from the other two groups

b– both scores are significantly different from the control group

c– the output group score is significantly different from the control group, but not the input group

phase, and the second post-test six weeks after the treatment phase. Results only for accuracy in performance on listening comprehension and written production of (a) pronoun form and (b) pronoun location are presented in table (i). Listening comprehension involved participants in looking at a picture and simultaneously hearing a native French speaker read four sentences, only one of which was grammatical and described the picture. The others were either ungrammatical or grammatical but did not describe the picture. Written production involved participants reading statements and questions with underlined DPs that they had to re-write as unstressed direct object pronouns.

> Question (i): How does the notion of 'output based instruction' in this study differ from Swain's (2005) view of the role of 'output' in developing L2 proficiency?
> Question (ii): How do you interpret the difference in scores at the first post-test one week after treatment and the second post-test six weeks after treatment?
> Question (iii): Compare the results of Erlam's study with those of VanPatten and Cadierno (1993) discussed in section 9.3. How do they differ? Can the difference be explained in terms of a difference in the tasks used?

FURTHER READING

For more on processing instruction see:

> VanPatten, B. (ed.) 2004. *Processing instruction: theory, research, and commentary*. Mahwah, NJ: Lawrence Erlbaum Associates.

For more on the effects of indirect negative evidence in L2 learning see:

> Gass, S. M. 1997. *Input, interaction, and the second language learner*. Mahwah, NJ: Lawrence Erlbaum Associates.
> Long, M. H. 2007. *Problems in SLA*. Mahwah, NJ: Lawrence Erlbaum Associates, chapter 4: Recasts in SLA: the story so far.

10 The Effect of Starting Age on Learning Second Languages

10.1 Factors Involved in Determining the Effect of Starting Age on L2 Learning

A former British Secretary of State for Education, Michael Gove, expressed the view that 'there is a slam-dunk case for extending foreign language teaching to children aged five' (*Guardian*, Friday 30 September 2011). This is a popular view. People are often heard to say that children are better foreign language learners than adults. As is often the case with generalisations of this kind, there is some truth in it, but the reality is more complex. Two factors must be taken into account in assessing the effect of starting age on the ability of L2 learners to meet the five challenges of second language learning identified in chapter 1: the segmentation, categorisation, syntax, semantics and context problems. The first is whether learning occurs predominantly in a naturalistic setting through interaction with speakers of the target language, or predominantly in a classroom setting where interaction is with a teacher and a controlled set of audio-visual and written materials. The second factor is the point at which the effects of starting age on meeting those challenges are measured: the early months after first exposure, several years after first exposure when learners have become communicatively highly proficient users of the L2, or some point in between these two. The aim of this chapter is to consider the effect of starting age on the acquisition of L2s, given these factors, and more specifically whether there is a 'slam-dunk case' for extending foreign language teaching to children aged five. The chapter begins by describing results from a selection of studies looking at the effect of starting age on learners in naturalistic settings.

10.2 Effects of Starting Age on L2 Learning in Naturalistic Environments

10.2.1 The Early Months after First Exposure

Snow and Hoefnagel-Höhle (1982) (henceforth S&H) is a classic study of the effects of starting age on the development of L2 skills in the early months of learning. They studied fifty-one native speakers of English who were acquiring Dutch in the Netherlands 'by "picking it up" at school or at work, with little or no formal instruction' (1982: 95). They divided their participants into groups by age of arrival in the Netherlands: three- to five-year-olds (n = 10), six- to seven-year-olds (n = 8), eight- to ten-year-olds (n = 13), twelve- to fifteen-year-olds (n = 9) and adults (n = 11). The majority of them were from similar socio-economic backgrounds (middle class). The three- to five-year-olds were estimated to be encountering Dutch at school for a minimum of thirty hours per week. The adults, by contrast, were not using Dutch regularly, although some were attending Dutch classes.

Participants were first tested within six months of their arrival, and then at two later points each separated by four or five months. The three tests covered the first year of consistent exposure to Dutch. A range of properties reflecting how learners were meeting some of the five challenges was tested. These are listed in table 10.1.

TABLE 10.1 Tests of abilities in Dutch used by Snow and Hoefnagel-Höhle (1982: 97–8)

Skill	Task
Pronunciation	Repeat 80 single words uttered by a native speaker, with picture support, immediately and after a delay.
Auditory discrimination	Choose one of two pictures on the basis of hearing a single word. (The names of the objects in the pictures differed minimally in phonological form, e.g. *man* /mæn/ 'man' vs *maan* /man/ 'moon').
Morphology	Produce an appropriate word in contexts like the following: 'Here's a picture of a wug. Now there are two of them. There are two ___ ?' (The task requires participants to use morphology productively with novel words like 'wug' (Berko, 1958)).
Lexicon	Point to the picture (out of 4) that corresponds to a heard word.
Verbal memory	Repeat sentences uttered by a native speaker. (These increased in length from 2 to 10 words.)
Translation	Translate 60 English sentences into Dutch.
Intuitions of syntactic well-formedness	Choose the grammatical sentence from pairs of sentences uttered by a native speaker. (One sentence was grammatical, the other not).
Story comprehension	Retell in English a story heard in Dutch.
Story telling	Tell, in Dutch, a story represented in a series of pictures.

The results from S&H's study can be summarised as follows. At the first time of testing, the ranking of the participant groups by overall score was:

| **Best score** | 12- to 15-years | > adults | > 8- to 10-years | > 6- to 7-years | > 3- to 5-years | **Worst score** |

Not only did the three- to five-year-olds have the lowest overall score, but they 'scored consistently worse than the older groups on all the tests', with one exception: pronunciation (1982: 103). This suggests that in the early months of learning a second language naturalistically, adolescents and adults are dealing with the five challenges more quickly than younger learners. And recall that the three- to five-year-olds were getting considerably more exposure to Dutch than the adults. The advantage in terms of amount of exposure did not convert into an early acquisitional advantage. These findings clearly run counter to the popular view of young children being better L2 learners, at least in the early stages.

While the performance of all participants improved at the second and third points of testing, S&H found important differences between the groups in speed of development. At the second testing, the eight- to ten-year-olds had overtaken the adults in auditory discrimination, verbal memory, intuitions of syntactic well-formedness, story comprehension and story telling. At the third testing they had also overtaken the adults in performance on morphology and translation. The six- to seven-year-olds had overtaken the adults on auditory discrimination at the third testing. S&H (1982: 103) conclude that 'all the tests ... showed a similar pattern: most rapid learning by the twelve- to fifteen-year-olds and adults during the first few months of acquisition ... and by the six- to ten-year-olds during the last three-quarters of the first year'. The twelve- to fifteen-year-olds maintained their rapid progress over the first year, while the adults started quickly but developed slowly. The evidence, then, is that over the first year of naturalistic exposure to an L2, adolescents are particularly fast learners. By comparison, in these early stages, three- to five-year-olds make slow progress.

Asher and Price (1982) found a similar pattern of higher performance by older learners in the early stages of learning in an experimental setting that nevertheless had the characteristics of naturalistic learning. They exposed participants to Russian in the form of aurally-presented commands acted out by a Russian-speaking experimenter over a one-week period. For example, learners might hear the Russian for 'stand', and the experimenter would stand up, or they would hear 'walk' and the experimenter would walk. The learners were asked to listen to the commands and imitate the actions of the experimenter. (There was another group who just listened, without acting out the commands – the L2 development in this group was almost identical.) The learners were exposed to increasingly complex commands as the programme developed over a week (e.g. 'walk to the door', 'walk to the window', 'pick up the book', 'put down the pencil', etc.).

Participants belonged to four different age groups: eight-year-olds (n = 16), ten-year-olds (n = 16), fourteen-year-olds (n = 16) and eighteen- to twenty-one-year-olds (n = 18). Tests of learning ('retention tests' in Asher and Price's terms) required

TABLE 10.2 Accurate actions performed in response to aural commands in Russian (based on Asher and Price, 1982: 81, Table 1)

Age	8-yr-olds (n = 16)	10-yr-olds (n = 16)	14-yr-olds (n = 16)	Adults (n = 18)
Mean scores	146/354	192/354	208/354	324/354

participants to listen to commands and act them out without the help of the experimenter. Some of the commands involved novel combinations of previously encountered commands. Retention tests were administered during the exposure phase, and two weeks after the programme had ended. The results of accurate 'act out' performance are presented in table 10.2. The total possible score is 354.

It is clear that in this task, in the very early stages of learning Russian, the adult group show superior retention over all the younger groups, including in this case the adolescents. This is somewhat surprising. The one area where young children might be expected to have an advantage over older learners is in 'picking up' language from simply hearing it. Yet this appears not to have been the case in this experiment testing the earliest stage of learning.

Fathman (1982) administered an oral production task to 140 immigrant children aged between six and fifteen who had been in the US for less than three years. These children spoke various L1s at home, and were acquiring English naturalistically at school. Some also had a one-hour English-as-a-second-language class per day, but others did not. The task aimed to elicit information about the children's use of twenty morphological forms and syntactic structures, for example use of articles, possessive 's, the regular plural -s, third person singular non-past tense subject–verb agreement, yes–no questions, wh-questions. Fathman used pairs of pictures to prompt participants to use the relevant forms/structures. For example, to elicit the preposition in, participants were shown a picture of a cat sitting by a box and a second picture of a cat sitting in a box. The experimenter would point to the first picture and say 'Here the cat is by the box'. She would then point to the second picture, say 'Here the cat is ___ ?' and encourage the participant to complete the description ('in the box'). Responses were scored as correct or incorrect. Fathman divided the participants by age at testing (six- to ten-year-olds and eleven- to fifteen-year-olds) and number of years in the US, from one to three, and calculated the mean score for each group. The results are given in table 10.3.

TABLE 10.3 Mean scores on a production test (% target-like) (based on Fathman, 1982: 118, Table 2)

	Years in US			
Age	1	2	3	Average
6–10	25.6	39.1	50.7	**38.5**
11–15	31.1	47.2	53.5	**43.9**

The eleven- to fifteen-year-olds achieved higher scores than the six- to ten-year-olds in each of the first three years of exposure to English, and an average score for those years that was significantly better statistically. However, the gap between the groups is closing by the third year.

The evidence from these three studies is representative of the findings in other studies of the effects of starting age on development in the early stages of naturalistic exposure. Adolescent and adult learners make more rapid progress than young child learners. Long (1990: 264) reviewed studies that had been undertaken up to 1990 and concluded that:

> most of the literature to date is … consistent with … the idea of a rate advantage for adults over children, and for older children over younger children, but with the advantage being temporary and applying primarily to developmentally early morphology and syntax. The advantage also operates in phonology, but seems to last for a shorter period.

10.2.2 Effects of Starting Age on Performance in Highly Proficient Users of the L2

A number of the studies of the effects of starting age on the eventual performance of communicatively highly proficient L2 speakers have employed a 'rating by native speaker' methodology. Recordings (or transcripts of recordings) of L2 speakers are mixed with recordings/transcripts of native speakers. Native-speaker 'raters' are then asked to judge randomised and anonymous sets for the nativeness of each recording/transcript. Other studies have compared L2 speaker and native-speaker performance directly in terms of their use of particular linguistic structures. The results from a representative selection of both types of study are described in this section.

Asher and Garcia (1982) got nineteen American high school students to rate the pronunciation of 101 speakers reading four sentences (for example, *It started to snow when we were about to leave for the mountains*). Seventy-one of the group were Spanish-speaking immigrants to the US from Cuba, the other thirty were native speakers of American English of a similar age. Most of the immigrants had been in the US for five years and were highly proficient users of English. Asher and Garcia divided them into three groups by age of first arrival (AoA). The 'raters' were asked to assign each recording they heard one of four grades:

A Native speaker
B Near-native speaker
C Slight foreign accent
D Definite foreign accent

Twenty-three of the thirty native speakers (77%) were given an A rating; none of the L2 speakers was rated as a native. The proportion of B–D ratings assigned to the L2 speakers, subdivided by AoA, is shown in table 10.4.

TABLE 10.4 Rating (%) of the nativeness of L2 speakers by age of arrival in the US (based on Asher and Garcia, 1982: 7)

	Rating			
AoA	A	B	C	D
1–6 yrs (n=19)	-	68	32	-
7–12 yrs (n=37)	-	41	43	16
13–19 yrs (n=15)	-	7	27	66

It can be seen that the L2 speakers who were first exposed to English before the age of six are considerably more likely than older starters to be rated as having near-native speaker pronunciation. Those whose AoA was thirteen or older are the least likely to be rated as near natives, with the seven- to twelve-year-olds coming in between. It appears, then, that although older L2 learners have an advantage during the early stages of acquisition, once a threshold of exposure to the L2 has been reached young starters can generally get closer to the pronunciation norms of native speakers of the target language.

Oyama (1982a) used a similar 'rating' design to assess native-like pronunciation of English by sixty Italian immigrants to the US, whose recordings were mixed with those of ten native speakers of American English. Participants were asked to read a short paragraph, and then to recount a brief anecdote of a frightening experience they had had (the latter being a measure of their pronunciation of English in spontaneous use of the language). Two native-speaker 'raters' were asked to judge each participant on a five-point scale from 1 (no accent) to 5 (heavy foreign accent). The L2 speakers were divided into three groups by AoA: six- to ten-year-olds, eleven- to fifteen-year-olds and sixteen- to twenty-year-olds. All participants had been resident in the US for between five and eighteen years. The mean ratings assigned to each group, and the effects of different lengths of residence (and hence differences in amount of exposure to English) are shown in table 10.5.

TABLE 10.5 Mean rating of L2 speakers by age of arrival and length of residence (based on Oyama, 1982a: 25–6, Tables 1 and 2)

	AoA							
	Born in US (n = 10)		6 to 10 yrs (n = 19)		11 to 15 yrs (n = 23)		16 to 20 yrs (n = 18)	
LoR	Para	Anecd	Para	Anecd	Para	Anecd	Para	Anecd
5 to 11 years			1.4	1.4	2.6	2.5	3.5	3.2
12 to 18 years			1.3	1.3	2.3	2.0	3.7	3.6
Native speakers	1	1						

Table 10.5 shows that the native speakers in the sample are given the highest rating (no accent) for both their reading of the paragraph and the telling of an anecdote. The L2 speakers who were first exposed to English between the ages of six and ten have mean ratings for both the paragraph and the anecdote that are close to 'no accent'. The L2 speakers with later AoAs have mean ratings that suggest they have perceptible foreign accents. Those who arrived at age sixteen or older are closer to the 'heavy foreign accent' end of the scale. There appears to be little difference in the rating that speakers receive when they are reading a paragraph or engaged in the spontaneous activity of recounting an anecdote. And once participants have been exposed to English for at least five years in a naturalistic setting, there appears to be little effect of longer immersion on performance.

Patkowski (1982) also used the 'rating of nativeness' technique to look at the effects of AoA on the syntactic, morphological and lexical choices made by L2 speakers in spontaneous speech during interviews. The participants were sixty-seven immigrants to the US speaking a variety of L1s. They all had a minimum of five years' residence. They were 'highly educated, upwardly mobile subjects who could be assumed to have been exposed to [English in] near optimal sociolinguistic conditions' (1982: 53). There were also fifteen native speakers of American English in the sample. Participants were interviewed for between fifteen and thirty-five minutes, and five-minute written transcripts were made of a section towards the end of the interview. Written transcripts were used to eliminate pronunciation differences.

Two native-speaker raters were trained and then asked to rate the randomised transcripts on a scale from 0 to 5, where 5 represented 'native performance'. All of the native speakers in the sample were given a 5 rating. The ratings given to the L2 speakers are displayed in table 10.6. The table shows the number of participants who received one of the ratings 3, 4 or 5, subdivided by AoA: arrival in the US before the age of fifteen or arrival after the age of fifteen.

The table shows that thirty-two (out of thirty-three) participants who arrived in the US before the age of fifteen were rated as native speakers, while only five (out of thirty-four) participants who arrived after the age of fifteen were given that rating. This suggests that where L2 speakers have had at least five years of exposure to English in a naturalistic setting, and are therefore likely to be highly

TABLE 10.6 Number of L2-speaker participants rated as 3, 4 or 5 (native) distributed by age of arrival (based on Patkowski, 1982: 56, Figure 1)

		Rating		
		3	4	5
AoA	Pre-15	1	-	32
	Post-15	8	21	5

proficient users, those who are below the age of fifteen at first exposure are considerably more likely to be rated as native-like by native speakers in their use of syntax, morphology and lexical items than learners who arrived after the age of fifteen.

The impressionistic rating by native speakers of other speakers' 'nativeness' is one way of measuring the effect of an earlier versus later start on L2 learning under conditions of naturalistic exposure to the target language. It is, however, a rather coarse measure. It is impossible to know what features of an individual's performance a rater is focusing on when giving a 'non-native' rating. A number of other studies have examined the effects of starting age on the use of specific linguistic properties by high-proficiency L2 speakers to gain a better understanding of how starting age might affect their mental grammars.

Long (2007: 50ff) reports the results of an unpublished study by Spadaro (1996) of lexical knowledge in thirty-eight immigrants to Australia who had been resident 'for substantial periods' and were using English 'extensively in their work, household, and so forth'. Spadaro subdivided them into three groups by AoA: under six (n = 13), seven to twelve (n = 15) and thirteen and older (n = 10), and compared them with a group of native speakers of Australian English (n = 10). Spadaro gave them the tests described in (1).

1. Tests of Lexical Knowledge Used by Spadaro (1996)

a. A 100-item written word association test. In word association tests participants are presented with a stimulus word (for example, *snow*) and respond with the first word that comes to mind (for example, *cold/ice/winter*) (see section 2.3 for discussion of word association tests).

b. A sentence completion test. Participants were presented with twelve incomplete sentences, such as *She agreed to _____ a kidney to save somebody's life, The drunk _____ over to the bus-stop,* and had to supply an appropriate filler (e.g. *donate, tottered/staggered*). To supply natural-sounding fillers requires considerable knowledge of the lexical items of the target language and the ability to make fine distinctions between potential fillers with similar meanings, such as *donate* versus *give* or *stagger* versus *shuffle*.

c. A lexical decision task. A list of twenty-four words was compiled, twelve of which were real English words, and twelve were plausible, but invented, words like *walker-by, high-brained*. Participants had to indicate the non-existent words.

d. A word naturalness test. Fifteen sets of four sentences were presented to participants. In three of the sentences the use of a key word (like *pass* in the illustrative example) is natural, but it is unnatural in the fourth sentence. Participants had to identify the unnatural use (example (iii) in the following):

i. Bessie passed a relaxing month in Provence
ii. Twenty years have passed since they last saw each other

iii. You've got the money you demanded – now pass the hostage

iv. The whole class passed the weekly test

e. An idiom completion task. Participants are presented with eighteen incomplete idioms and have to complete them. For example, *aches and* _____, *labour of* _____, *tie the* _____ ('pains', 'love' and 'knot' are the expected fillers).

f. An idiom expansion task. Participants are given ten key words from idioms, such as *gab* and *spick*, and have to complete the idiom (*gift of the gab, spick and span*).

g. An idiom correction task. Participants correct the error in twenty-five sentences like *I'm afraid you're growling up the wrong tree* (*barking up the wrong tree*).

h. A sentence naturalness test. Participants are shown eighteen sentences in some of which the use of idioms is structurally natural, while in others it is unnatural, for example:

i. The kids aren't pulling their weight with the housework. (natural)

ii. The bush was thoroughly beaten about by her. (unnatural)

Spadaro found no significant differences between any of the groups in their responses to tests (a) and (b). Furthermore, the L2 speakers whose AoA was under six were indistinguishable from the native control group on any of the other tests. However, the responses of the group whose AoA was between seven and twelve were statistically significantly different from the native-speaker control group on tests (c) to (h), and those who arrived at age thirteen or older were significantly different from the control group on tests (d), (e), (f) and (h). Differences in length of residence had little effect on participants' performance in the tests. It appears that, as far as lexical knowledge is concerned, all the participants of whatever starting age had acquired knowledge of the core meanings of a wide range of morphemes similar to that of native speakers, as shown by performance on the first two tasks. However, the later starters were less likely to identify invented words or the misuse of words (tests (c) and (d)) or know the constraints on the use of conventionalised expressions (idioms) (tests (e) to (h)). Long observes that 'they had weaker knowledge of the semantic boundaries and collocational properties of the items concerned' (2007: 53).

Johnson and Newport (1989) focused on the effect of starting age on knowledge of morphological and syntactic properties of English in forty-six L1 speakers of Chinese and Korean, and a group of twenty-three native speakers of American English. They were all given an aurally-presented grammaticality judgement task consisting of 276 sentences, 140 of which were ungrammatical. The morphological and syntactic properties tested are illustrated in (2).

2. Morphological and Syntactic Properties Tested by Johnson and Newport (1989)

Past tense:	Yesterday the hunter shot (*shoots) a deer
Plural:	The farmer bought two pigs (*pig) at the market
3ps S-V agreement:	A shoe salesman sees (*see) many feet throughout the day
Non-past progressive:	The little boy is speaking (*is speak) to a policeman
Determiners:	Tom is reading a book (is reading *book) in the bathtub
Pronouns:	Susan is making some cookies for us (*for we)
Particle movement:	Kevin called Nancy up for a date (*for a date up)
Subcategorization:	The man allows his son to watch (*allows his son watch) TV
Auxiliaries:	Leonard should have (*has) written a letter to his mother
Yes/no questions:	Can the little girl ride a bicycle? (*Can ride the little girl a bicycle?)
Wh-questions:	When will Sam fix his car? (*When Sam will fix his car?)
Word order:	The woman paints (*Paints the woman)

Participants listened to a tape of a native speaker of American English uttering each sentence twice. They had to respond by circling a 'yes' or 'no' answer on an answer sheet.

All participants were adults at the time of testing, and were all students or employees of American universities, using English on a regular basis. The L2 speakers were divided into four groups on the basis of AoA: three- to seven-year-olds, eight- to ten-year-olds, eleven- to fifteen-year-olds and seventeen- to thirty-nine-year-olds. All participants had had at least three years of continuous residence in the US, with the majority of them (35 out of 46) having at least seven years' residence. The accuracy scores of the participants are presented in table 10.7.

It can be seen that the L2 speakers whose first immersion in English occurred between the ages of three and seven achieved a range of scores which is almost identical to that of the native speakers, while those whose first immersion occurred at age seventeen or later do not fall within the same range. In fact, Johnson and Newport found statistically significant differences between the scores of the native speakers and those of every L2 group except those whose first immersion was between the ages of three and seven. They conclude that ' ... if one is immersed in a second language before the age of seven, one is able to achieve native fluency in the language; however, immersion even soon after that age results in a decrement in ultimate performance' (1989: 78).

TABLE 10.7 Mean accuracy scores of native and non-native speakers of English on an aurally-presented grammaticality judgement task (based on Johnson and Newport, 1989: 78)

AoA	Natives	3–7	8–10	11–15	17–39
	(n = 23)	(n = 7)	(n = 8)	(n = 8)	(n = 23)
Mean	268.8	269.3	256.0	235.9	210.3
Range	275–265	272–264	263–247	251–212	254–163

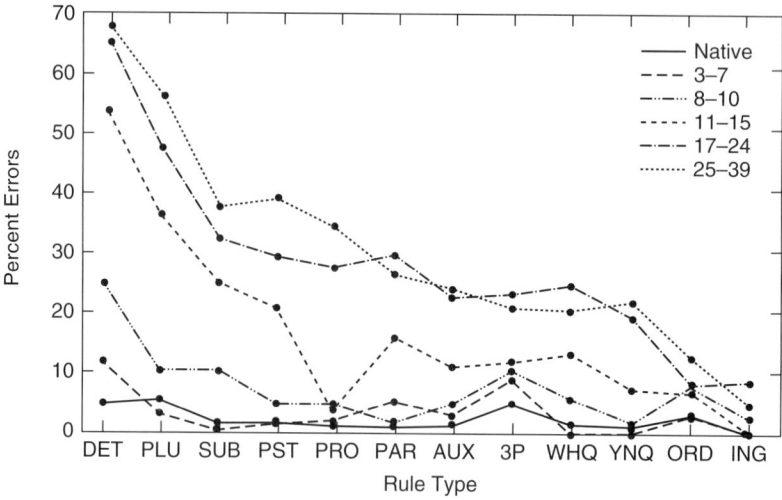

Figure 10.1 Graph from Johnson & Newport (1989: 87, Figure 3) Key – DET = determiner; PLU = plural; SUB = subcategorisation; PST = past tense; PRO = pronoun use; PAR = particle movement; AUX = auxiliary verb; 3P = third person non-past subject–verb agreement; WHQ = wh (information) question; YNQ = yes–no question; ORD = word order; ING = non-past progressive.

The degree of non-nativeness varied in relation to the particular grammatical properties involved. Figure 10.1 (Johnson and Newport's figure 3, 1989: 87) shows the percentage of errors made by each group on each grammatical property (i.e. percentage of responses accepting non-native forms).

The percentages of errors made by participants whose AoA was eleven or later in judging the grammaticality of sentences involving determiners (*the* and *a*), plural marking, subcategorisation (for example when to use *to* with a non-finite verb) and past tense marking are typically higher than percentages of errors on other phenomena. This property-determined accuracy in the later starters is discussed in section 10.2.3.

A study by DeKeyser (2000) replicated Johnson and Newport's study, this time with fifty-seven Hungarian-speaking emigrants to the US. DeKeyser did not divide his participants into as many AoA subgroups as Johnson and Newport. He simply divided them by AoA before sixteen (n = 15) and after sixteen (n = 42). All participants had been resident for at least ten years. The Johnson and Newport grammaticality judgement task was reduced to 200 items, with some of them replaced by items known to pose difficulties for Hungarian speakers (for example, the ungrammaticality of the plural affix with mass nouns like **informations, *furnitures*, and the omission of auxiliary *be* with progressives: **Tom working in his office right now*). Each dot in figure 10.2 represents an individual participant, located in relation to their AoA and score on the grammaticality judgement task (figure 1 in DeKeyser, 2000). The vertical dotted line marks the division between participants whose AoA was before and after age sixteen. The diagonal solid line represents the idealised trend in the data between AoA and grammaticality judgement test score.

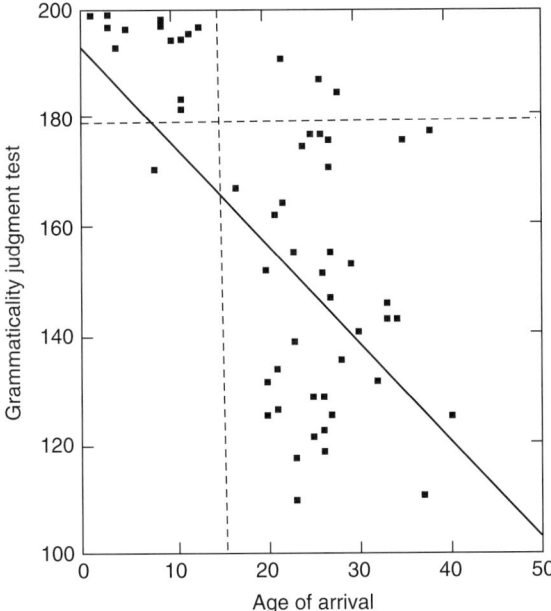

Figure 10.2 Scatterplot showing the distribution of scores of individual participants (from DeKeyser, 2000: 511, Figure 1)

It can be seen from figure 10.2 that fourteen out of the fifteen participants whose AoA was before age sixteen scored above 180 on the test, whereas only three of the forty-two participants whose AoA was after age sixteen did. The post-sixteen starters, then, are performing similarly to the post-seventeen starters in the Johnson and Newport study. However, starters between the ages of ten and sixteen appear to be performing as well as those whose AoA was below age five, in contrast to the findings of Johnson and Newport.

As Johnson and Newport had found, the participants in DeKeyser's study whose AoA was post-sixteen were more inaccurate on some properties than others. They were less accurate on the use of determiners, the ungrammatical plural marking of mass nouns and omission of auxiliary *be* in the progressive than on word order properties. The possible reason for this is discussed in the next section.

10.2.3 Explaining Effects of Starting Age on L2 Development in Naturalistic Learners

All researchers recognise that AoA has an effect on L2 acquisition in naturalistic settings. Observations like those described in sections 10.2.1 and 10.2.2 are incontrovertible. However, there are a number of different ways in which this effect has been interpreted. This section begins by considering possible explanations for AoA effects in highly proficient L2 users.

Johnson and Newport examined the correlation between AoA and grammaticality judgement task score in participants in their sample whose AoA was at or below age fifteen (n = 23) and those whose AoA was seventeen and above (n = 23). If AoA has a simple linear effect on performance, it would be expected that the older a person is when they are first exposed to the L2, the lower their score on the grammaticality judgement task would be: a 'negative correlation'. They found a significant negative correlation for the group whose AoA was at or below fifteen, but no correlation between AoA and test score in those who had arrived aged seventeen or older. They interpret this finding as providing evidence for a 'sensitive' or 'critical period' for the full acquisition of an L2 that lasts up to around the age of seven. The argument runs as follows.

Table 10.7 shows that the L2 speakers in their sample whose AoA was between three and seven performed within the same range as the native speaker control group. For speakers who first started learning English between the ages of eight and fifteen, there is a linear decline: the older a learner is at first encounter with English, the lower their performance in the judgement of grammaticality across a range of morpho-syntactic phenomena (see figure 10.1). However, this tendency to decline flattens out once learners are over sixteen. L2 learners whose first encounter with the target language is in their thirties are no less likely to acquire knowledge of the morphological and syntactic properties of the target language than learners whose first encounter is in their late teens or early twenties. This pattern of results is consistent with the idea that people have innate linguistic knowledge that fully guides the construction of mental grammars up to the age of about seven, but then progressively fades in influence over the next ten years. After those ten years, whatever language-learning capacities individuals have access to remains stable, at least for the next twenty years. What these language-learning capacities are is an empirical question. They might involve residual innate linguistic knowledge (that is, only some aspects of innate linguistic knowledge fade at the end of the sensitive period). Or completely different mental capacities might take over the learning task as innate linguistic knowledge fades.

While Spadaro's results on the effect of AoA on lexical knowledge in highly proficient L2 speakers are consistent with an early sensitive period for acquisition that begins to fade after the age of six to seven, DeKeyser's results show that AoA does not influence the performance of his L1 Hungarian participants on a grammaticality judgement task until after sixteen, suggesting that if there is a sensitive period during which innate linguistic knowledge is available to guide acquisition, it begins to fade at a much later age than claimed by Johnson and Newport.

DeKeyser also examined the correlation between AoA and performance on the judgement task. He found no negative correlation between AoA and test performance in those whose AoA was post-sixteen. In other words, a learner whose AoA was thirty was as likely to achieve the same score on the test as a learner whose AoA was twenty. This is consistent with Johnson and Newport's findings for participants whose AoA was seventeen or above. However, there was also no

negative correlation in the group whose AoA was pre-sixteen. This is inconsistent with the findings of Johnson and Newport and Spadaro. DeKeyser concludes
that seven to sixteen years is a period of transition during which some change
occurs in the ability to fully acquire an L2: 'Somewhere between the ages of six to
seven and sixteen to seventeen, everybody loses the mental equipment required
for the implicit induction of the abstract patterns underlying a human language'
(DeKeyser, 2000: 518).

Not everyone believes that age effects are the consequence of a sensitive period
for the application of innate linguistic knowledge to the learning task. Some
researchers argue that there is no specifically linguistic innate knowledge, and
that language is 'under the control of cognitive processes that are not unique to
a language learning module' (Bialystok and Hakuta, 1999: 172). Age effects are
simply the result of the general cognitive decline that humans undergo as they
age. Their ability to learn languages suffers as a result. If age-related changes in
the ability to acquire L2s are attributable to cognitive changes over the lifespan,
the prediction should be that decline in ultimate proficiency will be gradual and
constant.

Bialystok and Hakuta support this claim with evidence from a study based on
census data collected in 1990 from two groups of non-English speakers in New
York State: L1 speakers of Chinese and Spanish. Only informants who had been
resident in the US for ten years or more were included. This yielded 24,903 Chinese
speakers and 38,787 Spanish speakers. The factor that Bialystok and Hakuta correlated with AoA was self-reported proficiency. Informants had been asked on the
census form to say how well they speak English on the scale: 1 not at all; 2 not
well; 3 well; 4 very well; 5 speak only English. The results show a steady decline in
self-rating of proficiency from the earliest arrivals, whose rating was around 4, to
the oldest arrivals (aged sixty or over) whose rating was around 1. The pattern was
the same in both the Chinese and Spanish groups, consistent with a gradual and
constant decline in L2 proficiency the older learners are on first arrival.

The problem with these results, however, is that self-rating of proficiency is a
very coarse measure of the linguistic knowledge that speakers have. Individuals
may over-rate or under-rate their actual ability for various reasons. For example,
an L2 speaker may have knowledge of the target language that falls within the
native range, but self-rate as speaking 'not very well' because they are rather introvert by nature and feel that they are poor conversational partners. Similarly, sup-
pose that older people are generally more modest in assessing their abilities than
younger people. The results of the census data would then reflect changes in people's self-assessment of their abilities, not the actual abilities themselves. Studies
that look at changes in the use of linguistic properties are considerably more reli-
able as an indicator of possible AoA effects on the acquisition of L2s.

A different counter-argument to the claim that there is a sensitive period for the
application of innate linguistic knowledge in the L2 acquisition process proposes
that learners do indeed have access to such knowledge, and that access remains

TABLE 10.8 Mean accuracy scores of L1 Spanish speakers of L2 English on an aurally-presented grammaticality judgement task (based on Birdsong and Molis, 2001, Table 1)

AoA	3–7	8–10	11–16	17–44
	(n = 14)	(n = 6)	(n = 9)	(n = 32)
Mean	266.7	256.8	262.3	234.5
Range	273–261	268–244	267–257	268–161

fully available throughout life. Changes in performance with a later AoA are the result of other factors, but not the ability in principle to establish target-like mental grammars.

Birdsong and Molis (2001) conducted an exact replication of the methodology used by Johnson and Newport (1989), but this time with sixty-one immigrants to the US whose L1 was Spanish. AoA ranged from three to forty-four. Length of residence in the US was on average over ten years. As in the Johnson and Newport study, all participants were university-educated and were either students or employees of universities at the time of testing. The results from the study are presented in table 10.8. (A pair of grammatically ambiguous test items in the Johnson and Newport study was eliminated, giving a total possible score of 274, rather than 276.)

In contrast to the Johnson and Newport study, Birdsong and Molis found no negative correlation between AoA and accuracy on the grammaticality judgement task in the twenty-nine participants whose AoA was sixteen or below. But there was such a correlation in the group whose AoA was seventeen or older. The latter finding also contrasts with that of DeKeyser, who found no correlation between AoA and performance on the grammaticality judgement task in his post-sixteen arrival group. Birdsong and Molis cautiously conclude that the evidence from their study could be construed as falsification of the claim that there is a sensitive period for the application of innately-determined linguistic knowledge in the acquisition of L2s.

An alternative view is that discrepancies in the findings across the three studies (Johnson and Newport 1989, DeKeyser 2000 and Birdsong and Molis 2001) are consistent with a sensitive period for L2 acquisition early in life, since in all three studies young starters with long exposure to the target L2 in a naturalistic setting perform, as a group, within the native range on the measure used (a grammaticality judgement task). The point at which the sensitive period ends, and innate linguistic knowledge begins to fade, is less clear. However, when it does fade L2 learners unconsciously recruit other cognitive processes in the acquisition task to compensate. One source of compensation is grammatical processes present in the L1. Where learners identify similarities between the L1 and the L2, they map L2 forms onto L1 grammatical processes. Strikingly, a number of the properties tested in Johnson and Newport's grammaticality judgement task have similar realisations in English and Spanish, but are quite different in Chinese and Korean. Chinese, for example, lacks subject–verb agreement, does not mark verbs for past tense, does not have definite and indefinite articles, and does not have an obligatory plural affix for nouns. Spanish, like English, has all of these properties. One possible reason why the Spanish speakers in the Birdsong and Molis study with later AoAs appear to show higher levels of accuracy on the task than Johnson and Newport's Chinese and Korean speakers could be that they are drawing on the grammar of their L1 to model the distribution of forms in the L2 in the absence of guidance from innate linguistic knowledge. This is a view taken by DeKeyser (2000: 502–3): 'the more closely related the L1 and L2 are, the fewer structures have to be acquired from scratch, and the fewer structures, therefore, are eligible to show an age effect'.

A second potential factor compensating for loss of innate knowledge explored by DeKeyser is aptitude for language learning. A person's aptitude for language learning is typically measured by scores on tasks that aim to tap the following skills: an ability to distinguish speech sounds that contrast minimally and to associate speech sounds with written symbols; an ability to identify the grammatical function of sentence constituents (for example, distinguishing a subject from an object); an ability to rote-learn new words and meanings; an ability to infer grammatical rules from samples of an unknown language. The higher a person scores on such tasks, the greater their potential for learning an L2.

DeKeyser gave his participants a version of an aptitude test in Hungarian, identified each participant as of 'low' or 'high' aptitude, on the basis of their scores, and then correlated participants' aptitude scores with their scores in the grammaticality judgement task. For participants whose AoA was before sixteen, there was no correlation between aptitude and score on the grammaticality judgement task. That is, while some participants in this group of fifteen had low aptitude-test scores, this had no effect on their success in judging the grammaticality of English sentences. However, for those participants whose AoA was post-sixteen there was a significant correlation: participants classified as 'high aptitude' had higher scores on the judgement task than participants classified as 'low aptitude'. This again is consistent with there being a sensitive period for the application of innate linguistic knowledge. During that period, L2 learners' mental grammars develop as the result of an interaction between samples of the target language and pre-existing linguistic knowledge. General aptitude for language learning is irrelevant. Beyond the sensitive period, those who are most successful are those who are good at discriminating sound contrasts, at word learning and at grammatical analysis. They use these skills (unconsciously) to compensate for the loss of innate linguistic knowledge. L2 learners whose L1s realise grammatical properties in similar ways to the L2 and who have good aptitude for language learning have the potential for performing in tasks within the native range (as in the Birdsong and Molis study).

Abrahamsson and Hyltenstam (2008) have also found that high aptitude scores correlate with near-nativeness in L2 learners whose AoA occurs in adolescence or later, but not in learners whose AoA is before adolescence. The participants in their study were all native speakers of Spanish acquiring Swedish naturalistically. They were selected on the basis of samples of their speech being rated as near-native by native-speaker judges. There were thirty-one participants whose AoA in Sweden was eleven or below, and eleven participants whose AoA was between thirteen and twenty-three. Participants in both groups were matched for length of residence and self-reported daily use of Swedish. The results of an aptitude test showed that all of the thirteen- to twenty-three-year-old arrivals had above-average aptitude test scores, and that as a group they had significantly higher scores than the group of early arrivals. The aptitude test scores of the pre-eleven AoA group were not significantly different from those of a group of twenty native speakers who also took the test. In other words, aptitude for language learning played no role in the success with which native speakers and pre-eleven AoA L2 learners have acquired Swedish, whereas for the post-thirteen group aptitude for language learning appears to have played an important role. Only those with high aptitude scores were rated as near-natives by native-speaker judges.

Section 10.2 in a Nutshell

In the early stages of learning an L2 in a naturalistic (immersion) setting, adolescent and adult learners develop knowledge across a range of properties more quickly than younger learners. Three- to five-year-olds develop least quickly (Snow and Hoefnagel-Höhle, 1982). The gap between younger (six- to ten-year-old) and older (eleven- to fifteen-year-old) children in accuracy on measures of knowledge of morphology and syntax closes after three years of immersion (Fathman, 1982). Ability to achieve native-like performance when learners have had three or more years of immersion is affected by Age of Arrival (AoA) in a country where the target language is spoken. In ratings by native speakers of the 'nativeness' of the pronunciation of L2 speakers of English, those whose AoA occurred between one and ten years were more likely to be rated as near-native than those whose AoA was later (Asher and Garcia, 1982; Oyama, 1982a). A study of native-speaker ratings of 'nativeness' on syntactic, morphological and lexical properties found an advantage for those whose AoA was below fifteen years (Patkowski, 1982). Studies focusing on accuracy in the use of lexical (Spadaro, 1996) and morphological and syntactic (Johnson and Newport, 1989) properties of English report that those whose AoA was below six years are indistinguishable from native speakers on the measures used, but those with higher AoAs are significantly different. Johnson and Newport's participants were L1 speakers of Chinese and Korean. A replication of their study with Hungarian-speaking learners of English with at least ten years of immersion found native-like performance by speakers whose AoA went up to sixteen years.

Johnson and Newport (1989) found a significant negative correlation between AoA up to fifteen and accuracy scores on their grammaticality judgement task (i.e. the later the AoA the lower the score), but no correlation in participants whose AoA was seventeen to thirty-nine. This is consistent with a sensitive or critical period for L2 acquisition that ends around age seven, fades over the next ten years and then remains stable. Spadaro's (1996) results are consistent with this, but DeKeyser's (2000) study found no negative correlation between AoA and accuracy scores up to the age of sixteen in his Hungarian-speaking participants. This suggests that a sensitive period may continue up to age sixteen.

Some studies have argued against a sensitive period for L2 acquisition. A census-based study by Bialystok and Hakuta (1999) found a negative correlation between AoA and self-ratings of proficiency that continued throughout life. However, self-rating of proficiency is a coarse measure that might be skewed by extraneous factors. Birdsong and Molis (2001) replicated Johnson and Newport's study with Spanish-speaking immigrants to the US with at least ten years of immersion. They found no correlation between AoA and accuracy scores up to sixteen years (consistent with DeKeyser's findings) but a correlation between AoA and accuracy in those who arrived after age sixteen. Their conclusion is that the findings falsify the claim that there is a sensitive period for L2 acquisition. An alternative interpretation of the findings is that there is a sensitive period that ends at some point between the ages of seven and sixteen, after which the L1 and aptitude for language learning can compensate to some extent for the loss of access to innate linguistic knowledge.

10.3 Effects of Starting Age on L2 Learning in a Classroom Setting

This section describes a number of studies that have been undertaken of the effects of starting age on L2 learning outcomes in settings where the community in which the learner lives does not speak the L2 (for example, an L1 speaker of Arabic living in Riyadh learning English, an L1 speaker of English in the UK learning Chinese, and so on). In these contexts, exposure to the L2 largely occurs in a classroom for a few hours a week. The kind of language that such learners are exposed to can, of course, take different forms (see chapter 9 for discussion). In traditional language classrooms the emphasis is usually on learning pedagogically-oriented grammatical rules and lists of lexical items, then using those rules and those lexical items in various exercises. Less traditional approaches might foreground the learning of communicative functions (requesting, imparting information, persuading, etc.) in various task-based activities. Classes might involve the spoken and written forms of the target language to varying degrees. They might involve using the target language as a means of teaching other curriculum subjects (such as science, geography, religion). In the discussion that follows, where information about the kind of exposure learners have received in the classroom has a bearing on interpreting the effects of age at which learning first started, this will be given. Since classroom L2 learners are likely to have fewer encounters with the target L2 than naturalistic learners and to be exposed to a more controlled sample (selected by the teacher or the coursebook), the relevant point of first encounter will be described as Age of First Exposure (AoE) to distinguish it from Age of Arrival (AoA) in naturalistic learning contexts.

10.3.1 Effects of Starting Age on L2 Learning in Traditional Foreign Language Classrooms

A number of studies of the effects of an early versus late AoE on L2 development and attitude to language learning in traditional foreign language classrooms have been undertaken in the Basque and Catalan regions of northern Spain (see García Mayo and García Lecumberri (2003) for a selection of representative studies). Participants are typically bilingual speakers of Basque and Spanish or Catalan and Spanish learning English at the rate of two to three hours a week. In the Basque region, Cenoz (2003) compared three groups with AoE of four years, eight years and eleven years after they had received about 600 hours of exposure. That is, they were tested at ages nine, thirteen and sixteen. In Catalonia, Muñoz and Tragant (2001) and Muñoz (2003) compared two groups with AoE of eight and eleven after 200 hours of exposure (tested at ages eleven and thirteen) and after 416 hours (tested at ages thirteen and fifteen respectively). Participants' development in English was measured on factors like:

- the grammaticality of their utterances
- the extent to which they had a 'foreign accent'
- their ability to discriminate sound contrasts
- their oral production and comprehension skills
- their ability to write compositions
- their attitude to learning English and foreign language learning more generally

Larson-Hall (2008: 38) summarises the findings of these studies as follows: 'in almost every reported comparison it was found that earlier starters lagged behind later starters at least numerically and often statistically'. Just as in the studies of naturalistic L2 learners, in the early stages of learning English in the classroom the children with the youngest AoE lag behind older children and adolescents in the speed with which they acquire the L2. One advantage found in one study for the four-year-old starters in the Basque region

(Cenoz 2003) was that after 600 hours of exposure they showed more positive attitudes towards and motivation for language learning than older starters. However, in a study in Catalonia, Muñoz and Tragant (2001) found no difference in attitude to language learning between the eight-year-old starters and the eleven-year-old starters after 200 hours or after 416 hours. At 200 hours, between 64 and 71 per cent of participants responded positively to the question 'Do you like learning English?', and after 416 hours of exposure this had risen to between 81 and 89 per cent. This interesting finding leads Muñoz and Tragant (2001: 217) to suggest that 'accumulated instruction seems to have had a stronger effect' on positive attitudes to learning English than AoE. That is, the enjoyment that classroom language learners gain from learning a foreign language is the result of increasing exposure to it, not the age at which they begin to learn it.

Larson-Hall (2008) notes that a potential confound in the results from these studies is the age at which participants are tested. To keep the number of hours of input constant while testing for the effects of AoE, participants were necessarily of different ages at the time of testing (nine, thirteen and sixteen in the case of the Basque participants, and thirteen and fifteen in the case of the Catalan participants). Yet it is known that older teenagers have better test-taking skills than younger teenagers and pre-adolescent children. The older teenagers' proficiency in English may look better than it really is because they can use their problem-solving abilities to produce appropriate answers. While test-taking ability appears unlikely to have much influence on the extent to which someone has a foreign accent or is able to discriminate sound contrasts, nevertheless it is a factor that needs to be controlled for on other measures.

Althubaiti (2010) conducted a study that included such a control. She compared AoE in informants of the same age at testing. Her participants were fifty classroom learners of English in Saudi Arabia whose AoE was between three and eleven, and eighty-two learners whose AoE was twelve to thirteen. Participants were in their twenties at the time of testing. This resulted in the early starters having greater overall exposure to English (a mean of 1,021 hours) than the later starters (a mean of 819 hours). Althubaiti tested her participants' knowledge of the five syntactic and semantic properties listed in (3a–e), and also asked about their attitude to learning English.

3. Properties Tested by Althubaiti

a. Knowledge of English verb phrase ellipsis. In conjoined clauses where similar material is present in both verb phrases, the second occurrence may remain unpronounced, e.g. *John slept and Mary has slept too* may alternatively be produced as:

John slept and Mary has ___ too

However, there are some subtle constraints on what can remain unpronounced. *John slept and Mary was sleeping too* does not allow ellipsis:

    *John slept and Mary was ___ too

Althubaiti tested whether her participants knew these constraints (which are not the same in Arabic).

b. Knowledge of the ungrammaticality of pronouns in positions where pronouns are impossible in English (but possible in Arabic), for example:

    Which student does the teacher think (*she) can pass the exam?

c. Knowledge of the fact that lexical verbs do not raise above verb-phrase adverbs in English (they do in Arabic):

    The boy carefully crossed the street vs *The boy crossed carefully the street

d. Knowledge of the contexts in which progressive versus simple present forms of verbs like the following are semantically appropriate:

    Heidi is playing/plays tennis with Peter

e. Knowledge of the contexts in which simple past versus present perfect forms of verbs like the following are semantically appropriate:

    John lived/has lived in England

She found no observable AoE-determined difference in the performance of her participants on any of the properties tested in (3). The most proficient speakers in both groups distinguished the progressive/simple present contrast and knew that main verbs do not raise over adverbs, but did not know the constraints on verb-phrase ellipsis, allowed pronouns where they are impossible in English, and overgeneralised the use of the English simple past to contexts where the present perfect is required. She also found no effect of AoE on the attitude of participants to learning English. The learners who started English when they were twelve to thirteen were no less positive about learning English than the early starters. So even though the early starters had on average over 200 hours more exposure to English than the later starters and had started earlier, the older starters performed just as well. And because all participants were tested in their early twenties, test-taking ability was not a factor.

Observe that these results are different from those reported in the studies from northern Spain. In those studies the early starters 'lagged behind later starters' (Larson-Hall, 2008: 38). In Althubaiti's study, the early and late starters were indistinguishable in performance. The difference appears to be the result of length of exposure. Althubaiti's participants had had longer exposure to English. This appears to mirror the findings of studies of L2 acquisition in naturalistic settings. Later starters have an advantage in the early stages, but early starters 'catch up'. Further evidence that with longer exposure early starters not only catch up but also overtake later starters in classroom settings comes from a study by Larson-Hall (2008).

Larson-Hall's participants were L1 speakers of Japanese learning English in a traditional foreign language classroom setting, with four or fewer contact hours per week. Sixty-one participants had started learning English between the ages of three and twelve, and 139 at the ages of twelve or thirteen. They were all tested when they were college students (hence eliminating the potential 'age at testing' confound). Larson-Hall compared early starters and late starters with similar amounts of exposure to English and similar scores on an 'aptitude for language learning' test. The linguistic measures on which participants were compared were DeKeyser's (2000) grammaticality judgement task (see section 10.2.2), and an auditory discrimination task targeting the sounds /r/, /l/ and /w/ at the beginning of real and invented words like *ring, wing* and *ling* (contrasts known to be difficult for Japanese speakers). Participants were also asked to answer two questions relating to their attitude to language learning: 'How much do you like studying languages?' and 'How much do you like studying English?' on a scale from 10 (I love it) to 1 (I hate it).

A statistically significant difference was found between the early starters and the later starters on the auditory discrimination task when the amount of their exposure to English ranged between 1,200 and 2,200 hours. The early starters outperformed the later starters. The early starters were also more accurate than the later starters on the grammaticality judgement task but only once exposure to English ranged between 1,600 and 2,200 hours. This difference was statistically significant. So it appears that an early start in the classroom can lead to more target-like judgements of grammaticality and greater auditory acuity, but only once a certain threshold of exposure to the target language has been reached. And that threshold is quite high. To put it into perspective, consider a hypothetical traditional foreign language programme where students receive three hours of contact per week over a forty-week academic year (many real programmes offer less input than this). Ten years would need to be spent in such a programme before an early start made any difference to auditory discrimination, and thirteen and a bit years before it made any difference to the ability to judge the grammaticality of sentences in the target language. Given that most language learners at best spend seven or eight years in such programmes, there is no real advantage to an early start. Larson-Hall did find higher mean scores in the responses of the early starters to the two questions about liking studying languages and liking studying English (7.0 and 7.1) compared to the later starters (6.4 and 6.5), but this difference did not reach statistical significance.

10.3.2 Effects of Starting Age on L2 Learning in Classroom Immersion Programmes

Classroom foreign language immersion programmes are 'educational programmes in which two (or more) languages are used for academic instruction' (Genesee 2001: 1). They are an attempt to approximate the conditions of naturalistic L2 learning, and are based on the assumption that learning in a naturalistic context leads to better outcomes than learning in a traditional foreign language classroom. It is instructive, therefore, both to examine the effects of AoE in such programmes and to compare the performance of learners who have taken part in immersion programmes with those who have only been exposed to the target language in traditional foreign language classrooms.

The first documented immersion programme began in Quebec, Canada, in 1965 and was created to facilitate the acquisition of French by monolingual English speakers. (Canada is officially an English–French bilingual country, and in the province of Quebec the majority language is French, with English speakers representing only 15 per cent of the provincial population.) Following that early experiment, similar programmes were instituted across Canada, mostly as the result of 'parent initiative and commitment' to their children having access to both English and French as part of their educational training (Harley, 1986: 55).

Harley (1986: 54ff) investigates in detail the effects of AoE in three different types of immersion programme offered in schools in southern Ontario on the development of learners' knowledge of various properties associated with the use of French verbs. She compared three groups:

(i) A group of twelve early total immersion (EI) learners. These were monolingual English-speaking children who attended a half-day French kindergarten when they were five, and were taught 100 per cent in French for all of their first year of school (grade 1). Their teachers were native French speakers who understood and accepted English from the children, but who used only French themselves. Following this first year, the amount of teaching in French was gradually reduced, and teaching in English introduced so that by around the age of eleven they were receiving half of their instruction in French.

(ii) A group of twelve late immersion (LI) learners who had started conventional French-as-a-foreign-language classes of twenty to thirty minutes a day when they were around age eleven. At age thirteen they opted for an immersion programme for a year in which 55–70 per cent of the school day was taught in French, including subjects like maths, history, geography and science. The amount of teaching conducted in French was reduced when they were fourteen and fifteen to between 25 and 40 per cent.

Harley compared the EI and LI groups after they had each received about 1,000 hours of French input. However, because participants were at different ages at the time of testing (the EI group had a mean age of 6 years 11 months, the LI group a mean age of 15 years 4 months), the better test-taking ability of the teenagers is a potential confound, as discussed earlier. To partially control for this, a third group of participants was included:

(iii) A group of twelve early partial immersion (EPI) learners with a mean age of 15 years 5 months. Although similar in age to the LI group, these learners had had considerably more exposure to French: over 3,500 hours.

Harley used data collected from thirty-minute individual interviews with participants, a translation from French to English task, and a story repetition task (used only with the LI and EPI groups). The focus of the comparison was primarily the verb properties described in (4).

4.   Properties Tested by Harley

a.   Use of appropriate forms of verbs in obligatory contexts for the expression of present, past and future tense (e.g. *j'aide* 'I'm helping', *j'ai aidé* 'I helped', *j'aiderai* 'I will help')

b.   Use of appropriate forms to distinguish perfective and imperfective past interpretations (e.g. *j'ai aidé* 'I (have) helped' versus *j'aidais* 'I used to help, I was helping')

c.   Use of appropriate forms to mark subject–verb agreement in person and number (e.g. *j'aide* 'I'm helping', *nous aidons* 'We're helping')

d.   Use of verbs with a reflexive pronoun. A number of French equivalents of common verbs in English like 'fall asleep', 'wake up' and 'get up' require the reflexive pronoun *se: s'endormir, se réveiller* and *se lever*.

e.   The lexical variety in the choice of verbs that participants used.

The results of the comparison show that the EI and LI groups were indistinguishable in their performance on (4a) and (4b), but that the LI group were significantly more accurate on (4c–d), and used a greater variety of verbs than the EI group. These findings suggest that there is no advantage for an early start in immersion programmes when learners have up to 1,000 hours of exposure, with some advantages for later starters in terms of the acquisition of morpho-syntactic properties and lexical variety.

The comparison between the same-aged LI and EPI groups is interesting. It might be expected that the EPI group, with 3,500 hours or more of exposure to French, would generally outperform the LI group, particularly in view of Larson-Hall's finding that there are advantages for early starters once some threshold of hours of exposure has been reached. Although the EPI group did generally have higher scores on the measures tested, the differences only reached statistical significance in the use of past and future tense, and in the variety of lexical verbs used. Harley concludes that 'in formal syntactic rules of number agreement and word order, and in areas of the verb system which differ in subtle semantic ways from English, the amount of progress [the EPI group] have made appears to be quite similar to the late immersion students who have had much less in-school exposure to French' (1986: 93–94). Genesee (2001: 15), in a summary of research findings on the effects of immersion programmes aimed at teachers, administrators and parents, suggests that 'it may be that the natural ability to learn language that young children possess is not an advantage in school settings'.

10.3.3 Comparison of L2 Learners in Classroom Immersion and in Traditional Foreign Language Classrooms

García Mayo and Villarreal Olaizola (2011) report the results of a comparison made between classroom learners who have taken a partial immersion programme that they refer to as Content and Language Integrated Learning (CLIL) and learners who have taken traditional English-as-a-foreign-language classes. The participants were school students in the Basque region of Spain. Four groups were compared. A CLIL group was tested when they were fourteen or fifteen after one year of the programme (and a range of exposure to English of 875–910 hours). A second CLIL group was tested a year after they had completed three years of the CLIL programme (and had had a mean of 1,443 hours of exposure), when they were aged seventeen to eighteen. Two traditional EFL groups were also tested at age fourteen to fifteen (with a mean of 693 hours of exposure) and at age seventeen to eighteen (with a mean of 990 hours of exposure). The task that participants undertook was the oral narration of a picture story. The properties that García Mayo and Villarreal Olaizola focused on were morpho-syntactic: use of the third person singular non-past tense -s and past tense -ed affixes, and use of auxiliary and copula be. The results, in terms of percentage omissions of these forms in obligatory contexts, are presented in table 10.9.

These results suggest that partial immersion in the form of CLIL leads to no greater learning gains than a traditional instructional approach, at least with respect to the use of English verb forms.

TABLE 10.9 Omission of verb forms by CLIL and EFL learners (based on García Mayo and Villarreal Olaizola, 2011: 137, Table 3)

	Age 14–15		Age 17–18	
	CLIL	EFL	CLIL	EFL
-s	71%	72%	23%	12%
-ed	48%	22%	41%	44%
Aux *be*	2%	11%	0%	6%
Cop *be*	1%	1%	1%	0%

Section 10.3 in a Nutshell

Most studies of starting-age effects in the classroom measure learners in transitional development. Where learners have less than 1,200–1,600 hrs of exposure, there is no effect of an early start, and later starters show numerical and sometimes statistical advantages on performance measures. One study found that an early start leads to more positive attitudes to language learning (Cenoz 2003). Larson-Hall (2008) found a positive effect of an early start on phoneme discrimination after 1,200 hrs of instruction, and on grammaticality judgement after 1,600 hrs. An early start appears to have little effect in classroom immersion programmes: two years of late total immersion produces better effects than several years of early total immersion on general measures of L2 reading, speaking, listening and grammar (Harley, 1986). Content-based instruction (partial immersion) after three years produces no better effects on the performance of adolescent/young adult L2 learners (aged fourteen to eighteen) on English morphology than traditional EFL classes (Basque region study).

10.4 Concluding Remarks

The chapter began by asking whether the popular view that young children are better L2 learners than adolescents or adults is supported by empirical evidence. In addressing this question it is important to be clear about the point at which learning gains are measured (early in development or after a number of years of exposure to the target language) and whether learners are acquiring the target language naturalistically in immersion settings or in the classroom. A range of representative studies was reviewed and the general conclusion to be drawn from them is that young child learners do not have a learning advantage over older learners in the first few years of learning. Indeed, adolescent learners ranging in age from eleven to sixteen years develop knowledge of the L2 most quickly. This is true both in naturalistic and classroom settings. Learners who start acquiring an L2 as young children do eventually develop to a point where their performance is close to or identical with that of native speakers, in contrast to the majority of older learners. This is true where naturalistic learners have three or more years of immersion. It is only true of classroom learners when they have had over 1,600 hours of exposure, which in typical language classrooms means learning the language for more than ten years. Below that threshold of exposure adolescent learners perform just as well as young children. In practical terms, a foreign language curriculum for the classroom that starts with eleven- to thirteen-year-olds is likely to be more effective with better outcomes than one that starts with five- or seven-year-olds.

With learners who have had long exposure to the target language, the cause of the less target-like performance of older learners by comparison with younger learners across a number of measures has been the subject of debate. Some researchers have argued that there is a sensitive or critical period for L2 acquisition that begins to fade at some point between the ages of seven and sixteen (Johnson and Newport, 1989; DeKeyser, 2000). The assumption underlying this claim is that child learners of an L2 have access to innate linguistic knowledge (Universal Grammar), some aspects of which subsequently switch off. L2 learners who start when they are older compensate for the loss of this innate knowledge by using the L1 or general problem-solving skills to model target-language properties. However, these alternative strategies appear not to be as successful as UG. Successful older language learners may have an aptitude for language learning (DeKeyser, 2000; Abrahamsson and Hyltenstam, 2008).

A number of researchers have argued against the sensitive/critical period claim, however. Some have proposed a general cognitive decline that starts in later childhood and continues throughout life (Bialystok and Hakuta, 1999), although the evidence on which this is based (census data) is unconvincing. Others have cited evidence that L2 learners who start when they are older can be fully successful in acquiring the target language. Birdsong and Molis (2001) showed that Spanish learners of English who start learning as late as age sixteen can perform within the native speaker range on a grammaticality judgement task. And a number of studies discussed in previous chapters have shown that L2 speakers who started learning the L2 in adolescence or adulthood can acquire target-like competence on specific L2 properties.

Clearly there are some areas of L2 knowledge that are fully acquirable, whatever age a learner is when s/he starts learning, given sufficient exposure. But there are other areas where learners who start acquiring an L2 when they are older diverge persistently from native speakers, even after long exposure to the target language. The interplay between areas of L2 knowledge that are readily acquirable by all learners and areas where older learners appear to be persistently divergent is taken up in the concluding chapter, where the threads of discussion in previous chapters are brought together.

ACTIVITIES

1. TEST YOURSELF

(i)   Why is it important to distinguish early from later stages of L2 development in considering the effects of age of first exposure?

(ii)   Describe a study that has used native-speaker rating of L2 performance as a measure of how closely L2 speakers approximate to target-language norms.

(iii)   In Spadaro's (1996) study of high-proficiency L2 speakers of English, on the acquisition of which properties did age of arrival appear to have little effect, and on the acquisition of which properties did it have a significant effect?

(iv)   What are the similarities and differences between Johnson and Newport's (1989) and DeKeyser's (2000) studies of age-of-arrival effects on the acquisition of morpho-syntactic properties in L2 English?

(v)   How important is the L1 in determining the different results involving age-of-arrival effects in the studies of Johnson and Newport (1989), DeKeyser (2000) and Birdsong and Molis (2001)?

(vi)   How is aptitude for language learning involved in the debate about the effects of starting age on ultimate success in learning L2s?

(vii)   What did Muñoz and Tragant (2001) find in relation to attitude to language learning in early- and later-starting L2 classroom learners?

(viii) What is the range of exposure to the target language needed by early L2 classroom learners to surpass later L2 classroom learners on (a) auditory discrimination, (b) judgements of grammaticality, according to a study by Larson-Hall (2008)?

(ix)   How successful is L2-medium instruction (teaching content subjects through the L2) in promoting L2 acquisition?

2. BEST AGE TO INTRODUCE A FOREIGN LANGUAGE INTO THE SCHOOL CURRICULUM

Assume you are in a country where there are three levels of schooling:

From 5 to 7 years (elementary school)
From 8 to 11 years (middle school)
From 12 to 18 years (high school)

There is a debate about the best age to introduce a foreign language into the curriculum. The Ministry of Education asks for your advice, on the basis of your knowledge of empirical studies that have been conducted on the question.

What advice would you give?

3. AGE EFFECTS ON ACQUIRING GERMAN SOUNDS

Olson and Samuels (1982) asked twenty 9- to 10-year-olds, twenty 14- to 15-year-olds and twenty 18- to 26-year-olds, all monolingual English speakers with no previous foreign language learning experience, to listen to some aural exercises in the

TABLE (i) Mean rating of participants' pronunciation of German words by age (based on Olson and Samuels, 1982: 73, Table 2)

Age in Years	Pre-Test Rating /100	Post-Test Rating /100
9–10 (n = 20)	55	64
14–15 (n = 20)	57	73
18–26 (n = 20)	57	76

use of German sounds. The materials, which consisted of contrasting syllables or words and short sentences, contained thirty-three sounds that differ from English. They received this training over three weeks.

To test the effect of the training, participants were given a pre-test before training began that required them to repeat twenty-five aurally-presented short German words. They were given the same test after they had received the training. Two independent German-speaking judges were asked to rate each participant on a five-point scale, going from 4 (native-like pronunciation) to 0 (no attempt to pronounce the word). If a participant was rated as native-like on every test item the score would be 100 (4 × 25 items). Results from the pre-test and post-test are presented in table (i).

On the pre-test, no group was statistically significantly different from the others. On the post-test, both the 14- to 15-year-olds and 18- to 26-year-olds were rated as statistically significantly more target-like in their pronunciation than the 9- to 10-year-olds, but they were not different from each other.

Question: What conclusions do you draw from these findings? Can the results be said to reflect early acquisition of the sound system of an L2?

4. COMPREHENDING ENGLISH SENTENCES IN WHITE NOISE

Oyama (1982b) asked sixty Italian-speaking immigrants to the US and ten native English speakers to listen to twelve sentences read by a native speaker and to repeat whatever they had understood. They heard short declarative sentences of five to seven words like *Shepherds seldom lose their sheep, Young people like red apples, Robert put the dishes down*. The task was complicated by the fact that the sentences were accompanied by 'white noise' (a kind of electrical hissing similar to background noise to a radio programme when reception is poor) of varying loudness. Participants heard each sentence four times. The first time the white noise was very loud and the sentence was virtually incomprehensible even for native speakers. On the second, third and fourth hearings the white noise became progressively less loud. Participants were given a point for every time they correctly identified a word. There were sixty-eight words in the twelve sentences, so a possible maximum score for a participant who identified these words in all four of the sentence presentations is in principle 272 (68 x 4). In practice, scores were lower than this because the loudness of the white noise in the initial trials made comprehension very difficult. The mean score for the native speaker group was in fact 166.

TABLE (i). Mean comprehension scores: words in sentences presented in white noise to 60 L2 speakers of English with L1 Italian (based on Oyama, 1982b: 43, Table 1)

AoA in Years	LoR in the US in Years	
	5–11	12–18
6–10	141 (n = 8)	163 (n = 11)
11–15	132 (n = 12)	119 (n = 11)
16–20	124 (n = 9)	110 (n = 9)

Oyama analysed the mean scores of the Italian speakers by their age of first arrival in the US (AoA) and by their length of residence in the US (LoR). The results are presented in table (i) (n = the number of participants in each AoA/LoR group).

How do you interpret these results in terms of hypotheses about the role that age of first arrival and length of residence in an immersion setting play in determining success in an L2?

5. LANGUAGE PROFICIENCY AND APTITUDE IN FRENCH IMMERSION STUDENTS

Harley and Hart (1997) compared performance in L2 French and the relevance of language aptitude to that performance of two groups of English-speaking immersion students aged fifteen to sixteen. The first group (n = 36) had undergone early partial immersion (EPI): they were first exposed to French from the age of five to six when 50 per cent of their school curriculum was taught through the medium of French. The second group (n = 29) were late immersion (LI) students who had begun French in normal forty-minute-per-day French classes at age eleven, but switched to 50 per cent of their school curriculum taught through the medium of French at age thirteen. The EPI group had therefore had considerably more exposure to French than the LI group at the time of testing.

The two groups were tested on a number of measures of proficiency in French, four of which are considered here:

- Lexical decision – participants were given a list of 100 words. They were asked to 'cross out any words that they did not know well enough to say what they mean' (1997: 387).
- Listening comprehension – participants listened to five oral discourses on different topics and answered multiple-choice comprehension questions.
- Cloze test – participants read a three-paragraph text on the evils of money and materialism with twenty-five words omitted, and had to fill the gaps with appropriate items.
- Grammatical and lexical accuracy – following the cloze test, participants responded in writing in French to an open question: 'Is money indispensable to happiness in your opinion? Why or why not?' Their answers were scored for grammatical and lexical accuracy.

The results from these tests are presented in table (i) with an indication of any statistically significant differences.

Question (i): Are these results what you would expect in the light of the observations made in this chapter?

Harley and Hart then measured participants' performance on a language aptitude test and correlated the results with proficiency scores. Two elements of the aptitude test were 'memory for text' and 'analytical ability'. In 'memory for text' participants listened to two short narratives in English and were given six minutes to write down as much as they could remember. Each text contained twenty-four bits of information, and participants were scored on their recall of these bits. In the 'analytical ability' task participants were given a small corpus of data from an unknown language with English glosses. They had to 'infer how the new language system works and, for each of fifteen multiple choice items, select the correct way of expressing in the new language a stimulus statement provided in English' (1997: 386).

Table (ii) shows whether or not there was a statistically significant correlation between scores on these two measures of aptitude and performance on the French proficiency measures.

Question (ii): What conclusions do you draw from these results about the relationship between language aptitude and knowledge of L2 French in early partial immersion and late immersion learners?

TABLE (i) Mean scores on four tests of proficiency of French immersion students (based on Harley and Hart, 1997: 389, Table 2)

	EPI (n = 36)	LI (n = 29)	Significant?
Lexical decision /100	66	44	Yes
Listening comp. /17	8.9	7.8	No
Cloze /25	10.1	10	No
Gramm. and lex. accuracy (error-free sentences)	.91	1.4	No

TABLE (ii) Correlations (significant and non-significant) of measures of language aptitude and French proficiency (based on Harley and Hart, 1997: 390–1, Tables 3 and 4)

	Early partial immersion		Late immersion	
	Memory for text	Analytical ability	Memory for text	Analytical ability
Lexical decision	Yes	No	No	Yes
Listening comp.	Yes	Yes	No	No
Cloze	Yes	No	No	Yes
Gramm. and lex. accuracy	No	No	No	Yes

Question (iii): Harley and Hart (1997: 395) offer two possible explanations for these findings:

(a) 'One interpretation … is that when intensive L2 exposure begins around adolescence, language learning will tend to depend on different cognitive abilities from those that early learners rely on, with analytic ability being more intimately involved in L2 success for later learners.'

(b) Alternatively, the differences found could be an effect of different kinds of instruction in EPI and LI programmes, 'with initial instruction in early immersion oriented toward incidental learning and holistic processing of meaning in context, and in late immersion involving a heavier initial focus on the second language as a code to be taken apart and intentionally mastered'.

Given the observations made in chapter 9 about the effects of instruction on L2 learning and the observations made in this chapter about the effects of starting age on L2 development, which of these explanations do you find most convincing? Give reasons for your choice.

FURTHER READING

For further information about the critical period hypothesis see:

Birdsong, D. (ed.) 1999. *Second language acquisition and the critical period hypothesis.* Mahwah, NJ: Lawrence Erlbaum Associates.

Herschensohn, J. 2007. *Language development and age.* Cambridge: Cambridge University Press.

Birdsong, D. 2009. Age and the end state of second language acquisition. In W. C. Ritchie and T. K. Bhatia (eds) *The new handbook of second language acquisition.* Bingley: Emerald Group Publishing, pp. 401–24.

For an assessment of the advantages of a later start in classroom L2 learning see:

Pfenninger, S. E. and Singleton, D. 2017. *Beyond age effects in instructional L2 learning.* Bristol: Multilingual Matters.

11 Pulling the Threads Together – a Theory of How Second Languages are Learned?

11.1 Problems, Hypotheses and Theories

In chapter one, five problems that the L2 learner has to solve were identified:

- segmenting recurrent strings of sounds from the continuous stream of speech;
- categorising those sequences as morphemes with uniquely identifiable or meaning-modifying meanings, or dependency-marking functions;
- determining the possible ways in which morphemes combine into phrases, clauses and sentences in the target language (the 'syntax problem');
- identifying possible interpretations for phrases, clauses and sentences that go beyond the simple combination of the meanings of individual morphemes (the 'semantics problem');
- linking grammatical properties with aspects of discourse and the social context in which language is used (the 'context problem').

Subsequent chapters then presented a range of observations that have been made about how L2 learners deal with those problems and the effect that types of input and age of first exposure have on development, citing a representative sample of empirical studies.

The problems all relate to establishing a body of linguistic knowledge in the mind that can be deployed by an individual speaker to understand and produce sentences. There are other, non-linguistic aspects of learning an L2 that have not been considered here. For example, an individual's motivation for learning, her/his attitude to the target language and speakers of the target language, the extent to which an individual is an introvert or extravert, the kinds of strategies that an individual might use to help her/him acquire the L2, among others. These are all factors that affect a learner's interaction with samples of the target language – the 'input' – and the extent to which these samples are made available to the mental processes that segment, categorise and store linguistic information. Although they are potentially interesting areas for investigation in themselves, it is important to be clear that they are not factors directly involved in the establishment of a body of linguistic knowledge in the mind. (More information about studies of these non-linguistic factors in L2 acquisition can be found in the suggestions for further reading at the end of the chapter.)

Discussion of how L2 learners deal with the five problems often led to more than just presentation of the facts. In a number of cases attempts to explain the observations were made. This took the form of hypotheses ('informed guesses') which were tested against observed data. Hypotheses stand or fall by the extent to which they predict the observations made. A hypothesis can never be 'proved correct' because there is always the possibility that an as-yet undiscovered piece of information will emerge to falsify it. Such falsifications are useful because they narrow the range of potential lines of enquiry. For example, in the case of observations about how L2 learners of English use the functional morphology associated with finite verbs (tense marking and subject–verb agreement), six hypotheses were proposed:

• the 'apparent, but not real, optionality hypothesis' (section 3.2.1)
• the Aspect Hypothesis (section 3.2.2)
• the Missing Surface Inflection Hypothesis (section 3.2.3)
• the Morphological Deficit Hypothesis (section 3.2.4)
• the Feature Re-assembly Hypothesis (section 3.2.5)
• the Prosodic Transfer Hypothesis (section 7.3.2)

The first of these was falsified by the observation that both inflected and non-inflected forms of the same verb appeared in the speech of a Turkish-speaking L2 learner of English (section 3.2.1). The falsification of this hypothesis is useful because it shows that optionality in the use of functional morphology associated with the verb is real and requires explanation. The other five hypotheses are each consistent with some of the facts about the use of English finite verb morphology by L2 learners. None of them covers all of the facts; each needs additional hypotheses. For example, the Prosodic Transfer Hypothesis needs to explain why some Mandarin Chinese speakers accommodate English affixal verb morphology by incorporating it into the prosodic word (the only option allowed in Mandarin) while others do not, and typically omit all verbal inflectional morphology (section 7.3.2). There appears to be no single hypothesis currently that accounts for all of the observations about the acquisition of English verb morphology by L2 speakers.

A hypothesis makes use of independently-defined concepts. For example, the Missing Surface Inflection Hypothesis, the Morphological Deficit Hypothesis and the Feature Re-Assembly Hypothesis all make use of the concept 'morpheme', of the idea that there is a separation between morphemes and the forms that realise them, and of the proposal that morphemes are collections of features drawn from a set that includes [N], [V], [D], [past/non-past], [1, 2, 3 person], [number], [gender], and so on. These are defined within a general theory of language. Morphemes are the minimal meaningful syntactically-relevant units. The separation of morphemes from the forms that realise them is justified by the fact that two morphemes can be realised as a single unanalysable form, e.g. {V, write} + {tense$_{finite, past}$} is realised by the unanalysable form *wrote*. Features are required to distinguish the meanings of morphemes: {tense$_{finite, past}$} is different in meaning from {tense$_{finite, non-past}$}. These independently-defined concepts within a theory of language are used by a hypothesis like Missing Surface Inflection to offer an interesting account for why L2 learners of English might optionally use both inflected and uninflected verb forms in finite contexts, but rarely use inflected verb forms in non-finite contexts: learners have acquired the abstract tense morpheme with its target features, use inflected forms only when their feature specification matches the feature specification of the morpheme, but fail to access these forms on some occasions, substituting a less specified uninflected verb form (section 3.2.3).

VanPatten and Williams (2007: 2) describe a theory as 'a set of statements about natural phenomena that explains why the phenomena occur the way they do ... [It] also ought to make predictions about what would occur under specific conditions'. The 'statements' they refer to are hypotheses. They go on to propose an ambitious goal for a theory: 'we want a single theory to bring all of the observed phenomena under one umbrella' (2007: 4–5). Is it possible to have a single theory of second language learning that brings under one umbrella all the observations made in previous chapters? Given the current state of our knowledge, the answer is unclear. However, it is worth exploring what such a theory might look like, and that is what is aimed for in this chapter.

11.2 Innate Knowledge in a Theory of Second Language Learning

Few researchers deny that learning a language involves innately-determined capacities (O'Grady, 2008b: 620). However, an empirical question is whether there are innate capacities designed specifically for language (Universal Grammar), and if there are, how they interact with innate domain-general mental capacities that underlie thinking, planning, problem solving and so on, that might also be involved in the acquisition and use of language.

The ability to rapidly tally the frequency of co-occurring sounds/syllables in the stream of speech as an initial step in identifying form–meaning pairings (section 1.2) was argued to be a likely domain-general capacity (section 5.3). Parsing preferences for garden-path sentences like *The woman sold the house emigrated to Australia* (section 8.1) and relative-clause attachment preferences in sentences like *The dean liked the secretary of the professor who was reading a letter* (section 8.2.2) are arguably a response to domain-general limitations on our ability to compute information in real time. Speakers cannot entertain all of the possible grammatical analyses of a form or construction at the same time in real-time comprehension – *sold* can be both a finite transitive verb and a passive participle; *who was reading a letter* can merge with the closest local noun (*professor*) or with the whole direct object phrase – and so one analysis is applied preferentially, sometimes leading to the wrong interpretation. Even the fundamental generativity of language – the ability to produce and understand novel sentences – may be a particular implementation of a domain-general capacity to use a finite set of constructs to produce an infinity of novel patterns (section 5.1).

On the other hand, acoustic/articulatory features like [voice], [stop], [lateral] and so on, used for identifying and categorising the linguistic sounds segmented by domain-general frequency tallying, are plausibly elements of innate linguistic knowledge. The small set of lexical and functional categories like N, V, A, P, T, D, C, the features these categories encode ([animate], [number], [person], [finite], [definite], among others), and the syntactic rules that manipulate them (binary Merge, Move, Agree) are arguably part of UG. Poverty-of-the-stimulus cases like the effects of quantifier scope on interpretation (section 6.2.1), the Overt Pronoun Constraint (section 5.3) and constraints on the co-reference possibilities for anaphors like English -*self* forms and Mandarin Chinese *ziji* (section 6.2.2) are also strong candidates for consideration as properties of UG.[1]

How might these different kinds of innate knowledge – domain-general and UG – be integrated within a single theory of second language learning? In discussing optionality in the use of English verb morphology by L2 speakers (chapter 3) and the reason why temporarily ambiguous sentences like *The woman sold the house emigrated to Australia* might lead us up the garden path (chapter 8), reference was made to the role of 'working memory' in the real-time use of language, and the demands made when a lot of information needs to be computed. The overloading of working memory was an argument used by both the Missing Surface Inflection Hypothesis and the Morphological Deficit Hypothesis to account for why elsewhere or default forms for morphemes are accessed by L2 speakers where more specified forms are required. Reducing the burden on working memory may also be a reason for parsing preferences, as discussed above.

The proposal of a working memory (in addition to the traditionally-recognised categories of short-term and long-term memory) appears to have been first made by Baddeley and Hitch (1974). It is defined as 'an integrated system for holding and manipulating information during the performance of complex cognitive tasks' (Baddeley, 2000: 78). In Baddeley's (2007) model, working memory consists of three components, one dealing with language, one with visual and spatial information, and one with consciously acquired information of various kinds. These are distinct from, but feed and are fed by, short- and long-term memory. In an alternative conception, working memory is not distinct from short- and long-term memory 'but [is] rather [the] selective activation of items in long-term memory' (Sharwood Smith and Truscott, 2014: 60). That is, there is a single memory store, and when speakers use language for comprehension or production in real time the constituents involved reach

---

[1] It should be noted that some researchers argue that the properties attributed here to UG are derivable from the application of domain-general mechanisms to input. See Goldberg (2003), Ellis, N. (2006) and O'Grady (2008a). The position adopted here is that the evidence is sufficient for a case for UG to be made.

higher levels of activation than all other constituents that are not involved. Working memory for language is the set of the most highly activated elements at any given time.

Whichever conception of working memory is correct, one possibility is that it is the location where domain-general capacities and UG interact. The tallying of the frequency with which sounds/syllables recur in speech is coordinated in working memory by the domain-general capacity to compute frequency, drawing on phonetic and phonological features provided by UG. The information extracted from input is used to establish morpheme-like strings that are then stored in the language-specific Vocabulary of forms. These morpheme-like strings are available to working memory for future reinforcement through further encounters with the same strings and assignment of meanings.

Parsing preferences might be the effect of the interaction between domain-general tallying of the frequency of forms or constructions in input to which grammatical analyses have been assigned by knowledge that comes from UG. For example, English *sold* is either a finite, past-tense form or a non-finite participle. This analysis has been arrived at through the application of the UG-derived features [finite], [non-finite], [past]. Domain-general frequency tallying might establish that the finite, past-tense interpretation is more frequent in input than the participle interpretation, and assign a frequency index to both interpretations. Then in future encounters with *sold*, working memory will preferentially assign it the most frequent interpretation: the finite, past-tense interpretation. Or, from Sharwood Smith and Truscott's perspective, the finite, past-tense interpretation of *sold* will have a higher level of activation than the passive participle interpretation and hence will be applied first in parsing.

The UG-derived syntactic rules binary Merge, Move and Agree are involved in creating the structure of clauses like *This is the dog, The dog chased the cat, The cat caught the rat, The rat stole the cheese*. But working memory could be where a domain-general mechanism allows those structures to be recursively combined to generate potentially infinitely-long strings like *This is the dog that chased the cat that caught the rat that stole the cheese …* An alternative view is that generativity is specific to language so that recursivity is generated by binary Merge and Move themselves, without the involvement of domain-general processes.

A different kind of generativity was encountered in section 5.1 with examples like Penrose's sentence describing the birth of the notion 'mathematical proof'. This is a sentence you are unlikely to have ever encountered before, although you will have encountered the morphemes of which it is composed, and you can understand their novel combination perfectly well and determine that it is a grammatical sequence in English. This kind of generativity results from an interaction between language and thought. Thought initiates a novel conjunction of ideas which then finds expression through a novel use of language. More will be said about the interface between language and conceptual thinking in section 11.6.

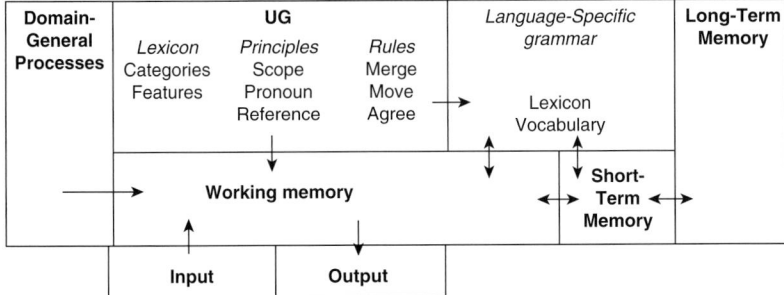

Figure 11.1 Possible components of a theory of second language learning and their interactions

The picture that is emerging is clearer if it is cast in diagrammatic form, as in figure 11.1. This is not an attempt to construct a model of the actual components and processes in the mind, just an expository device to keep what is being claimed explicit and clear. (For real attempts to construct a model of how language is represented in the mind, see Smith et al. (2011: chapter 6 and specifically p. 175) and Sharwood Smith and Truscott (2014: chapter 5 and specifically p. 161)).

In figure 11.1, the UG component is arbitrarily subdivided into a Lexicon that contains the universal set of categories (N, V, T, C, among others) and features ([voice], [stop], [lateral], [past], [1, 2, 3 person], [animate], [definite], among others), a set of principles that determine interpretations (scope, pronoun reference, among others) and constrain possible structures (like locality of movement – chapter 4, section 4.4.1), and the three rules Merge, Move and Agree. Empirical evidence is needed to determine whether such a subdivision is justified.

Input, which includes linguistic and non-linguistic information, is analysed by 'working memory' (WM) which uses both innate domain-general capacities and UG-derived knowledge to extract the linguistic information. Because WM is of limited capacity it must analyse current stimuli very quickly so that it can move on to the next incoming stimuli. It is assumed here that WM places analysed input in a temporary store that has greater capacity. This is 'short-term memory'. If the information placed in 'short-term memory' has a high level of activation (i.e. is memorable) it will be transferred to 'long-term memory'. If it does not have a high level of activation it will fade and be forgotten.

Linguistic information held in 'short-term memory' with a high level of activation will be transferred to the language-specific grammar, which is assumed to be a subcomponent of 'long-term memory'. This consists of a Lexicon, where abstract morphemes with their features are stored, and a Vocabulary, where forms with information about how they realise morphemes are stored.

In the very earliest phase of L2 acquisition, the segmentation phase, the language-specific grammar may contain only provisional phonetic specifications of forms in the Vocabulary that have been extracted from the tallying of recurrent strings in the stream of speech by domain-general statistical learning (supported by the phonetic features provided by UG). These will have their activation level raised when WM encounters the same recurrent strings in future input, and the morphemes they realise will begin to be identified as WM associates those strings with meanings.

There are several things to note about what is being proposed in figure 11.1. Firstly, the language-specific grammar consists only of a Lexicon of morphemes and a Vocabulary of forms. The rules that combine morphemes into phrases, clauses and sentences are part of UG and not specific to a particular language.

Secondly, there are bi-directional arrows between WM and short-term memory, between short-term memory and the language-specific grammar, and between short-term memory and long-term memory. This is to allow for the fact that the language-specific grammar and long- and short-term memory are not only capacities for storing information but are also involved in the production of language and other kinds of information. That is why there is an arrow going from WM to output. WM is involved both in the comprehension and production of language.

Thirdly, it is assumed that the more that morphemes in the Lexicon and forms in the Vocabulary are activated through WM and short-term memory, the less costly they are to WM in terms of attentional resource, allowing WM to concentrate on the analysis of the content of messages. In less proficient speakers processing language has a cost, requiring WM to juggle between paying attention to the content of messages and linguistic resources.

Finally, the language-specific Lexicon and Vocabulary store items from all of the languages that an individual speaks. There are no separate grammars for each language. This is consistent with the observation made in section 2.1 that initial acquisition of L2 lexical items involves L2 forms being connected to L1 forms and their associated L1 morphemes. When L2 forms later become connected directly to morphemes they remain within the same grammatical space and in effect compete with L1 forms. This is consistent with the finding of Dijkstra et al. (2000 – see activity 2 in chapter 2) that Dutch speakers who are highly proficient in L2 English react more slowly in identifying words that have the same form in Dutch and English but different meanings (like *room*, which means 'cream' in Dutch) than in identifying English words that have no form counterpart in Dutch. Such homographs activate two morphemes, one in Dutch and the other in English. The Dutch morpheme needs to be inhibited to make the appropriate decision, and this slows down reaction times.

Sections 11.1 and 11.2 in a Nutshell

The five problems that L2 learners have to solve identified in chapter 1 (segmentation and categorisation of morphemes from input, and solving the syntax, semantics and context problems) relate to establishing a mental grammar for the target language. An individual's motivation to learn, attitude to the target language and its speakers, personality (extravert or introvert) and learning style affect her/his interaction with input but are not directly involved in the acquisition of a mental grammar. Hypotheses about how learners deal with the five problems draw on independently-defined concepts, like 'morpheme', defined within a general theory of language. VanPatten and Williams (2007) have proposed an ambitious goal for a theory of second language learning of bringing all the observations under one umbrella. It is not clear whether this is possible but the current chapter explores what such a theory might look like. In such a theory innate domain-general and innate domain-specific (UG) resources need to be integrated, and one possible location for this integration is working memory (WM). Input feeds WM, which draws on domain-general processes and UG to analyse linguistic information. Because WM is of limited capacity, analysed strings are transferred to 'short-term memory', a temporary store with greater capacity. From here analysed strings may be transferred to the language-specific grammar, which is a component of 'long-term memory' and consists of a Lexicon of morphemes and a Vocabulary of forms. Syntactic rules are part of UG and not language-specific. Morphemes and forms become less costly in terms of the attention required from WM to process them the more they are activated. The language-specific grammar is a single store for all of the languages an individual knows.

11.3 The Role of Universal Grammar in a Theory of Second Language Learning

Given the outline in figure 11.1 of a provisional set of assumptions that a theory of L2 acquisition might need to make, it can now be considered how specific hypotheses follow from these assumptions. In relation to UG, researchers have taken three distinct views about how it is deployed in L2 learning. All agree that UG is fully accessible to child language learners, but differ in their view of continued accessibility to L2 learners beyond childhood. Bley-Vroman (1989), Schachter (1990) and Meisel (1997), among others, have argued for a Fundamental Difference Hypothesis. At some point during childhood, which could be any time between age seven and age sixteen (see section 10.2.3), UG becomes completely unavailable to L2 learners. This is what underlies the idea of a sensitive/critical period for language acquisition. As a result the grammars of L2 learners diverge persistently in some areas from those of native speakers. This is because they are based entirely on properties of the L1 grammar and the ability of domain-general problem-solving mechanisms to model L2 properties that diverge from the L1. In terms of the diagram in figure 11.1, this account would need to be interpreted as the Lexicon and Principles components of UG becoming inaccessible to WM. The rules would still be needed to construct phrases, clauses and sentences. L1 feature specifications of morphemes in the language-specific Lexicon would remain unchanged when L2 forms in the Vocabulary are associated with them.

Typical observations that are consistent with the Fundamental Difference Hypothesis that have been described in previous chapters include:

(a) the case of adult L2 learners of Dutch who optionally used Adj + Ø forms in attributive contexts that require Adj + e forms in contrast to child L2 learners who optionally used Adj + e forms in Adj + Ø contexts (section 4.7). The argument would be that while child learners have acquired or are acquiring the unvalued [ugender] and [udefinite] features assigned to adjectives in Dutch that come from the UG Lexicon, the adult speakers are using domain-general frequency tallying that determines Adj + Ø forms as the most frequent and hence most likely forms to appear in attributive contexts;

(b) the persistent use of L1 prosodic constraints by Mandarin Chinese-speaking L2 learners of English in the production of English affixal morphology (section 7.3.2);

(c) the persistent divergence of near-native speakers of Italian from native speakers in determining the reference of overt pronouns in contexts where null pronouns can also appear (section 8.3.3). This would result from the failure of the L2 learners to assign a [topic shift] feature derived from the UG Lexicon to overt pronouns in the language-specific grammar.

Other researchers argue that UG remains fully available to L2 learners throughout life (White 1985, 2003a; Schwartz and Sprouse, 1994; Epstein et al., 1996, among others). A particularly influential hypothesis has been Schwartz and Sprouse's (1996) Full Transfer/Full Access Hypothesis, which proposes that L2 learners have access to all the properties of UG, but initially assign all L2 forms the feature specifications of L1 morphemes. More will be said about this hypothesis in section 11.4 when the role of the L1 in L2 acquisition is considered. Proponents of the Full Access to UG hypothesis cite poverty-of-the-stimulus cases and target-like performance of very advanced-proficiency learners as evidence to support the position. Typical poverty-of-the-stimulus cases include the sensitivity of L2 learners to the Overt Pronoun Constraint on co-reference between null and overt pronouns and quantified expressions (section 5.3), to the effects of scope differences on interpretation (section 6.2.1), and to possible co-referents of reflexive anaphors (section 6.2.2). Typical cases of target-like performance include the valuing of the unvalued [ugender] feature of Spanish adjectives and German determiners that ensures agreement with the noun (section 4.7) or the acquisition of the [path] feature of English spatial prepositions like *into, under* in 'manner of motion along a path' expressions by L1 speakers of Spanish and Japanese (section 6.3).

Cases of persistent divergence, like the optionality shown by L2 speakers of English with L1 Mandarin Chinese in the production of affixal morphology (section 7.3.2) or the failure of near-native speakers of Italian to identify the [+topic shift] feature of overt subject pronouns (section 8.3.3), observations that proponents of the Fundamental Difference Hypothesis take to be evidence of the inaccessibility of UG, are explained as effects of the use of language in real time, of failure to fully 're-assemble' features through lack of evidence in input or of problems with pronunciation (as proposed by the Prosodic Transfer Hypothesis; see section 7.3.2). For example, the Missing Surface Inflection Hypothesis assumes that L2 learners have fully acquired the relevant morphemes with their target feature specification even when learners sometimes use an elsewhere form in contexts that require a more specified form. This kind of optionality arises when WM is dealing with a lot of information and accesses the elsewhere form from the Vocabulary, rather than taking the more costly option of searching for the specified form. In the case of the [+topic shift] feature of overt pronouns, L2 learners have acquired it, but fail to access it when the demands of keeping track of discourse information again overload WM so that overt pronouns take on the interpretation of null pronouns.

A third view of the role of UG in the acquisition of L2s by older starters is that it is partially available. The rules and principles of UG are still accessible, but some of the features in the UG Lexicon become difficult or impossible to access if they have not been instantiated in the L1. The features in question are the unvalued features involved in dependencies like [*u*gender], [*u*number], [*u*person]. These are referred to in the linguistic literature as 'uninterpretable' features, in contrast to their semantically interpretable counterparts [gender], [number], [person]. Semantically interpretable features that are not present in the L1 are still accessible to older starters. Advocates of this view (Tsimpli and Dimitrakopoulou, 2007; Hawkins and Casillas, 2008; Hawkins, 2012) cite cases like the acquisition of the [path] feature of English spatial prepositions (section 6.3) or the [definiteness] feature of English articles (by the Turkish speaker SD – White 2003b) (section 4.7.2) as evidence for the acquisition of interpretable features. They cite cases like persistent optionality in the use of affixal morphology (*contra* the proponents of Full Access to UG) and the persistent failure of L1 speakers of languages that lack articles (like SD) to recognise that English singular count nouns have an unvalued [*u*individuation] feature that needs to be valued by an individuating constituent like an article, demonstrative, numeral, as evidence of the difficulty L2 speakers have in accessing uninterpretable features from UG. This view is consistent with the separation in figure 11.1 of features of the UG Lexicon from principles and rules, and may require a subdivision of features into interpretable and uninterpretable.

The challenge for advocates of the partial access to UG position is to explain why L2 learners are as successful as they are (the converse of the challenge facing proponents of Full Access to UG who need to explain why late-starting L2 learners are persistently divergent from native speakers in some areas). The response is that learners will be successful in acquiring new properties involving interpretable features and principles of UG, they will be successful in acquiring properties that are the same in the L1 and the L2, but they will need to draw on domain-general learning mechanisms to model properties in the L2 that involve new unvalued features. For example, this approach would suggest that the Moroccan Arabic- and Berber-speaking adult learners of Dutch studied by Blom et al. (2008) who optionally use Adj + Ø forms in attributive contexts where Adj + e is required (section 4.7.1) have not accessed the [*u*gender] and [*u*definite] features of the adjective morpheme. Rather, a domain-general mechanism has tallied the frequency of Adj + Ø and Adj + e forms. Adj + Ø forms are more frequent and so will be more likely to be selected from the Vocabulary for insertion in an attributive-adjective position. The target-like performance on attributive adjective agreement with the noun in L2 Spanish and on determiner agreement with the noun in L2 German by English speakers (section 4.7.1) would also need to be explained as the successful application of domain-general learning, perhaps tallying of the co-occurrence frequency of specific adjective–noun and determiner–noun pairs.

Section 11.3 in a Nutshell

Three different perspectives have been taken on the role of UG in second language acquisition. Firstly, that beyond some point in childhood access to UG stops completely, making the L2 mental grammars of older starters fundamentally different from those of native speakers. They are based on the L1 and domain-general problem-solving mechanisms. Secondly, that language learners continue to have full access to UG throughout life; this perspective explains persistent divergence between older L2 starters and native speakers as the effect of language use in real time (overload of WM leading to the selection of elsewhere forms where more specified ones are required), lack of evidence from input for particular L2 properties, or problems with pronunciation. Thirdly, that older L2 starters have access to UG apart from unvalued (semantically 'uninterpretable') features; this perspective explains the success of older starters as the effect of access to valued UG features and principles, L1–L2 similarities and domain-general learning mechanisms that attempt to model properties of the target language.

11.4 The Role of the L1 in a Theory of Second Language Learning

Many examples emerged in previous chapters of the influence of the L1 on L2 development. Some of these were non-persistent L1 effects on early stages of development. For example, the early and temporary influence of L1 French on the acquisition of T to V movement in L2 English, and the influence of L1 English on the acquisition of V to T movement in L2 French (section 4.4.2); the use of native phones like [s] and [z] by L1 speakers of French to realise the English phonemes /θ/ and /ð/ in contrast to L1 Russian speakers who use [t] and [d] (section 7.2.4); the treatment of all English dynamic, durative verb phrases like *bake a cake, bake cakes* as atelic by L1 speakers of Bulgarian at an early stage of development, ignoring the effect of the presence of an article, in contrast to L1 Spanish speakers of similar proficiency (section 6.4). All of these L1 effects disappear as learners become more proficient.

Other examples were encountered of more persistent L1 influence. Italian speakers first immersed in English at age fifteen or later and with long exposure to English did not acquire the sub-phonemic Voice Onset Time values of stop sounds: [pʰ], [tʰ], [kʰ] (section 7.2.2); speakers of L1 Mandarin showing persistent optionality in the use of L2 English affixal morphology, as in the case of Patty, in contrast to speakers of L1s that also have affixal morphology like Turkish, as in the case of SD (section 2.7); speakers of L1s that do not have articles showing persistent optionality in using articles to license count singular nouns, in contrast to speakers of L1s that have articles (section 4.7.2), among others.

These examples of L1 influence are an empirical challenge for any hypothesis that claims there is no transfer of L1 properties into L2 grammars, as argued by Flynn (1987) and Epstein et al. (1996). An alternative hypothesis that is widely accepted is that in the initial state of L2 learning all properties of the L1 are assigned to newly encountered forms in the L2. This is the hypothesis advanced in Schwartz and Sprouse's (1996) Full Transfer/Full Access (to UG) Hypothesis: 'according to the FT/FA model, the entirety of the L1 grammar (excluding the phonetic matrices of lexical/morphological items) is the L2 initial state' (1996: 41). Referring again to figure 11.1, this proposal claims that the features of L1 morphemes in the language-specific Lexicon, but not their associated L1 forms in the Vocabulary (the 'phonetic matrices'), are initially linked to newly-acquired L2 forms. This needs a slight qualification in the light of the studies of picture-naming in an L2 versus L1-to-L2 translation by early-stage learners reported in section 2.1. Recently acquired L2 forms appear initially to be indirectly linked to L1 morphemes through a connection to the L1 form. It is still the case, though, that L1 forms are not transferred when a speaker produces the L2.

The Full Transfer/Full Access proposal means that, for example, when English speakers learn French, initially the feature of English T that blocks movement of the lexical verb to T is assigned to the French T, and when French speakers learn English, initially the feature of French T that requires verb movement to T is assigned to the English T. When English speakers learn Spanish or German, they initially do not assign a [ugender] feature to adjectives or determiners, because English adjectives do not encode such a feature, and so on.

Restructuring of the initially-transferred L1 properties is driven by encounters with input in WM that conflicts with L1-tranferred feature values. Schwartz and Sprouse propose that in some cases restructuring can occur quite rapidly. For example, the study by Yuan (2001) of the acquisition of the location of VP adverbs in Mandarin Chinese reported in section 4.6.1 showed that speakers of L1s with V to T movement (French, German) could rapidly acquire the non-verb movement property of Mandarin. It was suggested that this is because the evidence that learners encounter in input for non-movement of the verb is unambiguous. In other cases changes may take longer or may never occur at all if the data that would force change are ambiguous, obscure or even unavailable. For example, there is nothing in the English input that Japanese speakers encounter to lead them to pre-empt their L1-transferred resultative interpretation of English *be + ing* with dynamic, punctual verbs like *arrive* (section 6.3).

11.5 Properties and Transition in L2 Grammars

Gregg (2003: 838–49) draws a distinction between property theories of second language acquisition and transition theories. In relation to figure 11.1, a property theory is the set of constructs that are given under UG and in the language-specific grammar. A transition theory needs to explain how a state of knowledge in the language-specific grammar changes over time. Schwartz and Sprouse's (1996) Full Transfer/Full Access hypothesis embodies a proposal for transition in the form of restructuring from L1-transferred properties to L2 properties when WM identifies a conflict between a property in the input and the currently-held property in the language-specific grammar. However, as Sharwood Smith and Truscott (2014: 323) point out, Schwartz and Sprouse's account only allows for abrupt change. At one point a morpheme has L1 feature x, and at some later point it has L2 feature y. This instantaneous change from one state of knowledge to another is not typically what is observed in L2 acquisition. Rather, change occurs gradually. Sharwood Smith and Truscott cite a number of observations of gradual change to support this claim. One is a study by Westergaard (2003) of Norwegian-speaking adolescent learners of English. Norwegian is a verb-second (V2) language like German and Afrikaans (section 4.5.1). The participants in Westergaard's study quickly recognised that English is not a V2 language and began to allow the verb in main clauses to appear in third, fourth, fifth position. However, they continued optionally to use V2. Over the period of observation (fourth to seventh grades) the proportion of use of non-V2 constructions gradually increased: 2%, 14%, 38%, 61%, with no apparent sudden shift from V2 to non-V2.

Sharwood Smith and Truscott's proposal to account for gradual development is to allow L1 and L2 features to co-occur, presumably in two distinct L2 morphemes, in the language-specific Lexicon. Each feature/morpheme has its own level of activation. Activation level determines how accessible it is to WM. Morphemes with a high level of activation are highly accessible, while those with a low level of activation are less accessible. Under this proposal, initially in L2 acquisition morphemes with L1 features associated with L2 forms will have high levels of activation and L1 influence will be high. As learners encounter more examples consistent with the L2 features of morphemes, the activation levels of those features/morphemes will rise and there will be competition between them. Eventually, given sufficient exposure to the L2, morphemes with L2 features will have higher activation levels than morphemes with L1 features and so the speaker will predominantly be using target-language properties. For example, in the case of the Norwegian speakers unlearning the V2 property for L2 English, initially the C category for L2 English has the features of Norwegian, requiring a finite verb to move to C and a topic constituent to move and merge with C. Encounters with examples of non-V2 main clauses in English (like *At the weekend, I work in a café*) will lead the learner to establish a competing C for L2 English where the features that force V2 are absent. This alternative specification will increase in activation level as the result of repeated encounters through WM with English non-V2 main clauses until it has a higher level of activation than the C with Norwegian V2 features. This is what underlies the gradual pattern of development observed by Westergaard.

11.6 The Relation between the Language-Specific Grammar, Thinking, Discourse and Context of Use

Figure 11.1 shows language-specific grammars that are shaped by the properties of UG interacting with 'short-term memory', which temporarily stores information that has been extracted from input by WM. There is at least one other area of cognition that language-specific grammars need to interact with: general thinking. One of the functions of language-specific grammars is to convert incoming linguistic information gained through WM into a form from which propositional meaning can be extracted by the speaker, and to convert propositions formulated by the speaker into a form that can be externalised through language. This requires the language-specific grammar to interface with a component of mind that is often called the 'conceptual/intentional system' in the linguistic literature (for example, Chomsky 1995). This consists of a set of concepts and a mechanism for combining those concepts into propositions ('thoughts') that can be converted into linguistic messages for production or that can decode incoming linguistic messages. Consideration of the structure of conceptual representation is beyond the scope of the discussion here, but it is also likely to interface with UG, with domain-general processes and with 'long-term memory'. In the case of UG, categories and features are the linguistic counterparts of, and may derive from, a subset of concepts. For example, tense, person and number have conceptual counterparts in the form of time, participant role in interactions and enumeration. Domain-general processes of statistical learning, induction and deduction are central to thinking. And 'long-term memory' both stores information derived from general thinking and feeds thinking with existing information. Figure 11.1 is modified in figure 11.2 to capture these interfaces.

Another interface that has been proposed is between the language-specific grammar and discourse. Sorace (2005) and Sorace and Filiaci (2006) argue that persistent L1 influence and persistent optionality in highly proficient L2 speakers are not the result of limitations within the language-specific grammar itself, but

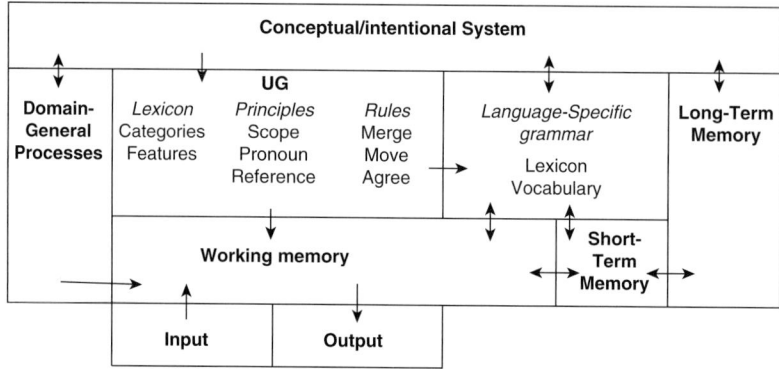

Figure 11.2 Possible components of a theory of second language learning, including an interface with the conceptual/intentional system

result from limitations on processing information where the language-specific grammar interfaces with non-linguistic components of mind, like discourse information (section 8.3.3). However, within the set of assumptions outlined in figure 11.2, it is debatable whether discourse information comes from a specific non-linguistic component of mind or whether it is information about the ongoing topic that is held in 'short-term memory' to which the language-specific grammar has access. The language-specific grammar needs to learn which of its features are conditioned by topic and focus information (like the topic-shifting effect of overt pronouns in null subject languages (section 8.3.3), the topic-shifting effect of movement in German and Spanish (section 8.3.2) and the focus-shifting effect of contrastive stress in English (section 8.3.1) and will do this from input information identified by WM that is temporarily stored in 'short-term memory'.

The learning of such links may require long exposure to the target language. Hopp's (2007) study of the parsing of appropriate and inappropriate German sentences in a discourse context found that only near-native speakers (with L1 Russian and L1 English), and not speakers of advanced proficiency, parsed word orders in the same way as native speakers. Studies by Hertel (2003) and Lozano (2006) showed that L2 learners of Spanish at an advanced proficiency level had not yet fully acquired the link between word order and discourse information, although they were moving in that direction (section 8.3.2). Once acquired as features of morphemes in the Lexicon, the language-specific grammar can implement discourse-conditioned grammatical properties in real-time comprehension and production. That implementation may also be influenced by the L1. Studies were reported in section 8.3.3 that suggested that L2 speakers of Dutch with null-subject Turkish L1 continue to allow overt subject pronouns to co-refer with a shifted topic, even though this is inappropriate in Dutch, in contrast to speakers of non-null-subject L1 German; and Japanese-speaking L2 learners of English continue to look for long-distance co-referents for reflexive anaphors in previous discourse, again even though this is inappropriate in English (Bertenshaw, 2009).

Knowledge of how language varies in relation to context of use (for example in the spoken versus the written modality, in formal versus informal registers, or in relation to conventions of politeness) may also be knowledge that the language-specific grammar acquires from information held in 'short-term memory' and that takes time to acquire. L2 learners of Canadian French need to establish that *on* 'we' is the form predominantly used in the spoken modality and *nous* the form that is predominantly used in the written modality. The immersion classroom learners studied by Rehner et al. (2003) had not yet established this distinction, and were using *nous* predominantly in both contexts (section 1.6.2). The L2 learners of French studied by Regan (1996) (section 8.4) had acquired the alternation between *ne* and *Ø* of French sentential negation (*ne/Ø ... pas*), but were only using them in proportions equivalent to native speakers (more use of *Ø* in an informal register than in a formal register) after a nine-month period of immersion in a French-speaking community.

Sections 11.4 to 11.6 in a Nutshell

Some L1 effects on L2 grammars are short-lived, others are persistent. A widely accepted hypothesis is that the initial state of L2 learning is 'the entirety of the L1 grammar' excluding L1 forms (Schwartz and Sprouse, 1996: 41). Where the L1 and L2 differ, change away from the L1 is driven by encounters with input in WM that conflicts with the L1-transferred property. Restructuring can occur quickly, can take time or may never occur at all if the evidence required from input is ambiguous, obscure or unavailable.

Schwartz and Sprouse's proposal entails abrupt change from the L1 to the L2 property. However, L2 development appears to be gradual, with long periods of optionality. Sharwood Smith and Truscott (2014) account for this by proposing competition between pairs of morphemes, one of which has the L1 feature and the other the L2 feature. The activation level of each determines how accessible it is to WM. With time and continued encounters with input the L2 morpheme will come to predominate.

Language-specific grammars and UG have an interface with a conceptual/intentional (general thinking) module of mind. Categories and features of UG are counterparts of, and may derive from, a subset of concepts. Sorace (2005) and Sorace and Filiaci (2006) argue that persistent L1 influence and optionality result where the language-specific grammar interfaces with non-linguistic modules of mind, which include a discourse module. However, it seems more likely that discourse information is information held in 'short-term memory' about the ongoing topic to which the language-specific grammar has access. The language-specific grammar needs to learn which of its properties are conditioned by topic and focus, and will do so from information supplied by WM to 'short-term memory'. Discourse-conditioned grammatical properties in the L1 may be transferred to the L2. Knowledge about how language varies in relation to context of use may also be derived by the language-specific grammar from information held in 'short-term memory'. Long exposure to the target language may be required before the links between the language-specific grammar and discourse/context-of-use information are acquired.

11.7 Concluding Remarks

Theories, as VanPatten and Williams suggest, aim to explain why natural phenomena 'occur the way they do' (2007: 2) and not some other way. VanPatten and Williams also propose the ambitious goal of explaining all of the observations that can be made about a natural phenomenon within the same theory (bringing them 'under one umbrella', 2007: 4–5). Assuming second language learning to be a natural phenomenon in need of explanation, in this chapter an attempt was made to sketch what a theory of second language learning that sought to explain the observations reported in the book might look like.

It was concluded that to explain a number of observations it is necessary to include an innate domain-specific set of linguistic predispositions: Universal Grammar (UG). This itself derives from a more general theory of language that is required to explain the nature of mature native grammars and the acquisition of native languages by children. It was also concluded that domain-general processes (frequency tallying, constraints on how much information can be processed in real time, and possibly the recursivity that underlies one kind of generativity in language) are involved. It was proposed that UG and domain-general processes are integrated in Working Memory (WM). They work together to parse (i.e. analyse) input and extract linguistic information that is then stored temporarily in 'short-term memory'. In the acquisition of an L2 the linguistic information held in 'short-term memory' may be added to the language-specific grammar and become long-term linguistic knowledge. The language-specific grammar consists of a Lexicon of morphemes with the features that determine their meaning and use, and a Vocabulary of forms that are specified for the morphemes that they realise. Both are heavily influenced by the L1 in early stages of development. Once established, this knowledge, together with the rules Merge, Move and Agree, are the basis for the spontaneous use of the L2 both in comprehension and production. Comprehension is the response to input; production is instigated in the conceptual/intentional component of mind as a proposition or set of propositions that then trigger the accessing of morphemes and forms from the language-specific grammar, and rules from UG.

Progress in understanding how second languages are learned comes from making explicit assumptions about what a theory of second language acquisition might look like and then testing hypotheses derived from those assumptions against empirical data. Whether they survive current testing and go on for further testing, or are falsified by empirical data, each serves a useful function in narrowing the range of possible explanations.

ACTIVITIES

1. TEST YOURSELF

(i) What did Saffran et al. (1996b) show by using an invented language made up of words like *bidaku, padoti, tupiro*? (Chapter 1)

(ii) What is the 'categorisation problem'? (Chapter 1)

(iii) What does a study by DeKeyser (1995) of an invented language called Implexan tell us about how L2 learners might deal with the categorisation problem in the very earliest stages of language learning? (Chapter 1)

(iv) What were the two tasks that Potter et al. (1984) gave L1 Chinese/L2 English speakers in order to find out how they store English words in their mental lexicons (understood as including the Lexicon and the Vocabulary)? What were their findings? What are the implications of the findings? (Chapter 2)

(v) Kroll and Curley (1988) replicated Potter et al.'s experiment with L2 learners who had less than two years' exposure, and L2 learners with more than two years' exposure. What difference did they find? What are the implications of their findings? (Chapter 2)

(vi) Do L2 learners store words in their mental lexicons in the same way as native speakers? (Chapter 2)

(vii) How does Williams' (2005) study of the learning of the novel determiners *gi, ro, ul, ne* in an English-based invented language suggest that learners might use innate knowledge when they are acquiring dependency-marking forms? (Chapter 2)

(viii) What do you understand by the Missing Surface Inflection Hypothesis explanation for optionality in the use of forms by L2 speakers (for example, using *bought* on some occasions and *buy* on others in clearly intended past tense contexts)? (Chapter 3)

(ix) What do you understand by the Aspect Hypothesis explanation for optionality in the use of forms by L2 speakers? (Chapter 3)

(x) How does knowledge of sentential negation in English typically develop in L2 learners? (Chapter 4)

(xi) How does the interpretation of sentences like *Was beisst die Katze?* and *Was hat die Katze gebissen?* in German by L1 speakers of English and Afrikaans suggest L1 influence on the acquisition of L2 syntactic rules (Grüter and Conradie, 2006)? (Chapter 4)

(xii) Which of the following aspects of linguistic knowledge might reasonably be assumed to be innate? Give reasons for your answers. (Chapter 5)

    a. German verb-second word order

    b. binary merger of morphemes to form phrases

    c. ability to 'tally' the co-occurrence frequencies of sounds

    d. the knowledge that left-dislocated constructions in English (e.g. *That play, it was terrible*) introduce new discourse information?

    e. the morpheme categories N, V, A, D, T, Neg, C

    f. the organisation of morphemes in the mental lexicon

    g. the knowledge that forms can have uniquely identifiable and meaning-modifying meanings, or a dependency-marking function

    h. the knowledge that adjectives that precede nouns have a 'qualitative' meaning (as in the French *cher bijou* 'cherished jewel') and adjectives that follow nouns have an 'additive' meaning (as in *bijou cher* 'expensive jewel')

(xiii) How are both transfer from a speaker's L1 and innate knowledge involved in the L2 acquisition of English articles? (Chapter 5)

(xiv) What effect does 'scrambling' an object DP in Dutch (e.g. *een aap* 'a monkey') over a quantified adverb (e.g. *twee keer* 'two times') have on interpretation? Were the L2 speakers of Dutch in Unsworth's (2005) study aware of this effect? (Chapter 6)

(xv) What is the difference between the co-reference possibilities of English reflexive anaphors like *herself* and the Mandarin Chinese equivalent *ziji*? Were English-speaking L2 speakers of Mandarin in Ying's (1999) study aware of the co-reference possibilities of *ziji*, or did they assume that *ziji* has the same co-reference possibilities as the English reflexive anaphors? (Chapter 6)

(xvi) How is 'manner of motion along a path' expressed in Spanish and Japanese? How do Spanish- and Japanese-speaking L2 learners of English express 'manner of motion along a path' in English? (Chapter 6)

(xvii) Why is it necessary to consider articulatory/acoustic features like [lateral], [voice], [labial] and [continuant] to determine whether new phoneme contrasts in an L2 will be easy or difficult to acquire? (Chapter 7)

(xviii) Where a speaker's L1 disallows consonant clusters in syllable onset and coda positions, what effect does this have on their pronunciation of an L2 where consonant clusters are permitted in syllable onset and coda position? (Chapter 7)

(xix) What linguistic properties are involved in creating 'garden path' sentences like *The woman sold the house emigrated to Australia*? Do L2 speakers of English parse sentences like these in the same way as native speakers? (Chapter 8)

(xx) What were the grammatical reflexes of discourse information (topic and focus) encountered in chapter 8? How successful are L2 learners in acquiring these grammar–discourse links? (Chapter 8)

(xxi)   What is the difference between positive and negative evidence about an L2? (Chapter 9)

(xxii)   What is Krashen's 'learning–acquisition' distinction, and what is his view of how they interact? (Chapter 9)

(xxiii)   In contexts where L2 learners are immersed in the target language, are children better learners than adolescents and adults? (Chapter 10)

(xxiv)   What positions have researchers taken on the role of Universal Grammar in L2 learning? What kinds of evidence have been used to defend each position? (Chapter 11)

(xxv)   What is the 'transition problem' for a theory of L2 learning? What solution do Sharwood Smith and Truscott (2014) offer for it? (Chapter 11)

2. DESIGN AN EXPERIMENT

You have observed the following asymmetry between *have* + *V-en* (past participle) forms (e.g. *have written*) and *be* + *V-ing* (progressive participle) forms (e.g. *is writing*) in the specific topicalising construction illustrated in (i).

i.   **a.** Joe asked Mary to write a feature for his magazine, and **write a feature she has**

   b. Mary told Joe she was going to sell her car, and *****sell her car she is**

Here a non-finite VP has moved to the left of TP, putting the auxiliary verb *have* or *be* in focus position. But whereas the verb can lose its past participle *-en* inflection in this construction (ia), it cannot lose its progressive participle *-ing* inflection (ib): the topicalised construction has to be *sell**ing** her car she is*. One explanation for this is that whereas *-ing* has a semantically interpretable [progressive] feature that cannot be deleted, the auxiliary *have* encodes the semantically interpretable [perfective] feature with *-en* being a pure dependency-marking morpheme encoding an unvalued [*u*perfective] feature that can be omitted in this topicalising construction. Since the construction displays the contrast between valued (interpretable) and unvalued (uninterpretable) features, it provides a domain in which to test the claim of the partial access to UG hypothesis that L2 learners have access to the rules, principles and valued features of UG, but may find it difficult to access unvalued features that have not been activated in their L1.

   Design an experiment that will test whether L1 speakers of French and Mandarin Chinese who are L2 speakers of English (a) know this kind of topicalising construction (while infrequent, it occurs productively both with auxiliary verbs and modals, e.g. *Jodie wants to join the club, and join the club she can/will/may*); (b) know the asymmetry described above.

   The factors that you will need to consider include: proficiency of the L2 speakers, their type of exposure to English (including age of first exposure), a method of data collection that will provide appropriate information on knowledge of the construction, information on how native speakers treat this construction, the procedure you will use to administer the test, and how you will score the raw data.

FURTHER READING

For more advanced discussion of second language learning set in the context of the study of language and of first language acquisition see:

Slabakova, R. 2016. *Second language acquisition*. Oxford: Oxford University Press.

For discussion of research into second language learning that takes account of its historical context see:

Snape, N. and Kupisch, T. 2017. *Second language acquisition: second language systems*. New York: Macmillan Palgrave.

Gass, S. M. and Selinker, L. 2008. *Second language acquisition: an introductory course*. Third Edition. Abingdon: Routledge.

For discussion of the role of theory in the investigation of second language learning see:

VanPatten, B. and Williams, J. (eds) 2007. *Theories in second language acquisition: an introduction*. Mahwah, NJ: Lawrence Erlbaum Associates.

Mitchell, R., Myles, F. and Marsden, E. 2013. *Second language learning theories*. Third Edition. Abingdon: Routledge.

For discussion of non-linguistic aspects of second language learning like motivation, personality factors and learning strategies see:

Dörnyei, Z. 2009. *The psychology of second language acquisition*. Oxford: Oxford University Press.

Ortega, L. 2009. *Understanding second language acquisition*. London: Hodder Education.

Cohen, D. 1998. *Strategies in learning and using a second language*. London: Longman.

GLOSSARY

Bold print within definitions is used for cross reference.

* Symbol that, by convention, is placed at the beginning of an expression that is ungrammatical, e.g. *I books borrowed, *She be late.

Symbol that, by convention, is placed at the beginning of an expression that is **grammatical** but infelicitous (i.e. unnatural in a given context), e.g. *What did Mary buy? #The bag was bought by Mary.* The new information in the second **sentence** is not in a focus position. The sentence is, however, grammatical and felicitous in a context like: *Who bought the bag? The bag was bought by Mary.*

[ ] Brackets that, by convention, enclose a phonetic symbol, e.g. [pʰ], [u], or an articulatory/acoustic or syntactic/semantic **feature**, e.g. [voice], [lateral], [animate], [past], [definite], [telic].

/ / Brackets that, by convention, enclose a **phoneme** symbol, e.g. /p/ vs /b/, /u/ vs /i/.

{ } Brackets that, by convention, enclose a **morpheme**, e.g. {mis-}, {align}, {-ment}

adjective (A): A category to which form–meaning pairings that describe a property or characteristic of the referent of a **noun** belong, e.g. *tall, hot, wooden.* Adjectives can merge with nouns to form noun phrases (*tall tree*), or with verbs like *be, become, appear* to form **verb** phrases (*be tall, become tall, appear tall*).

adverb (Adv): A category to which form–meaning pairings that describe time, manner, place, frequency, degree or reason belong, e.g. *now, quickly, home, often, extremely, consequently.* Adverbs can merge with **verb** phrases (*quickly write an email*), adjectives (*often sick*) and other adverbs (*extremely quickly*).

affix: A bound **morpheme** that must attach to a host morpheme. In English, affixes can be prefixes (e.g. *mis-align*) or suffixes (e.g. *align-ment*).

Agree: A rule of **syntax** that resolves dependencies between categories by copying valued **features** from one category to the unvalued features of another, e.g. [$_C$ Ø [$_{TP}$ [$_{ProN}$ she 3 person, singular] [$_{TP}$ [$_T$ finite, non-past, *u*person, *u*number] [$_V$ sing]]]] → [$_C$ Ø [$_{TP}$ [$_{ProN}$ she 3 person, singular] [$_{TP}$ [$_T$ finite, non-past, *u*person: 3, *u*number: singular] [$_V$ sing]]]] 'She sings'

agreement: A dependency between two categories. For example, in *Mary sings/We sing* there is agreement between the person and number features of the noun *Mary* or the pronoun *we* and the **tense (T) morpheme** that merges with the **verb**. This is reflected in the forms -*s* (third person singular) and -Ø (third person plural).

anaphor: A **morpheme** that takes its reference from a **determiner** phrase elsewhere in the same sentence, in an earlier sentence, or from a referent in the extra-linguistic context. **Pronouns** (e.g. *she, her*), reflexives (e.g. *herself, themselves*) and reciprocals (e.g. *each other*) are examples of anaphors.

antonym: **Words** that have opposite meanings are antonyms, e.g. *new–old, tall–short.*

article: A **morpheme** that belongs to the category **determiner (D)** and in English expresses definiteness (*the*) or indefiniteness (*a* used with singular count nouns and Ø used with plural count and **mass nouns**). The definite article signals the speaker's assumption that the referent of the accompanying **noun** phrase is already known to the hearer. The indefinite article signals that the referent of the accompanying noun phrase is assumed by the speaker to be new information for the hearer.

aspect: *Situation* (also called *lexical*) *aspect* is a subclassification of the action, event or state described by a **verb** phrase. A combination of three binary features is used to define situation aspect: dynamic/static, durative/punctual, atelic/telic (i.e. with or without an endpoint). For example, *run for hours, bake cakes, build houses* are dynamic, durative, atelic and are often called 'activities'; *run a mile, bake a cake, build a house* are dynamic, durative, telic and are often called 'accomplishments'; *find a gold coin, reach the gate, glimpse the sun* are dynamic, punctual, telic and are often called 'achievements'; *love chocolate, own a house* are static, durative, atelic and are often called 'statives'.

Viewpoint (also called *grammatical*) *aspect* is expressed by meaning-modifying morphemes like *be + V-ing* (progressive), *have + V-en* (perfective) that situate the action, event or state described by the verb phrase in relation to the moment of speaking and can shift its situation aspect. For example, *Mary is running a mile* situates the event as simultaneous with the moment of speaking and shifts the situation aspect from telic to atelic. *Tom has baked cakes* situates the event as having occurred prior to the moment of speaking and shifts the situation aspect from atelic to telic.

clause: An expression that includes one **subject** (overt or understood) and a **verb** phrase. For example, *Mary picked apples* (with overt subject *Mary*), *visiting her father in Normandy* (with understood subject), *to help out* (with understood subject), and *because she likes the fresh air* (with overt subject) are each clauses. They can be merged into a four-clause **sentence** where the understood subjects refer to *Mary*: *Visiting her father in Normandy, Mary picked apples to help out and because she likes the fresh air.*

cognitive reserve: The ability of the brain to compensate for damage to its neural structure, particularly from diseases that cause dementia.

complementiser (C): A category that expresses the 'force' of a **clause** – **declarative, interrogative** or **imperative** – and merges with the **tense** phrase.

control group: In experimental studies of L2 learner performance (e.g. those that involve grammaticality judgements, word association tests, deciding on the truth of statements and so on), a control group of native speakers allows the researcher to determine that the test used really does elicit the properties that are assumed to exist in the target L2. In studies of the effects of particular types of input on learning gain, a control group of learners who have been exposed to different input from that experienced by the experimental group acts as a baseline against which to compare the learning gain of the experimental group.

copula: A **verb** that links a **subject** and an **adjective**, **noun**, **determiner** phrase or **prepositional** phrase/**adverb**; *be, become* are typical copular verbs, e.g. *Tom is happy, Mary became president, Terry is the winner, Jill is in the garden/here.*

count and mass nouns: A count **noun** can merge with a plural **morpheme**: *doctors, liberties, children.* When singular it must be licensed by a **determiner**, e.g. **I borrowed book from library* versus *I borrowed a book from the library.* Mass nouns (e.g. *honey, sand, water*) do not merge with the plural morpheme and do not need to be licensed by a determiner, e.g. *I bought honey.*

declarative: A **clause** that makes a statement, e.g. *Mary bought a new bike.*

default form: A form that is frequent in input and is used by an L2 speaker in a context where the target language requires a less frequent form, e.g. the use of bare **adjectives** in Dutch by adult L2 speakers where that language requires adjectives to have an *-e* **affix**: **een groen appel* instead of *een groene appel* 'a green apple'; see section 4.7.1.

determiner (D): A category to which **morphemes** that modify the meanings of **nouns** in terms of definiteness, possession or proximity belong, e.g. *a/the/my/your/this/that hat.*

direct object: See **object**.

discourse: Uses of language that extend beyond a single **clause** and are typical of conversations, monologues and other extended uses of language.

elsewhere form: A form with under-specified **features** that is selected when forms with more specified features cannot be selected, e.g. the forms *writes, walks* are specified for selection when the **tense** category has the features [finite, non-past, 3 person, singular], and the forms *wrote, walked* are specified for selection when the tense category has the features [finite, past]. In all other specifications of the tense category, the forms *write, walk* are selected. They are elsewhere forms.

epenthesis: The insertion of a vowel to create an additional **syllable**, e.g. when Spanish speakers pronounce English words like *study* as *estudy.*

executive control: The mental processes that 'manage, integrate, regulate, coordinate or supervise other cognitive processes, such as attention and visual perception' (Valian, 2015: 5).

feature: A minimal component of meaning or sound from which **morphemes**, **phones** and **phonemes** are constructed, for example [animate], [definite], [past], [voice], [lateral], [nasal]. Some features are unvalued (semantically uninterpretable), e.g. [*u*number], [*u*person] and [*u*gender], and need to be valued by the semantically interpretable features of another category through the operation of the rule **Agree**.

finite and non-finite: A **tense** (T) category that has **features** expressing a defined time period like past or non-past is finite. A T category that has no feature expressing a defined time period is non-finite.

focus: New information in a **sentence** that the speaker assumes is not shared by her/his hearer/reader.

formula: An expression used as a single **morpheme** by an L2 learner that for a native speaker can be analysed into two or more morphemes. Also called an 'unanalysed chunk', e.g. the use of *dont* as an unanalysed sentential negator by an L2 speaker where a native speaker distinguishes *do + n't, does + n't, did + n't.*

gender: Grammatical gender is a division of **nouns** into subclasses. In some languages there are two subclasses, referred to traditionally in French and Spanish as masculine and feminine, and in Dutch as common and neuter. In German there are three subclasses: masculine, feminine and neuter. In the Bantu languages there are ten or more subclasses. The set of nouns in English is not subdivided by gender. Grammatical gender is often not realised in a change in the form of the noun itself, but in a change in the form of categories with which it has merged, e.g. **adjectives** and **determiners**, as in French: *une pomme verte* 'a green apple' (feminine) versus *un chapeau vert* 'a green hat' (masculine).

generative grammar: A mental grammar that allows a speaker to produce and understand a potentially infinite number of **grammatical sentences**. This encompasses both sentences that are novel combinations of **morphemes** that we can nevertheless understand (e.g. *Buttered toast has just crossed the finishing line in the London Marathon* may be pragmatically bizarre, but it is both grammatical and perfectly comprehensible) and sentences to which a new **clause** could be added ad infinitum, e.g. *This is the horse that chased the cow that kicked the dog that bit the cat that played with the mouse … .*

grammatical: Grammatical **sentences** conform to the norms of the **phonology, morphology, syntax** and **Lexicon** of a given language. Ungrammatical sentences violate those norms. The grammaticality of a sentence must be distinguished from its felicity (naturalness) in a given context. See the entry for # for an illustration of felicity.

head: The main word in a phrase that also determines how the phrase is labelled, e.g. [$_N$ grape] is the head of the **noun** phrase [$_{NP}$ [$_A$ sweet] [$_N$ grape]].

hyponyms: words whose referents belong to the same natural class. For example, *salmon, trout, cod, herring, haddock* etc. are hyponyms of *fish*, which is the superordinate word.

imperative: A **clause** that expresses an order or a command, e.g. *Bring me that book.*

indirect negative evidence: In language learning, making a learner aware that s/he may have used a non-target form through reformulating or recasting what they said or requesting a clarification, without referring to the non-target form directly. See also **positive evidence, negative evidence**.

indirect object: See **object**.

inflection: A meaning-modifying or dependency-marking **morpheme** that is realised by an **affix** or a change in the form of a host, e.g. *writes* and *wrote* are inflected forms of *write*.

interrogative: A **clause** that asks a question, e.g. *Did Mary buy a new bike?* (yes–no question), *What did Mary buy?* (a *wh*-question), *I wonder what Mary bought* (indirect/embedded question).

intransitive: See **verb**.

Lexicon: The Lexicon, with a capital L, is the mental store of **morphemes** minus their associated phonetic/phonological forms, which are stored in the **Vocabulary**.

mass noun: See **count and mass nouns**.

mental lexicon: The set of pairings of conceptual representations with linguistic forms stored in the mind/brain of a speaker. See also **Lexicon** and **Vocabulary**.

Merge: A rule of **syntax** that combines constituents to form **phrases**, e.g. [$_A$ good], [$_N$ book] → [$_{NP}$ [$_A$ good] [$_N$ book]].

modal verb: One of the forms *must, ought, may, might, will, would, can, could, shall, should.* In English these appear to be assigned to the category **tense (T)**.

morpheme: The minimal meaningful unit of syntactic structure. The **word** *misalignments* (N) consists of four morphemes: {mis-}, {align}, {-ment}, {-s}. {align} can be used on its own (is a 'free form') whereas {mis-}, {-ment}, {-s} must be affixed to another morpheme (they are 'bound forms').

morphology: (a) the structure of **words**; (b) the branch of linguistics that studies the structure of words.

Move: A rule of **syntax** that re-organises the **phrase structure** generated by Merge to create new phrase structure, e.g. moving the **tense (T)** category in [$_C$ Ø [$_{TP}$ she [$_{TP}$ [$_T$ must] [$_V$ leave]]]] to the **complementiser (C)** to form a yes–no question: [$_C$ must [$_{TP}$ she [$_{TP}$ [$_T$ e] [$_V$ leave]]]]?

negation: Sentential negation denies the proposition expressed by a **clause**. In English the sentential negator is the form *n't/not*, e.g. *I don't like your hat.* Anaphoric negation is a negative response to a yes/no question, e.g. *Do you like my hat? – No.*

negative evidence: Information provided to a language learner about what is ungrammatical in a target language. See also **grammatical, positive evidence, indirect negative evidence.**

noun (N): A category to which form–meaning pairings that describe people, things, places, ideas belong, e.g. *doctor, child, chair, library, liberty.* Nouns can merge with **adjectives** to form noun phrases (NPs), e.g. [$_{NP}$ tall tree], and with **determiners** to form determiner phrases (DPs), e.g. [$_{DP}$ a tree].

number: A morphological contrast that allows **count nouns** and **pronouns** in English to describe a single instance of the referent, e.g. *a chair, this book, it* (singular) or more than one instance, e.g. *chairs, those books, them* (plural).

object: A *direct object* is a **determiner** phrase (DP) (e.g. *the professor*), **noun** (e.g. *Mary*) or **pronoun** (e.g. *her*) whose referent is directly affected by the action described by the **verb**, e.g. *The mayor invited the professor/Mary/her to a reception.* An *indirect object* is a determiner phrase (DP), noun or pronoun whose referent is typically the goal or recipient of the action described by the verb, e.g. *Mary* is the indirect object in *The tax office sent a letter to Mary, The mayor offered Mary a drink, The professor wrote to Mary.*

obligatory context: Context in which the use of a particular linguistic form is obligatory if the **sentence** is to be **grammatical**. For example, a **count singular noun** must be accompanied by a **determiner** to be grammatical: **Mary bought new dress for party* versus *Mary bought **a** new dress for **the** party.*

paradigmatic distribution: Forms that are grouped together under one of the **morpheme** categories N, V, A, D, T, etc. form a paradigm, and are therefore in paradigmatic distribution, e. g. [$_N$ *sofa, couch, leaf, tree* ...], [$_T$ *must, might, ought, may, can,* ...].

parse: Assign **phrase structure** to, and extract meaning from, **clauses** as they are being heard or read in real time.

passive: A construction where the **subject** of a **transitive verb** is unspecified and a **direct object** moves to the subject position. In English this is implemented through the use of *be + V-en/-ed*, e.g. *e finished the essay on Friday* → *The essay was finished on Friday.*

person: A three-way classification of expressions that have animate referents (primarily **pronouns**), in relation to the speaker and hearer. A *first person* expression includes the speaker, e.g. *I, we, me, us* are first person. A *second person* expression excludes the speaker but includes the hearer, e.g. *you* is second person. A *third person* expression excludes both the speaker and hearer, e.g. *they, them, that herd of wildebeest* are third person.

phone: Any speech sound that is systematically used in a language. For example, $[p^h]$, $[p]$, $[t^h]$, $[t]$, $[k^h]$, $[k]$ are all systematically used in English, the aspirated sounds in **morpheme**-initial position, the unaspirated sounds following $[s]$.

phoneme: Phonemes are the categories into which sounds that distinguish **morphemes** are classified. For example, $/p/$ is a phoneme in English because it distinguishes *pin* and *nap* from *bin* and *nab*, and *kin* and *knack*.

phonology: (a) the sound system of a language; (b) the branch of linguistics that studies sound systems.

phrase: Any syntactic unit that results from the **merger** of two **morphemes**, a morpheme and a phrase, or two phrases. For example, *good book* $[_{NP} \{_A \text{ good}\} + \{_N \text{ book}\}]$, *a good book* $[_{DP} \{_D \text{ a}\} + [_{NP} \text{ good book}]]$ and *good book with a red cover* $[_{NP} [_{NP} \text{ good book}] + [_{PP} \text{ with a red cover}]]$ are all phrases.

phrase structure: Any linguistic expression that has resulted from the application of the syntactic rules Merge, Move and Agree to a set of morphemes.

positive evidence: In language learning, positive evidence is provided when a property of the L2 is present in the input a learner encounters. For example, English provides positive evidence that it allows double **objects** in **sentences** like *Mary sent her brother a letter, Tom bought Nigel a drink.* See also **negative evidence, indirect negative evidence.**

poverty of the stimulus: Knowledge that a speaker of a language has that cannot plausibly be explained as resulting from experience, from non-linguistic mental processes or (in the case of L2 speakers) from the L1. The poverty of the stimulus is one of the arguments used to support the existence of **Universal Grammar.**

preposition (P): A category to which form–meaning pairings that describe location, path, manner or cause belong. Prepositions typically merge with **determiner, noun** or **verb** phrases to form **adverb**-like expressions of time, place, manner, frequency or reason, e.g. *on Thursday, in the garden, through her efforts, at intervals, from eating too much chocolate.*

pronoun (ProN): A **morpheme** that may have **person, number** and **gender features,** but is not associated with a uniquely identifiable referent. A pronoun's reference is determined by association ('co-indexing') with a **determiner** phrase elsewhere in the **sentence,** in an earlier sentence, or from a referent in the extra-linguistic context. Examples of pronouns are *I/me/mine, she/hers.* See also **anaphor.**

quantifier: A **morpheme** that does not have a fixed reference but quantifies an expression with which it merges; *some, all, no, each, every* are quantifiers, e.g. *some* *languages, everyone, each participant, no journalist.* When two quantifiers are present in the same **clause** they give rise to different interpretations depending on which quantifier is within the scope of the other (scope ambiguity). For example, *everyone speaks some language* can mean 'There is one language everyone speaks' (*everyone* is within the scope of *some language*) or 'Each person speaks a different language, some or all of which are different' (*some language* is within the scope of *everyone*).

relative clause: A **clause** that is embedded in another through merger with a **noun**. That noun is co-referential with a DP in the relative clause that is null, e.g. *I invited the guest. The guest didn't turn up.* → *The guest [whom I invited e] didn't turn up:* [*whom I invited e*] is the relative clause.

semantics: The study of the meaning of **morphemes**, and the meaning of **phrases**, **clauses** and **sentences** that contain those morphemes.

sentence: Any syntactic expression that consists of one or more main **clauses**, and any number of other clauses that are dependent on the main clause(s). For example, each of the following is a sentence: *Mary picked apples* (one main clause). [*Mary picked apples*] and [*her brother picked plums*] (two main clauses conjoined). [*Visiting her father in Normandy*], [*Mary picked apples*] and [*her brother picked plums*] [*to help out*] [*because they both like fresh air*] (two main clauses and three dependent clauses).

subject: A **determiner** phrase (DP) (e.g. *the professor*), **noun** (e.g. *Mary*) or **pronoun** (e.g. *she*) that merges with a **tense** phrase (TP), e.g. *Mary* is the subject in *Mary left, Did Mary leave?, Mary met some friends, Mary was invited to a party, Rarely has Mary had so much fun.*

suppletive form: An irregularly inflected form of a **word**. For example, alongside regular non-past/past pairs of **verb** forms like *walk–walked, cough–coughed* there are pairs where the past tense form is suppletive (irregular) like *write–wrote, drink–drank, go–went, do–did.*

syllable: The minimal pronounceable unit consisting of at least a nucleus, usually a vowel, e.g. *a* [ə]. The syllable may also have an onset consisting of one or more consonants, e.g. *lea* [li], *flea* [fli], and a coda, consisting of one or more consonants, e.g. *ill* [ɪl], *ilk* [ɪlk]. The nucleus and coda together form a rhyme.

synonym: **Words** that have the same meaning are synonyms, e.g. *sofa–couch, help–aid.*

syntagmatic distribution: Words that co-occur in **phrases** are distributed syntagmatically, e.g. *black coffee, exchange gifts, extremely dangerous.*

syntax: The **phrase structures** that result from the application of the rules **Merge**, **Move** and **Agree**.

tense (T): A category that has **features** that express defined (past, non-past) or undefined time and merges with a **verb** phrase (VP).

topic: Information in a **sentence** that the speaker assumes is shared by her/his hearer/reader.

transitive: See **verb**.

unaccusative verb: An **intransitive verb** that describes a change of state. The **subjects** of unaccusative verbs typically do not instigate the action or event but are affected by it, e.g. *She died, The door closed, The sheets dried (in the sun).* In some analyses the subject of an unaccusative verb is initially merged in a direct **object** position and moved into subject position (Perlmutter, 1978).

unergative verb: An **intransitive verb** which does not describe a change of state and whose subject typically instigates the action, event or state that it describes, e.g. *We shouted, They ran.*

Universal Grammar: The set of **morpheme** categories, **features**, principles and rules that, by hypothesis, are innate and that guide the language learner in constructing a mental grammar for a specific language.

verb (V): A category to which form–meaning pairings that describe actions, events or states belong, e.g. *run, write, find, arrive, love, own* (lexical verbs), or to which forms that 'support' lexical verbs, like auxiliary *be* and *have* (e.g. *is running, has arrived*) belong. The support verb *do*, and the **modal verbs** (*must, ought, may* and so on) are forms that belong to the category **tense (T)**. A *transitive verb* has a direct **object**, whether overt or understood, e. g. *She drank the milk, He drinks* ('alcohol' understood). An *intransitive verb* has no direct **object**, e.g. *They ran, We shouted.*

Vocabulary: The Vocabulary, with a capital V, is the mental store of phonetic/phonological forms, each with a specification for the **morpheme** with which it is associated once the rules of **syntax** have applied. Where two forms have specifications that match the same morpheme, the more specified form is selected first in native speaker grammars. The less specified form is known as an **elsewhere form** and is selected only in contexts where more specified forms cannot be selected.

voice onset time (VOT): From the start of the production of a voiceless consonant (e.g. [t], [p], [s], [f]), the time it takes for the voicing of a following vowel to begin. The longer the delay before voicing begins, the more aspirated the consonant is perceived to be.

word: A form–meaning pairing that is assigned a category label (e.g. N, V, P, D, A) and that is not an affix. Words can consist of one or more **morphemes**. For example, each of the following is a word: *align* (V) (one morpheme), *mis-align* (V) (two morphemes), *mis-align-ment* (N) (three morphemes), *mis-align-ment-s* (N) (four morphemes).

word association test: In a word association test an informant hears a set of prompt words presented individually (e.g. *new, potato, brother*) and responds as quickly as possible with the first word that comes to mind (e.g. *old, onion, sister*). Responses are assumed to reflect the connections that the prompt and response words have in the mental lexicon.

REFERENCES

Abrahamsson, N. and Hyltenstam, K. 2008. The robustness of aptitude effects in near-native second language acquisition. *Studies in Second Language Acquisition*, 30, 481–509.

Adamson, H. D. and Regan, V. 1991. The acquisition of community speech norms by Asian immigrants learning English as a second language: a preliminary study. *Studies in Second Language Acquisition*, 13, 1–22.

Ahn, S-H. G. 2010. On steady-state interlanguage grammars of Korean English learners: focused on tense-agreement elements. *Korean Journal of English Language and Linguistics*, 10, 353–87.

Altenberg, E. P. 2005. The perception of word boundaries in a second language. *Second Language Research*, 21, 325–58.

Althubaiti, K. 2010. Age effects in a minimal input setting on the acquisition of English morpho-syntactic and semantic properties by L1 speakers of Arabic. Unpublished doctoral dissertation. University of Essex.

Anderson, B. 2008. Forms of evidence and grammatical development in the acquisition of adjective position in L2 French. *Studies in Second Language Acquisition*, 30, 1–29.

Ashby, M. and Maidment, J. 2005. *Introducing phonetic science*. Cambridge: Cambridge University Press.

Asher, J. J. and Garcia, R. 1982. The optimal age to learn a foreign language. In Krashen, Scarcella and Long (eds), pp. 3–12. (Reprinted from the *Modern Language Journal*, 1969, 38, 334–41).

Asher, J. J. and Price, B. S. 1982. The learning strategy of total physical response: some age differences. In Krashen, Scarcella and Long (eds), pp. 76–83. (Reprinted from *Child Development*, 1967, 38, 1219–27).

Ayoun, D. 2003. *Parameter setting in language acquisition*. London: Continuum.

Baddeley, A. D. 2000. Short-term and working memory. In E. Tulving and F. Craik (eds) *The Oxford handbook of memory*. Oxford: Oxford University Press, pp. 77–92.

Baddeley, A. D. 2007. *Working memory, thought and action*. Oxford: Oxford University Press.

Baddeley, A. D. and Hitch, G. J. 1974. Working memory. In G. H. Bower (ed.) *The psychology of learning and motivation: advances in research and theory*. New York: Academic Press, pp. 47–89.

Bautista Maldonado, S. 2011. The acquisition of English manner of motion and resultative constructions by native speakers of Spanish. Unpublished doctoral dissertation. University of Essex.

Benati, A. 2001. A comparative study of the effects of processing instruction and output-based instruction on the acquisition of the Italian future tense. *Language Teaching Research*, 5, 95–127.

Benati, A. 2005. The effects of processing instruction on the acquisition of the English past simple tense. *Language Teaching Research*, 9, 67–93.

Bennett, S. and Progovac, L. 1998. Morphological status of reflexives in second language acquisition. In S. Flynn, G. Martohardjono and W. O'Neil (eds) *The generative study of second language acquisition*. Mahwah, NJ: Lawrence Erlbaum Associates, pp. 187–214.

Berko, J. 1958. The child's learning of English morphology. *Word*, 14, 47–56.

Bertenshaw, N. 2009. The application of binding constraints by Japanese L2 learners of English. Unpublished doctoral dissertation. University of Essex.

Bialystok, E. 1999. Cognitive complexity and attentional control in the bilingual mind. *Child Development*, 70, 636–44.

Bialystok, E. 2009. Bilingualism: the good, the bad and the indifferent. *Bilingualism: Language and Cognition*, 12, 3–11.

Bialystok, E., Craik, F. I. M. and Freedman, M. 2007. Bilingualism as a protection against the onset of symptoms of dementia. *Neuropsychologia*, 45, 459–64.

Bialystok, E., Craik, F. I. M. and Luk, G. 2008. Cognitive control and lexical access in younger and older bilinguals. *Journal of Experimental Psychology: Learning, Memory and Cognition*, 34, 859–73.

Bialystok, E., Craik, F. I. M. and Luk, G. 2012. Bilingualism: consequences for mind and brain. *Trends in Cognitive Sciences*, 16, 240–50.

Bialystok, E., Craik, F. I. M., Klein, R. and Viswanathan, M. 2004. Bilingualism, aging, and cognitive control: evidence from the Simon task. *Psychology and Aging*, 19, 290–303.

Bialystok, E. and Hakuta, K. 1999. Confounded age: linguistic and cognitive factors in age differences for second language acquisition. In Birdsong (ed.), pp. 161–81.

Bialystok, E. and Sullivan, M. D. (eds) 2017. *Growing old with two languages: effects of bilingualism on cognitive aging*. Amsterdam: John Benjamins.

Birdsong, D. (ed.) 1999. *Second language acquisition and the critical period hypothesis*. Mahwah, NJ: Lawrence Erlbaum Associates.

Birdsong, D. 2009. Age and the end state of second language acquisition. In W. C. Ritchie and T. K. Bhatia (eds) *The new handbook of second language acquisition*. Bingley: Emerald Group Publishing, pp. 401–24.

Birdsong, D. and Molis, M. 2001. On the evidence for maturational effects in second language acquisition. *Journal of Memory and Language*, 44, 235–49.

Bley-Vroman, R. 1989. What is the logical problem of foreign language learning? In S. Gass and J. Schachter (eds) *Linguistic perspectives on second language acquisition*, pp. 41–68.

Blom, E., Polišenská, D. and Weerman, F. 2008. Articles, adjectives and age of onset: the acquisition of Dutch grammatical gender. *Second Language Research*, 24, 297–331.

Bloom, P. 1994. Generativity within language and other cognitive domains. *Cognition*, 51, 177–89.

Boeckx, C. 2008. *Aspects of the syntax of agreement*. New York: Routledge.

Bohnacker, U. 2006. When Swedes begin to learn German: from V2 to V2. *Second Language Research*, 22, 443–86.

Braine, M. D. 1963. The ontogeny of English phrase structure: the first phase. *Language*, 39, 1–13.

Broselow, E. 1983. Non-obvious transfer: on predicting epenthesis errors. In S. Gass and L. Selinker (eds) *Language transfer in language learning*. Rowley, MA: Newbury House, pp. 269–80.

Broselow, E. 1988. Prosodic phonology and the acquisition of a second language. In S. Flynn and W. O'Neil (eds) *Linguistic theory and second language acquisition.* Dordrecht: Kluwer, pp. 295–308.

Broselow, E., Chen, S-I. and Wang, C. 1998. The emergence of the unmarked in second language phonology. *Studies in Second language Acquisition*, 20, 261–80.

Broselow, E. and Park, H.-B. 1995. Mora conservation in second language prosody. In J. Archibald (ed.) *Phonological acquisition and phonological theory*. Hillsdale, NJ: Lawrence Erlbaum Associates, pp. 151–68.

Cabrelli Amaro, J., Flynn, S. and Rothman, J. (eds) 2012. *Third language acquisition in adulthood*. Amsterdam: John Benjamins.

Cadierno, T. 1995. Formal instruction from a processing perspective: an investigation into the Spanish past tense. *The Modern Language Journal*, 79, 179–93.

Carlisle, R. 1997. The modification of onsets in a markedness relationship: testing the interlanguage structural conformity hypothesis. *Language Learning*, 47, 327–61.

Carreiras, M. and Clifton, C. 1993. Relative clause interpretation preferences in Spanish and English. *Language and Speech*, 36, 353–72.

Carroll, S. and Swain, M. 1993. Explicit and implicit negative feedback: an empirical study of the learning of linguistic generalizations. *Studies in Second Language Acquisition*, 15, 357–86.

Cenoz, J. 2003. The influence of age on the acquisition of English: general proficiency, attitudes and code-mixing. In García Mayo and García Lecumberri (eds), pp. 77–93.

Cho, J. and Slabakova, R. 2014. Interpreting definiteness in a second language without articles: the case of L2 Russian. *Second Language Research*, 30, 159–90.

Choi, M-H. and Lardiere, D. 2006. The interpretation of *wh*-in-situ in Korean second language acquisition. In A. Belletti, E. Bennati, C. Chesi, E. DiDomenico and I. Ferrari (eds) *Language Acquisition and Development: Proceedings of GALA 2005.* Cambridge: Cambridge Scholars Press, pp. 125–35.

Chomsky, N. 1981. *Lectures on government and binding.* Dordrecht: Foris.

Chomsky, N. 1986. *Knowledge of language.* New York: Praeger.

Chomsky, N. 1988. *Language and problems of knowledge: The Managua lectures.* Cambridge, MA: MIT Press.

Chomsky, N. 1995. *The minimalist program.* Cambridge, MA: MIT Press.

Chomsky, N. 2000. Minimalist inquiries: the framework. In R. Martin, D. Michaels and J. Uriagereka (eds) *Step by step: essays on minimalist syntax: in honor of Howard Lasnik.* Cambridge, MA: MIT Press.

Chrabaszcz, A. and Jiang, N. 2014. The role of the native language in the use of the English nongeneric definite article by L2 learners: a cross-linguistic comparison. *Second Language Research*, 30, 351–79.

Clahsen, H. and Muysken, P. 1986. The availability of universal grammar to adult and child learners. *Second Language Research*, 2, 93–119.

Cohen, D. 1998. *Strategies in learning and using a second language.* London: Longman.

Colantoni, L., Steele, J. and Escudero, P. 2015. *Second language speech: theory and practice.* Cambridge: Cambridge University Press.

Comrie, B. 1976. *Aspect: an introduction to the study of verbal aspect and related problems.* Cambridge: Cambridge University Press.

Costello, W. and Shirai, Y. 2011. The Aspect Hypothesis, defective tense and obligatory contexts: comments on Haznedar, 2007. *Second Language Research*, 27, 467–80.

Crain, S. and Nakayama, M. 1987. Structure dependence in grammar formation. *Language*, 63, 522–43.

Crain, S. and Thornton, R. 1991. Recharting the course of language acquisition: studies in elicited production. In N. A. Krasnegor, D. M. Rumbaugh, R. L. Schiefelbusch and M. Studdert-Kennedy (eds) *Biobehavioral foundations of language development*. Hillsdale, NJ: Lawrence Erlbaum Associates, pp. 321–37.

Crystal, D. 1995. *The Cambridge encyclopedia of the English language*. Cambridge: Cambridge University Press.

Curtin, S., Goad, H. and Pater, J. 1998. Phonological transfers and levels of representation: the perceptual acquisition of Thai voice and aspiration by English and French speakers. *Second Language Research*, 14, 389–405.

Danan, M. 2004. Captioning and subtitling: undervalued language learning strategies. *Meta*, 49, 67–77.

DeKeyser R. M. 1995. Learning second language grammar rules: an experiment with a miniature linguistic system. *Studies in Second Language Acquisition*, 17, 379–410.

DeKeyser, R. 2000. The robustness of critical period effects in second language acquisition. *Studies in Second Language Acquisition*, 22, 499–533.

DeKeyser, R. 2007. Skill acquisition theory. In VanPatten, B. and Williams, J. (eds) *Theories in second language acquisition*. Mahwah, NJ: Lawrence Erlbaum Associates, pp. 97–113.

Dekydtspotter, L. and Sprouse, R. A. 2001. Mental design and (second) language epistemology: adjectival restrictions of *wh*-quantifiers and tense in English–French interlanguage. *Second Language Research*, 17, 1–35.

Dijkstra, A., Timmermans, M. and Schriefers, H. 2000. On being blinded by your other language: effects of task demands on interlingual homograph recognition. *Journal of Memory and Language*, 42, 445–64.

Donaldson, B. 2011. Left dislocation in near-native French. *Studies in Second Language Acquisition*, 33, 399–432.

Dörnyei, Z. 2009. *The psychology of second language acquisition*. Oxford: Oxford University Press.

Dugarova, E. 2014. Russian speakers' L2 Chinese acquisition of *wh*-topicalization at the syntax–discourse interface. *Second Language Research*, 30, 411–37.

duPlessis, J., Solin, D., Travis, L. and White, L. 1987. UG or not UG, that is the question: a reply to Clahsen and Muysken. *Second Language Research*, 3, 56–75.

Dupoux, E. Sebastián-Gallés, N., Navarrete, E. and Peperkamp, S. 2008. Persistent stress 'deafness': the case of French learners of Spanish. *Cognition*, 106, 682–706.

Dussias, P. E. and Piñar, P. 2009. Sentence parsing in L2 learners: linguistic and experience-based factors. In W. C. Ritchie and T. K. Bhatia (eds) *The new handbook of second language acquisition*. Bingley: Emerald Group Publishing, pp. 295–317.

Eckman, F. R. 1985. Some theoretical and pedagogical implications of the markedness differential hypothesis. *Studies in Second Language Acquisition*, 7, 289–307.

Eckman, F., Elreyes, A. and Iverson, G. K. 2003. Some principles of second language phonology. *Second Language Research*, 19, 169–208.

Ellis, N. C. 2006. Language acquisition as rational contingency learning. *Applied Linguistics*, 27, 164–94.

Ellis, R. 1988. *Classroom second language development*. New York: Prentice Hall.

Ellis, R. 1990. *Instructed second language acquisition*. Oxford: Blackwell.

Embick, D. and Noyer, R. 2007. Distributed morphology and the syntax/morphology interface. In G. Ramshand and C. Reiss (eds) *The Oxford handbook of linguistic interfaces*. Oxford: Oxford University Press, pp. 289–324.

Epstein, S., Flynn, S. and Martohardjono, G. 1996. Second language acquisition: theoretical and experimental issues in contemporary research. *Brain and Behavioral Sciences*, 19, 677–758.

Erard, M. 2012. *Babel no more: the search for the world's most extraordinary language learners*. New York: Free Press.

Erlam, R. 2003. Evaluating the relative effectiveness of structured-input and output-based instruction in foreign language learning: results from an experimental study. *Studies in Second Language Acquisition*, 25, 559–82.

Erteshik-Shir, N. 2007. *Information structure: the syntax–discourse interface*. Oxford: Oxford University Press.

Fallah, N., Jabbari, A. A. and Fazilatfar, A. M. 2016. Source(s) of syntactic cross-linguistic influence (CLI): the case of L3 acquisition of English possessives by Mazandarani–Persian bilinguals. *Second Language Research*, 32, 225–45.

Farwell, B. 1963. *Burton: a biography of Sir Richard Francis Burton*. London: Longman. Republished by Penguin Books (London) 1990.

Fathman, A. 1982. The relationship between age and second language production ability. In Krashen, Scarcella and Long (eds), pp. 115–22. (Reprinted from *Language Learning*, 1975, 25, 245–53).

Fazio, L. L. 2001. The effect of corrections and commentaries on the journal writing accuracy of minority- and majority-language students. *Journal of Second Language Writing*, 10, 235–49.

Felix, S. 1981. The effect of formal instruction on second language acquisition. *Language Learning*, 31, 87–112.

Felix, S. and Weigl, W. 1991. Universal Grammar in the classroom: the effects of formal instruction on second language acquisition. *Second Language Research*, 7, 162–81.

Felser, C., Roberts, L., Marinis, T. and Gross, R. 2003. The processing of ambiguous sentences by first and second language learners of English. *Applied Psycholinguistics*, 24, 453–89.

Flege, J. E. 1987. The production of 'new' and 'similar' phones in a foreign language: evidence for the effect of equivalence classification. *Journal of Phonetics*, 15, 47–65.

Flege, J. E., Munro, M. J. and MacKay, I. R. A. 1996. Factors affecting the production of word-initial consonants in a second language. In R. Bayley and D. R. Preston (eds) *Second language acquisition and linguistic variation*. Amsterdam: John Benjamins, pp. 47–73.

Flynn, S. 1987. Contrast and construction in a parameter-setting model of L2 acquisition. *Language Learning*, 37, 19–62.

Fortescue, M. D. 1984. *West Greenlandic*. London: Croom Helm.

Fromkin, V. and Rodman, R. 1998. *An introduction to language*. Sixth Edition. Fort Worth, TX: Harcourt Brace.

Fuli, L. T. 2007. Definiteness vs. specificity: an investigation into the terms used to describe articles in Gagana Samoa. Unpublished Master's dissertation. University of Auckland.

Gabriele, A. 2009. Transfer and transition in the SLA of aspect: a bidirectional study of learners of English and Japanese. *Studies in Second Language Acquisition*, 31, 371–402.

Gabriele, A. 2010. Deriving meaning through context: interpreting bare nominals in second language Japanese. *Second Language Research*, 26, 379–405.

García Mayo, M. P. and García Lecumberri, M. (eds) 2003. *Age and the acquisition of English as a foreign language*. Clevedon: Multilingual Matters.

García Mayo, M. P., and Villareal Olaizola, I. 2011. The development of suppletive and affixal tense and agreement morphemes in the L3 English of Basque–Spanish bilinguals. *Second Language Research*, 27, 129–49.

Gass, S. M. 1997. *Input, interaction, and the second language learner*. Mahwah, NJ: Lawrence Erlbaum Associates.

Gass, S. M. and Selinker, L. 2008. *Second language acquisition: an introductory course*. Third Edition. Abingdon: Routledge.

Gathercole, V. C., Thomas, E. M., Kennedy, I., Prys, C., Young, N., Viñas Guasch, N., Roberts, E. J., Hughes, E. K. and Jones, L. 2014. Does language dominance affect cognitive performance in bilinguals? Lifespan evidence from preschoolers through older adults on card sorting, Simon and metalinguistic tasks. *Frontiers in Psychology*, 5, article 11, 14 pp.

Geeslin, K. L. 2014. *Sociolinguistics and second language acquisition: learning to use language in context*. Abingdon: Routledge.

Geluykens, R. 1992. *From discourse process to grammatical construction: on left-dislocation in English*. Amsterdam: John Benjamins.

Genesee, F. 2001. *Second language immersion: a summary for teachers, administrators and parents*. Tallinn: Keelekuemblus Keskus.

Gibson, E., Pearlmutter, N., Canseco-Gonzalez, E. and Hickok, G. 1996. Cross-linguistic attachment preferences: evidence from English and Spanish. *Cognition*, 59, 23–59.

Goad, H., White, L. and Steele, J. 2003. Missing inflection in L2 acquisition: defective syntax or L1-constrained prosodic representations? *Canadian Journal of Linguistics*, 48, 243–63.

Goldberg, A. 2003. Constructions: a new theoretical approach to language. *Trends in Cognitive Sciences*, 7, 219–24.

Graddol, D., Cheshire, J. and Swann, J. 1994. *Describing Language*. Second Edition. Buckingham: Open University Press.

Gregg, K. R. 2003. SLA theory: construction and assessment. In C. J. Doughty and M. H. Long (eds) *The handbook of second language acquisition*. Malden, MA: Blackwell, pp. 831–65.

Grüter, T. and Conradie, S. 2006. Investigating the L2 initial state: additional evidence from the production and comprehension of Afrikaans-speaking learners of German. In R. Slabakova, S. A. Montrul and P. Prévost (eds) *Inquiries in linguistic development: in honor of Lydia White*. Amsterdam: John Benjamins, pp. 89–114.

Guasti, M. T. 2002. *Language acquisition: the growth of grammar*. Cambridge, MA: MIT Press.

Haegeman, L. 1985. Scope phenomena in English and Dutch L2 acquisition: a case study. *Second Language Research*, 1, 118–50.

Halle, M. and Marantz, A. 1993. Distributed morphology and the pieces of inflection. In K. Hale and S. J. Keyser (eds) *The view from building 20*. Cambridge, MA: MIT Press, pp. 53–109.

Hao, Y-C. 2012. Second language acquisition of Mandarin Chinese tones by tonal and non-tonal language speakers. *Journal of Phonetics*, 40, 269–79.

Hardeman, K. 2013. Gender and second language style: American learner perceptions and use of Mandarin *sajiao*. Unpublished doctoral dissertation. University of Hawaii at Manoa.

Harley, B. 1986. *Age in second language acquisition*. San Diego: College-Hill Press.

Harley, B. and Hart, D. 1997. Language aptitude and second language proficiency in classroom learners of different starting ages. *Studies in Second Language Acquisition*, 19, 379–400.

Harley, B. and Swain, M. 1984. The interlanguage of immersion students and its implications for second language teaching. In A. Davies, C. Criper and A. P. R. Howatt (eds) *Interlanguage*. Edinburgh: Edinburgh University Press, pp. 291–311.

Harley, H. and Noyer, R. 1999. Distributed morphology. *Glot International*, 4, 3–9.

Harley, H. and Ritter, E. 2002. Person and number in pronouns: a feature-geometric analysis. *Language*, 78, 482–526.

Hart, J., Berndt, R. and Caramazza, A. 1985. Category-specific naming deficit following cerebral infarction. *Nature*, 316 (6027), 439–40.

Hawkins, R. 2001. *Second language syntax: a generative introduction*. Oxford: Blackwell.

Hawkins, R. 2012. Knowledge of English verb phrase ellipsis by speakers of Arabic and Chinese. *Linguistic Approaches to Bilingualism*, 2, 404–38.

Hawkins, R. and Casillas, G. 2008. Explaining frequency of verb morphology in early L2 speech. *Lingua*, 118, 595–612.

Hawkins, R., Towell, R. and Bazergui, N. 1993. Universal Grammar and the acquisition of French verb movement by native speakers of English. *Second Language Research*, 9, 189–233.

Haznedar, B. 2001. The acquisition of the IP system in child L2 English. *Studies in Second Language Acquisition*, 23, 1–39.

Haznedar, B. 2007. The acquisition of tense-aspect in child second language English. *Second Language Research*, 23, 383–417.

Haznedar, B. and Schwartz, B. D. 1997. Are there optional infinitives in child L2 acquisition? In E. Hughes, M. Hughes and A. Greenhill (eds) *Proceedings of the 21st Annual Boston Conference on Language Development*. Somerville, MA: Cascadilla Press, pp. 257–68.

Henry, N., Culman, H. and VanPatten, B. 2009. More on the effects of explicit information in instructed SLA: a partial replication and a response to Fernandez (2008). *Studies in Second Language Acquisition*, 31, 559–75.

Herschensohn, J. 2007. *Language development and age*. Cambridge: Cambridge University Press.

Hertel, T. J. 2003. Lexical and discourse factors in the second language acquisition of Spanish word order. *Second Language Research*, 19, 273–304.

Holmberg, A. and Roberts, I. 2013. The syntax–morphology relation. *Lingua*, 130, 111–31.

Holobow, N. E., Lambert, W. E. and Sayegh. L. 1984. Pairing script and dialogue: combinations that show promise for second or foreign language learning. *Language Learning*, 34(4), 59–76.

Hopp, H. 2007. Ultimate attainment at the interfaces in second language acquisition: Grammar and Processing. Doctoral dissertation, University of Groningen. Published as *Groningen Dissertations in Linguistics*, 65.

Hopp, H. 2013. Grammatical gender in adult L2 acquisition: relations between lexical and syntactic variability. *Second Language Research*, 29, 33–56.

Hurford, J. R., Heasley, B. and Smith, M. B. 2007. *Semantics: a coursebook*. Second Edition. Cambridge: Cambridge University Press.

Inagaki, S. 2001. Motion verbs with goal PPs in the L2 acquisition of English and Japanese. *Studies in Second Language Acquisition*, 23, 153–70.

Ionin, T., Ko, H., and Wexler, K. 2004. Article semantics in L2-acquisition: the role of specificity. *Language Acquisition* 12, 3–69.

Ionin, T. and Wexler, K. 2002. Why is 'is' easier than '-s'? Acquisition of tense/agreement morphology by child second language learners of English. *Second Language Research*, 18, 95–136.

Ionin, T., Zubizarreta, M. L., and Bautista Maldonado, S. 2008. Sources of linguistic knowledge in the second language acquisition of English articles. *Lingua* 118, 554–76.

Ionin, T., Zubizarreta, M. L. and Philippov, V. 2009. Acquisition of article semantics by child and adult L2-English learners. *Bilingualism: Language and Cognition*, 12, 337–61.

Iverson, P., Kuhl, P. K., Akahane-Yamada, R., Diesch, E., Tokhura, Y., Ketterman, A. and Siebert, C. 2003. A perceptual interference account of acquisition difficulties for non-native phonemes. *Cognition*, 87, B47–57.

Jegerski, J., VanPatten, B. and Keating, G. D. 2011. Cross-linguistic variation and the acquisition of pronominal reference in L2 Spanish. *Second Language Research*, 27, 481–507.

Jenkins, J. J. 1970. The 1952 Minnesota word association norms. In L. Postman and G. Keppel (eds) *Norms of word associations*. New York: Academic Press, pp. 1–38.

Johnson, J. and Newport, E. 1989. Critical period effects in second language learning: the influence of maturational state on the acquisition of English as a second language. *Cognitive Psychology*, 21, 60–99.

Juffs, A. 2004. Representation, processing and working memory in a second language. *Transactions of the Philological Society*, 102, 199–225.

Juffs, A. 2009. Second language acquisition of the lexicon. In W. C. Ritchie and T. K. Bhatia (eds) *The new handbook of second language acquisition*. Bingley: Emerald Group Publishing, pp. 69–88.

Klein, W. and Perdue, C. 1992. *Utterance structure: developing grammars again*. Amsterdam: John Benjamins.

Koeneman, O. and Zeijlstra, H. 2017. *Introducing syntax*. Cambridge: Cambridge University Press.

Krashen, S. 1985. *The input hypothesis*. London: Longman.

Krashen, S. D., Scarcella, R. C. and Long, M. H. (eds) 1982. *Child–adult differences in second language acquisition*. Rowley, MA: Newbury House.

Kroll, J. F. and Curley, J. 1988. Lexical memory in novice bilinguals: the role of concepts in retrieving second language words. In M. Gruneberg, P. Morris and R. Sykes (eds) *Practical aspects of memory*, vol. 2. London: Wiley, pp. 389–95.

Kroll, J. F. and Stewart, E. 1994. Category interference in translation and picture naming: evidence for asymmetric connections between bilingual memory representations. *Journal of Memory and Language*, 33, 149–74.

Kumpf, L. 1984. Temporal systems and universality in interlanguage: a case study. In F. Eckman, L. Bell and D. Nelson (eds) *Universals of second language acquisition*. Rowley, MA: Newbury House, pp. 132–43.

Lardiere, D. 2007. *Ultimate attainment in second language acquisition: a case study.* Mahwah, NJ: Lawrence Erlbaum Associates.

Lardiere, D. 2009a. Some thoughts on the contrastive analysis of features in second language acquisition. *Second Language Research*, 25, 173–227.

Lardiere, D. 2009b. Further thoughts on parameters and features in second language acquisition: a reply to peer comments on Lardiere's 'Some thoughts on the contrastive analysis of features in second language acquisition' in *SLR* 25(2). *Second Language Research*, 25, 409–22.

Larson-Hall, J. 2004. Predicting perceptual success with segments: a test of Japanese speakers of Russian. *Second Language Research*, 20, 33–76.

Larson-Hall, J. 2008. Weighing the benefits of studying a foreign language at a younger starting age in a minimal input situation. *Second Language Research*, 24, 35–63.

Levelt, W. J. M. 1989. *Speaking: from intention to articulation.* Cambridge, MA: MIT Press.

Levin, B. and Rappaport Hovav, M. 2005. *Argument realization.* Cambridge: Cambridge University Press.

Li, P., Legault, J. and Litcofsky, K. A. 2014. Neuroplasticity as a function of second language learning: anatomical changes in the human brain. *Cortex*, 58, 301–24.

Li, P. and Shirai, Y. 2000. *The acquisition of lexical and grammatical aspect.* Berlin: Mouton de Gruyter.

Lightbown, P. 1992. Can they do it themselves? A comprehension-based ESL course for young children. In R. Courchêne, J. Glidden, J. St. John and C. Thérien (eds) *Comprehension-based second language teaching/L'Enseignement des langues secondes axé sur la compréhension.* Ottawa: University of Ottawa Press, pp. 353–70.

Lightbown, P. and Spada, N. 1993. *How languages are learned.* Oxford: Oxford University Press.

Lightbown, P. and Spada, N. 1999. *How languages are learned.* Revised Second Edition. Oxford: Oxford University Press.

Long, M. H. 1983. Does second language instruction make a difference? A review of the research. *TESOL Quarterly*, 17, 359–82.

Long, M. H. 1990. Maturational constraints on language development. *Studies in Second Language Acquisition*, 12, 251–85.

Long, M. H. 2007. *Problems in SLA.* Mahwah, NJ: Lawrence Erlbaum Associates.

Lozano, C. 2006. Focus and split-intransitivity: the acquisition of word order alternations in non-native Spanish. *Second Language Research*, 22, 145–87.

Lyons, C. 1999. *Definiteness.* Cambridge: Cambridge University Press.

Lyster, R. and Ranta, L. 1997. Corrective feedback and learner uptake: negotiation of form in communicative classrooms. *Studies in Second Language Acquisition*, 19, 37–66.

Mackey, A. 1999. Input, interaction and second language development: an empirical study of question formation in ESL. *Studies in Second Language Acquisition*, 21, 557–87.

Madox Ford, F. 1924. *Joseph Conrad: a personal remembrance.* London: Duckworth. (Re-issued as e-book #1054 by Project Gutenberg Canada: www.pgdpcanada.net)

Mai, Z. and Yuan, B. 2016. Uneven re-assembly of tense, telicity and discourse features in L2 acquisition of the Chinese *shi … de* cleft by adult English speakers. *Second Language Research*, 32, 247–76.

Major, R. C. 1986. Paragoge and degree of foreign accent in Brazilian Portuguese. *Second Language Research*, 2, 53–71.

Marsden, H. 2008. Pair-list readings in Korean–Japanese, Chinese–Japanese and English–Japanese interlanguage. *Second Language Research*, 24, 189–226.

McCarthy, C. 2008. Morphological variability in the comprehension of agreement: an argument for representation over computation. *Second Language Research*, 24, 459–86.

Meisel, J. 1997. The acquisition of the syntax of negation in French and German: contrasting first and second language acquisition. *Second Language Research*, 13, 227–63.

Mitchell, R., Myles, F. and Marsden, E. 2013. *Second language learning theories*. Third Edition. Abingdon: Routledge.

Montalbetti, M. 1984. After binding. Unpublished doctoral dissertation. MIT.

Muñoz, C. 2003. Variation in oral skills development and age of onset. In García Mayo and García Lecumberri (eds), pp. 161–81.

Muñoz, C. and Tragant, E. 2001. Motivation and attitudes towards L2: some effects of age and instruction. *EUROSLA Yearbook*, 1, 211–24.

Myles, F. 2005. The emergence of morpho-syntactic structure in French L2. In J-M. Dewaele (ed.) *Focus on French as a foreign language: multidisciplinary approaches*. Clevedon: Multilingual Matters, pp. 164–90.

Myles, F., Mitchell, R. and Hooper, J. 1999. Interrogative chunks in L2 French. *Studies in Second Language Acquisition*, 21, 49–80.

Neumann, S. B. and Koskinen, P. 1992. Captioned television as comprehensible input: effects of incidental word learning from context for language minority students. *Reading Research Quarterly*, 27, 95–106.

Norris, J. M. and Ortega, L. 2001. Does type of instruction make a difference? Substantive findings from a meta-analytic review. *Language Learning*, 51, 157–213.

O'Connor, J. D. 1973. *Phonetics*. Harmondsworth: Penguin.

O'Grady, W. 2008a. The emergentist program. *Lingua*, 118, 447–64.

O'Grady, W. 2008b. Innateness, universal grammar, and emergentism. *Lingua*, 118, 620–31.

O'Grady, W., Lee, M. and Choo, M. 2003. A subject-object asymmetry in the acquisition of relative clauses in Korean as a second language. *Studies in Second Language Acquisition*, 25, 433–48.

Ohta, A. S. 2000. Rethinking recasts: a learner-centered examination of corrective feedback in the Japanese language classroom. In J. K. Hall and L. S. Verplaeste (eds) *The construction of second and foreign language learning through classroom instruction*. Mahwah, NJ: Lawrence Erlbaum Associates, pp. 47–71.

Oliver, R. 1995. Negative feedback in child NS–NNS conversation. *Studies in Second Language Acquisition*, 17, 459–81.

Olson, L. L. and Samuels, S. J. 1982. The relationship between age and accuracy of foreign language pronunciation. In Krashen, Scarcella and Long (eds), pp. 67–75.

Ortega, L. 2009. *Understanding second language acquisition*. London: Hodder Education.

Oyama, S. 1982a. A sensitive period for the acquisition of a nonnative phonological system. In Krashen, Scarcella and Long (eds), pp. 20–38. (Reprinted from *Journal of Psycholinguistic Research*, 1976, 5, 261–85).

Oyama, S. 1982b. The sensitive period and comprehension of speech. In Krashen, Scarcella and Long (eds), pp. 39–51.

Papadopoulou, D. and Clahsen, H. 2003. Parsing strategies in the L1 and L2 sentence processing: a study of relative clause attachment in Greek. *Studies in Second Language Acquisition*, 25, 501–28.

Patkowski, M. 1982: The sensitive period for the acquisition of syntax in a second language. In Krashen, Scarcella and Long (eds), pp. 52–63. (Reprinted from *Language Learning*, 1980, 30, 449–72).

Pavesi, M. 1986. Markedness, discourse modes, and relative clause formation in a formal and informal context. *Studies in Second Language Acquisition*, 8, 38–55.

Penrose, R. 2004. *The road to reality: a complete guide to the laws of the universe*. London: Jonathan Cape.

Pérez-Leroux, A. T. and Glass, W. 1997. OPC effects in the L2 acquisition of Spanish. In A. T. Pérez-Leroux and W. Glass (eds) *Contemporary perspectives on the acquisition of Spanish*, vol. 1: *Developing grammars*. Boston, MA: Cascadilla Press, pp. 149–65.

Pérez-Leroux, A. T. and Glass, W. 1999. Null anaphora in Spanish second language acquisition: probabilistic versus generative approaches. *Second Language Research*, 15, 220–49.

Perlmutter, D. 1978. Impersonal passives and the unaccusative hypothesis. *Berkeley Linguistics Society*, 4, 157–89.

Pfenninger, S. E. and Singleton, D. 2017. *Beyond age effects in instructional L2 learning*. Bristol: Multilingual Matters.

Polio, C., Fleck, C. and Leder, N. 1998. 'If I only had more time': ESL learners' changes in linguistic accuracy on essay revisions. *Journal of Second Language Writing*, 7, 43–68.

Potter, M. C., So, K-F. S., von Eckardt, B. and Feldman, L. B. 1984. Lexical and conceptual representation in beginning and proficient bilinguals. *Journal of Verbal Learning and Verbal Behavior*, 23, 23–38.

Prévost, P. and White, L. 2000. Missing surface inflection or impairment in second language acquisition? Evidence from tense and agreement. *Second Language Research*, 16, 103–33.

Progovac, L. 1992. Relativized SUBJECT: long-distance reflexives without movement. *Linguistic Inquiry*, 23, 671–80.

Radford, A. 2009. *An introduction to English sentence structure*. Cambridge: Cambridge University Press.

Radford, A., Atkinson, M., Britain, D., Clahsen, H. and Spencer, A. 2009. *Linguistics: an introduction*. Second Edition. Cambridge: Cambridge University Press.

Rebuschat, P. 2008. Implicit learning of natural language syntax. Unpublished doctoral dissertation. University of Cambridge.

Regan, V. 1996. Variation in French interlanguage: a longitudinal study of sociolinguistic competence. In R. Bayley and D. R. Preston (eds) *Second language acquisition and linguistic variation*. Amsterdam: John Benjamins, pp. 177–201.

Rehner, K., Mougeon, R. and Nadasdi, T. 2003. The learning of sociolinguistic variation by advanced FSL learners: the case of *nous* versus *on* in immersion French. *Studies in Second Language Acquisition*, 25, 65–97.

Reinhart, T. 1976. The syntactic domain of anaphora. Unpublished doctoral dissertation. MIT.

Révész, A. 2009. Task complexity, focus on form, and second language development. *Studies in Second Language Acquisition*, 31, 437–70.

Roberts, I. (ed.) 2017. *The Oxford handbook of Universal Grammar*. Oxford: Oxford University Press.

Roberts, L. and Felser, C. 2011. Plausibility and recovery from garden paths in second language sentence processing. *Applied Psycholinguistics*, 32, 299–331.

Roberts, L., Gullberg, M. and Indefrey, P. 2008. Online pronoun resolution in L2 discourse: L1 influence and general learner effects. *Studies in Second Language Acquisition*, 30, 333–57.

Robison, R. E. 1995. The aspect hypothesis revisited: a cross-sectional study of tense and aspect marking in interlanguage. *Applied Linguistics*, 16, 344–70.

Roebuck, R. F., Martínez-Arbelaiz, M. A. and Pérez-Silva, J. I. 1999. Null subjects, filled CPs and L2 acquisition. *Second Language Research*, 15, 251–82.

Rogers, V. 2009. Syntactic development in the second language acquisition of French by instructed language learners. Unpublished doctoral dissertation. University of Newcastle-upon-Tyne.

Rothman, J., Judy, T., Guijarro Fuentes, P. and Pires, A. 2010. On the (un)ambiguity of adjectival modification in Spanish determiner phrases: informing debates on the mental representation of L2 syntax. *Studies in Second Language Acquisition*, 32, 47–77.

Saffran, J. R., Aslin, R. N. and Newport, E. L. 1996a. Statistical learning by 8-month-old infants. *Science*, 274, 1926–8.

Saffran, J. R., Newport, E. L. and Aslin, R. N. 1996b. Word segmentation: the role of distributional cues. *Journal of Memory and Language*, 35, 606–21.

Saffran, J. R., Pollak, S. D., Seibel, R. L. and Shkolnik, A. 2007. Dog is a dog is a dog: infant rule learning is not specific to language. *Cognition*, 105, 669–80.

Saito, M. 1999. *Wh*-quantifier interaction and the interpretation of *wh*-phrases. In M. Muraki and E. Iwamoto (eds) *Linguistics: in search of the human mind*. Tokyo: Kaitakusha, pp. 588–621.

Schachter, J. 1990. On the issue of completeness in second language acquisition. *Second Language Research*, 6, 93–124.

Schwartz, B. D. and Sprouse, R. A. 1994. Word order and nominative case in nonnative language acquisition: a longitudinal study of (L1 Turkish) German interlanguage. In T. Hoekstra and B. D. Schwartz (eds) *Language acquisition studies in generative grammar*. Amsterdam: John Benjamins, pp. 317–68.

Schwartz, B. D. and Sprouse, R. A. 1996. L2 cognitive states and the full transfer/full access model. *Second Language Research*, 12, 40–72.

Sharwood Smith, M. and Truscott, J. 2014. *The multilingual mind: a modular processing perspective*. Cambridge: Cambridge University Press.

Shea, C. E. and Curtin, S. 2010. Discovering the relationship between context and allophones in a second language. *Studies in Second Language Acquisition*, 32, 581–606.

Sheen, Y. 2010. Differential effects of oral and written corrective feedback in the ESL classroom. *Studies in Second Language Acquisition*, 32, 203–34.

Sheppard, K. 1992. Two feedback types: Do they make a difference? *RELC Journal*, 23, 103–10.

Singleton, D. 1999. *Exploring the second language mental lexicon*. Cambridge: Cambridge University Press.

Slabakova, R. 2000. Evidence of transfer: L2 acquisition of telicity in English by Spanish and Slavic native speakers. *Pittsburgh Working Papers in Linguistics*, 4, 188–200.

Slabakova, R. 2001. *Telicity in the second language*. Amsterdam: John Benjamins.

Slabakova, R. 2008. *Meaning in the second language*. Berlin: Mouton de Gruyter.

Slabakova, R. 2009. Features or parameters: which one makes second language acquisition easier, and more interesting to study? *Second Language Research*, 25, 313–24.

Slabakova, R. 2016. *Second language acquisition*. Oxford: Oxford University Press.

Smith, N. V. and Tsimpli, I. M. 1995. *The mind of a savant: language learning and modularity*. Oxford: Blackwell.

Smith, N. V., Tsimpli, I. M., Morgan, G. and Woll, B. 2011. *The signs of a savant: language against the odds*. Cambridge: Cambridge University Press.

Snape, N. and Kupisch, T. 2017. *Second language acquisition: second language systems*. New York: Macmillan Palgrave.

Snow, C. and Hoefnagel-Höhle, M. 1982. The critical period for language acquisition: evidence from second language learning. In Krashen, Scarcella and Long (eds), pp. 93–111. (Reprinted from *Child Development*, 1978, 49, 1114–28).

Sorace, A. 2005. Selective optionality in language development. In L. Cornips and K. Corrigan (eds) *Syntax and variation: reconciling the biological and the social*. Amsterdam: John Benjamins, pp. 55–80.

Sorace, A. and Filiaci, F. 2006. Anaphora resolution in near-native speakers of Italian. *Second Language Research*, 22, 339–68.

Spadaro, K. 1996. Maturational constraints on lexical acquisition in a second language. Unpublished doctoral dissertation, University of Western Australia, Perth.

Stauble, A. M. 1984. A comparison of a Spanish–English and a Japanese–English second language continuum: negation and verb morphology. In R. Andersen (ed.) *Second languages: a cross-linguistic perspective*. Rowley, MA: Newbury House, pp. 323–53.

Stenzel, K. 2005. Multilingualism in the Northwest Amazon revisited. In *Memorias del Congreso de Idiomas Indígenus de Latinoamérica-II*. Austin: University of Texas, pp. 1–28.

Sung, Y-T., Tu, J-Y., Cha, J-H. and Wu, M-D. 2016. Processing preference toward object-extracted relative clauses in Mandarin Chinese by L1 and L2 speakers: an eye-tracking study. *Frontiers in Psychology*, 7. http://journal.frontiersin.org/article/10.3389/fpsyg.2016.00004. Accessed 8 March 2017.

Swain, M. 1985. Communicative competence: some roles of comprehensible input and comprehensible output in its development. In S. M. Gass and C. G. Madden (eds) *Input in second language acquisition*. Rowley, MA: Newbury House, pp. 235–53.

Swain, M. 1995. Three functions of output in second language learning. In G. Cook and B. Seidlhofer (eds) *Principle and practice in applied linguistics: studies in honour of H. G. Widdowson*. Oxford: Oxford University Press, pp. 125–44.

Swain, M. 2005. The output hypothesis: theory and research. In E. Hinkel (ed.) *Handbook of research in second language teaching and learning*. Mahwah, NJ: Lawrence Erlbaum Associates, pp. 471–83.

Swain, M. and Barik, H. 1977. Report to Ottawa Board of Education and Carleton Board of Education re: evaluation of the 1976–77 French immersion program in grades 4–6. Ontario Institute for Studies in Education, Toronto.

Talmy, L. 1985. Lexicalisation patterns: semantic structures in lexical forms. In T. Shopen (ed.) *Language typology and syntactic description*, vol. 3:*Grammatical categories and the lexicon*. Cambridge: Cambridge University Press, pp. 57–149.

Talmy, L. 2000. *Toward a cognitive semantics*, vol. 1:*Concept structuring systems*. Cambridge, MA: MIT Press.

Thomas, M., 1989. The acquisition of English articles by first- and second-language learners. *Applied Psycholinguistics*, 10, 335–55.

Tinkham, T. 1997. The effects of semantic and thematic clustering on the learning of second language vocabulary. *Second Language Research*, 13, 138–63.

Tomaselli, A. and Schwartz, B. D. 1990. Analysing the acquisition stages of negation in L2 German: support for UG in SLA. *Second Language Research*, 6, 1–38.

Trahey, M. 1996. Positive evidence in second language acquisition: some long-term effects. *Second Language Research*, 12, 111–39.

Trahey, M. and White, L. 1993: Positive evidence and preemption in the second language classroom. *Studies in Second Language Acquisition*, 15, 181–204.

Traxler, M. J. 2012. *Introduction to psycholinguistics: understanding language science.* Chichester: Wiley-Blackwell.

Trenkic, D. 2007. Variability in second language article production: beyond the representational deficit vs. processing constraints debate. *Second Language Research*, 23, 289–327.

Truscott, J. 2007. The effect of error correction on learners' ability to write accurately. *Journal of Second Language Writing*, 16, 255–72.

Tsimpli, I. M. and Dimitrakopoulou, M. 2007. The interpretability hypothesis: evidence from *wh*-interrogatives in second language acquisition. *Second Language Research*, 23, 215–42.

Unsworth, S. 2005. *Child L2, adult L2, child L1: differences and similarities: a study on the acquisition of direct object scrambling in Dutch.* Utrecht: LOT Netherlands Graduate School of Linguistics.

Vainikka, A. and Young-Scholten, M. 2007. Minimalism versus organic syntax. In S. Karimi, V. Samiian and W. Wilkins (eds) *Clausal and phrasal architecture: syntactic derivation and interpretation. Papers in honor of Joseph Emonds.* Amsterdam: John Benjamins, pp. 319–38.

Vainikka, A. and Young-Scholten, M. 2011. *The acquisition of German: introducing organic grammar.* Berlin: de Gruyter Mouton.

Valian, V. 2015. Bilingualism and cognition. *Bilingualism: Language and Cognition*, 18, 3–24.

VanPatten, B. (ed.) 2004. *Processing instruction: theory, research, and commentary.* Mahwah, NJ: Lawrence Erlbaum Associates.

VanPatten, B. and Cadierno, T. 1993. Explicit instruction and input processing. *Studies in Second Language Acquisition*, 15, 225–43.

VanPatten, B. and Williams, J. (eds) 2007. *Theories in second language acquisition: an introduction.* Mahwah, NJ: Lawrence Erlbaum Associates.

VanPatten, B. and Wong, W. 2004. Processing instruction and the French causative: another replication. In B. VanPatten (ed.) *Processing instruction: theory, research, and commentary.* Mahwah, NJ: Lawrence Erlbaum Associates, pp. 97–118.

Weinberger, S. 1997. Minimal segments in second language phonology. In A. James and J. Leather (eds) *Second language speech: structure and process.* Berlin: Mouton de Gruyer, pp. 263–311.

Wells, J. C. and Colson, G. 1971. *Practical phonetics.* London: Pitman.

Wenk, B. J. 1979. Articulatory setting and de-fossilization. *Interlanguage Studies Bulletin*, 4, 202–20.

Werker, J. F. and Tees, R. C. 1984. Cross-language speech perception: evidence for perceptual reorganization during the first year of life. *Infant Behavior and Development*, 7, 49–63.

Westergaard, M. 2003. Unlearning V2: transfer, markedness, and the importance of input cues in the acquisition of word order in English by Norwegian children. *EUROSLA Yearbook*, 3, 73–101.

White, L. 1985. The pro-drop parameter in adult second language acquisition. *Language Learning*, 35, 47–62.

White, L. 1991. Adverb placement in second language acquisition: some effects of negative evidence in the classroom. *Second Language Research*, 7, 133–61.

White, L. 2003a. *Second language acquisition and Universal Grammar*. Cambridge: Cambridge University Press.

White, L. 2003b. Fossilization in steady state L2 grammars: persistent problems with inflectional morphology. *Bilingualism: Language and Cognition*, 6, 129–41.

White, L. 2007. Linguistic theory, Universal Grammar and second language acquisition. In VanPatten and Williams (eds), pp. 37–55.

Williams, J. N. 2005. Learning without awareness. *Studies in Second Language Acquisition*, 27, 269–304.

Williams, J. N. 2009. Implicit learning in second language acquisition. In W. C. Ritchie and T. K. Bhatia (eds) *The new handbook of second language acquisition*. Bingley: Emerald Publishers, pp. 319–53.

Wode, H. 1976. Developmental sequences in naturalistic L2 acquisition. *Working Papers on Bilingualism*, 11, 1–31.

Wode, H. 1981. *Learning a second language: An integrated view of language acquisition*. Tübingen: Gunter Narr Verlag.

Wolter, B. 2001. Comparing the L1 and L2 mental lexicon: a depth of individual word knowledge model. *Studies in Second Language Acquisition*, 23, 41–69.

Yang, Y. and Lyster, R. 2010. Effects of form-focused practice and feedback on Chinese EFL learners' acquisition of regular and irregular past tense forms. *Studies in Second Language Acquisition*, 32, 235–63.

Ying, H. G. 1999. Access to UG and language transfer: a study of L2 learners' interpretation of reconstruction in Chinese. *Second Language Research*, 15, 41–72.

Yuan, B. 1998. Interpretation of binding and orientation of the Chinese reflexive *ziji* by English and Japanese speakers. *Second Language Research*, 14, 324–40.

Yuan, B. 2001. The status of thematic verbs in the second language acquisition of Chinese: against inevitability of thematic verb raising in second language acquisition. *Second Language Research*, 17, 248–72.

Zareva, A. and Wolter, B. 2012. The 'promise' of three methods of word association analysis to L2 lexical research. *Second Language Research*, 28, 41–67.

Zhao, X. 2008. The syntax and interpretation of overt and null arguments in Chinese and their acquisition by second language learners. Unpublished doctoral dissertation. University of Cambridge.

Zsiga, E. C. 2013. *The sounds of language: an introduction to phonetics and phonology*. Oxford: Wiley Blackwell.

Zubizarreta, M. L. and Nava, E. 2011. Encoding discourse-based meaning: prosody versus syntax. Implications for second language acquisition. *Lingua*, 121, 652–69.

INDEX